Tony Samara:
A Modern Shaman...
and Beyond .

Tony Samara.

To Martin,
With much love,

Tony

Tony Samara:
A Modern Shaman...
and Beyond

Book One: Journeys

Book Two: Teachings

by
Nomi Sharron

ANTONY ROWE
PUBLISHING

Published in 2010 by Antony Rowe Publishing
48-50 Birch Close
Eastbourne
East Sussex
BN23 6PE
arp@cpi-group.co.uk

A catalogue record for this book is available from the British Library

ISBN 9781905200979

Printed and Bound in Great Britain by
CPI Antony Rowe, Chippenham and Eastbourne

FSC
Mixed Sources
Product group from well-managed
forests and other controlled sources
Cert no. SGS-COC-2953
www.fsc.org
© 1996 Forest Stewardship Council

Acknowledgements

To my agent, Diana Tyler, and to Susan Smith and the team at MBA, thank you for all your help and continued support.

To everyone who shared the Rainbow House, the Ashram, and to the wider 'Ashram community': Kaya [Mayana], Ilyana [Rebecca], Satprem, Angelina and Gabriel, Regina, Gesine, Sud Ram, Shayna [Indira], Martim, Fernanda and Alfonso, Marina, Alex, Mladen, Kira [Natalia], Jamie, Constanza, Estrella, and the 'van' family: Jo and Andy and daughters Hanna and Yasmin – thank you all for being part of my journey as I began to write these books.

To Sabrina and to Paula, thank you for coming into my life in Portugal – and staying; and for sharing your spiritual wisdom, your humour and your unconditional love. You are each a blessing in my life.

To Nura [Michi] and Wahido, thank you for adopting me as an 'honourary grandmother' to Myron and your new baby. I feel privileged to be part of your family.

My thanks to others who became part of my life in Portugal, and greatly enriched it: Lublic [Jordi], for circle dancing and for the gift of the Labyrinth; Jutta, for inviting me to teach circle dance at Faust and for your generous heart; Gabriella, for yoga and healing; Tertit, for a beautiful place to start writing these books; Reinhart, for good teeth and inspiring conversation; Wendy, for delicious food that also nourished my soul; Satya [Ana], for your infectious laughter; Katja, for special time at Quinta da Pombal; Christiaan O. for offering other ways of connecting; Daniel C. for your gentle hospitality; Sally, Henri, Michelle and everyone at Quinta Mimosa, for sharing your space and opening your hearts to me; and Naomi, for bringing ever more light into my life – yehi or!

And a big thank you to the children of the community, Shana, Sai and Shara, for 'pushing my buttons', for your endless curiosity and love of life, and for your laughter.

To Satprem, Nura, Wahido, Sud Ram, Soroya, Sabrina, Jutta and Kaya, thank you so much for sharing your experiences of working with Tony [which appear at the end of Book Two].

My thanks to Yutke for 'recognizing me' and giving me a home on Kibbutz Hardouf for several months, where I sat overlooking the glorious hills of the Galilee in northern Israel, and rewrote, and rewrote…

To Alan, Nick, Keith, and all the trustees, wardens and staff at Claridge House, the Quaker House in Surrey, who provided a haven of peace for me to edit when I came back to England and needed to escape the busyness of London.

To Rivka, Nitzan, Sabrina, Gwen – immense gratitude for reading chunks of the manuscript, in different drafts and stages, with such dedication; for your encouragement, your insights, your wisdom, for pushing me to explore ever more deeply, and for giving so generously of your time. And huge thanks to Daniel S. for your meticulous reading of several drafts of the manuscript, and for playing 'devil's advocate' all the way; it was enormously helpful – but you didn't win!

To my beloved son Nitzan – thank you for encouraging me to leap without a safety-net to catch me if I fell; love everlasting.

My profound and abundant gratitude to Tony for inviting me to write about you and your teachings; I didn't know what I was letting myself in for! You pushed open the door to my spiritual questing, and gave me this amazing opportunity to journey. There is no going back. And huge thanks to Sylvia for your intelligent and insightful comments on the text, and for your on-going and invaluable help and support for the project.

And to my unseen guides, the lodestar of my life, boundless gratitude for blessing me with your unconditional love, your infinite wisdom, and your smiles.

My heart is overflowing…

Tony believes that the name Samara derives from the Hebrew word 'shamar' which means 'guarded' or 'protected'.

Some names in Book One have been changed at Tony's request.

Book One
Journeys

"I thought I was going to the Amazon to save the Rain Forest. But I realize that I'd gone to save myself. The real journey of our lives is the journey into ourselves… "

Tony Samara

Content

Introduction: How I came to write this book   9

1   Beginnings – Early Visions, Dreams and Aspirations   27

2   The Zen Buddhist Monastery – Unbroken Meditation, and Beyond   48

3   The Amazon Rain Forest – the First Forest Shamans   65

4   Deeper into the Rain Forest – the *Ayahuasqueros* [Ayahuasca Shamans]   90

5   The Andes Mountains: Bolivia and Southern Peru – the Quechua Shamans   110

6   The Andes Mountains: Northern Peru – the *Huachuma* [San Pedro Shamans]   128

7   Moving On – The Caribbean/Australasia/Europe   142

8   Shamanic Wisdom for Our Time   157

Introduction
How I came to write this book

Tony Samara came into my life in a curious way. So curious, in fact, that it was clearly destined to be. In fact, meeting with Tony was to change my life, though of course I was unaware of it at the time.

I was sitting at the large old pine table in my kitchen in London, drinking coffee and talking with my son. In a random kind of way, I noticed a small buff-coloured leaflet on the table. I glanced at it, then picked it up and looked at it more closely. It was a leaflet giving information about Shamanic retreats being held in Portugal, lead by a Shaman called Tony Samara. The leaflet gave dates of retreats from the beginning of the year. Nothing odd in this, you might think. But what was odd was the fact that this was now October, so the leaflet must have been about a year old – and I had no recollection of ever having seen it before.

I had no knowledge of it arriving in the post, of opening an envelope with it inside, or of anyone giving it to me. I had not picked it up at my local health shop, which boasts a shifting plethora of interesting 'mind/body/soul' leaflets, nor at the library. I was absolutely sure that I had never set eyes on this leaflet before. It was simply there, sitting on my kitchen table. Now I acknowledge that tidiness is not one of my strongest traits, and I tend to spread my papers to fill, or more usually overflow, the space available. But I *had* cleared the kitchen table more than once during the past year, and the leaflet had not been there. Where had it come from?

I was intrigued. I stared at the leaflet; it stared back at me, provocatively. In some absurd way, it seemed to be calling to me. There was a photograph of Tony on the back, wearing a cowboy hat and a smile of immense warmth and gentleness. His eyes seemed to look at me, and into the very depths of my being. He also looked incredibly young and drop-dead gorgeous. This had to be worth a telephone call. His wife answered and then put Tony on the line. I asked, in my best businesslike manner, if he could send me some more material about his work. No, he said, he doesn't have any other printed material. What did I want to know?

I wasn't sure what I wanted to know. Perhaps I had asked for more material as a way of stalling, of putting off a decision I was beginning to feel compelled to make. I continued talking to him, asking questions that would now embarrass me. He answered with great patience and, I felt, faint amusement. But his voice was unbelievably gentle and something in his manner drew me to him. Feeling inexplicably pulled along a path I was not sure I wanted to take, I said I would call him back later, and put the phone down.

I told my son that a strong desire to go to one of the retreats advertised in the leaflet was creeping up on me. He smiled and said "go for it" as though it were the most natural thing in the world. But to me it seemed crazy. I had no money, the retreats were in some far off place I'd never heard of in the south of Portugal, and my knowledge of Shamanism was limited to the sorcery of Don Juan in the books of Carlos Castaneda, that I'd read years ago as a student. And the retreat that most attracted me started in less than two weeks' time. What was I doing?

I called Tony back.

"I'd like to come to the Intensive," I blurted out hurriedly, before 'good sense' got the better of me.

"Of course."

"But it starts very soon, I suppose it's fully booked?" Hoping, perhaps.

"It's been booked up for months. But an hour ago, we had a cancellation." [Later, I would discover that Tertit, who would become my landlady in Portugal, had been the one to cancel; making space for me. The synchronicities of the universe!]

And so it went, problems arising and being resolved before I had time to change my mind. I telephoned four or five travel agents, asking for a cheap flight to Faro, the nearest airport to the retreat centre. [This was before I was dragged reluctantly into the twenty-first century and had access to the Internet.] No cheap flights were available at such short notice. Disappointed, but also relieved, I told my son that I couldn't go. The universe may have been trying to nudge me in a certain direction, but not at British Airways prices!

I sat staring into my empty coffee mug, willing it to divulge some secret that would guide my course of action. Then the telephone rang. One travel agent had found 'just one' cheap flight to Faro for the dates I had requested. I only need one, I said dryly. I booked for a week, as Tony had suggested, although the retreat was to last only five days. I made another mug of coffee – I was still addicted to coffee then – and drank it with mounting excitement, and not a little trepidation. I knew, in some inexplicable and not really conscious way, that my life was about to change; forever.

I arrived in Monte Mariposa, the Mountain of Butterflies, on a windy afternoon in late October. I was exhausted, washed out, on the verge of collapse. I had M.E. [Myalgic Encephalomyelitis, also known, rather inaccurately, as Chronic Fatigue Syndrome] and it was taking its toll.

I had had M.E. for four years at that time, and the symptoms were still quite severe. Travelling was an enormous challenge and although I used a wheelchair at both airports, and was met at Faro airport by one of Tony's helpers, by the time I arrived at Monte Mariposa my whole body was aching with fatigue; I could barely function.

But even through my exhaustion, I was charmed by my first sight of the Mountain of Butterflies. Set deep in the hills of the Algarve, not far from the village of Santa Catarina, it was a picturesque place, with magnificent views across rolling countryside. Carved into the hillside, the main building – which housed the office, a large kitchen and dining room and some space for other mind/body workshops

– was at the top of the hill. The large space specially built for Tony's retreats, and referred to by everyone as the 'Temple', was down in the valley.

The Temple was a large simple structure built of natural wood, with all four 'walls' made of floor-to-ceiling glass panels that could slide open. The accommodation, also in the valley, was in small wooden cabins, each furnished with two beds, two shelves and a few hooks: sparse but adequate, and the simplicity appealed to me. But the toilets and showers were halfway up the hill, up many rough-hewn, uneven and very steep stone steps. Walking with difficulty, with a stick, I wondered how on earth I would manage the climb. And I needed to use the toilet frequently!

As I stared up the hill in disbelief, uncertain of what I had let myself in for, I noticed that people were also staring at me. Indeed, I surely cut a strange figure. Everyone I saw seemed to be about twenty-two years old, in robust health and bursting with energy. With my stick, my long dark hooded cape and my body bent over from the weariness of the journey, I must have looked like an ancient witch. People told me later that they had wondered what on earth I was doing there. At that moment, so did I.

I was greeted and shown to my cabin, where I desperately needed to rest. Perhaps after a long night's sleep I would feel a little better the next day, able to cope with whatever was on offer. But I was in for a big surprise. I would be woken later, I was told, as Tony would be starting the retreat at sunset and working through the night. When he does Ceremony, Tony likes to work with the more subtle energies of the moon. I explained that I could not possibly work at night, that I was ill, incapacitated with exhaustion and needed a long night's sleep at the best of times – and this was definitely not looking like the best of times. I was told not to worry, to have a rest, and that everything would be fine. Too exhausted to argue, I collapsed onto the bed and slept.

At sunset, I woke to find a blond woman with a beautiful smile bending over me and gently nudging my shoulder. She helped me, or rather half carried me, to the Temple. And there began one of the most extraordinary experiences of my life.

Tony Samara was standing in the doorway to welcome me. Whether it was a trick of the light as the setting sun was reflected through the glass walls of the Temple, or my own dazed state that created that first image I had of him, I don't know. But Tony appeared at that moment as some kind of ethereal being, exuding love and peace that seemed almost other-worldly. With his long dark curly hair and piercing green eyes, he also projected astonishing physical beauty, but without a hint of sexuality. He had a quiet charisma about him that sucked you in; it was easy to understand why both women and men fell in love with him.

He greeted me and showed me to a mattress and told me that it was fine to sleep when I felt the need, that the work continued on the energetic level whether we are asleep or awake. I started to ask questions – as always, I had a lot of questions – but he hushed me, saying that I didn't need to understand anything intellectually, I just needed to allow myself to experience whatever would happen.

He said that if at any time during the night I needed him, I had only to call; but anyway he would be with me before I called. And he was.

About thirty people had gathered on the mattresses spread around the perimeters of the Temple. Beside each mattress a plastic bowl, a glass, a toilet roll and a saucer with a few segments of orange on it, had all been carefully laid out. I wondered aloud if they had some strange Shamanic symbolism – mundane objects transformed through Ceremony into something exotic and meaningful. All would be revealed, I was told. Be patient. [Something I would hear with irritating frequency when working with Tony!] The other participants all seemed to know what they were doing, why they were there and what would happen during the Ceremony. They had all worked with Tony before, and most, though not all of them, had attended previous Intensives.

I learnt the next day that Tony virtually never allows anyone who has not worked with him before to join an Intensive. [Now, he no longer advertises them, and attending an Intensive is by his invitation only.] Months later, when I was interviewing him for this book, I asked him why he had let me join – assuming that, in his great wisdom, he had recognized that I was 'special'. "You're so intellectual, talking to you at one of my retreats would not have helped you. You needed a serious jolt to get you out of your brilliant mind." So far, so good. Then he smiled his inscrutable smile and added, "You were so stuck, Nomi. Nothing short of an Intensive would have got you moving." Never make assumptions!

The large space of the temple was intensely quiet; the only sounds, the breathing of participants and the wistful crackling of the wood-burning fire. The sun had set and the darkness was punctured by myriad stars pushing through the glass walls on all sides. I lay on my mattress, drinking in the magic of the atmosphere, curious for the Ceremony to begin. Then Tony started to speak in a low, gentle voice that created an enchantment of its own. He told us to reserve judgement, as far as possible not to think about what was happening – in fact, not to think at all; just to allow ourselves to experience whatever came up. He explained that we would be drinking a special herbal concoction, the juice of a cactus plant that comes from South America, where it is used in Shamanic Ceremony.

Tony had become a Shaman in the Amazonian Rain Forest some ten years before. He had studied the healing powers of Shamanic herbs and their ability to work on the emotional and spiritual levels, as well as the physical. After many years of working with the *Huachuma,* Shamans who specialize in using healing herbs, he had created his own Ceremony, geared to helping people in the West – with our different sensibilities and reference points – to open up to our spirituality. The plants that Tony uses are specially grown and prepared under his guidance, so that the spirit of the plant – the essence of the work with Shamanic herbs – remains within the juice.

This juice is a strong concoction that purifies the blood, cleans out the bowels and eliminates toxins from the whole body. When taken in Ceremony, it can also help us to remove the masks we wear in our daily lives and let go of the constant buzzing of our busy minds. It can take us to a place beyond the limitations of the material world, beyond our self-imposed restrictions and clever mind games. It can enable us to transcend the limits of our belief systems and the judgements that they create, and move into a space of deeper knowing. It can help us to relinquish the fierce hold of the 'reality' created by our ego, our culture-bound and conditioned thought patterns, and let go of assumptions about ourselves, the world and our place in it. It can open up a space within that is normally hidden, not conscious, enabling us to get in touch with our highest self, taking us on a journey to that place of divinity deep inside us and allowing us to explore its truth.

This herbal remedy works differently for each individual. Like every good teacher, it starts each journey from the known and familiar place where the traveller is at the time. It does not bombard the system with extraneous sights and wonders, but gently leads more deeply into the source of each person's own being. Unlike potent hallucinogenic drugs, it does not create experiences beyond the self; rather, it removes our inhibitions so that we can move more deeply into our own inner selves. It may also connect us to nature spirits, to great spiritual masters of the past and to our own spirit guides. It may show us scenes from our past that we need to work with, or take us back into past lives.

In Peru, where Tony learnt its secrets, this herbal remedy is also used for healing many diseases, including cancer. But in Ceremony, its purpose is cleansing and purification – physical, emotional and spiritual. It must be used, however, with correct intention, and should only be taken under the guidance of an initiate.

Tony begins his journey around the darkened Temple, the only light coming from the flickering fire and the stars shooting through the glass walls.

Tony comes to each person individually and pours each one a glass of the special herbal liquid. Then he sits with them as they drink it, watching, guiding, encouraging. Though there may be thirty people taking part in Ceremony, each person experiences an individual journey. This is not a 'sharing retreat' and there is no contact among the participants during Ceremony itself. Each person relates directly, and only, to Tony, as the guide – and to him/herself, focusing on the inner journey; there is no comfort zone of shared sympathy and camaraderie. Rather like childbirth, once the process has begun it takes its own relentless course; there is no escape.

Tony knelt beside my mattress, poured me a glass of the juice and waited. I don't know what I expected, but certainly not what I was given. The juice looks like green slime, smells awful and tastes foul – the most disgusting drink I have ever tried to force down my throat. After two sips, I felt nauseous and couldn't drink any more. Tony encouraged, cajoled, persuaded. "I will sit with you while you drink," he told me in his soothing, gentle voice, at the same time letting me know that there was no way out: he was not leaving until I had finished the glass. There were thirty people in the room, but he had all the time in the world to sit with me. He told me to hold a piece of orange to my nose as I drank, and to suck on the orange when I'd finished, so that

I didn't vomit. He explained that the juice was cleaning me out inside, emotionally as well as physically, and that I should try to hold it in as long as I could.

Somehow, I managed to finish the glass and lay back on my mattress, feeling sicker than I could remember. My mind seemed to have disappeared; I was without context or gravity, floating in an unrecognized limbo, entirely without thoughts. At first this felt frightening, then perfectly natural; I realized, somewhere deep in my being, that thoughts are only a small part of us and we don't have to live in our minds. Indeed, that living too much in our minds is the strongest factor in keeping us 'stuck'. Then I started to feel as though I were curled up inside my body, looking at it from the inside. I seemed to fluctuate between being inside my body, and outside observing it. I was intensely aware of my physical self in a way that I had not been before, finding it both beautiful and absurdly funny. And then I was flooded with sensations, coming too fast to grasp.

My first vision was of a little man inside my stomach, perhaps six inches tall, wearing a denim suit and peaked worker's cap, sweeping out my stomach with a long broom. He had the most impish blue eyes and a smile to die for. I had an uncanny feeling that I knew this man, and had to remind myself that he was walking around inside my body and was only six inches tall! This image was to recur many times during the night.

Then I started to see flashing lights, and swords cutting through me in swift brutal strokes and I screamed in terror. Suddenly, I became aware that Tony had been sitting by my mattress for some moments before I screamed. He offered no reassurance, no sympathy; just his presence to help me through whatever I needed to go through. And he made it very clear that this was my journey, and I would have to do the work. He told me to trust: in the universe, the Divine, in my own higher intuition and wisdom. Trust was the first lesson, he said, letting go of conditioned beliefs and old mind patterns, moving into my body and my heart. Moving into the unknown, without fear.

The night was long and hard. After two or maybe three hours – I seemed to have lost contact with time – Tony came to give me another glass of the herbal juice which I found more disgusting than the first. I drank it, knowing that there was no escape; I held an orange segment to my nose, willing myself not to vomit, to stay with the experience. I visited several past lives – terrifying, painful and strikingly real – and was also shown incidents from this life. Some I saw as though watching a vivid, brightly-technicoloured larger-than-life film in slow motion. Others were not so much seen as felt, the pain of old traumas surfacing and engulfing me. Images and sensations, pain and grief, swirled through me; my mind was suspended and there was no way out, but in. Tony talked with me again, encouraging me not to try to understand, not to judge, not to suppress, just to allow myself to feel and live through whatever came up. And intermittently, my little cloth-capped worker kept sweeping and smiling inside me. After perhaps five or six hours, the visions subsided and I slept.

I needed to be helped to the toilet several times that night. [And the next night. By the third night, I was able to go by myself.] On one of my excursions that first night, I stayed outside for a while. I wanted to drink in the night air, look at the stars, feel the peace and perfection of the universe in this magical place. I felt myself to be huge, the centre of all worlds, and at the same time infinitesimal, a tiny speck in the vastness and wonder of the cosmos. I looked around the garden and saw angels, many angels, about four feet tall, dressed in white and pale blue, their wings folded behind them, standing in the branches of the trees. To me, that night, they were real.

At about five o'clock in the morning, Tony brought me a third glass of the dreaded juice. After two sips, I could hold back no longer and I vomited my guts out. Now I understood what the plastic bowls and toilet paper were for, and why all the glass panels that made up the walls of the Temple slid open. No hidden Shamanic symbolism here! Staying on my mattress, I opened the glass panel behind me, put my head out into the cold night air, and filled my plastic bowl, again and again. I vomited until there was nothing left to vomit. I felt that I was retching up my illness, all the physical toxins that my little peak-capped 'friend' was cleaning out, and a lifetime of fears and emotional 'baggage' that had been stored in my solar plexus. Though vomiting is such a basic physical act, it is also ridding the system of emotional pain that is held in every cell of the body. I lay back on my mattress exhausted, but with a profound feeling of release and relief.

I must have slept, for the next thing I knew a weak October sun was heralding the dawn, the fire had gone out and people had moved their mattresses to form small intimate groups. Tony had disappeared. I was invited to curl up with a group of five or six people who all seemed to be connected physically, arms and legs intertwined in such a way that it was difficult to see where one body ended and another began. A fitting metaphor, perhaps, after a long night of spiritual journeying, that we are all interconnected; in fact, that we are all one. We talked a little and laughed a lot, as though we had been life-long friends; a welcome release from the rigours of the night. Then, hunger getting the better of us, we went in search of food.

After breakfast, I slept for most of the next day, surfacing only to eat an early lunch, the last food we would be given before breakfast the following morning. [The Shamanic herbs that Tony uses should always be taken on an empty stomach.]

At sunset I made my way to the Temple and lay on my mattress, curious to see what this second night of Ceremony would bring. But although the first night had been difficult and very painful, I was quite disappointed when nothing much seemed to happen on the second night. Tony told me that he was "being kind" to me, that I needed to absorb the experiences of the previous night, and I should just rest; the work would continue on the energetic level. I managed to keep down one and a half glasses of the juice without vomiting, and slept most of the night.

The third night I was again nauseous and only by a great act of will managed not to vomit until after I had drunk the second glass of the slimy green liquid. That night, too, nothing seemed to happen: no visions, no past lives, no dreams, no relived experiences from this life. Nothing except physical pain and nausea, which seemed to engulf my whole body. Tony said that of course many things were happening, and were being processed through my body. I should not try to understand with my mind, just allow the experiences to unfold in their own way, and trust the innate intelligence of my body. But my body then felt like one raw open wound, pulsating with pain, and I was not overly encouraged when Tony told me that gradually, over the next weeks and months, I would come to see the wisdom of what I had been shown.

During the day after the third and last night of Ceremony, we ate and slept and then gathered in the Temple in the late afternoon. We were to perform a closing ceremony, the Shamanic Dance of the Universe, bringing the energy of Spirit deep into our bodies, renewing our life force after the cleansing and depleting effects of the last three nights. Tony told us that in South America, Shamans often perform this dance for seven or eight hours without a break. But he would be kind to us: we would dance for just two hours. I laughed; though feeling healthier than when I arrived, there was no way I could keep going for more than about three minutes. I said that I would be happy to watch. No, said Tony, start. We will put a mattress in the middle of the circle, and if you feel that you cannot continue, you can rest on the mattress, and so still be a part of the dance.

We stood in a circle and joined hands, moving slowly two paces to the right, then two paces to the left, chanting *Haya Hu* as we danced, invoking Great Spirit to be with us. This is a Shamanic chant, *Hu* meaning "Spirit" and *Haya* meaning "come to me". I was intrigued that although we moved the same number of steps in both directions, the circle gradually moved round to the right. [I subsequently learnt that this is because moving to the right represents moving towards the future, the left, moving back to the past; and that even when we take an equal number of steps in both directions, we are always moving forwards.]

After a very short while, I felt that I could not go on but somehow, perhaps with the energy I had absorbed during the nights of Ceremony, I seemed able to push out my boundaries of physical endurance and kept going, just a little longer. Again and again, as exhaustion overtook me and I felt on the point of collapse, the energy in the room seemed to lift and sustain me, and the people on either side of me, holding my hands, seemed to support me and carry me forward on the breath. This happened many times. I kept going. *Haya Hu,* I chanted, *Haya Hu.* And Spirit came to me. When Tony drew the dance to a close, I was surprised: I thought we were going to dance for two hours? We had been dancing for two hours and twenty minutes!

Before I booked my flight to come to Portugal, Tony had told me that the Intensive lasted for five days, but that I should book for a week. And in fact the day after the Intensive finished proved crucial for me. Tony spent a couple of hours talking with me privately, helping me to process the experiences of the nights of Ceremony, enabling me to absorb and understand in an experiential way the spiritual journey upon which I had embarked, giving a context to my questioning and questing.

I stayed in the valley for two more days, after the end of the retreat. Everyone had left, including Tony. Though the office at the top of the hill was quite busy during the day, I was entirely alone in the valley. And it was wonderful, a gift to myself, a time of being in the beauty and stillness of nature, alone with my soul. A time of getting to know a quieter, calmer self.

And more extraordinary things were to happen before I left. On the morning of the penultimate day, I woke feeling queasy and out of sorts. A residue of the work of Ceremony, perhaps: toxins deeply buried in the cells, moving out into the blood stream before being released from the body. Before he left, Tony told me that there was still some food in the kitchen in the valley, which should be enough to last me for those two days. That morning I certainly didn't feel like eating breakfast, but I really wanted some herbal tea to settle my stomach. I went to the kitchen but could find no tea anywhere: no packets, no tea bags, no tea plants. Then suddenly I noticed, brewing on the stove, a large urn – filled with Louisa tea. Through the morning, as I started to write about my experiences of the previous few days, I sipped several mugs of the gentle balm, grateful to the thoughtful person who had made it.

Later that day, I went up the hill to the main house to thank Wendy, who had been feeding us on the retreat, assuming that she had made the tea. But she hadn't. Nor had anyone else at Monte Mariposa. I asked her to check; someone there must have made it. She checked; they hadn't. Could someone perhaps have visited and made it? No, only the staff were there and none of them was responsible for the tea. And I was entirely alone in the valley. There was no other human who could have made the tea. No-one. Another visitation of angels?

Tony came back the next day and again we spoke. I had been fascinated by the Shamanic aspects of his work, and wondered if he could recommend some books for me to read. He explained that although his teachings were rooted in Shamanism, they were no longer classical Shamanism, and that he had now moved along a spiritual path beyond. This was his own work and there were not as yet any books published about it. However, he was in the process of writing a book about his teachings; I would have to be patient. I don't know what prompted me to ask him if he had a publisher; he said that he didn't. I told him that I was with a good literary agent and that if he would like me to, I would be happy to pass the manuscript on to her when it was finished. And so we left it.

I returned to London and realized that my life would never be quite the same again. The changes that I had begun to make on my journey through M.E. continued at an accelerated pace. But now I was aware that the changes were on the inside. My son said that I had a glow about me that he had not seen before. I still had M.E. but I was learning that there is a 'healthy' way to be ill. To those observing my life from the outside, it perhaps did not look very different from the way it had looked before. But my perceptions were changing; the limitations of my old worldview were disintegrating and a growing consciousness of spirituality now informed my life. There was no going back.

All my life, spiritual questing had woven itself like a *leitmotif* through all my activities. Throughout a difficult childhood and troubled teenage years, it had been a constant companion, a comforting familiar presence in a dark world that I didn't understand and couldn't relate to. But in all the busyness of my adult life as I pursued a career as an actor, it had been pushed into the background, a small flame flickering forlornly on a back burner, though never entirely extinguished; waiting patiently until I was ready to engage with it.

I continued to work on my book – my journey through my M.E. and the spiritual blessings it had brought me. I was now able to bring to my writing a deepening spiritual perspective, and realized that the journey – and the book – were no longer just about healing M.E. I seemed to be in touch with spiritual forces that I had not been aware of before, of 'being guided' in some inexplicable and indefinable way. My healing journey was about healing my life.

I was also eager to return to acting. Although I was still not well enough to sustain a performance in the theatre, I felt that I could cope with television and film work. I now understood that all forms of creativity are to be nurtured and valued, that my intermittent doubts about acting as some demon within seeking vainglorious recognition were the result of a limited and conditioned mind-set and that acting, like all artistic endeavour, when undertaken with right intention, is also an expression of the spiritual. Indeed, all creative work is spiritual, as we open ourselves up as a vessel to the Great Creator. Coming to this realization was liberating.

So it was that, a few weeks later, I was invited to a casting for a part in Roman Polanski's film "The Pianist", set in the Warsaw ghetto during the holocaust. I mention this because it showed me very powerfully how change on the inside manifests in our actions in the outside world. Previously, a casting had been a most stressful experience for me; I would first rehearse endless dialogues in my head of what to say to the casting director, how to react in every possible scenario, and then berate myself afterwards for my perceived inadequacies and stupidity in not profiting from the opportunity offered to me. Now I had no 'game plan', just a strong feeling that this was work I wanted to do. I came from a still centred place within, open to whatever would come up, not needing to control anything, and so was able to be completely in the moment. After a second audition, I was offered the role.

Filming with Polanski was a unique experience that took me to the heart of my creativity; as we transcended the horror of the subject matter, it became powerful and uplifting. Filming is about being in the moment, being open and aware of everything that is happening in the moment and reacting to it in character. You learn your lines, of course, but then you must allow them to become just the outward symbol of the inner journey of your character; in fact, of your own inner journey, that takes you at that moment through a particular time in your character's life.

Playing a woman who had lost her husband and her mind during the horrors of life in the Warsaw ghetto, was not an easy journey. And all the time, you must also be conscious that you are filming; as you play out your scenes, you need to be aware of where the camera is, where your mark is, and all the other technical trappings of filming. It struck me that this was the perfect metaphor for our spiritual journey: to be fully in the moment, fully aware of everything around us in the physical world, but conscious that the real journey takes place within.

Some months later, a manuscript arrived in the post from Tony. As I read, my excitement turned to disbelief. It was incomprehensible, as though cobbled together by a bureaucratic committee trying to write a PhD thesis. Where was Tony's magic? His humour? I could not possibly pass this on to my agent; she would clearly think I'd lost the plot.

I telephoned Tony and told him, very gently, that of course it was only my opinion, but I thought that the manuscript needed more work. Fine, he said, will you help me? At that stage I really didn't know. I didn't see a way of moving through the confusion, but I said that I'd think about it. Some days later I called him to say that I'd be happy to spend a few days with him [he was staying in Dorset at the time] and see if we could come up with a working plan for the book.

Tony met me at the bus stop and took me to the house in which he was staying, a rambling old cottage with a large wild garden where his equally wild four-year-old son, Sai, could play. I was introduced to his wife, Sylvia, and baby daughter, Shara. During the course of the next few days, I was fascinated to watch the family interaction. Tony, spiritual guide to thousands, being the happy family man: cooking, rocking Shara, trying to cajole Sai into eating *something*. [Karma, perhaps, catching up with him for the anxiety he had caused his parents when he had refused to eat as a child!]

I was also in for a pleasant surprise: Tony in fact, had not written the manuscript he'd sent me. It had been put together by several other people after attending some of his retreats. So, we spent the next few days working through ideas and I began to form a concept of what the book could be. In the end, although the manuscript was dotted with interesting information, I decided that I would rather not use it at all. Tony agreed to give me *carte blanche*; it would be my book, however I chose to write it. He invited me to spend August with him back in the Algarve, so that I could interview him and begin to form a structure for the book.

August in the south of Portugal is hot; in a little wooden hut down in the valley, it was unbearably so. But at least this hut had its own shower and toilet, and a tiny kitchenette built onto the porch.

I was again alone in the valley, this time self-contained; but without transport, I was dependent on others for food and all necessities. Tony was now living in another valley, a fifteen-minute drive away on the other side of Santa Catarina, and several people who were working with him had moved into that valley to be near him. From time to time, one or other of them would appear, bringing me supplies of food or anything else I needed.

So began my month in Portugal. Tony would visit, appearing out of the blue when he could find the time. I would learn later that Tony never had time for anything, and I thought this strange for a spiritual teacher. [My assumptions about how a spiritual teacher should be, says Tony. Never make assumptions!] But somehow everything always got done, although often to the great frustration of those working closely with him. A lesson to teach us patience? Perhaps. My own journey with Tony towards patience was peppered with not a little irritation and annoyance, and a great deal of questioning about the connection between a spiritual teacher's life and teachings.

I never knew when Tony would visit me. At first I was cross – after all, I had come to Portugal specifically to interview him for the book – and found his behaviour disconcerting. But I came to realize that this was also an important spiritual lesson: trust. Trust in the universe, trust in Tony to be there when needed, trust in my own process of working. And once I let go of the need to control my timetable, everything flowed. If Tony didn't come when I had a bunch of questions for him, I would move on to something else that I could write without him. And so I began to relinquish preconceived ideas of how things 'ought to be', to open up to the gifts that the universe was showering upon me, and to connect more deeply with my own intuition and creativity.

In spite of the intense heat, it was a glorious month. I would rise early with the sun, while it was still cool and a gentle breeze danced through the trees. I would greet the new day with great joy and gratitude, thankful for the perfection of the universe, for having been brought to this place, physically and spiritually. The only human in the valley, I would share my morning prayers with the trees, the hills, the sounds and smells of Mother Nature; with the abiding peace that embraced me and joined with the growing peace within.

And I would sing. For me, this was a major breakthrough because at the age of six – six! – I had been told by a particularly delightful schoolteacher to "mouth the words only, but do not sing" at the end of term concert, because the sound that came out of my mouth was so tuneless. Since then, I had never, ever, sung where I could be overheard, or even where I couldn't; in fact, I wouldn't even sing to myself alone in the bath. I had totally accepted 'the fact' that I couldn't sing. Now I found myself singing from my depths, from my soul, unafraid, singing out across the valley, with the caution button turned off, and the volume turned full up. The trees didn't seem to mind. It was liberating!

A gentle pattern of living emerged. Each day I would make fruit juice for breakfast [Tony had lent me a juicer] and sip it slowly, sitting on the steps of my porch, looking out across the beauty of the valley. During the morning, I would pick fresh figs and savour their deliciousness. I felt as though I were living in another time; or connected, perhaps, to some past life as a peasant woman. I had a strong sense of *déjà vu,* a feeling of knowing this place in a way beyond my current connection with it.

Then, in the shade of the old fig tree, I would spend the mornings writing. I interviewed Tony to learn the facts of his life and his journey through Shamanism; a skeleton upon which I would later put flesh. As I wrote, I would have more questions for him; and his answers invariably led me to still further questions. In the heat of the early afternoons, I would rest on a mattress on my porch – it was much too hot to be inside the hut. After dinner, when the fierce heat of the day had abated, I would go for a short walk. And then I would sit in the stillness of the valley, watching the trees and listening to the silent sounds of the universe. Learning just 'to be' – a difficult step for me. I felt very blessed.

I had come to Portugal to interview Tony and start structuring the book. My plan was to take copious notes and then return to London and write. But a week before I was due to leave the valley, I had a change of heart. Why would I want to go back to London, to spend a grey and rainy winter living in a small flat carved out of the bottom part of an old terraced house, with people crammed on either side of me and above me, enveloped by the noise and the busyness of a big city, to write a 'spiritual' book about a Shaman who was living a thousand miles away? And, indeed, was living in an idyllic place where the sun shines most of the year round, and I could have the peace and stillness so perfect a backdrop for writing.

My son met me at Luton airport and after a hug of welcome asked me jokingly when I was going back to Portugal. I laughed, and told him that he had pre-empted my surprise. I had found a flat near the valley where Tony was living, owned by Tertit – the woman who had cancelled her place on the Intensive at the last minute, thus freeing a space for me. I planned to go back in a few weeks, as soon as I could sort out what needed to be done before I left London.

The flat, a pleasant three-room apartment that abutted Tertit's magnificent villa, was a big change from the wooden hut in the valley. As well as being vastly more spacious and comfortable, it was at the top of a hill with magnificent views on all sides.

Tertit was an insatiable traveller, and spent most of that winter in North Africa. Again I found myself living quite alone, and discovered that I loved the experience. For I didn't feel alone at all. The views across the hills were stunning, the draw of nature strong: I felt embraced by the universe, totally peaceful, at one with the natural world and with myself.

I stayed at Tertit's apartment for six months, writing, reading and spending some time each day sitting on the terrace looking out across the hills, just being. At some point during this time, an almost blind diabetic husky dog turned up on my doorstep and 'adopted' me. He followed me around and sat at my feet as I worked. I fed him and we became friends. He 'invited' me to take him on walks [my health was slowly improving]. He watched over me and I felt protected by him. Once, when I fell over and hurt my leg he galloped over to me and lay huddled against my body until I was able to get up. His presence became an important part of my life.

I got into the habit of sitting out on the terrace with the husky as dusk fell, looking out across the darkening hills, with no human in shouting distance. When there was a full moon, he would howl. And I would hug him, and sometimes I would howl, too, echoing his call to the wild, wanting to reconnect to my wilder, primitive self. I had been asking Tony for some time what my 'totem animal' was, and he said that he wouldn't tell me, that I would know myself. Now, I knew: my totem animal was wolf.

During this period Tony would visit me intermittently, though now I needed his physical presence less and less. He had told me the bare bones of his life, enough for me to be able to weave around it the clothes of his story, without needing further input from him. So I spent my days writing, reading widely on Shamanism, and imperceptibly moving forward on my own spiritual journey. I also made friends with some of the people around Tony and with others I met, and began to create a life for myself in Portugal.

But the winter was hard. It was bitterly cold, the houses in the Algarve being built against the intense heat of summer, not the icy cold of winter. It rained frequently, and when it really bucketed down there was usually a power cut – which meant no heat, no light, and no computer. On those dark days I stayed in bed with a hot water bottle and several layers of sweaters, the only way to keep warm, and wrote by hand under the bedclothes. Or I simply gave up and read.

I knew that in mid March I had to return to England where I was scheduled to lead my own healing retreats. Tony knew this too. I had hoped to have sketched out a *very* rough first draft of the book by then. But at the beginning of February Tony dropped a bombshell: he was leaving – and I was forced to take a break from the book. At first, I was furious: how dare he leave just like that, with no warning, when I had come to Portugal, at his invitation, specially to write a book about him? Then I tried to persuade him to go a month later; at least this would give me a month, if not six weeks, and I would write fast! But no, he was leaving and that was that; there was no question of Tony changing his plans. So there was nothing for it. I calmed down and used the time to travel around Portugal. In fact I discovered many interesting places and wonderful people, several of whom have become 'forever' friends.

Back in England, as well as leading my own healing retreats, I spent time visiting with friends and catching up. I found that I was becoming more drawn to being with 'spiritual' friends, and was moving away from my previous involvement with political peace-making activity. I still cared passionately about the issues and the people, but was now moving towards Einstein's view that "no problem can be solved by the same consciousness that created it.". The political realities at the core of any problem can only change by imbuing them with spiritual awareness.

I went back to Portugal in late summer, again to Tertit's flat, and continued writing. But with the approach of winter, an opportunity to move came up and I decided to take it. I had spent one winter entirely alone and I knew I could do it; I didn't need to do it again. It was time for something different.

And different it was! Tony by this time had left the valley and was living next to some land in the hills near Bouliquieme, where he would establish his first Ashram. I was invited to move into a large villa nearby [which we affectionately called the 'Rainbow House' as each of the six bedrooms was painted a different colour] to share with eight other adults and a five-year-old girl. Everyone in the house was working in some way with Tony, and so we were profoundly connected: a loosely-knit 'spiritual' community. It was also eight mirrors showing us who we really were, warts and all. It was a time of sharing, loving, struggling; of great compassion as we learnt to give unconditional love, to others and to ourselves. It was a time of looking inward and facing ourselves in ways that were not comfortable; a time of opening up to welcome the future without fear – and without assumptions. A time of moving out of our comfort zone and forward with growing consciousness on our own journeys through life.

And so it was that I spent a difficult, challenging and rewarding winter in the 'Rainbow House', continuing to work on myself, and on the first draft of this book…

In ancient times, those magical times when our ancestors first walked upon the earth, the human race recognized itself as part of the natural world, and acknowledged the natural world as part of itself. The unity and harmonious order of Creation was apparent to all. All creatures that walked the earth, flew across its skies or swam in its oceans were understood by humans to be interconnected and interrelated. The ebb and flow of night and day, of seasonal differences, of the changing weather, held mystery as well as practical application. The life of dreams and of the waking world were interwoven; the physical and the metaphysical embraced one another without separation. Visible and invisible worlds were known to be entwined, and our ancestors walked the sacred path between the two.

This was the world inhabited by the first Shamans...

Chapter One
Beginnings
Early Visions, Dreams and Aspirations

The crystal chandeliers hanging from the high ceiling of the grand dining hall sparkled with a thousand colours. As the crystals gently swayed, the light seemed to spin in circles, whirling and dancing like rainbows of stars. The constant movement of the light bedazzled the little boy as he gazed upwards, transported into a magical world. Three-year-old Tony Samara was held spellbound by the chandeliers in the ornate Cairo mansion that was his grandfather's home. His first remembrance of light, touching the Divine.

As a small child, Tony spent many happy hours at the home of his grandparents, in a busy and colourful quarter in the centre of Cairo, near the river Nile. Long before Tony was born, his grandparents had settled in Egypt. Tony believes that his ancestors hailed originally from the Caucasus Mountains of South Eastern Europe. Certainly, he has always felt a strong affinity with the people and the culture of this area, as though he knew that his roots had been planted there long ago.

Several centuries before, these ancestors had made the long trek across the Caucasus Mountains, down to the Ottoman Empire. More a tribe than a family, they were like a many-branched candlestick, each branch separate from the others, yet firmly bonded at the roots. Wherever they went, they had all prospered, and by the beginning of the twentieth century, they had become wealthy and influential.

But all that was to change. After the First World War, the Ottoman Empire became embroiled in successive power struggles. Growing unrest and insurrection ensued, destabilizing and changing the political map of this region forever. In the instability thus created, many wealthy landowners were losing their lands and their fortunes. Tony's perspicacious grandfather saw what was happening and decided to leave, managing to escape to Egypt with a large part of his wealth intact. Egypt at that time was a stable and liberal society, the 'Switzerland' of the Middle East. It was a centre of learning, with a rich intellectual, artistic and cultural life, and attracted to it from abroad many leading figures in the world of the arts and academia. Many languages could be heard in the streets and bazaars; many cultures intermingled in a climate of openness and gracious living.

Qasim Samara, Tony's grandfather, soon began to feel at home in Egypt, and was able to establish himself without too much difficulty. With his brilliance in languages [it was said that he spoke seventeen fluently!] his business acumen, his intellectual gifts and his worldly sophistication, he soon became a respected member of the political and social elite. His home became a centre for gatherings of interesting and influential people.

And so his son Zoran, Tony's father, was also born into an affluent family. It was a large, complicated family, full of strong personalities and the kind of self-confidence that comes with long-inherited wealth. Like all affluent families in Cairo at that time, the household also included many loyal servants. Zoran, like his brothers, was educated in the best private schools. His mother, Suhara, enjoyed running a large and busy household, but still found time to supervise her sons' homework and ensure that they studied hard. Qasim, the archetypal patriarch of the family, was strict but always just. His children revered him and did what was expected of them; no-one would have dreamt of questioning his authority.

At sixteen, Zoran Samara was sent to a private college in England to broaden his horizons, as was customary among wealthy Cairene families at that time. Certainly he did broaden his horizons – though perhaps not in the way that his father had intended! The college to which his father sent him attracted many able students from abroad, and Zoran surrounded himself with fascinating people from many countries and many different backgrounds, often with new and provocative ideas. He would spend long nights with them discussing art, literature, philosophy, politics – whatever students in the late 1950's were wont to spend their time discussing. He spoke several languages, was charming and good-looking, and apparently very popular with his peers. His life was exciting and full.

At one of the student parties that he went to with his friends, Zoran met Julia Andersen – and it was love at first sight for both of them. Her background could not have been more different from his. Born in Skien, Norway, of mixed Scandinavian descent, she grew up in a cold northern climate, a far cry from the colourful, hot and exotic Egypt of Zoran's childhood. Her parents were Lutheran, decent hard-working people who brought up their children with traditional values, to have simple, unpretentious aspirations. But the young Ms. Andersen was high-spirited and independent, and not one to be limited by what she felt to be the narrowness and conservatism of her milieu. While still in her teens, she left home to travel and experience the world. Eventually she arrived in England, where she intended to study English.

Julia and Zoran married and set up home in the southeast of England. And there, in 1965, Tony was born. A year and a half later, his brother Mark followed him into the world. But their time in England was shortly to end. Zoran was summoned back to Egypt by his father, who wanted his growing family around him. Qasim secured a position for his son in an organization affiliated to the United Nations. Later, Julia obtained an excellent job working at the Norwegian Embassy. Tony was two years old when the family moved to Cairo; this was to be the first of many moves in his life.

Zoran didn't take well to his new life in Egypt. He had become used to the cool sophistication and lack of rigid rules of 1960's England, with its order, essential honesty and sense of fair play, and he didn't want to leave. He certainly didn't appreciate the Middle Eastern way of life, the unpredictability and chaos, the street scenes with the child beggars, the donkeys getting in the way of the traffic, the kids who insisted on cleaning your car windows with dirty rags, leaving the windows dirtier than before. But it was inconceivable even to think of disobeying his father; and being a dutiful son, Zoran fulfilled Qasim's wishes with good grace. In time, he acclimatized to the life of a wealthy and well-connected Cairene.

Julia, on the other hand, immediately fell in love with Egypt. She loved the colour and diversity of life in Cairo, and adored what to her was her husband's exotic family. And they immediately took to this blond Nordic beauty and embraced her and her children with great warmth. Julia made many Egyptian friends of all social strata, and mixed as easily and enthusiastically with the local *fellahin* as she did with members of the Diplomatic Corps. She seemed to have an uncanny interest and insight into the lives of the poor and dispossessed. Altogether, she loved her new life in Cairo.

Cairo, magical, mystical, memorable, became the colourful backdrop of Tony's formative years: the pyramids, the Nile, the bazaars, the diversified mixture of people, the labyrinthine alleys of the city and its mysteries.

Although still a very young child, Tony was fascinated by the buzz of ideas, by the contrasting lives of the very wealthy and the very poor living in such close proximity; by the hieroglyphics and the ancient cultures that still lived and breathed just beneath the surface of the city; by the exotic mix of cultures that filled the streets, and very often his parents' house as well. The Egypt of his early childhood, exotic and mysterious, was to have a profound effect upon him, although he would not understand this until he was in his early thirties, and had travelled far on his spiritual path.

As a small child, Tony was enchanted by the bazaars: the bright colours of the richly woven carpets and tapestries; the pungent smells of herbs and strong spices, cardamom and wild thyme. And the sounds: the sing-song Arabic shouts of the coffee vendors balancing their trays of tiny coffee cups as they pushed through the crowds in the bazaars; and the tired grunts of the donkeys mingling with the wail of the distant *muezzin* calling the faithful to prayer.

Tony often went with his mother or grandmother to the bazaars, which were cool even in the heat of the day, as the narrow alleyways were covered over with large carpets providing rich tapestries and welcome shade. They always bought something: small brass trinkets, candlesticks, colourful mats, or freshly ground coffee beans with cardamom seed to make strong Turkish coffee. And Tony loved it all: the mystery and adventure, the flies and the dust; and the people – strange, colourful, larger than life figures who, although this was Cairo, could have walked straight out of Lawrence Durrell's "Alexandria Quartet". Such fertile ground from which a small boy's imagination could blossom.

Egypt at this time was at the crossroads of many different cultures, and a wide variety of mystical sects flourished there: the Sufis, the Jewish Kabbalists, the Copts [the Coptic church is the oldest Christian church in the world, but in Egypt it had also become a mystical sect]. There was great religious fervour and a mosaic of ritual practice among the different religious groups, all powerfully painting the ambience of the city. Tony loved visiting the different Quarters of the city – Moslem, Jewish, Copt – each with its own characteristic flavour and atmosphere. He would stay there for hours on end, fascinated by the strange rites: the chanting of the Copts, the dancing of the Sufis, the whispered magic of them all.

But most of all, he felt an intuitive affinity with the Greeks. When he was older, he would understand why. The ancient Greeks espoused a doctrine of balance and interconnectedness among the physical, emotional and spiritual aspects of life, and aspired to live in harmony with nature; something that was later to become supremely important to Tony. It was this deep spiritual link with the natural world that would draw him to the Shamanic way of life. He also felt very much at home in the Greek temples, which were places of healing as well as prayer. And the fact that the Greeks were a Mediterranean people resonated strongly with him, even at that early age.

At the end of the 1960's, Cairo was a tolerant and inclusive place, and foreigners were an accepted and welcome part of the life of the city; indeed, it would have been a much poorer place without them. The different sects mingled freely and respectfully, although they kept to their own traditions. It was an easy-going, pluralistic society; the city belonged to all her inhabitants. Spiritual power hovered over the city, unseen but ubiquitous and deeply felt. There was a strong unbroken connection to the Biblical Pharaohs; the pyramids were just up the road, and a frequent site for family picnics.

Cairo was a place of great contrasts: the open desert and the greenery along the river Nile; sheep and donkeys nonchalantly crossing busy roads in the chaos and honking of the traffic; the juxtaposition of washing strung out across the narrow back streets, of women dressed in the traditional *gallabiya* beating carpets hung over the railings of their balconies; and the ultra modern hotels boasting shops as fashionable as any in Paris or London.

The Maadi district, to which the Samara family had moved from the centre of Cairo, was lush and green and elegant, full of trees and flowers and the sounds of birds all year round. In the evenings, dressed in their best clothes, the family would often take walks along the wide boulevards, and meet other families doing the same thing. There was an old-fashioned charm and grace about these occasions, a formality that was amiable while being respectful of each other's privacy.

As a small boy, one of Tony's favourite and magical places to visit was the home of his grandparents. Their house, much larger and grander than his parents' home, was filled with ornate furniture, antiques, original paintings by well-known artists, hand-woven Persian carpets and many rare *objets d'art*, all of which fascinated him. Qasim and Suhara Samara were famous for the great dinner parties they hosted in the grand dining room, lit by those magical chandeliers, when wealthy diplomats or distinguished visiting professors or artists would be their guests. The long table in the dining hall would be laid with delicate lace cloths, and set with the finest china and silverware; many delicacies of local and international cuisine would be served, and praised, during the course of the evening.

Although the atmosphere at these dinners was warm, they were also formal occasions, and children were expected to sit still and keep quiet. Tony loved those dinner parties, to which he was taken from the age of four. He would eagerly follow the conversation of the adults, which would roam across history, philosophy, current affairs, the arts, and whatever were the special fields of expertise or interest of the visitors. He was insatiably curious, and his questions would usually be treated with great seriousness and respect by the visitors, and with gentle indulgence by his grandfather, who was secretly very proud of him.

If his intellect was engaged at the ornate dining table of his grandfather, his heart belonged 'below stairs'. The huge kitchen was the hub of the household, with its buzz of energy and infectious excitement, as exotic dishes emerged from raw ingredients. Tony would watch the cooks and their assistants, fascinated, as they patiently prepared delicious feasts of five, six or seven courses. Above all, he loved listening to their stories; cooks always seemed to have great stories to tell, their own personal "Arabian Nights". It was in that kitchen that he absorbed, in some profound way that was not conscious, that people are people, to be respected, loved and valued, irrespective of their class, their education or their wealth.

His grandfather always behaved rather formally towards Tony and his brothers, though he clearly adored them. But his grandmother was much more approachable, a warm and affectionate woman, with a soft lap and comforting arms. One day when he was visiting her, Tony developed a bad tummy-ache. His grandmother gave him love and comfort, but also some 'magic' medicinal herbs, and he soon felt much better.

During his childhood, Tony was to suffer increasing bouts of undiagnosed sickness, which his grandmother cured with her 'magic' herbs. He was very curious to know what she had given him, for the medicines with which the regular doctors tried to cure his illnesses never had any effect. Suhara showed her grandson the herbs from which she had brewed a strong green tea, and explained how they grew and how they had helped to cure his stomach-ache. She served the tea in delicate china cups, as though it were all part of some special ritual.

And perhaps in a way it was. It brought Tony instinctively close to the wisdom of herbal and plant remedies, which were known and made usually by the older women, and handed down from one generation to the next. His grandmother also 'read' his teacup when he had finished drinking, and said that one day he would marry a dark haired, pretty woman from another country – which later proved to be true! She explained the symbols of the tealeaves and how they contained the spirits of the plants from which they came.

31

All this awakened in Tony a feeling of the rightness of natural remedies, of ceremony and blessing. It also reaffirmed an intuition that his distrust of the impersonal and non-holistic care of the doctors who had treated him, was well founded. For a long time after this, he associated feeling better with Suhara. He became fascinated by her 'tea cups' and herbal remedies. His later study and use of medicinal herbs may well have originally been sparked by the childhood cures of his Egyptian grandmother.

More than anything in those early years, Tony loved walking or cycling alone by the river Nile. He would watch the boats and the fishermen, the tinkers selling lavender and jasmine flowers, the boat people cooking corn on open coals. And men sitting around all day, languidly smoking their *nargillas* as though they held all the answers to the meaning of life.

One day, while he was cycling alone by the river, he saw a strange gathering of people just ahead in a place that was usually deserted. Ever the curious child, he left his bike, joined the crowd and asked someone what was going on. One of the men explained that they had found a baby crow that must have fallen out of its nest, and they were debating what to do with it. They said that crows are a bad omen, and they had to get rid of it. Drowning it was the most humane course of action they proposed. Seeing Tony's horror, and no doubt also his expensive clothes, they said that if he wanted to he could buy the crow from them. Tony gave them all his pocket money and took the little bird with him.

At home, he made a small cage for the tiny crow, put it on the veranda of his bedroom, and fed it every few hours with a small feeder. [His parents would become used to the many stray creatures he would bring home to nurse, throughout his childhood.] He lavished devoted care on the tiny bird and slowly it began to recuperate. The crow's parents, with homing instincts much stronger than those of humans, found it and would visit every day, circling and squawking around the veranda. Every morning Tony would open the cage door and the little bird would hop out, flap its tiny wings and make a few hesitant attempts to fly; but, unable to take off, it would return to the cage. One morning it succeeded, and flew off with its parents, squalling with delight. Tony was sad to see it leave, but he was also filled with deep joy for that little crow, leaving its cage and flying off to freedom.

Perhaps this was his first lesson in unconditional love and detachment. Whatever, this episode awakened in him a profound love of all creatures, and a respect for their own place in the universe; for the right of all beings to be free.

"Why? Why? Why? *Why?*" This was the perennial question on the young Tony's lips as he struggled to understand the world around him. Constantly questioning any adult who was willing to listen, and many who were not, he would relentlessly keep up this monosyllabic chain of questions. It would only cease when that precocious, stubborn four- or five- or six-year-old mind was satisfied – or when one of his parents took pity on the adult being 'tortured'. He wasn't purposely making a pest of himself; he just wanted to know; everything. This need to know and understand everything has remained a lifelong drive, leading Tony in many diverse, and sometimes difficult, directions in life.

As well as being a precocious child, and perhaps also an annoying one to adults with little patience, Tony was also hyperactive. He would regularly get up at four o'clock in the morning, disturbing the entire household, and then be on the go all day until his weary mother would finally get him into bed at eight or nine or ten o'clock at night. His inexhaustible energy has been one of the great gifts of his life; now, as an adult, he is able to sleep for just four or five hours a night and thrive. But for those entrusted with his care as a small child, life was not easy!

But it was his imagination and intuition that would both get him into a great deal of trouble, and would also be his salvation. Since he was very young, Tony had inhabited a world of dreams and visions, of spirits and angels and invisible beings, which were as much a part of his reality as his family, the bazaars and the river Nile. In these visions, which thronged with people quite real to him, he saw the Pharaohs in their great palaces, the ancient Egyptians toiling along the river. He saw the lives of the ancient Greeks, their temples, their ritual baths, their sporting arenas. He saw native American ceremonies, stunning in their mystical power. These stories unfolded before his eyes like a technicolour adventure film.

But when he related what he had seen to his parents, they were dismissive, saying that it was "just his imagination". He was deeply hurt and didn't understand their scepticism. For he really saw these events, absolutely clearly, and in great detail; they had a strong narrative flow and showed the minutiae of the lives that peopled them. Later, as an adult, when his own visions transported him into other worlds, he was able to validate in books what he was seeing in his visions; nobody could undermine these experiences, or take them away from him. But as a young child, he felt diminished by his parents' mistrust of this side of his imagination.

Not only did he see visions, Tony also assumed that everyone else did as well. In fact, he thought it very odd when he learnt that other people did *not* see visions. To him, they were a normal part of the world he inhabited. Later, at school, when he was accused of "letting his imagination run wild", or even of lying, he realized that not everyone shared this reality. He was also intuitive and highly sensitive to atmospheres, and often felt things that were about to happen; or he would 'know' things that he could not possibly have known in the normal course of events [this was when he was three or four, before he had learnt to read].

And so it began: as other people created a schism in the wholeness of his reality, trying to separate the physical world from the mystical, which to Tony were one, he became ever more curious to know why this was so. Instinctively, he was drawn to people who had mystical qualities, an aura of being connected to other worlds, whoever they were: a Coptic professor of Egyptology who was an occasional guest at his grandfather's table; his parents' old cook with the strong arms and the wondrous stories; a coffee vendor in the bazaar who was a Sufi. The things that he saw and felt and sensed were more important to him than the physical environment in which he lived.

The summers of Tony's Egyptian childhood were especially happy times. The family would decamp to Alexandria to escape the intense heat, humidity and pollution of Cairo in summer. Zoran, who had to remain at his post in Cairo, would join them for weekends.

Every year, they rented a villa on the beach, where the children were able to run around without restriction, and without having to be careful of traffic, thieves or strange people. They were allowed to play with the local kids and visit each other's homes with no constraints, in a way that was impossible in the class-conscious society of Cairo. During these summers, Tony made some good friends with children he would never have met at home. He also loved the open life-style, the Mediterranean atmosphere, the olives growing in nearby groves, and the fresh fruit that could be picked and eaten straight from the trees.

The sea, wild, relentless, was spectacular, and Tony and his brothers spent most of the summers in the water; they had a wonderful time, swimming, splashing each other, jumping the waves with the fish that darted between their limbs. Tony was born by the sea, and during those summers in Alexandria he formed what was to become a lifelong love affair with oceans. He also spent a lot of time collecting shells and stones, feeling a deep connection with them, a sense that they contained something beyond the physical.

Those summers were also, perhaps, one of the happiest times for his parents. They were on holiday, they were relaxed, and they had more time to spend with each other, and with their children. Their bonhomie rubbed off onto the kids too, and everyone enjoyed the whole of each summer in excellent spirits. The fresh air was good for Tony's physical health, his parents' stress-free mood was medicine for his over-sensitive emotions, and the freedom was balm for his soul. He flourished.

When he was five, two important events occurred in Tony's life. They were probably not connected in a causal way, but were certainly perceived to be in his young eyes: his second brother, Richard, was born, and Tony was sent to school.

The school chosen for him was the French Catholic School, a small establishment and one of the best private schools in Cairo. In retrospect, this seemed an odd choice, since his parents were neither French nor Catholic. At home, they spoke English among themselves and Arabic with the servants, and both Zoran and Julia were confirmed, even zealous, atheists. Tony learnt French at school easily, as small children often do pick up foreign languages. But neither of his parents was fluent in French, making help with his homework difficult; after one year he was transferred to the British school.

Tony had been happy at the French school, which was informal and relaxed, and close to home. Classes were small and intimate, the teaching often individual and mostly met the needs of a bright and inquisitive little boy. But the British school was situated in the heart of Cairo, an hour's journey from home. He hated that journey; it was uncomfortably hot and he suffered terribly from car-sickness. Two hours travelling a day, and he was just six years old; this was a nightmare that he never forgot. He also hated the school: the regime was rigid, the discipline strict. Tony was clearly highly intelligent, and even more stubborn; he would not be told what to do. So he started to play up and cause trouble; he was duly punished and his life at school became miserable.

The school, indeed, physically resembled a prison. Around the playground was a high fence, more to keep the pupils in, it seemed, than to keep intruders out. Zoran would usually drive his son to school, and drop him at the school gates. As the little boy ran into the playground and the gates clanged shut behind him, he entered another world. Far from the noise and bustle and chaos of the Cairo streets, the bazaars, the colours and the smells, all of which he loved, this was an ordered, pristine, austere world, where authority held sway – and Tony couldn't wait to escape.

At lunchtimes, he would go with other pupils into the playground and across to the fence, where some of the local kids were selling sweets or little cakes. They were very poor, often dirty and dressed in rags. Tony wondered a lot about their lives, and would get very angry about the injustice that created such poverty among such wealth. He would think about his own privileged life and feel great empathy for those children, who were literally on the other side of the fence. So, each day, he would spend some of his pocket money buying a few sweets from them.

On one such day, looking into the eyes of the little boy selling sweets – a boy no older than he was – Tony saw in his eyes such beauty, a deep haunting impenetrable stillness. In some inexplicable way, Tony understood: this child was freer than he was.

If one word could sum up Tony's needs as a child, it would be his need for freedom. He fought constantly against the constrictions of his milieu, always trying to push out the boundaries of what was possible. His parents could not understand him, but they were intelligent and caring and tried to accommodate his needs, not force him into their mould. But his yearning for real freedom went beyond over-stepping the bounds of normal childhood restrictions. As well as needing the freedom to explore this world in whatever direction it took him, he also needed to pursue his quests in the world of his visions and dreams.

A brief period of respite from the rigours of the British school came as political events overtook private concerns. In October 1973, the Samara family was evacuated to Cyprus to escape the turmoil of the war against Israel. The family consisted of Julia, Tony, and his two young brothers; they had to go without Zoran, who could not leave his job in Cairo. It was a difficult and stressful time. Julia had to cope alone, in a strange place, and with the constant worry of the situation back home in Egypt. Then Tony became ill.

Illness as a reaction to circumstances was to establish itself as a pattern in his life: any disharmony in his surroundings, emotional upset or stress, would manifest in him as physical sickness. Many years later, it was discovered that he had thalasemia, a rare blood disorder that prevents the blood from absorbing oxygen properly. This meant that he was particularly sensitive, physically, to pollution of any kind, and it proved to be one of the reasons that he would find living in a city so stressful when he was older.

As a child, his illness was not diagnosed, and no-one knew how to treat it. Tony would become ill as a reaction to a change in the air quality, a change in climate, a change in atmosphere, a change in the emotional interactions of those around him. His mother coped amazingly well in the difficult circumstances; but she was becoming increasingly anxious. She was far from home, without her husband, without her extended family, without her loyal servants, and with three young children to care for. When her eldest son stopped eating, she became sick with worry. He was skeletally thin and survived by drinking lots of water and eating three or four spoonfuls of Philadelphia cheese a day. And nothing else.

This pattern of not eating when circumstances are out of balance or not harmonious, continued for many years. While many people 'comfort eat' their way through unhappiness, Tony simply stopped eating altogether. When he started to run a high fever in Cyprus, Julia took him to the hospital. But the doctors there were unable to discover what ailed the sick child and could not help him. Then he started to have terrifying nightmares.

Tony's childhood, in fact, was marred by illness, and by doctors whose treatment he often experienced as worse than the effects of the illnesses themselves. When as a young adult he went to live with Shamans, he learnt that most of them had also experienced serious or chronic illnesses during their early lives and that this frequently preceded initiation as a Shaman. He learnt from them how to understand the teachings of illness, and its significance in becoming a healer. In their view, the wounded healer healed becomes the most powerful medicine man or woman. Tony learnt the Shamanic wisdom that sees illness as a physical symptom of emotional or spiritual imbalance.

But this was all much later. As a child, the frequent bouts of illness were a miserable inconvenience to Tony, keeping him in bed when he wanted to be out exploring the streets or playing by the river. And of course his illnesses were a grave concern to his parents.

One night, during an early period of illness, he became aware of a 'presence' in the room with him. It was clearly not his mother, nor one of his brothers. In fact, it had no visible form. But Tony felt it strongly, moving around the room, watching him intently. It was not at all frightening; in fact, it felt soothing and rather comforting, and by morning the illness had completely disappeared.

From that time on, this 'guardian angel' would visit him frequently and, no matter how ill he became, Tony knew that he was being taken care of and would recover. He was also conscious of this spirit being looking after him when he was well, guiding his journey through life. This was the first of many spirit guides that he would encounter during his life.

After some weeks, the family returned to Cairo, shaken by their experiences in Cyprus. Egypt, meanwhile, had also been shaken – by its swift defeat by Israel, which at that time was perceived as David slaying Goliath. The atmosphere in the streets of Cairo was now tense; people had withdrawn into themselves and the colour and gaiety of the city seemed overcast by a grey pall.

Julia and her children settled back into their old life, but something had changed. She and Zoran seemed to be pulling in different directions and there were growing tensions between them. Tony, ever sensitive to emotional atmospheres, picked up on this; and once again it manifested as physical sickness.

Tony was sent back to the British school, but was very unhappy there and continued to feel unwell. Frequently, so as not to have to go to school, he would 'make himself' ill – the lesser of two evils in his eyes. He found the actual school work exceedingly easy and exceedingly boring, and hardly studied at all. Being bright, and understanding what was wanted of him and how to 'play the game', he managed to get by and even got good results. But his father knew what he was really capable of and showed his disappointment.

Life was becoming increasingly difficult for Tony. He hated school, the rigidity and lack of freedom, and although he had lots of friends there was no-one with whom he could communicate deeply about the things that mattered to him. He could find no acceptable outlet for his drive and energy, his gifts and intuition, and seemed thwarted at every turn. He had an unquenchable thirst for knowledge, but wanted to learn what he wanted to learn, not what others wanted to teach him. He was miserable.

His bouts of illness became more frequent and of longer duration. Whenever he was particularly unhappy, he would 'take refuge' in illness, suffering a real 'sickness of the soul'. The world that was presented to him, the one which he was supposed to inhabit – and which everyone else seemed to inhabit with such ease – didn't make any sense to him. Try as he would, he could not fit into the niche that was so carefully carved out for him. He was looking for something more, something beyond, something indefinable. He was lost, unhappy and – in the midst of a loving family – he felt isolated in his world. Alone.

More and more, Tony turned inwards, beginning what would become a lifelong quest for spiritual wisdom and Enlightenment. More and more he would spend time alone, seeking for something beyond the physical, the tangible, the visible.

He realized very young that no-one outside himself could provide answers; if he sought in the right way, he knew that the answers would come from within. Spirituality of any kind was alien to Julia and Zoran, and they did not understand what drove their firstborn son. And so he learnt not to share this side of him with them, or indeed with anyone else.

But he loved his family; and there were two people with whom he especially loved to spend time: his brothers. He would often lead them in imaginative and wild games. One day, after being shown many visions in Egypt, he decided to recreate an Egyptian town. He took the doors off all the cupboards in the house – and there were many of them – dismantled much of the furniture and, with the enthusiastic help of his two young brothers, built 'houses' on the large front balcony.

Having the run of the house, they took all the slats off the beds and made tracks for cars and a railway. Beautiful silk bed-sheets were transformed into Bedouin tents. Finally they lit candles underneath the sheets to illuminate the tents, miraculously managing not to set fire either to the sheets or to themselves. The younger boys copied everything their big brother did, and the three of them had a wonderful time playing in their 'town'. But when their father came home, and the boys invited him to join in the fun, he was furious and lost his temper. A chastened Tony couldn't understand why.

His unhappiness at school was growing along with his sickness and finally his parents, at their wits' end, transferred him to the local state school. And he loved it! He made friends with local Egyptian children, though they came mainly from very different backgrounds and very different homes. But they were authentic and unpretentious and fun. Tony began to enjoy real friendship, and he thrived.

The local school offered other important advantages: firstly, it was close to home and so there wasn't the horrendous two hours a day of travelling, which had made Tony so sick. Secondly, instruction was in Arabic, which he loved – the language of the city and its mysteries. And then every morning the whole school held a ceremony of saluting the flag; a ritual that he found totally bizarre, and totally fascinating. But perhaps the best thing about attending this school was the fact that it was a Moslem school and, as Tony was not a Moslem, he had time off every day while the other children studied their faith. He was free to play, to roam and to read.

Ever since he had learnt to read at the age of four, Tony was a voracious reader. He read anything and everything he could lay his hands on. He was fascinated by ancient history and books about other cultures and would always see himself playing a role in the stories. He loved to read about the North American Indians, and in stories of "Cowboys and Indians" he always sided with the Indians, with whom he felt a kind of mystic affinity. He would read about present-day tribes in Africa, living the same lives as their ancestors had many centuries before. He read books about animals, different religions, astronomy – whatever was available. Reading became one of the real pleasures of his life. Books were his greatest friends taking his imagination on wonderful journeys to magical places where he would spend many exciting hours, absorbed in other worlds. He never felt alone with a book.

This was the best of times and the worst of times for the eleven-year-old Tony. He had become friends with an Egyptian girl who lived nearby, and went to his school. Although she was of a different class and older than he was, they did everything together and became inseparable – walking to school, playing by the river, strolling through the alleyways of the city, visiting each other's homes, telling each other about their lives, sharing secrets. At last he had found a friend who was a real soul mate. Their very different backgrounds, social class and home lives were totally irrelevant to their friendship. Until one day, when she became interested in an older boy, and Tony was left behind. His friendship with her had been entirely innocent and he couldn't understand her change of attitude. He mourned the gap she left in his life, in his heart.

But other, more serious, changes of heart were afoot. Zoran and Julia were moving in different directions. They had been growing apart for some time, with undercurrents of tension becoming more and more manifest. Each in their different ways was absorbed in their job, which was both an important part of their lives to each of them, but also an escape from the difficulties at home. They spent less and less time together, and when they did they were tense and ill at ease. It was becoming more apparent that each had a very different worldview and neither was any longer able, or willing, to compromise.

Julia was very idealistic. As she found her place in Egyptian society, she also became politically radicalized and involved in socialist politics. Being strongly concerned about the lives of the poor she supported Gamal Abdul Nasser's thrust towards nationalization, although the policies that he was advocating were the antithesis of the way she lived and, more importantly perhaps, of her husband's views and everything he stood for.

Zoran, on the other hand, was a realist. He foresaw the corruption that would follow in the wake of Nasser's reforms and, indeed, history would prove him right. Political arguments in the Samara household were caused by strongly held views; but also, of course, they were a cover for more serious emotional rifts. And finally, feeling unable to continue living in the current situation, Julia decided to leave her husband.

She had few options; moving to England seemed the obvious choice. She spoke fluent English, as did her children, and she had loved the time she'd spent in England before her marriage and during its early years; she had many happy memories of England.

Falmouth, in Cornwall, captivated Julia's heart. Before she left Cairo, she had a vision of where she would live: a charming and pretty little harbour, with small boats lining the coast – a picture postcard village. Falmouth turned out to be the picture of her vision. She fell in love with it on first sight, and found it to be not only picturesque, but also a place of deep healing and renewal. She found a little house in Redruth, nearby, and the family settled in. They would not see Zoran again until many years later.

Redruth was the mining capital of Cornwall. The community at that time was made up of mining families whose ancestors had lived in those parts for hundreds of years. They were conservative people, with a strong sense of place, of honesty and decency, and conformed to the values and moral codes of past generations. They had limited exposure to anything beyond their own horizons. But Julia felt a great affinity with the simplicity of their lives and their hard-working ethos. Echoes, perhaps, of her Norwegian background. [Years later, the area bred an 'alternative' culture, with a very good art college and film school, and a strong spiritual community.]

Julia brought her family to Cornwall because she thought the sea air and the countryside would provide a healthy environment in which her children could grow up. But she hadn't bargained on the culture shock, which for Tony was intense. He longed for the Mediterranean culture that he'd left behind, the mixing of the different communities and sects, the magic of the Nile, the buzz of the bazaars; for the smells and the flavours and the heat. Mostly, he missed the liberal/intellectual life he had taken for granted, the free exchange of ideas, the artistic current of the city, the interesting and colourful people who had visited his parents' home and the house of his grandparents; and the unseen but strongly felt mysticism that had pervaded his experience of Cairo.

With the onset of puberty, Tony's problems were exacerbated and his emotional suffering became intense. His whole world since leaving Egypt had been turned upside down, and there was nothing stable to hang on to. He felt his parents' separation keenly; their war became internalized, their battles became his inner conflict. Tony loved and needed his father, but in expressing this he saw that he was hurting his mother and he felt that he had to be protective of her and support her at all costs. The only way that he could cope was by pushing away his father and his love for him. So he distanced himself from his father's world and everything he stood for: his culture, the rich tapestry of their life together in Egypt, even his grandparents. And by doing this, he also denied a huge part of himself and set up a painful inner conflict that would take many years to heal.

Materially, too, the circumstances of the Samara family were totally transformed. At one stroke, they had come from living in a fairy tale castle of magic and abundance, to a cold little house on the windswept Cornish coast; from a large bustling household with loyal servants and close extended family, to being alone – just Julia and the three young children – in relative poverty.

Tony remembers it as a very difficult time for his mother. The emotional turmoil of her divorce from his father, while he begged and cajoled her to return to Egypt, might have floored a weaker woman. She also greatly missed her former life in Cairo, her job, her rich cultural and social connections, her entertaining of interesting people from many walks of life.

What sustained her in those first weeks and months in Cornwall was the fierce love that she had for her sons, and her determination to make a success of their new life. Gradually, the anger of the boys, who didn't understand why they had been uprooted to England and longed to go 'home', started to abate. Peace and harmony began to blossom within the home, after the conflicts and tensions of the past years in Egypt. This deep well of love and caring among them created an indelible bond with which to face the harshness of their new life. Together, Julia felt, nothing could break them.

When the family arrived in Cornwall in 1977, Tony was just twelve years old. After a very short settling-in period in his new home, he was sent to school, the local comprehensive, which was an eye-opening experience for him. On his first day at school, he slowly walked towards a large and foreboding old building, and was confronted by a population and an atmosphere that was so alien to what he had known in Cairo. How would he fit in?

Tony was a complete outsider, with several added strokes against him: he spoke 'classical' [read 'posh'] English, in contrast to everyone else's local dialect; he loved books and learning, ideas and culture, and was definitely not interested in the limited pursuits of the other children: 'hanging out', watching television and smoking. He was mercilessly ridiculed, bullied and ostracized. The teachers didn't notice, or didn't care to notice, or didn't care. With no-one to turn to, Tony kept himself, and his pain, to himself.

On his first visit to the school canteen, he was horrified to see the way that the food [greasy and unappetizing] was slapped onto the plates [greasy and cracked] and then gobbled up by the pupils. He thought nostalgically of his grandparents' house in Cairo, the formal dinners, the elegance and grace. He remembered, incongruously, that by the time he was four years old, he had known which of five forks to use for which course. The boy behind him in the canteen queue noticed his distress, and spat onto his plate to shock him. Tony thought of his grandparents with longing.

For his brothers, the upheaval seemed less traumatic. They fitted in at their primary school and made friends. But Tony did not make friends. He had always been a loner, but now, for the first time in his life, he felt completely alone, unprotected in this stark and unfriendly environment. He adored his mother and felt that as the oldest of the three boys he needed to be protective towards her; it was out of the question to add to her problems by burdening her with his own troubles.

So he withdrew into himself, and again started to look inward. Nothing in his new world made any sense; and denying the large part of himself that he had left behind with his father in Egypt, he could see no purpose in his life. He looked to books for salvation. He started to read books on psychology, trying to understand relationships and what goes wrong; but they were too theoretical. Desperately unhappy in the world of physical reality, he began to examine other worlds. He tried to get hold of books on religious experience, mysticism, esoteric paths – anything that could be a portal into other worlds; but there was not much in the local library! He read the lives of the saints, the prophets, biographies of people who had led extraordinary lives, overcoming great difficulties, seemingly supported by forces beyond the physical. And he talked more and more with his 'angel guide'.

His great solace at this time was being alone in nature. Tony felt sustained by nature, connected to the natural world, happy in its embrace. He also had one real friend – a large border collie called Sheppy, with whom he went everywhere: long walks across the fields or in the woods, or walking for hours by the sea along the sandy beach. The sea, as always, was his favourite place to be. Walking along the wind-swept beach, often in drizzling rain, he would share his inner world with Sheppy, and return home calmer and more at peace.

He also loved to spend time in a small graveyard that overlooked their house. Wild couch grass grew among the graves and was very green and fecund from the English rainfall. And there were many old bushes that grew, unattended and wild. Tony used to think that the place was haunted. At night, the bushes took on strange shapes, and the graveyard had a kind of eerie beauty, a mystical energy that somehow resonated with the Cairo of his early childhood. Often, he would creep out of the house at night, after his mother had gone to bed, and walk around the cemetery alone, fascinated by the stillness of the place.

Being out in nature was also an escape from the girls who had started to chase him at school. At fourteen he was strikingly handsome, and with the girls' burgeoning womanhood they were becoming sexually interested in him. He did not return the compliment, and did his best to get away. On one memorable occasion, he was literally being chased by a girl across a field. She simply would not take no for an answer. In order to get away from her, he jumped over a fence, and badly sprained his ankle. At the time, it seemed a price worth paying!

The highlight for Tony in this rather dark period of his life was the family trips to Falmouth at weekends. This enchanting place boasted a thriving cultural life, an art college, and many little cafes along the promenade, where you could sit and watch the people arriving from France and the Continent in their little yachts. To Tony it represented breathing the fresh air of cultural and intellectual ideas, as well as the fresh air of the sea. His mother loved these trips, and it felt that they were a happy family again.

As they slowly acclimatized to the changes in their lives, life started to become easier. New experiences, unknown in Cairo, were transformed from an ordeal into an adventure. So for instance, a trip to the launderette became a family outing. As the three boys watched the clothes spinning in the machine with great fascination, Julia would chat to the miners' wives and, being outgoing and friendly and quite unpretentious, by the end of the 'outing' she had overcome their resistance to newcomers and made friends. Then they would all go out for fish and chips at the local chip shop – not quite the *haute cuisine* of Tony's grandparents' dinners, but great fun nevertheless.

Going to the local shops was also an adventure. Often, Tony would be sent by himself to the bakery to buy fresh bread. He would always be greeted by the baker in the same cheery voice: "Hello, love! D'you want a pastie then?" It took a while to get used to being called "love" by everyone. But certainly, it was a mark of acceptance. Sometimes the local fishermen would come to the house and offer Julia fresh fish from their latest catch for almost nothing: crabs and lobsters, and occasionally mussels. The fact that they were also poor now helped them to make friends with the local people.

Gradually, they became part of the local community. Julia enrolled at the local college and began to study Marketing and Communications. When she was busy with exams, one of the neighbours would take the younger boys to school. And the local policeman must have been a little in love with her, for he turned a blind eye to her driving illegally, gently 'suggesting' that it might be a good idea if her battered old car were to pass its road test.

And so, in time, they adjusted to their new lives. Tony welcomed the new closeness with his mother. As the oldest son, and in the absence of his father, he became her confidante and was able to give her a lot of support. He did well at school, despite its shortcomings, and was expected to pass ten GCSE's with straight A's. And then he found a wonderful old bookshop in Falmouth and was again able to indulge his passion for reading. Life in Cornwall was, after all, beginning to look a little brighter.

When Tony was fifteen, and going through the worst rigours of adolescence, there was to be another devastating upheaval in his life. Though they had been living very frugally, the money that Julia had managed to bring with her from Egypt had finally run out. She was loath to leave Cornwall, which she had grown to love intensely. But in the circumstances, the only option was to return to her family in Norway, where her parents could give her material as well as emotional support. And so they were on the move again. Tony was distraught at this new and untimely disruption.

The culture shock on arriving in Oslo, though very different from their arrival in Cornwall, was no less traumatic for him. He knew not a word of Norwegian, and it was quite unlike any other language he had come across. And if England had been cold after Egypt, Norway was freezing – temperatures hovering around minus 20. Emotionally insecure, unsettled and without an anchor, Tony became even more reclusive. He felt that he was in a deep spiritual crisis, and knew that he needed a spiritual teacher, but didn't see how to find one. His mother did her best to be supportive, but didn't understand his needs.

His time at highschool in Oslo was not happy. Although the school did not shock him in the primitive ways that the comprehensive school in England had, Tony now faced other problems. Uncomfortable with the language and the new environment, and naturally shy, he did not easily make friends. He felt unable to express himself sufficiently well to give a good account of himself in this strange language and, being a perfectionist, this made him feel inadequate and inferior.

His peers at school tried to be friendly, and some of them did help him with the language. But he had to learn from scratch, and spent the entire first year at high school arduously struggling to get his head around Norwegian. Being bright and determined, and not a little stubborn, he managed to conquer the language, and eventually went on to complete his high school courses with honours, gaining the highest marks in the school at graduation. His Norwegian classmates were none too pleased, but his mother was immeasurably proud of him.

But it would be a long while before Tony would make any real friends. Again, books and ideas became his companions, not people. His experience of feeling 'different' from others was growing and he needed to unravel this and try to make sense of it. Naturally intellectual, he began to read seriously: history, philosophy – specially the ancient Greeks – psychology, sociology. He wanted to explore his own background, its historical and sociological context; to unearth the mechanisms of relationships, and understand how they work, and why they don't.

The obvious next step was to find out why he didn't seem able to make good and nurturing relationships himself, and what the causes of his deep unhappiness were. His mother, seeing his deep distress, suggested that he see a psychologist. He did his homework and found a therapist with an excellent reputation for treating troubled teenagers.

He went to a couple of sessions, but was horrified at the neat way the therapist tried to fit everything personal into psychological theory. Whenever Tony tried to explain things differently, he was told that this was his 'defence mechanism' preventing him from dealing with the real issues. He went a couple more times to make sure that he hadn't made a hasty judgement and also, perhaps, because he really wanted the therapy to work. Clearly, he was looking for salvation and hoped that in psychotherapy he would find it. But his negative feelings towards the whole process were reaffirmed. The shrink did his best to get him hooked. Tony fled.

His unhappiness continued, but there was one bright spark in his life at that time: he was able to renew his relationship with his Norwegian grandparents. When Tony was living in Cairo, they had visited from time to time to see their grandchildren, whom they clearly adored. And Tony, their first grandchild, had a special place in their affections. They were unpretentious, genuine people, and Tony loved them deeply. His grandfather had a great love and knowledge of classical music, which he passed on to his eldest grandson – the love, anyway! They spent many happy hours together, just the two of them, alone with Beethoven, Mozart or Bach.

But most of all, Tony loved the family occasions with them. In the summers, they would all go to the grandparents' little cottage in the mountains and go climbing. They, like Tony, were both nature lovers, and spending time in the wilds of the mountains together created a special bond between them. And in winter there was Christmas to look forward to, when all the family gathered at their house to celebrate together and enjoy the special blessings of a close-knit family unit; and the special family tradition of placing the golden angel at the top of the Christmas tree. His Norwegian grandparents, so different from the grandparents he had left behind in Egypt, were also in their way the centre of a large and loving family. In spite of the traumatic upheavals of his life so far, Tony felt embraced by love.

The years that he spent as a high school student in Oslo were intense and rigorous. People around him were smoking and drinking heavily, and some were experimenting with drugs. In reaction to this behaviour, Tony vowed that he would never smoke, drink, or take drugs – a vow that he has found easy to keep. He also decided to become super healthy.

But it was not enough just to refrain from 'poisoning' his body. Ever the perfectionist in whatever he undertook [not in comparison to others so much, but in pushing himself to the absolute limits of his own capability] his body had to be the healthiest body possible. So he started to train as an athlete, running up to ten kilometres a day, and then running in marathon races. When he began to do well in marathons, he felt the need to push his body still further. So he started training for the triathlon, an exhausting marathon of running, swimming and cycling.

Along with the difficulties of his school studies in Norwegian, and his vociferous appetite for reading – he would devour three or four serious books a week, and remember what he had read – he kept up his athletic training all through high school. Looking back, it is difficult to know where such inexhaustible energy came from. Tony was simply interested in everything, and it seemed that as his interests grew, so did his supply of energy. Time expanded to accommodate all his needs.

Like most teenagers, Tony was searching for 'the Meaning of Life', longing for something more, something beyond the mundane world of daily life, beyond the physical, the tangible, the visible. A deep spiritual yearning had remained at the centre of his life since his earliest childhood stirrings. But now this needed to be manifest; it was time for action. Angered by the terrible poverty, injustice and suffering in the world, he became involved in politics; 'obsessed' would perhaps be a more accurate description. But clearly, his politics were driven by his spiritual questing.

He joined the left-wing socialist party in order to help solve the problems of the world. He was very idealistic and very focused: the answer to all the world's suffering was simple – socialism. If everyone became a socialist, the world's wealth would be redistributed and there would be no more poverty or injustice, oppression or fear or greed, and so no more wars. And once these ills had been eradicated, we could all live in spiritual harmony with each other and with the universe.

Tony took his politics very seriously indeed. He organized debates, distributed leaflets and tried to spread the word: socialism would purge the world of all its evils. But soon, of course, talking politics was not enough. He needed action; and action meant living his politics. When he was sixteen, he decided to go and live on a kibbutz in Israel – true socialism in action. But his mother, aghast, very firmly put her foot down.

Tony's next plan was to go to Nicaragua and fight with the Sandinistas, who were struggling to create a just and compassionate society in the face of rampant and corrupt capitalism. Again, Julia's foot came crashing down. But, buying time, she did agree that she would give her blessing to whatever her firstborn chose to do, once he had graduated from high school. Little did she know what she was letting herself in for; for by then, he would be guided in an altogether different direction.

Gradually, Tony became disillusioned with politics – the infighting, the factions, the endless arguments. He was plagued by the idea that life had no meaning, and his quest for inner peace gradually took over his life. He became a regular visitor to the large central Oslo library, and to the many bookshops dotted around the city. He was on a spiritual mission. He started to read books about religion and spirituality, holy texts and books of ancient wisdom; mysticism, Sufism, the Kabbalah. Everything he could lay his hands on. He journeyed more deeply into his own psyche and spirit, learning lessons that were rocketing him inwards and forwards, showing him answers to questions he had yet to articulate.

His reading moved more intensely into the realm of the spiritual, the mystical and the esoteric. But ultimately, reading alone was not enough. He was looking for real answers, not intellectual sophistry. He decided that he needed some form of spiritual practice, and so he began to check out different religions to see what they had to offer.

His quest began nearest home: the Lutheran Church espoused a formal outward practice that didn't resonate with him at all; it was conservative, it appeared to have no real depth, and was closed to all forms of questioning. The Catholic Church proved to be rich in ceremonial, which appealed to him at that time, but seemed lacking in relevance. The Benedictine monks, gentle and lovely people though they were, were living in their history.

Eventually, after ploughing his way laboriously through everything religious or spiritual that Oslo had to offer, Tony found a resonance in Buddhism. He began to attend meetings of a local Buddhist group, and go to out-of-town weekend retreats. He told his mother nothing of this; he knew instinctively that she would not have understood, and certainly would not have been in sympathy. [The weekend retreats became 'stay-overs' at newly-acquired friends' houses.]

As he moved more deeply into Buddhism, he began to meditate, at least two hours a day. Somehow, time seemed to expand to encompass all his different activities. He kept up with his studies, his reading, his physical training; but gradually Buddhism was taking over at the centre of his life. After a while, he felt guided towards Tibetan Buddhism, and finally landed in the lap of Zen Buddhism. Tony had come home.

When he turned eighteen, at the end of May 1983, he seemed to be on the brink of a brilliant university career. He had studied sociology and social sciences at school and, graduating with top marks and greatly encouraged by his teachers, he was set to read sociology at university. But nobody had taken account of what was happening within him. How could they have done? Nobody knew, not even his family.

It was gradually becoming clear that university and 'worldly pursuits' were of no interest at all to Tony; what he wanted to do was to go and live in a Buddhist monastery. With help from Buddhist friends and guides, he chose the Mount Baldy Zen Buddhist Monastery in Los Angeles.

For some time during his last year at high-school, Tony had been working in the evenings at Kodak developing films, to make money to pay for the Buddhist courses and retreats. After paying for the courses, he had invested the remainder of the money in some shares, and actually made quite a large profit; enough to cover the fare to the United States and the expenses of staying at the monastery. He was independent, confident of his path, and aching to go.

He had intended to tell his mother of his plans a week or so before he left. She knew nothing at all of his spiritual life, or the fact that he was getting up at five o'clock every morning to meditate for two hours before going to school [and meditating for at least another hour before going to bed]. But a month before he was due to leave, Richard had come into his room while he was meditating. He was actually wearing a long white Indian robe and sitting in the lotus position – hardly something that could be argued away as part of 'normal' life!

So he told his mother of his plans. He reminded her of the kibbutz and Nicaragua, and she could brook no opposition. But she probably also saw something in him then, a kind of radiated peace and calm, that made her realize that she didn't need to worry about her firstborn son; that he knew what he was doing.

And what he was doing was absolutely clear: he was going to spend the rest of his life as a Zen Buddhist monk.

Chapter Two
The Zen Buddhist Monastery
Unbroken Meditation, and Beyond

At Los Angeles airport, towards evening, Tony was met by one of the monks from the Mount Baldy monastery. He was dressed in the traditional long black robes of a Buddhist monk, though the heat of the Californian summer was stifling, even at this late hour. From the airport it was a short drive to a nearby monastery where Tony was to spend the night, one of a group of Zen Buddhist monasteries which followed the teachings of Roshi Sasaki.

This monastery had originally been a huge mansion house, built by a wealthy Spaniard in the early twentieth century for his own personal use. An elaborately ornate building, it stood in sharp contrast to its surroundings in a poor black neighbourhood where the monks, who converted it into a monastery, had bought it very cheaply. Tony immediately fell in love with the place: the splendid decorations, the bells and the gongs, the slightly New Mexican flavour; above all, the contrast with the recent austerity he had experienced in Norway. This taste of the exotic brought back memories of his early childhood in Egypt. Sleeping beneath a picture of Kuan Yin, the woman who represents the feminine side of Buddhism, he felt a great connection with the place, and with himself. He was completely at peace with the world.

Next day, after an early breakfast with the monks, Tony was taken to Mount Baldy Monastery. The first sight of it created a fairy-tale picture; situated at the top of Mount Baldy, the highest mountain in California, and blending in with the natural beauty of the surroundings, it was awe inspiring. Mount Baldy is the only mountain in the whole range where it snows heavily; winters at the monastery would be beautiful to look at, but very harsh to experience.

In contrast to the ornate Spanish mansion-house monastery, Mount Baldy had originally been a scouts' camp. It was a bare and simple structure, with separate small wooden huts set among the pine trees. The accommodation was in dormitories, ten or twelve monks to each room. They were sparsely furnished, just a bunk bed and a small locker for each monk. When Tony arrived, he was greeted by a young Japanese monk and given his robes, sandals, bowl, mug, chopsticks and wash-cloth – from now on all that he would own in the world. Then he was taken to meet the head of the monastery.

Roshi Sasaki, a Grand Master of Zen Buddhism, was the spiritual head of Mount Baldy, and of many other Zen monasteries in Los Angeles and around the world. He would visit them in rotation spending a few weeks in each, sorting out any difficulties, guiding, teaching by the example of his presence as well as by the profundity of the Zen Buddhist knowledge he espoused. Roshi was Japanese, and conducted all the ceremonies in Japanese; one of the other monks translated what was necessary into English.

Roshi had spent almost his entire life in a monastery. His parents had first placed him in the care of monks when he was just eight years old, not as an act of cruelty, but because they saw his spiritual potential and were sure that they were doing the right thing. This is not an uncommon practice in Japan, where many children who seem to be receptive to spirituality are given to monks to be raised by them.

Roshi had become a Spiritual Master at a young age, and soon had a large following among Zen Buddhist monks. But then he left Japan. Although at that time there were some nine-and-a-half million practising Zen Buddhists in Japan, Roshi had left because he felt that the majority of Japanese, selling their souls to the work ethic and the company store, were not yet ready for spiritual Enlightenment. Many Japanese monks had followed him to California, settling there in one or other of his monasteries.

Zen Buddhist monks around the world considered Roshi to be on a par with the Pope; the eighteen-year-old Tony was naturally nervous before meeting him. He had been told that there would be a special ceremony to welcome him to the monastery; he was feeling both curious and a little overwhelmed. But it turned out to be a private ceremony with just Roshi present, and another monk who translated. Tony felt very humble in the presence of one of the truly enlightened beings of our age. It seemed to him that Roshi carried centuries of spiritual wisdom in his bones.

Roshi was a small, slight man with the traditional shaved head of a Buddhist monk. He was seventy-five when Tony first met him, though he didn't appear to be more than forty. He looked at Tony and smiled, his piercing brown eyes, shining with light and love, looking at him, and into him. It was as though he were seeing into the very heart of him, and still smiling. Gaining courage, Tony smiled back, holding his gaze for what seemed like a timeless moment. He didn't know why he was so privileged, but his audience with Roshi lasted for half a day, not the usual half-hour granted to welcome novice monks.

Although that first meeting was informal by Japanese standards, to a Westerner it seemed very formal and ceremonial. Before meeting with Roshi, Tony had been shown all the necessary protocols and was expected to perform them to the letter. On approaching him, he bowed low, as befitted a greeting to a great Master, touching his forehead to the tips of Roshi's toes. Then, as he rose, he lifted his hands, palms upwards, to symbolize an openness to receive his blessings and to connect to his own higher self.

Roshi asked many questions, and seemed interested to talk about every aspect of Tony's previous life. Nothing seemed too trivial or too insignificant: his life in Egypt, England, family, university, politics, friends, his reading, even athletics and sport. Funnily enough, though obviously by design, the one thing that he did not touch on was Tony's spiritual involvement and practice.

After talking at great length, the two men drank Japanese tea together, slowly, ceremonially, as was the Japanese custom, where the movements of preparation, serving and drinking the tea are all prescribed. Today, there are many different tea-drinking traditions in Japan, but Roshi adhered to the twelfth century tradition, introduced during the Song dynasty in China by the Zen monk, Eisai. This tea ceremony was originally performed in monasteries by Zen monks to help them stay awake through long hours of meditation.

After the tea ceremony, a delicious meal that had been specially prepared for the occasion was eaten. Then Roshi gave the new young 'recruit' some traditional Japanese sweets, to sweeten his arrival – the only time that he was ever given such a delicacy in the monastery. When the Master smiled at the end of the ceremony, Tony felt that the whole universe had blessed him. He went back to the dormitory and rested for the remainder of the day, feeling peaceful and happy; this was a dream come true.

There were about thirty monks living permanently in the monastery when Tony arrived, including Leonard Cohen, the famous Canadian poet/song-writer. Many other famous people, mostly American, mostly connected to the world of show business, would come for a week's or a month's retreat. But Mount Baldy was a traditional Zen Buddhist monastery, with no frills. It gave no quarter to trendy, rich or famous people, or those filled with their own importance; everyone wore identical robes, ate the same food and slept in the same dormitories.

Visitors who came on retreats – and there were always ongoing retreats, which would swell the numbers of people staying in the monastery to about seventy – were treated in the same way as the permanent residents. The only concession was that visiting males did not have to shave their heads as the monks did [nor did Tony, as a novice monk]. Men and women were treated equally, though assigned to separate dormitories. The accommodation was simple and sparse, the food plain and monotonous, the regime rigorous.

Monks did not take a vow of poverty, but the monastery was not a place of material plenty. The physical running of the monastery was financed by donations from the world community of Zen Buddhists – mainly from those in Japan and California where Roshi had many affluent followers, and by visitors who came to stay for retreats. As well as this, in order to obtain food several monks would go each evening to the market and ask for alms, and would always be given the leftovers. This, remember, was California, where people were open to 'spiritual' giving. Besides this, each monk was asked to pay for his/her keep for the first three months, to see how they attuned to monastic life. After this initial period, if they made a commitment in good faith to remain at the monastery, their stay would be free.

The physical path of Tony's life thus far had been paved with traumatic upheavals, none of them of his choosing. From the exotic and colourful ambience of 1970's Cairo, with its heat and flies, its mysticism and mixture of traditions, through the insular limitations of a small English mining town, to the cool and unexpressive Norwegian culture, he had lived two separate lives: the physical self living in the material world of school, examinations, politics, books, friends, athletics, the pursuit of ideas; and the spiritual self, seeking other worlds, living other visions, knowing other truths. He had lived both lives fully extended, with all his energy, but they had been separate, and he had often had the feeling that he was divided from himself, living many fragmented lives simultaneously.

Now, in this austere and isolated monastery, where he was without books – any books, which must have been a severe deprivation for an insatiable reader – without political involvement, without personal possessions, without family, friends, physical activity of any kind, without anything, in short, to link him to his former life, or to the material world, he acknowledged that this time he had moved of his own volition. He looked around at the other monks, he looked at Roshi exuding peacefulness and love, and he knew he had come home.

During his last year in Oslo, as well practising Zen Buddhist meditation for several hours each day, Tony had begun to study its history and rituals, thinking that he should perhaps gain some academic knowledge of the life and traditions that he was about to embrace.

Buddhism, both religion and philosophy, was founded in North Eastern India in the fifth century BCE, based on the teachings of Siddhartha Gautama, later known as the Buddha. Its goal is the escape from human suffering, the perfecting of the cycles of rebirth and reincarnation, and the attainment of Nirvana. It emphasizes the strict observance of moral precepts, and meditation as its major practice. The purpose of deep and prolonged meditation is to release the power that the mind has over us and bring us to a state of no-mind, what Buddhists call *mushin*. In this state, we see things as they truly are. *Mushin*, an empty vessel with no attachments of any kind, is the true mirror of our purest and most compassionate self, our deepest consciousness.

During his lifetime, the Buddha established the Buddhist monastic order [*sangha*]; his teachings were then transmitted orally by his disciples. He also adopted some ideas from the Hinduism of his time, notably the doctrine of karma [that we reincarnate many times, bringing with us each time those things from previous lives that we have not dealt with and need to work out in our current life]. But he rejected many of its other doctrines, and all of its gods.

The basic tenets of Buddhism are summarized in the Four Noble Truths. They were formulated by the Buddha in his first sermon, given near Benares, in India. These truths state: one, that suffering exists; two, that desire, or greed, is its cause; three, that the cessation of suffering is possible; and four, that the way to accomplish this is to follow the Eightfold Path.

This Path consists of right understanding [faith in the Buddhist view of existence], right thought [the resolve to practise the faith], right speech [avoidance of falsehoods, slander, and abuse], right action [abstention from taking life, stealing, and improper sexual behaviour], right livelihood [rejection of occupations not in keeping with Buddhist principles], right effort [development of good mental states], right mindfulness [awareness of body, feelings, and thought], and right concentration [meditation]. It is also called the Middle Path, because it steers a course mid-way between sensuality and asceticism. Following the Path leads to a release from suffering and the attainment of Nirvana. Though differently interpreted, these Four Truths are recognized by virtually all the major schools of Buddhist practice, including the Mahayana and Theravada traditions.

Today, the various branches of Buddhism throughout the world have a combined following of about four hundred million people. Zen Buddhism, the branch of Buddhism that particularly attracted Tony, was founded in China around the sixth century of the Common Era, where it was known as Chan. It soon divided into two schools, the Northern School, which believed in gradual Enlightenment, and the Southern School, which believed in a sudden flash of Enlightenment. By the eighth century, the concept of sudden Enlightenment had died out and only the Northern School survived.

In the twelfth century, Zen became fully established in Japan, where it is now the most important faction of Buddhism. During the early years of its long history, Zen Buddhism often came under the influence of indigenous religions, faiths and cults – especially Shinto in Japan, with its majestic shrines and rituals – and incorporated many of their ideas and observances into itself; at the same time, in its turn, it influenced them.

For hundreds of years, Zen temples in Japan were centres of learning, art and culture, as well as places of rigorous austerity and contemplative mysticism. But by the nineteenth century, it had distilled and refined its beliefs and practices to become the religion that we recognize today. Zen Buddhism is now widely practised in all parts of Asia, and there are many Zen centres in Europe and North America, most notably in California, where it has a significant following.

Zen claims to transmit the essence of Buddhism through experiencing the Enlightenment achieved by the Buddha. It teaches that the 'Buddha-nature', or potential to achieve Enlightenment, is inherent in everyone, but lies dormant through ignorance. This state of higher consciousness [*satori*] can be awakened in anyone: not by studying scriptures or holy texts, not by the worship of images or adherence to the form of any ceremonial rites, nor even by the practise of good deeds, but through a strict discipline of specific meditations that teach us to control the mind and break through the boundaries of logical thought. It was this that had fascinated Tony and brought him to Mount Baldy.

But academic knowledge was no preparation for the reality that greeted Tony at the monastery; the harshness of the regime could aptly be compared to a military training camp. Every task of the day [bar going to the toilet] was carried out in unison, slowly, ritualistically, and never varied. The purpose of this was to bring consciousness into every moment, into every action; to focus fully on the present task, as though it were the most important job in the world. And by bringing consciousness into every action, to imbue it also with deep spirituality.

The monastery was run democratically, although Roshi clearly enjoyed a special position. The head monk ran the monastery organizationally and made out the work rotas; everybody had a turn of cooking, cleaning, working in the office – and cleaning the toilets. It is said that when you can clean toilets, day in, day out, in a state of deep joy, you are truly living your spirituality. Everyone also had a turn of wake-up duty. This consisted of banging the gong, which was hung in a tree, very slowly and rhythmically, for several minutes, gradually increasing the speed and the volume. This happened at the unearthly hour of 3.30 every morning, which meant that the duty monk had to get up at 3.15.

The monastery residents rose and went straight to the meditation hall where they meditated for half an hour. Then at a sign from the leading monk, they all got up and formed a single line behind him, to perform the 'walking meditation' on the way to the showers. Everyone stood quite still for a few moments, breathing rhythmically, in unison. Then the head monk would start to chant, and everyone would join in, still standing quite still. The sign to move was the striking by the head monk of a small gong-like instrument. On the first strike, each person moved his/her right foot, on the second strike the left foot moved forward, on the third strike, the right foot again; and so it continued in slow rhythmic formation, for the ten minutes or so that it took to walk from the meditation room to the showers. When everyone had showered and dressed, they again lined up behind the head monk for the ritual walk back to the meditation hall, where they would sit and meditate until 6.30.

At 6.30 breakfast was served; meals, too, were all part of the meditation ritual. The duty monk for that day would bring round a large bowl of food, and stop beside each resident in turn. Still sitting and meditating, each person would fill her/his small bowl from the large one. Then, together, everyone would chant the blessing over the food. The head monk would lift his chopsticks, a sign to start eating; when he put down his chopsticks, everyone stopped eating, whether they had finished or not. [I use the masculine form here, as although there were women monks, Roshi and all his substitute head monks were men.]

More blessings were chanted after the food was eaten; then another bowl was brought round into which any leftovers were put, and with it a bowl of water for the monks to wash their cups, bowls and chopsticks. Then they dried them with a little cloth, wrapped them in it, and put them, inside the cloth, into their robes. Each monk carried this little parcel around with him at all times, the only personal possessions that any of them owned.

Meditation continued throughout the day, for every aspect of life in the monastery was, in fact, part of a meditation. Buddhism teaches that everything we do in life should be part of mindful meditation, so that each moment becomes filled with deep consciousness. At Mount Baldy, meditation always followed the same pattern: Roshi would lead the chanting of the *sutras* [the Buddhist holy texts] in Japanese, accompanied by a musical instrument. If he were away at a different monastery, another monk would lead the chanting. At the beginning of the day, he would play a gong-like instrument carved from wood, sometimes shaped rather like a frog, played slowly and rhythmically, like a drum, giving a very earthy resonance. As the day wore on, the rhythm of the chanting and the drumming would gradually speed up.

The monks continued to meditate until eight in the evening, with lunch served at midday, and dinner in the late afternoon. The ritual for all meals, and the food itself, never varied. There was no break in the meditative state, except for sleep. There were no distractions whatsoever; even casual talking among the monks was discouraged, although novices are allowed to ask questions when they first arrive, until they have learnt to follow the procedures.

Meditation has existed in some form in most religions since ancient times; but in Buddhism it is the central practice, the portal to Enlightenment. *Zazen*, sitting meditation, is a primordial practice, developed in the wake of the Buddha's teachings. Through *zazen*, the practitioner reaches a deeply meditative state, letting go of all attachment, belief and thought, entering an ego-less state of here/ now nothingness. Regular and prolonged practise leads to a purification of body and mind, connecting us to the timeless perfection of the Divine.

One aspect of the ancient practice of yoga, *dhyana* [the Sanskrit word for "concentrated meditation"] became the basis of the meditation practised in Zen Buddhism. This stresses the importance of deep rhythmic breathing – connecting us to the rhythm of the universe – upright posture, and complete stillness of body and mind. At Mount Baldy, there were three different types of meditation: the silent meditation, the chanting meditation and the story meditation.

In the silent meditation, Roshi would recite *koans* told by the Zen Master. A *koan* is a seventeen-word paradoxical statement or question used as a discipline in Buddhist meditation. Roshi would move among the monks, giving each one an individual *koan* depending on their level of understanding. The effort to solve a *koan* is designed to exhaust the analytic intellect and the will, leaving the mind open for response on a deep intuitive level. One *koan* frequently used in the monastery was the well-known, "When both hands are clapped a sound is produced; listen to the sound of one hand clapping." After the head monk had recited the *koan*, everyone would meditate on it for many hours, in silence.

In the chanting meditation, the Buddhist *sutras* would be chanted by everyone in Japanese, led by the head monk. Sometimes, a simple translation would be given before the chanting began. In the third kind of meditation, Roshi would give a talk in which he would tell stories about great Buddhist Masters and go deeply into their meaning. Someone would translate from the Japanese and then everyone would meditate and reflect upon their meaning.

At eight o'clock in the evening, the tree gong would be sounded to mark the end of official meditation for the day, and everyone would go to bed. Everyone, that is, except Tony. He had always felt compelled to push himself to the extreme, whatever he was doing, to extend the boundaries of what was possible, to reach the physical limits of endurance and then try to move beyond them. And so meditation for him, too, although a profoundly spiritual practice, also contained echoes of what had driven his marathon running and his political engagement as a teenager. He needed to do more than was expected of him, more than anyone else. And if his thoughts had wandered at all during the day of meditation, he would also see these extra hours of sitting as necessary to 'pay for' his weakness.

And so he would stay on in the meditation hall and meditate on his own until midnight. Sometimes one of the other young men would join him. At midnight he would go to bed, to be woken just three and a half hours later, to start the whole process all over again. Once more, his energy level was extraordinarily high, though now it seemed to be of a different quality; for a long time he survived on three and a half hours sleep a night, with seemingly no ill effects.

Time in the monastery didn't exist in the way we understand it in the 'real' world. There were no clocks, no watches. No-one knew what time it was, nor even which day of the week [although the head monk always knew when it was 3.15 in the morning!] Night and day, the changing seasons and the rhythms of monastery life were the only measures of time.

The winters at Mount Baldy were particularly harsh. The monastery was high up in the Californian mountains and the temperature fell to well below freezing. The small wooden huts and the grounds were covered in snow, creating an idyllic picture – but a harsh physical reality.

The walk from the meditation hall to the showers across the snow, in slow rhythmic formation, with the chanting and the beating of the gong may have been spiritually uplifting, but physically it was gruelling. Most of the monks had special shoes for walking in the snow. But Roshi and a few of the other Japanese monks walked barefoot. So Tony, of course, walked barefoot too. Testing himself against his own boundaries, he felt that if he could do this, not just once as a test but every day throughout the freezing winter, then he could do anything.

Women were admitted to the monastery, both as visitors to retreats, and as fully-fledged monks. The men's and women's quarters were quite separate, but all the activities of the monastery were carried out together, and the sexes were treated completely equally. The monastery was celibate, though no vow of celibacy was expected, as indeed no vows of poverty or obedience were expected; they were simply part of the fabric of monastery life, a way of focusing each monk's total energy on his/her spiritual purpose. However, lay monks could be married and live out in the world, and come to the monastery on a daily basis. Then, their first spiritual duty was to care for their family. But for the overwhelming majority of monks who lived at Mount Baldy, their prime relationship was with Roshi, and their first responsibility was to look after the monastery.

Tony's own test came a few weeks after he entered Mount Baldy. Every now and then, the monastery was open to public viewing. On this particular occasion, a party of university students had come to learn about its philosophy and practices. Each monk was assigned to look after a small group of students. Tony's group of three included a most attractive young woman who was quite obviously taken with him. He walked around the buildings and the grounds with her, explaining every detail of life in the monastery and its significance. She said that she found it all fascinating, and asked if she could come back the next day and learn more. Tony, who had a free day, readily agreed. He would often walk alone in the mountains when he had a rare day off, connecting deeply to nature; this time he would enjoy her company.

But that night was to be a long night of the soul for Tony. He meditated long and hard, looking into the deepest recesses of his soul. In the end, he decided not to keep the appointment with the young woman. He had found her interesting and very attractive and did not want to be distracted in any way from his spiritual purpose.

By his own admission, Tony was 'fanatical' about being a monk; he gave all his energy to his spiritual calling, meditating until midnight each day. When he went to bed each night, for just three-and-a-half hours, he was longing for sleep, not for a woman. The young woman called that day, the next day, and every day for the rest of that week. Tony stayed deep in meditation. And so it was that he made the decision to adopt celibacy for life.

I have written in some detail about the practices of the monastery because the detail is crucial to understanding the Zen Buddhist approach to spirituality, and the way of life that Tony had embraced – a way of life that paved his future spiritual path.

Zen offers a tough spiritual discipline, the only path towards true Enlightenment. Zen Buddhists believe that all the suffering in the world – wars, greed, poverty, oppression, disease – is caused by ignorance and attachment to the ego and the senses. There is no way in which human beings can prevent the negative forces in the world from reeking havoc unless we become fully conscious. This means becoming fully conscious of the real person within, being in continuous contact with the 'Buddha-nature', the 'no mind' nature. We cannot begin to see this if we are attached to our mind, to our senses, to our perceptions and beliefs, to our own limited vision of the world; to a belief that sees the physical world as 'reality' and responsibility for creating it as nothing to do with us.

To a Buddhist, becoming truly conscious means letting go of all attachment, so that real spiritual consciousness can shine through. This means of course letting go of all material possessions – but that's the easy part. More difficult, perhaps, is letting go of the ego with its false aspirations, and the mind with its clever tricks that keep us stuck in a limited and ultimately damaging view of the world that holds that material reality is all there is. Through regular and deep meditation, we are able to let go of all our worldly clutter and focus our attention on our deepest inner selves, and so move along the path towards true spiritual Enlightenment.

There are essentially two schools of Buddhist thought concerning the purpose of human life: the Little Boat School and the Big Boat School. The Little Boat philosophy holds that the sole purpose of our existence on this earth is to reach Enlightenment, and that karma dictates that we will be reborn again and again until we do. Enlightenment is attained through deep and prolonged meditation, in which we should spend our entire lives; any other activity is a deflection from our true goal and a waste of time and energy. This school of thought holds sway today among Buddhists in most of Asia, and especially in Thailand. Here, it is believed that one person becoming truly enlightened has a ripple effect on the rest of humanity, and benefits all.

The Big Boat philosophy has a wider interpretation: our first purpose is to become enlightened, but then it is our duty to go out into the world and teach and share our wisdom. Karma is not only a matter of personal spiritual growth and advancement, but also concerns our path in the world; how we help to shape it and how we raise consciousness. And of course, reaching Enlightenment may anyway take a lifetime, so the teachers would frequently be quite old.

Roshi adhered to the Big Boat philosophy and founded many monasteries where he taught monks the Buddhist path towards Enlightenment. Then, when they were ready, they too would go out into the world and start to teach. In this way, monasteries would grow up around a spiritual Master, where monks would spend years or decades studying the true path. Many monks, of course, do not reach Enlightenment in this world, but would stay at the monastery their whole lives, becoming more and more deeply spiritually aware. They would *de facto* be following the Little Boat philosophy and, through their own growing spiritual awareness, raise the spiritual consciousness of the world.

When Tony arrived at Mount Baldy at just eighteen years of age he truly felt that he had found home, and intended to stay in the monastery for the rest of his life. Despite the physical hardships and the rigours of the regime, and what may seem to those outside as great deprivation, he was living in a state of spiritual bliss that became ever more joyous as the work deepened. It was absolutely clear to him that his life's work was spiritual, that his path lay through Zen Buddhism and that Roshi was his spiritual teacher.

But after about a year and a half at the monastery, another current began to stir within him. He felt that it was no longer enough for him to enjoy this spiritual bliss for himself; he needed to take spirituality out into the world, to try to do something for humanity. He recognized that the same urge that had originally driven him in Oslo to almost obsessive political involvement as a way of solving the world's problems, was the same drive that was now pushing him through his spirituality to try to help the world. But from this new Buddhist perspective, he understood that the only chance of solving any of the world's major problems was through spiritual consciousness.

Tony realized that he needed to study and he needed to teach. And so he made one of the most difficult decisions of his life: he would have to leave the monastery. This was in no way because he was bored or fed up or finding the rigours of monastery life hard to bear; nor was it because he craved anything in the outside world. On the contrary, he would have been happy to stay in this state of bliss forever. But he felt impelled by some guiding hand to move on. Knowing that Roshi subscribed to the Big Boat school of thought, Tony knew that eventually he would have to leave the monastery and go out into the world to teach. So perhaps he was not really changing course, just leaving fifty years early!

Telling Roshi was one of the hardest things that Tony had ever had to do, and he felt Roshi's disappointment keenly. Although Roshi had never said anything in so many words, Tony felt that he was 'being groomed' to be his eventual successor. But he also knew that Roshi would understand his decision. If he were going back to be a part of the world, and to be a spiritual teacher, taking with him the practices of the Zen Buddhist monastery, it was clear that Tony needed to live in the world, and he needed to study. He decided to go to university. And how happy this decision would make his parents, though for different reasons.

Roshi listened attentively, smiling all the while. Then he made a very seductive proposal: that Tony study at the University of California in Los Angeles, and continue to live free of charge at the monastery as a lay monk. Though this was a very tempting offer, Tony felt that it would be too easy. He needed to be self-sufficient; he needed to do it alone. When he told Roshi this, the Master said simply, of course you must go. Then he laughed heartily. It took Tony many years to understand that laughter.

Roshi created a most beautiful parting ceremony. It was similar to the welcoming ceremony – a private session with just Roshi and Tony, and the monk who translated for them. Roshi told Tony that Mount Baldy was his home and that he would always be welcome to return. Then he gave his blessings for the journey. Afterwards a party was held in Tony's honour, to celebrate his time at the monastery. Some of the monks had prepared special food, which tasted delicious after the monotony of the monastery diet.

And then it was time to leave. Tony was curious, even a little fearful maybe, to be leaving the womb that had been his home for nearly two years. The thought of moving back into the world must have been scary; would it be the same world that he had renounced two years earlier? And how different would it appear to him now, seeing it with new eyes?

Tony looked sorrowfully back at his friends in the monastery. And at Roshi… He loved him deeply and had loved his time there. But now he had to move on.

From Mount Baldy, Tony went to the Spanish mansion-house monastery where he had stayed when he had first arrived in Los Angeles – how many lifetimes ago that seemed now. He spent a couple of weeks there, attending some meditations, but not being fully part of the monastery life. He helped a few of the monks working in the gardens and earned a little money doing so. Slowly, at this 'halfway house', he began his adjustment to the world.

He decided to go back to England, to Cornwall. Although at first he had not been happy there as a child, he loved the sea, and thought that it would be a good idea to spend a little time there, getting used to the outside world, before going on to university in England. He also had very little money, and this was a relatively cheap place to live. And he carried with him his Buddhist faith that 'the universe' would take care of him. [This, by the way, does *not* mean abdicating responsibility for one's own needs, but rather not trying to control it, being open to opportunities and in tune with whatever the universe would provide.] He rented a small cottage by the sea, and found odd jobs to keep body and soul together; or rather to provide for his body – his soul was now well able to take care of itself. And of course he was still meditating for several hours each day.

As the days turned into weeks and he began to feel restive, an unexpected visitor appeared. Zoran Samara, with whom he had had virtually no contact since the family had left Egypt when he was twelve, had nevertheless made sure that he received regular reports about his oldest son [and, indeed, all his sons] all through the years. He had been worried about Tony's stay at the monastery, feeling perhaps that he was being brainwashed. Now that he had left, Zoran decided to visit and see for himself how his firstborn son was doing.

They spent a week together. Living in simple circumstances and without any distractions of work, status or other people, his father offered Tony a side of him that he'd never seen before; a glimpse, perhaps, of the warm human being beneath the skin of position and power. Spending unhurried time together each day, they began to get to know each other as real people, and clearly liked what they found. Although still worlds apart, they formed the beginnings of a real bond.

One day, as they sat together watching the sea, Zoran made Tony an offer: he would support Tony through university, with no strings attached. He could study anything he wanted to, anywhere in the world. Was this an expression of his relief that his son was finally 'coming to his senses' and would start to live normally, in the real world? Perhaps he was also happy to welcome the opportunity of behaving like a 'real father' after so many years *in absentia.*

After many weeks in Cornwall, Tony knew that he didn't want to stay in England. He knew that he wanted to go to university, but didn't know where. Then one night he woke up startled: the universe had dramatically come to his aid with an extraordinary vision, in which he was 'guided' to go to New Zealand. He found out as much as he could about the major universities there and made preparations for his journey. But again, the hand of destiny intervened: there was a terrible earthquake in New Zealand, and all plans to go there had to be scrapped.

Tony took another look at his vision: perhaps it needed just a little nudge up the road? The University of New England in New South Wales, Australia, accepted him to study for a degree in marine biology – the closest academic subject, he thought, to the world of nature, his great love.

Before university started, he decided to go back to Norway and spend some time with his mother, who had missed him greatly, and his grandmother, who was ill. He spent a few weeks with them and his brothers, who were delighted to see him, catching up on their lives, and enjoying the closeness of being part of an ordinary loving family again.

But there were still a few months left before the semester began. Tony wanted to follow his spiritual path and explore it in contexts other than the monastery. And he was itching to travel; not as a tourist, but in a way that would have spiritual meaning.

The call of India was very strong. It wasn't exactly the 'guru trail' that attracted Tony; rather, he wanted to visit the places that were sacred to Buddhism: where the Buddha was born, where he sat, where he meditated, where he spoke to his followers, where he had died.

Arriving in India was a great culture shock. The filth and poverty were ubiquitous and devastating to behold. And nobody seemed to care. The Indian middle classes easily justify their indifference: if someone is desperately poor, it is his/her caste, or karma. Either way, their lot in this life is pre-ordained and therefore not the concern of anyone else to try to change it or alleviate their suffering. No-one is angered by the situation; everyone just smiles, and accepts that "that's the way things are".

Tony arrived with very little money, and 'lost' it all in the space of a few days. This happened in two very different incidents, which together show the huge contrasts that make up modern India: profound spirituality at one end of the spectrum, and rapacious greed at the other.

On his first day there, Tony had met a rickshaw 'taxi' driver, and they started to talk. The driver explained the root cause of his dire poverty: he didn't have the money to buy a rickshaw and so he had to rent one, and nearly all the money he made went on paying rent to the owner. He was trapped forever in this vicious circle of poverty; he could never make enough to feed his family, and there was seemingly no way out. Tony listened to the man's story, and then gave him enough money to buy a rickshaw, about half of everything he had at the time. The look in the driver's eyes as he accepted the money – total disbelief, total belief – showering blessings upon Tony, was worth more than any money could buy.

The second incident was not such a happy one. A trader had noticed Tony hanging around the railway station, and came over and offered to help. He said he could introduce him to a friend of his who sold the most wonderful Indian artifacts very cheaply. Tony readily agreed: he could take them back with him to the university campus and make good money. He thanked him and arranged to meet with them both the next day. It was only later, when he was hungry and wanted to buy something to eat, that he realized the whole thing had been a hoax: as the trader had engaged his attention in conversation, his wily accomplice had stolen all his money.

With no money at all, it was time to walk the streets as a *Sadhu* [an Indian 'holy man' who owns nothing in the world, and is fed by the 'universe', rather like the Buddhist mendicant monks]. Tony had anyway never intended to see India as a tourist. Now the universe was providing him with the perfect opportunity: to walk as a *Sadhu*. And it rather appealed to him. It was an act of supreme trust that he could relinquish all material goods and know that he would be taken care of; spirituality made manifest in a very concrete way.

So it was that Tony spent nearly five months in Varanasi, situated on the banks of the Ganges River in South Eastern Uttar Pradesh. He avoided the 'gringo trail' and lived like a pilgrim. Walking as a *Sadhu*, he found that when he was really hungry he would always be fed, either by people in the street, or by visiting the monasteries where food was given as a matter of course to *Sadhus*.

Varanasi is a uniquely spiritual place, where many avatars, gurus and spiritual teachers and seekers of all kinds have made their home. And a bonus of his pilgrimage was that he met many extraordinary people, whom he would not have met had he been living like a tourist. One such person, whom he encountered at a monastery, was a maharaja, who lived in a very grand mansion house that was falling apart because he didn't have the money for its upkeep. [Being rich can be an expensive business, he told Tony.] Tony stayed with him for many days, and was fed delicious Indian cuisine, and fascinating Indian history.

Varanasi is one of the oldest continuously inhabited cities in the world, and was the site of a prehistoric Aryan settlement. It is a place that has become sacred to both Hindus and Buddhists. One of the seven sacred cities of Hinduism, it has numerous shrines, temples and palaces, and miles of steps down for ritual bathing. More than a million Hindus visit the city each year, on a kind of pilgrimage. There are also sacred Buddhist temples there, and just north of Varanasi is Sarnath, where the Buddha delivered his first sermon.

Tony spent a lot of time in the temples, walking around them and sitting in them for many hours. He began to understand the extraordinary power that emanates from these sacred buildings, and felt a strong connection that fore-ordained his later explorations of Shamanism in the Andes. The temples, too, were a good place for meeting other spiritual seekers and talking with them. And Indians love to talk: philosophy, religion, and every outreach of both.

Walking as a *Sadhu* gave Tony a certain invisibility, and so it was a good way to observe the many different sides of India: the obscene poverty of the masses, the filth, the disease, the corruption; and the gentle spirituality and compassion that somehow permeates India in spite of this. Just before he left, he witnessed first hand the juxtaposition of the extremes of life in India. The airline on which he was flying out made a mistake with his ticket and he missed his flight. Being put up in a five-star hotel till the next flight out, two days later, he was able to observe the vulgar wealth of India's educated 'yuppies' that sits in such close proximity to the abject poverty of the masses: the cost of two drinks at the hotel bar would have fed an average Indian family for three months.

The few months that Tony spent in India were fascinating, horrific and salutary. He fell in love with the country and felt that he had been shown the 'soul' of India. He was beginning to learn what true compassion is: spirituality manifest in action. It was absolutely clear to him then, if he still had any lingering doubts about having left the monastery, that his place was definitely in the world. His real journey was just beginning.

In September 1985, three-and-a-half months after his twentieth birthday, Tony went off to Australia to begin his studies at the University of New England in New South Wales.

This proved to be a mixed experience for him. His time at the monastery had left him vulnerable to the ways of the world, with few social skills, and no small talk; at first it was hard to make friends. University life also presented another challenge: all through school, he had been used to being top in everything, without too much effort. Even in Norway, he had mastered the language and graduated top of his year. But having spent two years in full time meditation designed to let go of his mind, he now found it difficult to get back into intellectual pursuits. And being a mediocre student did not appeal to him at all!

But he did enjoy the diversity of campus life: it had an international flavour, with students coming from America, Europe, Japan, Asia, and some from Africa. There were also older people, in their forties and fifties, taking advantage of Australia's generous grants system to attend university in middle age. The weather was great, the timetable 'liberal' with much free time, and being a student offered a comparatively easy 're-entry' into the world.

Tony decided not to divulge the fact that he was a Buddhist to his fellow students; he did not want to have to 'justify' his beliefs and practices. Unlike his highschool days, he had no interest in being involved in student politics. But after a hesitant start, he did begin to mix more with other students, and gradually he made friends – all with women. Women liked him because he treated them courteously and as an equal. But he found it difficult to communicate with the men, who were exceedingly macho, and seemed to be interested only in rugby, beer and 'Sheilas'.

Over time he established good friendships with several women, but he wasn't interested in becoming involved in an intimate relationship. He wanted to honour the promise he had made to himself on leaving the monastery, to remain celibate.

This was because he didn't want to be distracted from his spiritual path, which he saw as the real purpose of his life. He still felt that he was a monk; this was his reference point, from which everything else stemmed. He also felt that he was incomplete, and therefore inadequate to be in a relationship. He didn't want to try to find his happiness or fill his incompleteness through someone else. If, later in his life, he were to have a relationship, it could only be when he had let go of all neediness and attachment. For now, he was on a mission to become enlightened, and this was all-absorbing.

Because he didn't become involved with any woman, although several made it obvious that they were interested, it was assumed that he was gay. But when it became clear that he didn't hang out with men either, people simply became confused. No-one knew how to deal with someone they couldn't label and put in a box. But eventually, this led to an unusual outcome: men started to befriend him. They saw that the women really liked him and his gentle ways, and so would ask him to 'plead their cause', acting as an intermediary between themselves and the women with whom they wanted to become more intimately involved. But like Viola pleading for Olivia's love on Duke Orsino's behalf, it often backfired – and the women fell in love with Tony instead!

During his second year at university, Tony became involved in the conservationist movement, and in particular with a dedicated group of people engaged in the preservation of the rain forest, the 'hot issue' of the day. This began to take up more and more of his time; although of course he was still connected to the monastery by an umbilical cord of spiritual practices, which were to last throughout his life. Indeed, meditation has remained at the centre of his life, wherever he is in the world, and whatever else he is doing.

Before the end of his second year at university, however, he became dissatisfied with the course in marine biology; it was too theoretical, and Tony wanted to be out there, doing. 'Out there' at this stage meant going to South America to work in some way to save the rain forest, an issue about which he now cared passionately. He decided to give up his university studies and follow his heart to the rain forest.

The Friends of the Rain Forest, the student group with which he had been involved, connected him to a 'green' organization in Brazil, which put him in touch with people who had worked with people who had worked in the rain forest. It seemed serendipitous and healthy, this 'people chain' stretching halfway around the world, hands joining across continents to enable one individual to go and work in the rain forest.

He was given a small grant from the Friends of the Rain Forest, in return for which he was to send back regular reports about his experiences in the Amazon. He had also managed to save quite a bit from his student grant, mainly because he was used to eating so little after his two years in the monastery and saw no reason now to spend a lot of money on food.

He flew from Australia to Miami to Brazil, and then travelled across land to the borders of Peru and the Trading Post that would be his last port of call before setting out into the heart of the Amazon Rain Forest.

As he began his journey, Tony may not have been sure what he was looking for; but he knew, with certainty, that he would find it.

Chapter Three
The Amazon Rain Forest
Meeting the First Forest Shamans

The Trading Post on the borders of Peru, where Tony landed one early June morning, was a squat, ugly place, reflecting its unplanned beginnings and haphazard growth. It was the end of the road, literally as well as metaphorically; after this, all travel was by canoe along the river.

A half-way house between Western civilization and the Amazonian Rain Forest, the Trading Post represented the worst of both worlds: the deterioration and corruption of tribal life, and the runaway rampages of capitalism and urban pollution. It was also filthy: raw sewage floated in the river, rubble sat on the unpaved streets waiting for collections that never came. All around, the detritus of years of indifference and neglect was visible.

Most of the people who lived at the Trading Post were *Mestizos,* people of mixed race, combining Indian and European heritage. They had originally been pure native Indian, but many generations of intermarriage with Europeans had thinned their native blood, and much of their ancient pride and nobility of spirit had disappeared along the way. In South America, the term *Mestizo* had acquired social and cultural connotations: a pure-blooded Indian who had stooped by adopting European dress and customs, and was often used pejoratively.

The *Mestizos* seemed to be living in a cultural and spiritual limbo, neither belonging to their ancestral tribal roots nor embracing the advantages of Western modernity. The society was changing too quickly and was destroying itself in the process. European visitors had brought with them diseases previously unknown in the rain forest; and sudden wealth, which the residents seemed unable to use for their own real benefit, was instead corrupting them.

The community, though perhaps this term is somewhat euphemistic, comprised about five hundred people; there was no cohesive ingredient to create any real sense of community. Tribal rites and ceremonies had long been discarded, and no new unifying practices had arisen to replace them. There was a feeling of transience, both about the place and about the lives of its inhabitants.

The men were all traders, trading up and down the rivers. They would travel by canoe to the nearby villages, collecting rubber [dripped into bowls by cutting the bark of rubber trees] which brought a high price in Europe, and bringing back fish, seeds and medicinal herbs. Villagers living in the small communities along the rivers would also bring goods to the Trading Post to sell.

The traders living at the Post sold on the goods that they'd collected to the Europeans, who visited every few weeks. They were paid mostly in dollars and made good money. In fact, there was nothing for them to do except make money – and drink. There was one run-down school, one small clinic-cum-hospital – and a bar on every corner, almost always full, gushing out loud European and South American music at all hours. Of course it was only the men who drank in the bars; this was a society with machismo carved into the DNA of the entire male population. While the men were busy making money and drinking, the women stayed at home, compliant, cooking and cleaning and looking after the children.

The Trading Post was on the edge of the rain forest and so had a tropical climate. The heat was unbearable, as the trees had been cut down and there was no shade anywhere. The humidity was worse. After spending a few days there as a reluctant visitor, while waiting for river transport, Tony was very glad to leave.

Traders took him up river in a long canoe, which a few days earlier had still been a tree. This was a kind of river 'bus' taking about ten passengers. The inside was carved out, and a small motor had been stuck, rather perilously Tony thought, onto one end. It took a full day's canoeing to reach the small transit camp, from where our traveller would be collected. This was a sort of riverside 'Bed and Breakfast', a one-family house where villagers and traders would stay on their way up and down river. The river, or more accurately rivers – the rain forest is sodden with an intricate web of rivers, small and large, flowing into and out of each other – were dotted with similar places, about one day's canoeing apart. All the riverside Bed and Breakfasts offered similar fare: breakfast was fish [which Tony didn't eat as he was a strict vegetarian], beans and rice; bed was two hooks on which to hang your hammock.

The Amazon River is a vast snake of water, the largest river in the world in volume, and second only to the River Nile in length. Its origins are within a hundred miles of the Pacific Ocean in the Peruvian Andes, and it flows almost four thousand miles across northern Brazil into the Atlantic Ocean. It has more than one thousand known tributaries, several of which are more than a thousand miles long. It is said that the river was given its name by European travellers in the sixteenth century, after they had engaged in battles with fierce tribes of women, whom they likened to the Amazons.

Originally many indigenous peoples lived along the rivers but, as waves of foreigners, exploring the rivers from the mid nineteenth century on, had sought to enslave them, they had moved further and further inland. Opened up to world shipping in the 1860s, the river traffic increased exponentially with the coming of the rubber trade. Now, the native people were used to foreigners and were happy to trade with them, but they didn't necessarily like them.

The village to which Tony would be taken was four days' journey away by canoe. Everything along the rivers happens at a leisurely pace. You move when there is a canoe available; it could be the next day, or the next week. Time was slowing down; there was nothing for Tony to do but be patient and wait.

After a few days, some people from the village where Tony would be living arrived in a dug-out canoe. Six or seven men climbed out of the canoe, and tied it to a tree on the riverbank; they totally ignored Tony. This was his first contact with Shamans, though he had no idea that they were Shamans, or indeed, what a Shaman was. To him they were simply native inhabitants of the rain forest, dressed in 'Western' clothes: in the intense heat and humidity, shorts and a T-shirt seemed the only sensible option.

At first light next day they set off, the Shamans still paying scant attention to their white-skinned passenger. Tony didn't seem to mind. At last, he was on his way into the rain forest, feeling excitement and trepidation in equal measure. Perhaps in some as yet unarticulated way, he knew that he was about to embark on an experience that would change his life forever.

The villagers spoke a strange dialect, a mixture of Portuguese and Spanish, with a smattering of their old native tongue. It was unlike anything Tony had ever heard, and he understood not a word. A leisurely four-day trip along the river with people from a strange culture, who spoke an incomprehensible language, was a daunting experience. But it also afforded ample time for reflection, and Tony made good use of it. He had been glad to leave 'civilization' behind, and was ready to welcome whatever lay ahead. With the gentle lapping of the water against the sides of the canoe, he felt embraced by a deep sense of peace, and a profound trust in his travelling companions and the universe.

But these feelings of peace and calm were short-lived. As they moved along the river, the Shamans began bucketing water out of the canoe – the only way to stop it from sinking. Tony felt sure that he was going to drown. Every time they hit a rock or a log, which was quite frequently, he was jolted out of his senses. Suddenly, doubts flooded in. What could have possessed him to come? Had he taken leave of his senses? What was he doing here, thousands of miles from everyone he knew, from everything familiar, totally cut off from the outside world, alone with people with whom he could not communicate? Had his adventurous spirit taken him one leap too far?

In one flash, the two years of growing spiritual awareness that he had experienced in the monastery seemed to evaporate. His logical, Western-trained mind took over, plunging into fear mode and the "what if?" syndrome. What if they had an accident? What if he needed to go to hospital? What if they couldn't get there in time? Who would let his family know? One way or another, he was convinced that he was about to die. And so our intrepid hero spent that first day, riddled with fears and apprehension.

In the evening, the party stopped at another riverside 'Bed and Breakfast'. Money rarely changed hands at these places; the visitors would either bring goods – seeds or medicinal herbs, perhaps, from further up river – or they would do favours: taking a message to someone in another village, or delivering a parcel. The natives would survive on gifts from villagers, augmented by fishing and gathering fruit that grew wild in the forest.

These stopovers along the rivers were all one-family houses, though there were usually many children, and often more than one wife. Tony had been told to bring the children sweets, which were unobtainable on the river, and so instantly bought their favour. And the children were wonderful: curious, open and uninhibited. White people were not a complete novelty on the rivers, as they had been coming to the rain forest for some time by then. And although they had no common language, they managed to communicate: Tony with wild gestures, the children with smiles and lots of laughter.

On the second day on the river, Tony had his first experience of Shamanic wisdom. One of the men at the front of the canoe pushed away a branch of a tree that was obstructing their way, and was stung by killer bees. Tony's first thought was that he was glad it hadn't happened to him. But he also felt great pity for the man who was suffering such agony, and became really afraid for him. But to his utter astonishment, the Shamans in the canoe began laughing and falling about in merriment. It didn't make any sense; and it seemed extremely uncaring and cruel.

Later, when he had been living in the Shamanic community for some time, and was able to communicate with them verbally a little, Tony asked the Shamans why they had laughed at the man's suffering on the canoe. His answer from the Shamans was to pose another question: "Is real compassion expressed through feelings of fear and negativity?"

They explained that the man's energetic body had been experiencing fear and pain and that Tony's anxiety would only have brought more negativity to his energetic body. It was like a parent panicking and screaming when a child falls and hurts herself, so compounding the situation. Then, the child would have to deal with the parent's fear as well as her own pain; whereas, if the parent was calm and reassuring, the child would know that nothing really bad had happened, and her recovery would be more easily effected.

True compassion, the Shamans explained, means helping an injured person to take away the trauma of the pain. By laughing, they had helped to draw the fear out of his body. The man was in shock and in danger of dying. If everyone in the canoe had reacted as Tony had, their anxiety would have fed strong negativity into the situation and the man would surely have died. Through laughter, the Shamans had turned the energy around and the man had healed. Tony felt humbled; he began to wonder what this culture was that the Western world dismissed so derisively as 'primitive'.

Gradually, over the rest of that four-day canoe journey, it began to dawn on Tony that his real purpose in coming to the Amazon had not been to save the rain forest, but to save himself. That by understanding the rain forest and the people who inhabited it, he would also come to understand himself and his own spiritual journey. The Shamans living in the village where he was to stay would be his first teachers, a portal into this ancient system of wisdom that would become an essential part of Tony's life and work.

Shamanism is a tradition of knowledge not bound by time, location or culture. It has always been with us, since the first humans walked the earth. It has spanned time and space, through the millennia and across the planet. It is a sacred path, opening up an awareness of the interconnectedness and oneness of all life. It offers a way of awakening our deepest consciousness to the perfection and harmony of the natural world and all life within it.

Shamanism is a bridge between worlds: the world of physical reality and the world of spirit; a way of being that brings the spiritual into every aspect of daily living. It is a way of life that acknowledges the divine within ourselves and within all life forms. In its highest aspirations, it is a manifestation of pure intention and unconditional love.

It is generally accepted that Shamanism, as old as humankind itself, existed as part of prehistoric cultures. It is the most ancient form of communal religious/ spiritual experience extant today, predating the great monotheistic religions of the world by many thousands of years. It was prevalent in the Neolithic Period and the Bronze Age, and was practised among peoples living in the hunting/gathering stage of early human development. It was carried forward, somewhat altered, amongst peoples who had reached the animal-rearing and horticultural stage, and evolved among more developed societies that bred cattle for production. Different traditions of Shamanism have existed, in some form, throughout human evolution.

Early records of Shamanism, archaeological and anthropological research, show that it was originally found in vast areas of the Arctic, North and Central Asia among the Ural-Altaic and Paleo-Asian peoples and among early hunters in Siberia. From here it spread to South East Asia, Indonesia, Oceania, aboriginal groups in North America and, much later, to South America, Australasia, and northern Europe.

During its long history, Shamanism has changed and adapted, incorporating into itself many of the ideologies and practices that were widespread amongst the general populations among which it flourished. Through the centuries, some Shamanic ideas were introduced, too, into the dominant religions where it was prevalent. Today, some form of Shamanism is practised on all five continents of the globe. In some parts of the world, notably in Central and North Asia, it is the principal religious force, second only to Islam. More usually it co-exists, amicably or uneasily, with other forms of religious and magical practice.

Native South American Shamans, with whom Tony was to live and study, trace their lineage back to the beginning of time, long before any kind of written records were kept. They remember the stories of the old folk, handed down the generations from grandmother to granddaughter, that speak of a time when Mother Earth was young and her wisdom was embraced by all. A time when spirits roamed the earth freely, and humans would converse with animals, birds, trees and stones – their ancestors. They talk of their roots among all the children of Mother Earth: the four-legged people, the tree people, the stone people, the winged and the finned ones. They talk of their unbroken connection to the Source of the All That Is.

The Shamanic path is a path of sacred power, of connecting directly to the unseen force of Spirit, of journeying to other realms of existence in altered states of consciousness. The Shaman sees the cosmos as incorporating many realms: the Upper World of the Sky, where the spirits live, and where the Shaman travels to connect to spirit knowledge, wisdom and visions; the Middle World, the visible world of Mother Earth which we humans inhabit; and the Underworld, where the Shaman may travel to bring back lost souls or conquer evil spirits. In the Shaman's reality, all these realms are interconnected and together form the consciousness in which he lives.

The term 'Shamanism' is open to many different schools of interpretation: spiritual, psychological, sociological, ethnological; the definition will depend upon whom you ask. It has variously been defined as incorporating religion, magic and sorcery, mysticism, medicine and healing, visions, mythological concepts, communication with spirits and ecstatic experiences in altered states of consciousness [this latter being essential in all definitions of Shamanism] and psychopomp [escorting the souls of the dead to other worlds].

Down the centuries and across the globe, Shamanism has undergone many developments, reversals, metamorphoses, a difference of emphasis as now one aspect, now another, has become dominant, influenced by shifting cultural, tribal and religious traditions and historical and geographical context. But its fundamental beliefs of the sacredness of nature and the interconnectedness of all life forms, has remained unchanged.

The word 'Shaman' has several possible derivations. The Vedic word *sram* means "to heat oneself up" and may have been influenced by Paleo-Oriental civilizations. But the most commonly accepted derivation is from the Manchu-Tungus word *saman,* formed from the verb *sa,* meaning "to know"; so Shaman literally means "one who knows". But it is more usually interpreted as "one who knows ecstasy", the ecstatic state being the *sine qua non* of Shamanism.

Classical Shamanism may be defined as that practised today in North Asia, where it is more highly ritualized and more specifically articulated than among other peoples. This model is followed, with adjustments to local culture and tradition, by Shamanic communities everywhere. Many primitive religions held some beliefs that may be similar to those of Shamanism – belief in spirits and other supernatural beings and communication with them, belief in magic and sorcery, ecstatic visions and out-of-body experiences – but were not actually Shamanic. The ecstatic experiences of Shamanism have always exercised a powerful influence on other religious ideologies, mythologies and ritual practices.

In Shamanic wisdom, everything within Creation is seen as interconnected and significant. The physical and the spiritual, the visible and the invisible, the known and the unknown, heaven and earth, were seen not as separate entities, but as divinely linked parts of the All That Is. The spiritual paradoxes that inform the different realms of existence were held within humans as part of the secrets of Creation. The breath of life within all species, in all worlds, is one. The Source of everything was understood as being one indivisible whole, which exists within everything.

Since ancient times, Shamans have been the keepers of the sacred knowledge of life, the guardians of ancient wisdom. Their wisdom came from the spirit world, from Mother Earth, from nature and everything within it; from their understanding of their place within the natural world. They were the bridge between worlds, guiding their tribes along the path of divine knowledge, reminding them that all trees and plants are sacred, that birds, not being earth-bound, perceive and communicate a higher perspective that can enlighten humans, and that all animals speak to those who listen.

Shamanism calls on us to respect all life and not to assume that we humans are lords and masters over any other life form. In fact as a species we are very young, all other beings having an evolutionary history far longer than our own. They have inhabited the earth for millions of years and have accumulated great wisdom; we are the newcomers and we would do well to acknowledge this.

To the Shaman, animals are our parents, trees and plants our grandparents, rocks and minerals our great-grandparents; and all have knowledge to impart. We may think that we have superior intelligence but this is only one kind of intelligence, and a very limited kind at that. All life forms were created by the same Spirit and contain consciousness, a manifestation of the intention of their spirit in physical reality. Accordingly, we should act towards them with humility, reverence and respect.

To Shamans, the cosmos is a web of interconnecting strands of energy, like beams of light, every strand connected to every other strand, and all connected to the Great Web that is the universe. This Web links all parts of creation within the visible world, all realms of existence, all levels of consciousness, past and future in an infinite present, through all time and through all space. The Shaman uses the concept of the Web to explain the wholeness and harmony of the All That Is, the infinite movement and circularity of everything that exists in creation, without beginning, without end, in an infinite flowing dance of life.

Tony arrived in the village that was to be his home in the rain forest in a state of shock. While still at university, he had spent a lot of time researching and preparing for his trip to the jungle. He had worked out regularly in the gym and was physically in fine fettle. He had read everything he could lay his hands on about the rain forest, and had spent long hours questioning people in the environmental movement.

At the Trading Post he had bought the five pieces of essential equipment necessary for survival in the jungle: a machete to cut through deep foliage; a small knife for peeling fruit and vegetables; a compass to find his bearings at all times; a hammock and mosquito net to rest in; and a pot for water – there is always water, for wherever you are in the forest you are near a river. He felt that he was well prepared and well informed. But nothing, nothing, could have forearmed him for the challenge and the brutal discomfort of actually being in the rain forest. It bore no resemblance whatever to the paradise on earth that he had imagined.

The sheer vastness of the forest and the huge variety of its plant and animal life was overwhelming. As well as covering an area of thousands of square miles, it also extends vertically, with many layers of vegetation and animal habitation. The tropical heat and the humidity are excessive, though no-one in the rain forest ever sees the sun. This is because the trees, densely packed together, link branches some fifty to a hundred feet above the ground to form a kind of ceiling, thick and sturdy enough to walk on, which blots out the sun. And so the climate on the ground is always hot and sticky, all year round, with no marked seasonal variations.

Many small animals live on this 'ceiling', feeding and escaping from predators in the thick foliage. Beneath this canopy, the next layer is home to many varieties of small trees, lianas and epiphytes, and many South American wild beasts which have adapted to walking and climbing short distances in the difficult terrain. Burrowing animals, such as armadillos and caecilians, are found below the soil surface, where millions of micro-organisms also live, helping to decompose much of the organic litter accumulated by other plants and animals from all layers.

The noise of the forest is deafening: birds, monkeys, insects, an incessant chattering, clicking, buzzing, a cacophony of caterwauling to assault the ears twenty-four hours a day. And the flies and the mosquitoes – armies of them, constantly on the attack. Snakes are huge and poisonous and ubiquitous, and a snake bite can prove fatal. Tony felt that all his senses were being relentlessly bombarded with no cessation; the reality of the rain forest left him reeling.

Those first weeks in the village proved unexpectedly difficult. Nature, Tony's first spiritual home, now felt scary. The rain forest was overwhelmingly powerful, with strange unknown forces at work that he didn't understand; he felt helpless, completely at its mercy. He realized then how precarious life is, and felt insignificant in this vast expanse of alien territory. He was also aware of feeling distrust and fear, compounded by the fact that he couldn't communicate with anyone. Not for the first time in his life, though now, perhaps, with the most frightening consequences, he felt a complete outsider.

And the villagers made no particular efforts to be friendly. But after all, why should they have? They hadn't asked this strange young white man to come and they weren't sure what he was doing there. And their lives were hard enough, without having to cater to foreign visitors: a constant struggle against the harsh and unrelenting environment of the rain forest, a struggle for survival.

Tony had been advised to stock up at the Trading Post with items that would be useful for the villagers – machetes, knives, staple foods, anything they might need that was unavailable in the rain forest. Then he was able to give them these items in exchange for his keep. Both sides seemed satisfied with this arrangement. Tony stayed with one family for a while, then moved on to another, then another. It was all very informal, and no special relationships developed with any of the host families. They simply provided a place to hang his hammock.

The village was small, about a dozen families, some with several wives, and most with lots of children. They lived in family units, in simple wooden huts made from bamboo, the barks of trees, or whatever was at hand. All the huts in the rain forest are built on high stilts, as the ground is permanently sodden, and snakes and other crawling creatures abound. There are no windows, just spaces for light and air. The only 'furniture' was hooks for the hammocks. But the huts were used only for sleeping, all year round. The temperature never fell below thirty degrees centigrade; lives were lived outside.

The life of the village was communal, and revolved around three things: work, food and whatever was necessary for survival; the children, their education into the ways of the community and their spiritual development; and the Shamanic rituals and ceremonies. There was also some social interaction with neighbouring villages along the rivers. The work was divided along gender lines – it was the only way to cope with the rigours of life in the rain forest. Simply maintaining the community and getting enough to eat took up a major part of each day. There was actually an abundance of food in the forest – but also an abundance of animals to get to it first!

The men fished, gathered food from the forest, built and took care of the canoes, mended the fishing nets and hammocks and kept the huts in a good state of repair. They did all the hard physical work; but still they seemed to have plenty of time to sit around and talk. The women, who always seemed to be busy, picked the food grown in the village, cooked all the food and kept the houses and the children clean. They prepared the herbal remedies and medicines, and each woman was responsible for the health of her own family. And much of the time the younger women were pregnant.

Although most of the villagers were not initiated Shamans, the life of the community was lived according to Shamanic practices, guided by the Chief Shaman who was head of the village, and in harmony with the rhythms and cycles of the natural world. Life was lived day-to-day, moment to moment, with full awareness, and a strong sense that everything was as it was meant to be. All the work seemed to be joyous, and was often accompanied by singing. The women especially, going down to the river together to wash the clothes, would sing: songs praising nature, songs to the trees, the river, the spirit of the moon; songs to *Pachamama,* Mother Earth.

The day started at sunrise, and ended at sunset. A small breakfast would be eaten at home, but the rest of the meals were cooked and eaten communally. Although nothing seemed to be officially planned or organized, everyone knew what was happening at every stage of the day. Except for Tony! Nobody bothered to tell him 'the rules', or where he should be at any given time. Sometimes people would disappear, and suddenly he would realize that they had all had lunch. The meals, though communal, always seemed to be impromptu, and were never eaten at the same place. Tony spent a great deal of time trying to find out where lunch would be each day, mostly unsuccessfully; he always seemed to be hungry. But after a while, as he managed to blend in to the rhythms of village life, some of the women took pity on him and would save him food.

Fired by great idealism and enthusiasm, Tony had come half way round the world to 'save the rain forest'. But actually he seemed to be doing very little. He worked with the men for a few days, mending fishing nets or toiling in the rice paddies; but he found the men's work physically too gruelling in the heat and had to stop. Then he worked for a while with the women, but the men didn't like this at all, so he stopped this as well. So, most of the time he just wandered around, watching people, trying to understand what was going on and learning as much as he could. And he spent a lot of time with the children.

The children spent most of their days happily by the river, playing and swimming and laughing a lot; they seemed to be free to do as they wished. But they were all expected to help out with the work of the community. The older boys would work with the men, learning how to build and maintain the huts, the canoes and the hammocks. The older girls would look after the younger children, and help the women with the cooking. The younger children, boys and girls, would collect herbs, clean out the cooking pots, carry things from one place to another, and help out in small ways wherever needed.

The education of the children seemed to be very *ad hoc*. There was no school and no formal schooling. But in spite of the informality of their education, the children learnt the two things that were essential for them to know: how to survive in the rain forest, and how to live in harmony: with themselves, with the community and with nature. If you asked any of them who their mother was, they would tell you "The Forest".

Growing up in a Shamanic community, the children's spiritual development is an intrinsic part of their lives, as natural and unquestioned as breathing. They would learn about the different spirits that are part of the Shamanic culture and their role in the life of the community, the interconnectedness of all life forms and the power of nature, and the expectations of the tribe to see them grow in spiritual wisdom. Children are brought up by the whole community, and parents have no special status with their own kids, though mothers take care of the physical well-being of their own children. From an early age, they are taught to be responsible for themselves. And being part of a larger community, with many adults to turn to if they have problems or worries, seems to obviate some of the more dysfunctional relationships that often exist between parents and children in the West.

The social mores and organization of the community are generally caring and compassionate. No-one lives alone. Personal problems can always be shared, and nobody is ever left to suffer on their own. And indeed, there does not seem to be much emotional suffering around. Of course there are jealousies, irritations, anger. But the dramas that we so often create around our suffering in the West seem to be unknown in the rain forest. However, there is no place here for an individual to buck the system. Conformity is taken for granted, and indeed without it survival would be put at risk.

There are few sexual taboos in most Shamanic communities, and sexuality is uninhibited. Before marriage, sex is free and open, and experimentation with different partners is accepted as the norm. But after marriage, which usually happens in the mid to late teens, everyone is expected to remain faithful. However, marriage could include more than one wife for a man [though not, apparently, more than one husband for a woman].

If a man wished to marry a second wife [or, occasionally, even a third] his first wife had to agree. She was the matriarch, she ran the household, and she made the decisions. Sometimes a man would try to persuade or cajole his first wife into letting him marry someone who had taken his fancy. But often she would agree gladly: there would be another pair of hands to help with the work, with the children, and someone for her to boss around, for she would retain the status of 'chief wife'. Or maybe her sexual drive had diminished with age, and she preferred her husband's sexual activities to remain under her roof – and under her thumb!

A man would also be expected to marry his wife's unmarried or widowed sister. This marriage would not necessarily be consummated; it was considered an act of kindness and generosity, a way of ensuring that all unmarried women in the community were taken care of, for a woman could not survive on her own. [Compare, for instance, the similar ancient Judaic custom, where a man is obligated to marry his brother's widow and take care of her and her children, unless she objects.]

Extra-marital affairs, however, as opposed to second marriages, were frowned upon, and social pressure on the couple would be brought to bear by the whole community. But it would all be out in the open; nothing was secret or hidden and there seemed to be little sexual game playing or hypocrisy. If there were sexual jealousies, the women would try to work things out among themselves. It seems that it was always the women who sorted things. In a way, they had more authority in relationships than the men.

Growing old in a Shamanic community seems to happen with confidence and grace. The old people are greatly respected and honoured. Being an Elder is a title worn with pride, and also carried with it great responsibility: the passing on of the wisdom and the stories of the community to the young, making sure that the old ways were not forgotten. Old people did not have to work, though they could continue as long as they wished [no forced retirement here]. And when they could no longer look after themselves, the whole community shared the responsibility for their care.

Living harmoniously was more than a rule of the community; it was their natural way of being. But of course even Shamanic communities are made up of individuals, with the same human weaknesses as the rest of us: jealousy, resentment, anger, loves and hates. And they have their own mechanisms for dealing with them. If someone were feeling angry or negative, a small group would visit them and give them a chance to talk through their emotions. If there was more serious antisocial behaviour, or if someone else had been hurt, a full meeting of the village would generally be convened. The person feeling angry or jealous or hurt would be given full opportunity to explain his/her feelings, or unacceptable behaviour, and suitable help for them would be prescribed. Help and support were the order of the day, not punishment *per se*; although reparations would usually be ordered if someone else had been hurt or offended.

For Shamanic communities, living this way was an expression of their harmonious relations with each other and with the natural world. But to a Western sensibility, living with everything exposed in this way, with everyone knowing everything about everyone else, and where privacy and deviation from the norm are unknown concepts, this way of life might invoke outrage or horror.

For children justice was swift, and often humiliating. While Tony was living in the village, he witnessed a very rare occurrence. A boy had molested a young girl, and a meeting of the whole community was called. Punishment is always decided upon by consensus, in a special ritual. In this case, the boy was forced to drink foul-tasting herbs, which had the added effect of loosening his mental control. Then he had to stand in the middle of the circle and explain to the whole village what he had done and how he felt. That boy learnt lessons he would never forget.

Tony, too, was learning much. He had now been staying in the village for several weeks, and was beginning to feel a little better, not so much of an outcast. He had become more used to the ways of the villagers and started to blend into their way of life. He also made huge efforts, aided by much hilarity from the children, to pick up something of their language, and was duly rewarded for his efforts: the community slowly began to accept him and he was allowed to follow the Shaman around and watch everything he did.

The role of the Shaman is, of course, central to the practice of Shamanism and to the religious/spiritual/mystical life of the community. The Shaman, in fact, is called on to play many roles: at different times, he may be any combination of priest, ecstatic, visionary, medicine man, seer, tribal head, judge. His functions are social as well as sacred. He may also be a singer and poet, a dancer and visual artist, a sorcerer and magician. He is not only the spiritual centre of his community; he would also be the keeper of his tribe's wisdom and knowledge:

sacred, secular and societal. But his central role is that of ecstatic, entering into trance-like states in order to travel to the spirit world and learn and be guided by its wisdom. [Many Shamans are women, but to obviate the continual use of he/she, and because almost all the Shamans with whom Tony worked were men, I shall use the masculine pronoun.]

The Shaman, blessed with transcendent knowledge, has an overview of his tribal culture and is seen as the focus and re-enforcer of the basic values of his community. He will define the relationships among the members of his tribe and is responsible for ensuring their harmony and well-being. He will determine the way the community relates to the environment, to the cosmos and to the spirits, and will act as a link between the community and the spirit world. Rooted in ancient Shamanic lore and custom, it is his vision of 'how life should be' that prevails.

The traditional role of the Shaman within the community may, for easier accessibility, be divided into four main areas of activity; though, of course, they are all interconnected and equally important. Firstly, he is a 'wise man', consulted by the community on all human matters in which extra help or guidance is needed. He may foresee events in the distant future, discover the whereabouts of a lost animal, or forecast the prospects for good fishing or hunting. He also plays a crucial role in solving disputes within the community, marital or any other kind. In this role, most Shamans are called upon to be arbitrator, politician, judge and psychologist too.

His second role is as healer, and he will have more than ordinary knowledge of the properties and preparations of all the local healing herbs and plants, and will be expert in their use. Shamans believe that physical sickness is a manifestation of imbalance or disharmony in the heart or soul, and he will always address the cause first, often invoking the guidance of the spirits. Only when he has addressed the root cause of the sickness will he deal with the symptoms, generally using medicinal herbs to treat the physical condition. There are also some plants that are helpful in relieving emotional imbalance.

Special ceremonies will have accompanied every stage of the growing and picking of the plants, to ensure that their 'healing spirit' remains within them. Healing ceremonies and rituals would be carried out in which the Shaman would minister to the patient, and it was not unusual for other family members or a small group of friends to be present. If a person has become seriously afflicted, a special healing ceremony might be held involving the whole community.

Shamans believe that illness could also be caused by the displeasure of spirits, so the Shaman's first task would be to ascertain which spirits were involved and then appease them. Sometimes, a soul has been 'caught' by spirits who are angry with it, and in this case the Shaman will need to liberate the soul. Or a person may be seriously ill because evil spirits have invaded his body, and then the Shaman's job is to drive them out. In all these cases, the Shaman will use his own expertise together with the wisdom and guidance of the spirits.

Thirdly the Shaman has a crucial role as spiritual teacher and guide, ensuring harmony among the community and with the natural world. In this role the Shaman, by the way he lives and purports himself – with humility, with reverence for all creation and with gratitude to the spirits – sets an example to his whole community. He is the bridge between the physical world and the world of spirit. He also plays an essential part in all rites of passage: birth, marriage and death. And he is the central figure in all rituals and ceremonies, which dominate the life of a Shamanic tribe.

Fourthly, the defining characteristic of the Shaman is his ability to 'travel' to other dimensions and spiritual realms, a reality beyond that of the physical world; his ability to communicate directly with the transcendent world. Able to fall into an ecstatic state at will the Shaman, it is believed, is able to communicate with the spirits either by experiencing an 'out-of-body' state, in which his soul leaves his body and enters the spirit world, or by acting as a vessel for the spirits' guidance. Or, he would stay in his body but move his consciousness into other dimensions.

The Shaman does not work alone; the power and knowledge that informs his work comes from his spirit guides and helpers. They are the bridge between the physical world of the Shaman and non-ordinary planes of consciousness that he is able to inhabit. They accompany his journeys through the cosmos, bringing him knowledge and wisdom that he could not access in the physical world, instruction in magical techniques, a new vision and perspective to guide his work. They are his connection to the Divine.

These spirit helpers may appear in human form, as great masters and spiritual teachers, or as angels; but generally they manifest as animals or birds, sometimes as trees or plants. Occasionally, the Shaman would shape-shift and inhabit the body of another being, usually an animal or a bird, thus availing himself of the animal's special powers. In the Amazon, for example, it is very common for a Shaman to take on the form of a jaguar, often his totem animal. [A totem is an animal species that offers its power to a Shaman, who then enters into sacred relationship with it. So, for instance, if his totem animal is jaguar, he connects to the power of the species 'Jaguar', not to an individual animal.] Thus, the Shaman is able to move with the speed and power of the jaguar, on land and in water, and see in the dark with jaguar eyes. He would also have access to the wisdom stored in the jaguar's spirit memory.

On these journeys, the Shaman would be able to communicate as he would with a human, with any life form that he encountered: animal, bird, tree, plant, water, sky, stars, the moon; and of course with Mother Earth. Experience in these other realms not only granted the Shaman the extraordinary wisdom of these other dimensions, it also gave him deeper knowledge of material reality, which he was able to bring back and use for the benefit of his community in his work in this world.

In most Shamanic tribes, the special position held by the Shaman precludes him from the normal work of the village, and he will be supported by the whole community; they will bring him food, see that his clothes and lodging place are well maintained and that all his physical needs are taken care of. This is done out of respect for the importance that is attached to the *role* of the Shaman, not the specific individual. Some communities boast many Shamans; most will have more than one, in which case one would act as Chief Shaman. Very occasionally, a community may find itself without an initiated Shaman, and then it would share that of a neighbouring village.

Becoming a Shaman is not usually a matter of choice; indeed, in most Shamanic traditions no-one voluntarily takes on this role. For the Shaman does not hold a position of power to be sought after like that of politicians in the West; rather his role is one of service, and often will have involved great personal suffering. The Shaman is 'chosen' for his role by the spirits. The spirits are the supernatural forces that are at the heart of Shamanism: the spirits of nature, the Underworld, the sky, the spirits of totem animals and ancestors. They are all seen as having supernatural power and play a central role in the practice of Shamanism. Where Shamans use the term 'spirits', we may think of God, the Almighty, the Divine, Great Spirit, or the All That Is.

Once chosen, a Shaman cannot avoid his destiny; though most know from a young age that this is their 'calling' and accept it as inevitable, usually with grace. If he does try to resist, the spirits have ways of breaking his resistance: he may be struck by illness or ill fortune, he may be tortured by terrifying dreams or have frequent accidents. Often, the chosen one may be tormented for years and suffer greatly, until finally he surrenders to the spirits and accepts his vocation.

Even if he does not resist, the Shaman in most cases will have suffered from serious physical sickness, undergone a psychological crisis or spiritual trauma, or had a close encounter with death. His own suffering is seen as the bestowal of a gift, acting as the gateway to his Shamanic powers. He may indeed have suffered terribly for many years, but not only will he have survived his ordeal, he will have healed himself in the process. So the tortures of the flesh become a portal to initiation, a vehicle to a higher level of consciousness. For only through his own experience can he truly know the mystical landscape of disease and death. The healed healer is a powerful physician. Tony now sees his frequent bouts of illness as a child as the driving force that led to his later work as a Shamanic healer; certainly, he felt that it had much in common with a Shamanic 'apprenticeship', and was a precursor of his own Shamanic initiation.

The selection of a Shaman by the spirits will usually take place before birth and so he is born to his role. He may even possess physically distinguishing marks, such as more teeth than normal, or six fingers or toes on one hand or foot; sometimes, he will have an extra bone in his body. These distinguishing marks are seen as a physical sign that he is the choice of the spirits. Some Shamans are neurasthenic epileptic. [Some sceptics dismiss Shamanic ecstasy as an epileptic fit. This might possibly account for the Shaman's easy access into the ecstatic state, but not for the spiritual work that he is able to perform there.]

In some communities, a person would become a Shaman by 'inheriting' the soul of a deceased Shaman, but it is still the spirits who have chosen him. Occasionally, an old Shaman would choose an exceptional young person of the community, one who had manifested a strong attraction to healing or spiritual practice, perhaps, to follow in his footsteps. In some cases, the whole clan would choose a candidate, but he would only be initiated as a Shaman if his ecstatic experiences were considered to merit this. Sometimes, the Shamanic role was revealed to a person through dreams or visions, or during an experience with hallucinogens. There were also instances of individuals choosing to become Shamans, usually by showing a great affinity with the sacred or the metaphysical from an early age; but in some communities they were considered to be less powerful than those Shamans chosen directly by the spirits.

The Shaman will serve as an 'apprentice' for many years, working with initiated Shamans who will guide him through his ecstatic experiences and 'journeys' to other realms, showing him the territory of non-ordinary reality, mapping connections to the wisdom of the spiritual world. When he is ready to take on the work of a Shaman, he will undergo what is often an agonizing initiation. Through all this, the ultimate goal of the Shaman is to become a bridge between realms, the servant of his community, not its master; the healer of sickness, preserver of harmony and balance, and guardian of the planet.

Tony, relaxed and at ease with himself after his first difficult weeks, began to enjoy the life of the village. It was now accepted by everyone that he didn't do any physical work; perhaps the Shaman intuitively knew that he had a different kind of contribution to make. Released from the need to earn his keep in this way, or to prove himself, Tony was free to spend time with the children, playing and learning.

He would go down to the river each day and swim with them, play games and just have fun. And he learnt to copy them and do what they did: if they got out of the water in a great hurry, so did he – maybe they had just seen a piranha! He followed the kids around [this way he also got fed] and gradually started to feel safe. The children still laughed a good deal when he was around, but he did not feel any longer that they were laughing *at* him. He was beginning to pick up the local dialect and could now communicate a little with the villagers.

He also spent time learning all he could from the Shamans. Under their guidance, he began to look at suffering in a very different way, to understand that it is actually caused by imbalance; and that recognizing this imbalance is the key to healing. According to Shamanic wisdom, healing is a transformation of mind and spirit to the point where we understand how to achieve balance in our everyday lives, in our thoughts and activities, and also in our deepest feelings. And that suffering as we normally define it in the West is an illusion that we ourselves create, manufacturing dramas which we then see as reality, instead of looking into our hearts and souls to transform the imbalance within.

Living with the Shamans and learning their ways, Tony began to realize how resistant he had been to the wisdom of the rain forest, how caught up in his own ideas and preconceptions. Now he was opening up to the forest, beginning to accept its rhythms, its wisdom, no longer trying to control it with his mind. He realized profoundly and experientially what he already knew through his rigorous practice of meditation in the Zen monastery, that the human mind has a powerful and dominant hold over us; if we allow it to control us, it limits our experiences and keeps us from moving forward. Shamans say that all the information we need for this life is encoded in the deepest part of our being. All we need to do is open ourselves up to this knowledge and let it embrace us.

Finally, came the real mark of Tony's acceptance into the community: he was to be invited to their rituals. He was greatly looking forward to attending his first ceremony; he now had a strong feeling that this was the real reason for his journey to the rain forest and his sojourn with the Shamans. But before he could attend the Shamanic rituals, his body had to undergo purification. He thought that by eating only healthy vegetarian food and undertaking special fasts to detoxify his body [helped by his strict Buddhist training and the simplicity and leanness of the fare at the monastery] his body was already purified. He was taken aback when villagers told him that his body was so polluted they could smell it. They said that, like everyone else from the 'outside world', he carried the past in every cell of his body, and before he could join in any ceremonies it had to be cleansed of all past attachments it was holding.

He was given a vile-tasting concoction of herbal remedies, which he was told to sip slowly. Then he started to vomit, and he vomited for seven days. Every part of his body felt weak and exhausted. He vomited until he had nothing left to vomit, and still he retched. He realized that he was bringing up not just physical slough, but also the negativity of his mind and emotions that were programmed into his body; all the baggage of twenty-two years of living in the West. The environment in which he had grown up had not nourished the process of real healing; instead, sticking-plaster remedies to his illnesses and suffering had constantly been sought through doctors and psychologists, all to no avail. Now, in a week of retching up his guts, he was bringing out all the sickness of the past, vomiting up everything that had kept him, albeit unconsciously, stuck in past diseases of the heart and soul.

Now that his body had been cleansed of toxins, past baggage and attachments, and he had become receptive to the spiritual wisdom of Shamanism, Tony was considered ready to attend his first ceremony.

Shamanic rituals and ceremonies are not just spiritual practices; they are part of the fabric of survival in the rain forest. If you don't listen to the spirit of nature in the jungle, and follow its purpose, you won't survive. There are special rituals for every aspect of life in the community: work, relationships, rites of passage. If you want to prosper in any aspect of your life, you must always ask the spirits for their blessing.

There are rituals, for example, to determine each step of the food process: blessing the land, asking the trees for permission to cut them down to prepare the land for planting, blessing the planting. All the spirits of nature would be invoked to bless a prosperous harvest, and then the reaping would have its own ceremony. The Shamans would listen to the spirits of the ancestors, to the old people, to sages and spirit guides, and to the spirits of the river, the trees and plants, the animals and birds, and of course to *Pachamama,* Mother Earth. There might also be a special ceremony asking the spirits to watch over the growing food so that the monkeys didn't get to it first!

Ceremonies are held at particular times of the year, according to the cycles of the moon and the rhythms of nature; to call on the spirits to bless the harvest, hunting or fishing, or a particular project of the community, or to counteract the failure of a food crop; to mark rites of passage, to resolve disharmony within the community, or in fact whenever a community has a particular need.

Sometimes an individual will request a ceremony, usually to sort out a personal problem or when special guidance or blessing is needed from the 'other world'. A pregnant woman might want a ceremony to ask the spirits to protect her unborn baby, someone about to start a journey might ask for the journey to be blessed, or a wife might seek help to keep an errant husband from straying. If the Shaman agrees that it is necessary, a ceremony would be held; it might be performed with just the family or a small group of villagers present, not the entire community, but always presided over by the Shaman.

But mostly, ceremonies and rituals would take place at special times of the year, when the astrological and energetic forces were favourable. At such times, they could be held every evening, at sunset, and the whole community would attend, including children from the age of puberty. These ancient and timeless rituals are the true heart of the community, linking it forever with its sacred past, and its future generations.

Ceremonies differ from one Shamanic tribe to another, incorporating the practices of their ancestors and their traditions, their culture and specific ways of connecting to the spirits and, very often, will be overlaid with tribal superstitions. Geographic terrain will also impact on the form and content of ceremonies: those in the Amazon Rain Forest, for example, would be very different from those in the Andes Mountains, or those held by Shamanic Eskimos where the icy ocean plays a central role.

But that said, there is a *leitmotif* that seems to run through all Shamanic rituals. Usually they are held at dusk, outside in a special place of power, with the whole community present, sitting in a circle on the ground with the Shaman in the centre. They would include drumming, rattling, chanting, dancing, the use of smoke and fire, and usually the drinking of a sacred drink – in all of which the whole community will participate, not just the Shaman. Though the accoutrements of the rituals may vary within different Shamanic traditions, as may the dress of the Shaman and the artifacts that he employs, central to all Shamanic ceremonies everywhere is the ecstatic trance of the Shaman and his communication with the spirits.

In many communities, the Shaman will wear special ritual robes. These will often be decorated in a way that helps the Shaman to imitate an animal, commonly a deer or a bear, or a bird. Or they may be elaborately embellished with animal likenesses, such as snakes, lizards and frogs. The most usual headdress is a crown made of antlers, or a headband into which feathers of particular birds have been sewn. The footwear is also symbolic, most often made from deers' hooves, birds' claws or bears' paws.

Many artifacts are used during the rituals, each possessing symbolic meaning particular to that tribe. The process of making the drum, the rattle, the whistle or the feathered headdress, and of gathering artifacts such as crystals, bones, plants and stones, is a deeply sacred one. Special songs, chants and blessings will accompany every step of this process.

The most important artifact used in Shamanic rituals, and the most ancient, is the drum. This is often oval rather than round in shape, has only one membrane and is highly decorated with symbolic depictions. The role of drumming is central to the ceremony; the slow ritual thudding of the drums beats to the rhythm of a heartbeat, the rhythm of the universe. It can modify the vibrations of being, so enabling consciousness to flow with the energy of spirit, moving from the physical to the immaterial world. The slow rhythmic drumming both helps to induce altered states of consciousness in the Shaman, and is also an invocation to the spirits to come to his aid.

The rattle is another significant artifact, symbolizing the movement of cosmic forces that expand in all directions, and is thought in some communities to contain the spirits of ancestors. The gentle rhythmic shaking of the rattle was used as an aid for surrendering the conscious mind and acting as a tool of transformation, helping movement from one reality to another.

Feathers were commonly used in Shamanic rituals, either as artifacts or as part of the Shaman's robe or headdress. Often they were made into healing wands, staffs and prayer arrows [a spiritual 'weapon' used to defeat evil spirits]. Feathers were regarded as having special energy and the feathers of certain birds were considered to bring with them particular powers. Feathers also symbolized weightlessness, consciousness not bound by gravity or limited by space or time.

Many Shamans use a medicine shield, made of animal skin stretched over a wooden frame. This would be decorated with feathers or beads, and representations of the particular animals that were that Shaman's main source of power and protection. The medicine shield represented his connection to his personal medicine and spiritual power.

Other important artifacts used in rituals included stones, crystals, necklaces, pouches, animal paws, sacred herbs, whistles for calling the Shaman's allies in the spirit world, bones of animals or ancestors, smoke, fire, staffs, pipes and plants. Their prominence and symbolic meaning within the ceremonies would vary from one community to another, but essentially their function was two-fold: to give a visible and meaningful focus for the community who were participating in the ceremony, and to help the Shaman reach his ecstatic state, his gateway to the world of spirit.

Among some Shamanic peoples, dance and drama were incorporated into their rituals. The Shaman, bedecked in splendid robes and highly decorated mask, would start by raising his voice in song to the spirits. Fire would frequently be used to create fantastic shadows as the Shaman – actor, singer, dancer, conjurer – wove his magic. The energy levels would be raised by the drumming and the chanting and the fire and the shadows, which provided a great theatrical show for the whole village. But behind the histrionics lay the serious purpose of helping the Shaman on his way to the spirit world, to access its transcendent wisdom and knowledge with which he would continue to inspire the spiritual life of his community.

The process that had begun as a purification of his body was now to culminate in Tony's participation in the defining ritual of the Shamanic community: the ayahuasca ceremony.

Ayahuasca is considered by Shamans to be 'spiritual medicine'. It is the central ingredient of every Shamanic ceremony in the Amazon, the gateway to another world. Ayahuasca is made from the bark of the ayahuasca vine [*banisteriopsis*] which grows in thick coils round the trunks of trees in the rain forest, mixed with the leaves of various wild bushes [usually *psychotria viridis*] that grow there in abundance. When correctly prepared in the right combination, and with right intention, the substance is extremely potent.

Special rituals accompany each stage of the preparation of the ayahuasca. Firstly, the Shaman selects the plants that he wants to use. Then he visits them many times while they are growing and talks with their spirits to ensure a successful harvest. Before the plants are harvested, the Shaman makes sure that it is astrologically an auspicious time for picking, and asks the nature spirits for guidance. Special songs are sung to the plants making sure that they are happy to be cut down at this time, and thanking them for their blessings. Every step of the process is carried out in agreement with nature.

Only an initiated Shaman knows [and guards zealously] the secrets of the ayahuasca, although the whole village may be involved in its preparation, under his watchful eye. When the plants are harvested, they are ground together and then boiled for many hours in river water until the essence is extracted. The river, and the water drawn from it, will also have been blessed. While the ayahuasca is being prepared, songs are sung to the spirits of the plants asking them to remain in the plants to protect the drinkers from evil spirits. [Ayahuasca can be used for good or evil purposes; some Shamanic communities were tempted to use it for sorcery and 'black magic'.] The preparation of the ayahuasca is always carried out with great joy, for Shamans believe that only what is prepared with joy nourishes, both the body and the soul.

At dusk, at the appointed place of power, the whole community gathered for the ceremony. But one final act was required of Tony before he could participate fully in the ayahuasca ceremony: proof, perhaps, of his commitment to the Shamanic path. This was a purification ritual: a fire-walk across burning embers, which had been specially prepared earlier in the day. A huge log fire had been left to burn down, and then the embers were raked onto the ground covering a large area of some twenty feet, and giving off a fierce heat.

Some way from the fire, the villagers sat in a circle on the ground, the Shaman in the centre. As always, he was dressed in his special robes, elaborate and colourful, decorated with huge animal likenesses. On this occasion, his headdress was made of an intricate weave of feathers, his face was painted, bright and startling, and his feet were adorned with symbolic footwear made of birds' claws.

Gradually, the villagers began singing, clapping, chanting, rattling, and drumming, slowly and rhythmically. This making of music is to attract the spirits of nature – spirits of the earth, the lakes, the mountains, trees, animals, birds, the sky and the moon. The Shaman also knows the sacred songs of the higher spirits: of angels, fairies, sages, of spirit healers of all kinds. Now he leads the singing to these spirits, asking to be graced with their power and wisdom.

At a signal from the Shaman, some of the villagers took hold of Tony and danced around the edges of the embers with him, working themselves into a frenzy. Tony was paralyzed with the knowledge that this was to be his baptism of fire, literally, and there was no escape: he would have to walk across the burning embers. He continued dancing round with the villagers, willing himself to conquer his terror. The heat emanating from the dying embers was intense. He was consumed with fright. He tried to get behind the fear; after all, the worst that could happen was that he would burn his feet!

He summoned all his spiritual energy for the task and suddenly, at that moment, he found himself walking alone across the embers, without knowing quite how he had got there. He hadn't consciously made a decision, but when he let go of the fear, he just found himself doing it; walking on fire! There was no sensation of heat at all, and his feet did not burn. He crossed the fire, back and forth, three times, feeling nothing, and emerged totally unscathed. The sudden rush of adrenalin had broken the fear barrier; it was easy. Overcoming the fear, he had pushed out the boundaries of what was possible. Connecting to an awakening consciousness, everything becomes possible; a lesson that he would apply constantly in the future.

The singing, chanting, rattling and drumming continued, increasing in speed and volume. Then it was time for the ayahuasca potion to be handed ceremoniously around the circle. Now Tony was invited to drink with everyone else. He was excited, curious, open to whatever would happen. He knew that this 'spiritual medicine' has mind-altering properties. But nothing could have prepared him for what followed.

During all the months that he had spent in the rain forest, he was still keeping up his Buddhist practices, meditating for about four hours a day, connecting ever more deeply to his spiritual self. It was a productive and growthful period for him, emotionally and spiritually; he had endless time for working on himself, with himself, moving more and more deeply within himself. It was a time of serious reflection, of connecting profoundly to his spiritual self, with no distractions. But nothing had readied him for the experience he would have when he drank the ayahuasca.

Suddenly, he found himself in another world, a parallel world – the world of spirit. In a flash, he saw the unique importance of the rain forest; he understood that it was the lungs of the world, the great spiritual centre connecting us all to God or Great Spirit. Creating harmony in their daily lives in the way that they live with the rain forest and the other creatures that share it, was a reflection of the work that the villagers did in this parallel, energetic world. The meaning of this was revelatory.

Tony watched and absorbed, stunned and overwhelmed. It was as though everything that was happening bypassed his mind and entered directly into his soul. Instantaneously, everything started to move at a hugely accelerated pace; it was like being caught up in a movie that had been fast-forwarded a thousand times. The Spirit of Ayahuasca, the essence of the universe, was speaking directly to him. A guide appeared, and revealed extraordinary spectacles that could fill a modern library, but there were no words to describe them. At that moment, words were a limitation, a total irrelevance.

Then in a flash, Tony saw and perceived and knew and understood everything, all that is, simultaneously. Everything was one, everything was connected with everything else; all people, animals, plants, all of nature, all spirit, was all one, with no separation between anything. Every minute particle of life was interconnected with every other particle, and was also the entire universe.

And suddenly he knew, in the depths of his being, that his whole life had been leading towards this. He understood that his guiding spirit had always been watching over him, moving him through his earliest childhood spiritual 'knowing' and questioning, his illnesses and suffering, through his adolescent visions and dreams and questing, to the spiritual lessons of the Zen Buddhist monastery to bring him here, in a miraculous coalescence of time and place. His whole life had, in fact, been preparing him for this. And in that moment of epiphany, he saw that the Spirit of Ayahuasca had accepted him to become a Shaman, that this was his destiny if not his choice, and all he could do was accept it with grace, and trust.

During the next few weeks, attending ceremonies and drinking ayahuasca every night, Tony was to live totally in this altered state of consciousness, an intense and all-embracing state that can best be described as 'dynamic ecstasy'.

On these journeys into changed reality, he met a whole spiritual community that existed in another dimension. Many teachers manifested: great Shamanic Masters, sages, angels. The work was intense; guides would appear, disappear, reappear, but it was unclear whether they had any physical reality or were 'living' only in this other dimension. Some, it later transpired, were living in the physical world, but thousands of miles away.

The whole sensation was one overwhelming entity of being, indivisible, encapsulating all experience, in all worlds, in all time; everything happened simultaneously, and in the same place, although things were happening in many different dimensions. Time and space were one, yet in this other realm were completely meaningless concepts; everything, everywhere, and through all time, existed co-instantaneously. Tony seemed to be learning the accumulated wisdom of many lifetimes, condensed into weeks or hours or moments. Now he completely understood the real meaning of Shamanism. The entire code of Shamanic wisdom had been vouchsafed to him, abstracted into one moment of true Enlightenment. He had reached the heart of Shamanism.

The villagers realized that something extraordinary had happened to him; they were communicating now without words, spiritually, telepathically. When Tony 'came down' from this altered state of consciousness, after several weeks of being 'somewhere else', the villagers intuitively knew that they needed to look after him. And they were diligent in their care. They walked with him to his hammock, they fed him, they stayed with him until they were sure that he was able to function again in the physical world.

During the weeks that followed, most of the villagers were very supportive, but a few became jealous. It was clear that Tony had been 'chosen' to play a special spiritual role and had been blessed in an extraordinary way. In just a few months, he had received and understood what would normally take the local people, steeped as they were in Shamanism and the culture of the rain forest, many years to learn.

Tony was to discover that not all the native people were as highly evolved as the Shaman. With the new eyes he had been given, he began to see the limitations of the village. In spite of the spiritual centre of community life, people were still caught up in their social and cultural needs, and their ceremonies seemed largely conducted to address these needs. But they were not taking spirituality any further than this, exploring its depths for its own sake, going beyond personal and social quests, moving into a place of oneness with the All That Is.

In his altered state of consciousness, the limits of their spiritual work became apparent to Tony. Their concept of battles being fought between the forces of good and evil seemed simplistic to him, even puerile. He now understood that evil does not exist; only a human perception of evil, created by our own negative thoughts, by a lack of spiritual consciousness. In the universe, everything is perfection. All the trappings of the Shamanic rituals now appeared quite unnecessary; indeed, they seemed to be a distraction from the real spiritual work. The singing and the chanting and the drumming that they used to call the spirits, were simply a diversion. For the spirits do not attend upon our calling of them; they are there, always, everywhere – and also within us. We just need to stop making a noise and listen to the silence around us; to hear, to acknowledge, to be open to receive.

Now that he saw with such clarity the limitations of their work, Tony realized that there was nothing further for him to do in this community. But his 'call' to Shamanism had also brought with it an awesome responsibility; it was clear that he needed to take the work of Shamanism further. So it was, as he grounded himself after his other-world experiences, that he acknowledged the first stirrings that it was time to move on.

This village had introduced him to Shamanism, or perhaps it had been the instrument through which the universe had given him an almighty push. He realized that the gateway to his altered state of consciousness and the wisdom that it had shown him was through drinking ayahuasca; he needed to work with this more deeply. It was time to find the *Ayahuasqueros,* Shamans who took the ceremonies of ayahuasca to a more profound spiritual level.

Tony waited for a sign. And one came, as signs do, in a most unexpected way. One afternoon, he was particularly hungry. So he went looking for banana trees, which had proved an excellent source of sustenance in the past. Suddenly, as if out of nowhere, a large cluster of banana trees appeared. Tony went for them, looking straight ahead, and not looking where he put his feet – and stepped straight onto a snake. It was very large, very green to camouflage it in the undergrowth, and very poisonous. There was a loud whack as the snake bit into his calf. Tony jumped back, white with fear. The snake lifted its head till it was on a level with his and stared into his eyes. It was mesmerizing. Tony stared back, transfixed; he could not move his eyes away. He realized that he was going to die of snake poison out there in the forest, all alone. He was petrified.

Then his whole life flashed before him, a kaleidoscope of visions, people, events: his childhood in Cairo, the bazaars, the Nile, the grand dinners, his grandmother's soothing arms, the school in Cornwall and his dog Sheppy, his mother and his brothers eating fish and chips, his friends in Oslo and their political meetings, Roshi and the Zen Buddhist monastery. He told his parents that he loved them and asked their forgiveness for letting them down by dying so ignominiously, so far from home.

It is unclear how long they stood there, the snake and the human, staring into each other's eyes, but it seemed to the human an eternity. Eventually, with withering disdain, the snake slithered away. Still paralyzed with fear, Tony glanced down at his leg and saw, in utter amazement, that the snake had bitten into the straps of the knife he carried strapped to his boot; it had not bitten his leg.

This episode proved to be a great learning experience for Tony. He realized that he wasn't dying at all. But his mind had acted as though he were, and he had felt all the terror of imminent death that his mind had created. This was a gift from the universe, a great opportunity to understand the ways in which we give our minds power over us. It was an invitation to explore more deeply spiritual wisdom and inner 'knowing'. It was indeed time to move on.

A few days later, a small canoe left the village with one white passenger on board, and sailed into the heart of the rain forest.

Chapter Four
Deeper into the Rain Forest
The *Ayahuasqueros* [Ayahuasca Shamans]

Travelling up river from the Shamanic village that had been his first home in the Amazon to the second village, was a very different experience from Tony's first journey from the Trading Post into the Amazon Rain Forest.

This time, there was no fear. He was completely at ease with himself and his surroundings, no longer an outsider. He was familiar with the ways of the river and the river people, and the spirits of the water. As his journey meandered along many rivers, in many canoes, taking him further and further into the depths of the rain forest, Tony was truly living wherever he found himself, savouring each moment, not just passing through, in place or time.

As he let go, more and more, of the certainties that he had brought with him to the Amazon, he made space to welcome the unknown. He didn't know where his journey would take him, what his ultimate destination would be, or when he would reach it. He only knew that he was being guided towards it, both by spirit guides and by the native people who hosted him along the way and sent him on to the next place as though they had some secret map of his journey. Time had ceased to exist in the ways in which it is normally defined. Waiting for a canoe to move from one place to another could be a matter of a day or a week; however long it took, that was fine.

During this leisurely time spent along the rivers, Tony was intensely aware that this was a spiritual journey as well as a physical one; the journey into the depth of the rain forest was also a journey into the depths of himself. It was a blossoming of total trust, openness, of welcoming the unknown without fear.

He stayed at many different villages along the rivers as he waited for his next canoe, or for a 'sign' that it was time to move on. Now that he was in no rush to go anywhere, he really enjoyed his time with these river families. Although he still had only a rudimentary knowledge of the main river dialect, he was able to communicate enough to get by, and gestures, smiles and laughter happily filled the gaps in his language. He became part of whatever was happening in each place, just going with the flow.

Tony was self-sufficient now, not needing to rely on anyone else for his survival. He still had some goods that he'd bought at the Trading Post and was able to exchange these for food with the families with whom he stayed along the rivers. He had also learnt how to collect the fruit from the trees and outwit his four-footed friends in getting to it before they did. He knew that whatever he needed would appear; he felt totally accepted by his hosts and swathed in the love of the universe.

The further up river he travelled, the more welcoming the native people seemed to be; partly, of course, this was because he had changed, both perceiving the reality that greeted him differently, and therefore also inviting different responses. Where before his journey had been fearful, now it was amazing. He realized how much the way we experience our lives is a matter of our perception: how we ourselves in fact create the world that we see. And how this very act of seeing differently – with open hearts as well as open eyes – reflects back to us a different reality. This was a time of opening up and connecting to what was around him, of feeling completely in tune with nature, with the synchronicities of the universe and with the lives of the indigenous people.

The inhabitants of the villages along the rivers had barely enough to live on, yet they always shared what little they had. They were warm-hearted and generous, and they looked after Tony really well, feeding him, and giving him two hooks... Mostly, his native hosts refused to take any money, though he still had a little left. But he was able to do small favours for them and act as a messenger as he travelled further up river. He was greatly moved by the total trust that people showed him: often they would give him large parcels or important packets to deliver. There was a knowingness and trust about them that everything would happen as it was meant to. He began to love the native people, and felt increasingly that he belonged to the rain forest.

Wherever he landed, the villagers seemed to recognize that, although he had white skin and the greenest of green eyes, he was not an outsider, and he was warmly welcomed. A far cry from the seeming indifference of his first hosts, and his original feelings of loneliness and isolation. Now, everywhere he went, he had the opportunity of watching the local people and learning their ways. And they were happy to share their time and their knowledge. In places where he stayed for many days, he was able to study the local plants and herbs and began to recognize the similarities and the differences between the plants in different areas. The villagers were happy to help, and would demonstrate how to make simple herbal remedies for common ailments. Thirsty for knowledge of the natural ways of these river people, Tony was eager to learn all he could about the Shamans' concept of health and healing, and he questioned his hosts avidly. What he learnt would profoundly change his approach to health, and inform all his later healing work.

The Shamanic perception of health and healing is very different from ours in the West.

Since ancient times, Shamans have known and practised the secrets of natural remedies and healing. In spite of huge cultural variances among different Shamanic communities, and the fact that they may have been separated by seas and oceans for thousands of years, they seem to have discovered independently the same secrets and developed similar remedies. This remarkable correlation among the methods of healing used by Shamans across the world is a mark, perhaps, of their intrinsic value and authenticity; developed in isolation over centuries, they have yet turned out to be so similar to one another.

Health to a Shaman is synonymous with harmony: harmony of body/mind/spirit within the individual, and harmony between the individual and all other life forms: human, animal, plant, and the whole of the natural world. Good health is a manifestation of the way each person walks the sacred path of life, of right relationship between the individual and the whole, and of attuning oneself to the harmony of Great Spirit and the will of the Divine.

To the Shaman, there are relatively few causes of physical illness and they are very specific: illness is the result of emotional or spiritual imbalance, emotional trauma, bereavement, conflict in a marriage or in personal relationships, an alienation of the heart or soul; illness can be karmic [unfinished business, left over from a previous life, that has not been dealt with]; or it is a direct result of interference from the spirits. But whatever the cause, illness is always seen as a gift that provides an opportunity for learning and growth.

The Shaman is the healer *par excellence* within his community, but is not a doctor in the way that we understand the term in the West. He does not cure a passive patient of a physical illness. Rather, he is a 'partner in healing' with the person who is sick, the possessor of sacred knowledge which can help to bring about wellness of body, heart and soul.

The Shaman will help his patients to transcend their normal vision of reality, including their definition of themselves as sick. He will show them that they are not alone in their struggle against illness but that he is with them, emotionally and spiritually, accompanying them along the whole difficult journey, and will not desert them. In all cases, the Shaman's conquest of his own disease and 'death' will act as a guide in teaching that seeming adversity is actually a blessing, given to us to illuminate and transform. By guiding patients on their own journey, rather than 'imposing' a cure, he brings them not only healing, but also a source of wholeness and personal empowerment.

In Shamanic wisdom, physical sickness is seen as only the tip of the iceberg, signs of a disturbance in the natural flow of energy. In order for a person to heal, the spiritual or emotional cause of the disease must be found and addressed. If the symptoms are causing great discomfort or pain, they may be alleviated meanwhile by herbal remedies. But it is the cause of the illness that the Shaman treats; then the symptoms will disappear and the patient will return to a state of balance and harmony.

If illness is the result of interference from the spirits, there are two possibilities: either there is something in a person's body that should not be there, or something is lost or missing that is needed. In the former case, the Shaman will go through a process of extraction to rid the person of the 'foreign body'; in the latter case he will retrieve the lost energy or power, or in some cases, a lost soul.

The Shamanic concept of a soul wandering off from a person's body, or being enticed by spirits, is not so far-fetched if we think of it in symbolic terms. Part of a person's soul may be stuck in some past trauma, which is preventing the person from feeling whole and being able to move on. Rather than analyze the situation, as a psychologist in the West might do, the Shaman disentangles the soul from the past trauma and returns it whole to its owner.

We may think of this 'loss of soul' as the loss of a person's life force. We have probably all, at some time, experienced a sharp fall in our energy levels, a loss of libido, a feeling of being dejected or dispirited. And what is 'dis-spirited' if not a loss of connection with our soul? The Shaman's healing process of returning a person's lost soul – that is, the power of their life force – is perhaps not inferior to lengthy psychoanalysis or a doctor prescribing anti-depressant drugs.

Medicine too, in Shamanic understanding, is very different from our definition in the West. It is what maintains harmony and balance, a manifestation of Spirit within each individual life. It is what we have when we are well, not something we take when we are ill: our own personal power that sustains us at all times. Medicine to the Shaman is the power within: it is the depletion of a person's medicine power that results in ill health. Being in contact with our medicine power is being in alignment with all the forces of creation; it fuels the intention to act in accordance with Great Spirit. This power is everywhere, part of the All That Is, freely available to everyone who walks with sacred intent. This power is a gift of the gods, and we abuse it at our peril.

During the many weeks that Tony spent along the rivers, he learnt that there are special rituals for healing diseases of every kind. Sometimes the Shaman would work one-to-one with the person who was sick. Sometimes, family members would be invited to attend as well; or, if the illness were deemed very serious, the whole community would gather for a healing ceremony. Usually the Shaman would start by creating a psychic field around the sick person, by blowing sacred smoke around him/her so that the negativity of the sickness could be pulled through this field and not return. The Shaman would administer to the sick person, but others would be involved, singing, chanting, drumming, rattling, sometimes dancing. The Shamans often saw this healing process as a battle between the forces of good and evil. So the spirits would be invoked to help the forces of good be victorious.

Tony studied with many different Shamans in the rain forest, and proved to be a diligent student; gradually he was allowed to work with some of them in their healing practices. He learnt the great importance of plants in Shamanic healing work, and their different uses. Often it is the spirit essence of the plant made into a sacred drink that helps the Shaman, not the actual plant.

It is interesting to note that when a sacred drink is imbibed for healing purposes, it is taken by the Shaman, and not by the patient, as we might have expected. It is an aid to the Shaman's work, transporting him to other realms of reality, where the wisdom that he gains will be brought back with him and applied in his healing work.

As well as inducing an altered state of consciousness, the sacred drink will help the Shaman to see into the body of the patient, as though it were completely transparent, and thus he will be able to 'see' the illness and effect healing. Occasionally, both Shaman and patient will drink. Mostly, healing ceremonies are performed at dusk or at night, when cosmic energies are most favourable.

One particular group of Shamans along the river, who had been especially helpful in teaching Tony their healing ways, asked him to describe Western medical practices and training. Tony explained that medical schools only accepted the brightest and most able students and that medical training lasted for many years.

"And how much of this training is spent in attuning with Mother Earth and the healing powers of nature?" the Shamans wanted to know. "And how much time is given to learning about the spiritual and emotional causes of illness?" The Shamans were astonished that our medical training seems to be one of learning about illnesses and 'techniques' of eradicating them, but no time is spent on what they consider to be healing. "Your doctors deal with illnesses, but not with people," was how one of them succinctly summed up our medical profession. "They need to learn about healing."

All this while, as he moved in a leisurely way further up the rivers, Tony was also living in a parallel reality, in an altered and heightened state of consciousness.

He was working especially with the spirits of nature, the spirits of the rain forest, the rivers and the trees, the animals and *Pachamama*. He was learning the unwritten and enduring laws of nature, and was being taught the hidden powers as well as the healing properties of different plants and trees. The nature spirits were affirming and expanding the knowledge he was gaining from the native people. In short, he was being given a crash course on the healing aspects of Shamanism and how to apply them, and was gradually able to build up his own medicinal arsenal. Later on, when he moved more deeply into the rain forest, the Shamans were astonished at his knowledge, but confirmed that everything he had learnt from the spirits was correct.

In this parallel reality, he continued working with great Shamanic Masters: spirits of the dead, or some who were alive but living hundreds or thousands of miles away. He was interacting only with their consciousness, but he was aware of them as intensely physical beings. But, being spirits, they were entirely unpredictable. They would appear or disappear at any moment, quite beyond the laws of physical matter. And the river people accepted that Tony was partly 'somewhere else'; it was not an unknown phenomenon to them, after all.

One of the spirits who appeared at this time was that of an Indian Master, a Hindu, not connected in any way with Shamanism. He appeared every day, for many days, and he was absolutely real, in the flesh; in no way did he seem to Tony to be an apparition or a vision. He started expounding the secrets of the universe, adding more and more detail, spinning an intricate web of separate threads that, when woven together, created one vast and astonishing new picture. He explained the nature of pure consciousness in a way that Tony was able to understand completely; as he elaborated it all seemed so obvious and so simple, yet far beyond anything that Tony had ever encountered before. He clarified the concept of dualism, the way in which we all see the world in two ways: our ego perception of the world, and the world outside us; subjective and objective reality. But to see the world split in this way is to create a false reality. If we are living in our pure heart, connected to our Higher Self, there is no place for the personal desires of the ego and the 'reality' that this creates; and so there is no division of the world into two, no separation; everything is one, whole, complete and perfect.

Those many visits of the Indian Master were mysterious, magical and momentous. He seemed to be imparting all the wisdom of the universe, down the ages and across continents; as he explained it, all knowledge is one. Tony's mind would have long been beyond boggling, had he been trying to grasp this information with his mind. But he was absorbing it with his spirit, which was also the whole of him.

The spiritual reality of those weeks along the river intensified. Many different spirits appeared to Tony, and all had great knowledge to impart. Some were those of Shamanic ancestors, others were of native Elders or sages. And still others were angelic beings, particularly connected to sources of light; they had a luminous glow about them, quite different from other spirit guides. After a while, there seemed to be fewer Shamanic teachers, but guides from many other traditions, long dead, or living a long way away.

Particularly during this time, many South and North American native Indian guides manifested. Their teachings were similar to those of Shamanism: a deep respect for and love of nature. They demonstrated to Tony how to listen to the breath of the earth, how to communicate with stones and rocks that hold memories from all time, how to know when it will rain by watching the way birds are flying. They explained that we can learn from all creatures, including the smallest and most insignificant; ants, for example, can teach us much, but generally we are too arrogant to notice. But if we were just to watch, we might observe thousands of ants all gathering in a certain place; Shamans know that this is a sign that energy is trapped there. In the rain forest, this information could be vital.

It is a spiritual truth that all creatures are of equal worth and all have a role in the interconnected web of life; only we humans think that we are superior. These guides stressed again and again: listen to nature, it teaches us everything we need to know.

An important spirit guide who also appeared frequently at this time was an Egyptian Pharaoh. His particular teachings were mathematics and the laws of physics. He explained in great detail how the ancient Egyptians had built the Pyramids. They had designed them according to specific astrological calculations, taking into account the relative positions of the sun, moon, stars and planets, and had then worked out mathematical formulae for their construction. [Incidentally, all the information that this Pharaoh imparted proved to be correct when it was checked out later.]

This knowledge opened up a whole new world for Tony. But more important than all the erudition that was imparted to him, fascinating though this was, was the profound spiritual connection he made with the Pharaoh. This reawakened Tony's mystical connections to Egypt, and would have far-reaching implications for his future.

Simultaneously with profound new perceptions and the vast amount of knowledge that was being given to Tony at this time, he was also being shown many different aspects of himself that he hadn't previously known, or perhaps hadn't wanted to acknowledge; now he was being forced to confront this 'mirror'. And with his growing wisdom came the realization that the more he learnt, the less he knew. At the same time, he was interacting with the native people around him in the physical world. He now felt very grounded and could move with ease between the two worlds. He was able to 'come down' from these trips by himself and function normally, although his visits to the spirit world were by invitation only: unpredictable and beyond his control.

Tony's journey up river to the heart of the rain forest, and his parallel journey in the world of spirit, were clearly interlinked; his physical movement was an accurate mirror of his spiritual evolvement.

The journey along this web of rivers, flowing and ebbing into each other, took him along many circuitous routes, so that he was never moving forward in a straight line; a perfect metaphor for his spiritual journey which, too, was circular. The meaning of this became very clear to him: our linear perception of progress is quite nonsensical; circular movement *is* the way we move forward.

Now, wherever he found himself, Tony spent much of his time in the spirit world [and of course he was still meditating several hours a day, a practice that has never left him]. If beforehand he had been gently sauntering along his spiritual path, now he was galloping ahead at full speed. In all the villages along the rivers there were ayahuasca ceremonies which he was invited to join, and he spent many intense nights in other worlds. Some were alarming, as he had to grapple with completely new ways of seeing, and his visions were crowded with many extraordinary things happening simultaneously. But mostly he felt calm and peaceful, as he was embraced by new wisdom.

Gradually, as he grew more accustomed to the ways and the inhabitants of other realms, his spiritual experiences became both more profound and less frightening. He now felt confidant that his spiritual journey was his own, which was enormously empowering, but also very humbling. He was no longer a visitor to other worlds, for they were his worlds too; but at the same time he was aware of being a minute speck in the vastness of the cosmos. He felt profoundly grateful to all the spirits who came to offer help: gurus, masters, sages from many traditions. He absorbed everything they had to offer with great zeal and enthusiasm, but didn't follow any particular school. It was now abundantly clear to him that at the centre of the universe are immutable truths, waiting to be known; it didn't matter who the guide was who led the way or opened the doors.

The greatest teacher for Tony in the physical world, and the one who most influenced his path, was Roshi, the Zen Buddhist Master. But in the spirit world, all the people who appeared to him became his teachers. And the first lesson that they taught was the one that Roshi had first tried to implant: let go of all attachments. This didn't only mean letting go of material possessions, which in the rain forest is hardly difficult! It meant letting go of attitudes of mind, of preconceived ideas, of beliefs, of 'agendas'; of an investment in outcome and, most importantly, of attachment to ego.

It also meant letting go of competitiveness. Since he was a very small child, Tony had always needed to be the best in whatever he did: the top of the class, the greatest athlete, the most dedicated political activist. Now he needed to let go of this self-image of having to be the best; he needed to move into another space where he could accept that whatever happened, happened, without judgement. And that whatever he did, if it came from a place of right intention and love, was the perfect way of doing it. And the process was never-ending. As he learnt one lesson, other guides would miraculously appear, with yet more lessons, to bring him to a deeper understanding.

As his spiritual journey took him more deeply into himself, further along the path towards the heart of Shamanic wisdom, so his physical journey was filled with happy synchronicities. Wherever he landed along the river, he felt that he had come to the right place, that these were exactly the people he needed to be with at this time. Perhaps they could add to his knowledge of herbal medicine, or maybe he could help someone who was sick. By now, the natives accepted that he had some Shamanic powers, and were happy to let him make use of them. And they were completely supportive of his spiritual journeying, whether they understood much, or little, of its content.

The weeks along the rivers turned into many months, and there was no indication of how long this journey would last. The native people were not constrained by any concept of time; they lived in the moment, according to the rhythms of nature and their intuition about their spiritual journeys. They were truly free beings. Tony was learning from them to relinquish his Western concept of time.

And the rivers themselves seemed to be a rich intertwining grapevine of information; the very water seemed to be whispering with knowledge. In each village, new suggestions were offered and Tony would be guided forward. Someone would know of a particular Shaman in a certain village that they thought he should meet; or another would mention a place where the ayahuasca ceremonies were particularly powerful. And so, with the spirits and the river people colluding for his benefit, he was moved from one place to another, up and down the rivers in a seemingly roundabout way, but always forward on his journey, deeper into the heart of the rain forest – and into his own heart.

The image that greeted Tony on his arrival at the place that was to be his new home in the village of the *Ayahuasqueros* was a glorious sight. A startlingly beautiful native girl, with huge dark eyes and the most amazing mass of wild dark hair, was standing before him and smiling at him.

After many days on the canoe on the last lap of his journey, seeing nothing but water and jungle foliage, and the handful of men with whom he was travelling, he wondered whether she might be a mirage. But she was real, wonderfully, marvellously real, with an ethereal beauty that was much more than physical. Suddenly, as he gazed at her, quite enchanted, her hair began to move. And then he realized that it was not hair at all, but a small monkey sleeping on her head!

The villagers here were all native Indians, not of mixed blood as those in the first village had been. Immediately, Tony felt comfortable among these people. There was a deeper consciousness of life here, possibly because they had been less 'contaminated' by outsiders, a more profound connection to the natural world. And the easy contact of the villagers with animals was particularly appealing to him; many animals were kept as pets, especially small birds and cute little monkeys that slept on people's heads!

Although there was a group ethos of spirituality here, as there had been in the first village, there were major differences between them. In the first village, all spiritual journeying was limited to what was shared by the whole community; there was no such thing as an individual spiritual quest. Here, there were no set limitations; each person could journey alone as far as he or she felt able. A sense of rightness, about the place and the inhabitants, prevailed.

Just as he had heard so much about these *Ayahuasqueros* before meeting them, so it was that Tony's growing reputation had preceded him. His new hosts were very curious about him, eager to know what he knew and what he could do, and excited by the revelations and understanding that he shared with them. The months that he had spent on the rivers on his way there, the extraordinary experiences that had accompanied his journey, both physical and spiritual, had all been preparing him for this new, deeper encounter with Shamanism.

The *Ayahuasqueros* lived apart from the surrounding communities, more deeply embedded in the interior of the forest. Many of them were single and lived alone, devoting all their time to their spiritual journeying. Some were married and lived in small family units. But although they lived way off the beaten track, even by the standards of the rain forest, they were known about in all the surrounding communities, and indeed much further afield. People who needed them would always find them.

A large part of their work involved helping and healing. People came seeking all kinds of help: to be healed from physical illnesses, to solve marital problems, infertility, or maybe to restore their medicine power when they felt that someone was trying to steal it from them. They came from the surrounding villages, either individually, or in families or small groups. They came from across the Amazon and from as far away as Lima. And people from cities throughout South America, often when they had exhausted all other possibilities of healing, would come to the *Ayahuasqueros* seeking to cure their cancers, AIDS or other serious diseases.

The *Ayahuasqueros* spent a lot of their time growing and preparing ayahuasca, as well as the many herbal remedies that they used in their healing work. They worked communally to provide for their daily needs, single and married people being equally cared for. They would eat together from the abundance of vegetation in the rain forest, supplemented sometimes by fishing. Much of their food would also be supplied by the people who came to them for help. Money was rarely exchanged.

As well as their healing work, one of the main roles of the *Ayahuasqueros* is to perform the Shamanic ceremonies and rituals for all the nearby villages, and of course for their own small community. A few days after Tony's arrival in the village, there was great excitement as a 'grounding ceremony' for the baby of a neighbouring community was to be held that night.

Shamans believe that for the first half year of a baby's life, its soul is still hovering between worlds; it has left the world of pure spirit, but has not yet fully entered the world of physical reality. During this time, the soul may still be unsure if it is committed to a physical reincarnation and so everything is done to ease its passage into the human realm.

So, for the first six months of its life the baby does not touch the ground. It is carried everywhere by one of its parents or another member of the community. At night, it sleeps in a hammock with its mother; during the day, it may rest in a small hammock tied between trees wherever its mother is working. [Mothers normally return to work a few days after giving birth; although to say 'return to work' is misleading; work is an integral and inseparable part of life in a Shamanic community and not something separate that one 'goes to'.] Shamans believe that in this way, keeping the baby between heaven and earth, its passage between realms is helped and the shock of entering the physical world is lessened. When the baby is six months old, a grounding ceremony is held.

On this occasion, the whole of the neighbouring village accompanied the parents and the baby. All the members of both communities gathered at dusk on the ceremonial ground. Tony was excited to have been invited. Everyone sat in a circle, chanting and clapping, as the baby, carried aloft by its parents, was slowly paraded round the circle. Then the villagers gave the baby small gifts: protective amulets, crystals, stones or rocks that had particular significance, beads, feathers of birds considered to have special power, and would each offer a blessing for the baby's earthly journey. Later, many of the gifts would be hung around the baby's hammock to protect it from evil spirits.

Then the baby was handed to the Shaman, who disrobed it and placed it naked on the earth in the middle of the circle, presenting it to *Pachamama*. Special songs were sung, invoking the spirits of the earth to receive the baby, to complete the passage of its soul into this incarnation and to protect it during its physical life. Blessings for its sojourn here, to be grounded and enriched with the abundant gifts of Mother Earth, were intoned.

The Shaman then brought the baby to greet the elements of nature: the stars, the moon, the trees and plants of the forest, the wind and clouds; and as he greeted each element, he would invoke their spirits to watch over this new earthling. He would offer the baby to Father Sky and Mother Earth, and thank them for this gift of new life to the community.

Next, the Shaman presented the baby to the Four Directions, and asked the Spirits of each Direction to give its special blessings to the baby. Shamans believe that each Direction has special gifts and energies that we can tune into and receive: East [representing dawn, spring] for the blessings of Earth, the body; South, [noon, summer] for Air, the mind; West [evening, autumn] for Fire, the spirit; and North [night, winter] for the blessings of Water, the emotions.

All the while, the Shaman sang and chanted power songs, asking all the spirits of nature to bless and protect the baby from malevolent forces. He invoked their help as the baby's true parents, to watch over the child and bless it with good health and a long life, to guide it on its human journey, walking the Shamanic path. Finally, the Shaman placed a tiny drop of ayahuasca on the baby's tongue, symbolising its acceptance into its earthly community, while simultaneously ensuring its everlasting bond with the world of spirit.

At the end of the ceremony, the baby was taken by the Shaman to its 'placenta tree'. It was explained to Tony that this was a special tree chosen for each baby where, after its birth, its mother's placenta would be buried. The Shaman would choose a special place of power, under an ancient tree that would have within it the memory of great wisdom, and bury the placenta there. It was believed that the child would then have a special affinity to this place, visiting it often throughout its life, imbibing its knowledge, its wisdom and its special power. At the end of the grounding ceremony, the Shaman takes the baby back to its 'placenta tree', reconnecting it to its birth into this world, and asking for protection from the tree throughout its life.

During these first months in his new home, Tony's work with the *Ayahuasqueros* was growing in intensity. He was now accepted as a Shamanic healer and was trusted to carry out some healing work among the surrounding communities.

But mainly, he was involved in his own process of learning. He was working simultaneously on two levels: firstly, with the *Ayahuasqueros* on the physical level, studying their herbs and plants, nature, the healing powers of the rain forest itself.

And secondly, he was working in the non-physical realm, with guides and masters who were moving him at great speed along the road towards Enlightenment.

At the centre of his spiritual work now were the ayahuasca ceremonies. Although these play an important role in all Shamanic practices along the Amazon rivers, the *Ayahuasqueros* use the 'sacred drink' as a portal into much more profound spiritual experience. Their ceremonies take place almost nightly, as they were often held for just small groups of people coming from neighbouring villages, not necessarily for whole communities. Tony took advantage of their frequency and attended all the ceremonies.

As in most Shamanic traditions, *icaros* were central to the *Ayahuasqueros'* rituals. *Icaros* are sacred songs, songs of power, that were thought to be another portal into the world of spirits. Shamans believe that sound was the first thing to be created, and the whole history of the cosmos is imprinted in sound. The universe is full of sounds, not only the myriad calls of animals and birds, the rushing ebb and flow of seas and oceans, the soughing of the wind, but also the sounds of plants, trees, rocks, sky, the earth itself.

Sound is the prayer of the universe made manifest. These sounds are beyond the range of our normal hearing; we need to be spiritually attuned to the silence of the universe, which is impregnated with the essence of all sound, to be able to hear them; for only in silence do these sounds resonate. And there is no real silence: the 'silence' of the universe is filled with living energy, which manifests as sound. Each human soul, too, has its own unique sound, audible only to the spiritual traveller.

Of all the many sounds used in Shamanic ritual – drumming, rattling, clapping, etc. – the voice of the Shaman himself is the most pivotal. It is the instrument of sacred manifestation, carrying within it the ancient symbols of Shamanism, the mythical past, the ancestral stories, the enduring primordial practices. It holds within it other voices: the spirits of the dead, the songs of the gods, the music of the elements, the echoes of the Underworld. It weaves together the world of physical reality and the invisible worlds of the cosmos. The Shaman's voice can give spiritual context to the pain of human existence and the reality of death. The paradise of the mythological era in which the magic of Shamanism is rooted, reinforces meaning in present-day practice.

Every Shaman has his own sounds, and is literally 'en-chanted': chanted into a magical and mysterious place on the breath of sacred sound. Often, the sounds of his chants will resemble different birdcalls or the cries of animals; sometimes, they will sound like the archetypal cry of the universe, unlike anything identifiable to the ordinary human ear.

Each Shaman has his own unique *icaros,* one of his strongest connections to his own medicine power. Shamans believe that *icaros* are gifts that come directly from the spirits and are called forth by him through his deep connection with them. He does not create an *icaro,* rather it is an incarnation in sound of a spiritual experience that he undergoes. In North American Shamanic communities, the word for 'spirit' and the word for 'song' is the same. Spirit awakens song, song is the embodiment of spirit manifest in sound.

In Shamanic tradition, an *icaro* has three main purposes. It is sung at ceremonies and rituals as a 'wake-up' call to the spirits, invoking the spirits of ancestors, spirit guides and teachers, and totems from the animal or plant worlds. It can be used to help the Shaman 'travel' to the spirit realms, and often the power song is not only the vehicle for the Shaman's journey, it is also the medium of his transformation. And thirdly, the *icaro* plays a powerful role in Shamanic healing.

Icaros do not necessarily have words, although they may have. In essence, an *icaro* is the chant of the Shaman: the music of the universe, sung by the spirits, incarnated on his breath. The power of the *icaro* is present in the intention behind the sound. Very often, it is a chant of just a few notes, endlessly repeated in slightly differing patterns, frequently sounding quite monotonous to the Western ear. If the Shaman is singing with words, the melody will come first and will dictate the words, which then seem to rise up of their own accord.

Often, the words of an *icaro* will create a narrative of the Shaman's psychic experiences, providing language to describe an epic journey of the soul. The words may describe the topography of the spirit world, and the Shaman's travels around this 'map'. They may be particular words of the spirits that the Shaman's community needs to hear at that time.

As well as the individual songs of the Shaman, there are many *icaros* that are part of the heritage of the tribe. They tell the stories of the lives of the ancestors, their heroic deeds, their wisdom and knowledge; epic *icaros,* recounted and celebrated in every generation. Tony was told about a Shaman who long ago in a time of drought had sung an *icaro* for rain. And then the rain came. So this *icaro* became part of the culture of this tribe; each generation sings it and talks about the time when Black Wolf first sang "The *Icaro* of the Rain".

The words of an *icaro* may weave a poem, a story, new or already known for centuries, that has meaning to a particular community. Sometimes a Shaman would add his own words to a traditional *icaro* melody. And in all tribes, there are *icaros* that a grandmother sings to her grandchild, the way that her grandmother sang to her, and her grandmother before her.

During ceremonies, when the Shaman is singing an *icaro,* he might encourage the whole community to join in a kind of 'chorus' that everyone would know, repeating some of the sacred chants with him. This has the effect of altering the consciousness not only of the Shaman, but of the listeners as well; opening up the energetic body, the emotional centre, the intuition, of everyone present. When this happens, it feels as though the song is inside you as well as all around you, as though your whole body is tingling with it, as though the sound were massaging your skin.

A Shaman will have many *icaros;* different power songs are connected to different ceremonies, and to healing different illnesses. Coming to him from spirit, they become a sacred tool of his work. Each song also collects a spiritual 'history', holding within its memory each occasion on which it has previously been sung. Its spirit contains the suffering and crises of each Shaman who has sung it, but also their transcendence and redemption. And so each time it is repeated it brings with it the power and the illumination of all its former singings, remembrance of earlier transformations. Each healing journey, guided by the Shaman and undergone by the patient, is not then just a reflection of the current situation, but is also part of a larger story, woven through the fabric of Shamanic tradition. Thus, when a particular *icaro* is called up to be used in healing, the patient will benefit from the collective Shamanic consciousness of its singing.

There are *icaros* for every kind of sickness, serious and more trivial. However, the connection between the *icaro* and the sickness may not be apparent to anyone but a Shaman. For example, if a person is complaining of terrible stomach pains, the Shaman may chant 'The *Icaro* of the Snake'. This *icaro* is traditionally used to release the life force present in the base energy centre, and the snake has a very powerful stomach. So, if a person's life force is blocked in the stomach, creating stress and anxiety and manifesting as pain in the physical body, singing 'The *Icaro* of the Snake' will release the blockage and transform the energy and so the pain will disappear.

Often the power of a sacred song to heal may affect the Shaman as well as the patient. When witnessing a healing ceremony of a very sick person carried out by an *Ayahuasquero*, Tony saw that by singing the *icaro,* the Shaman's own feelings of exhaustion and malaise completely disappeared. It seems to be a remarkable feature of the *icaro* that it can heal the singer as well as the 'sung to'. But in fact when the Shaman sings an *icaro*, he is tapping into the sacred sounds of the universe, breathed through him by the spirits, and carrying their higher wisdom.

During his stay with the *Ayahuasqueros,* Tony was privileged to witness several special ceremonies marking different stages of the life cycle.

The further into the depths of the rain forest the Shamans lived, the more celebratory the rites of passage seemed to be. Ceremonies were held to mark every stage of the human journey: birth, puberty, marriage, death. Rituals were colourful and noisy, full of singing and dancing, rattling and drumming, fire and smoke, with the use of many artifacts. The presence of the spirits was the dominating force, and Tony was clearly able to feel them.

Puberty was not generally celebrated with ceremonies for the whole community. It was a natural rite of passage, from childhood to adulthood, which would be marked within the peer group and gender. When boys reached puberty, they would be expected to prove themselves as men. They would be given certain 'manly' tasks to perform, such as walking through the forest by themselves at night, going fishing and being expected to make a good catch, or identifying and collecting plants with particular powers, maybe growing in a more dangerous part of the forest. Once they had proved themselves, the boys' acceptance into the society of men would be celebrated by a 'men only' party. Tony felt privileged to be invited to one such celebration. After the celebration, the boy was expected to work with the men.

When girls began to menstruate, the women would hold a ceremony, usually down by the river, which they believed had strong feminine energy. It would be held at the first new moon after the onset of menses, to emphasize the deep connection between woman and the lunar cycles. The new moon represented rebirth, the beginning of new life for the young girl initiated into womanhood. The ceremony would include much dancing and singing, but not the drumming and rattling and noise prevalent at male rituals.

And then the telling of stories would begin, women's stories, full of old women's wisdom and the power of the ancestors, tapping deeply into women's spiritual energy and power, into the profound mystery of birth and fertility. Some of the women Elders might tell stories of their own youth, revelling in their past adventures and frequently recounting their early sexual encounters. Often, they would give the young woman advice on handling men; now that her menses had begun, she was free to express her sexuality. Talking would generally last late into the night. From then on, the girls would join the women, for work – and for singing and gossiping by the river.

Another women's tradition is the moon-lodge. Every woman at the onset of her menstruation each month would go to the moon-lodge, a small hut set a little apart from the community, where she would stay throughout the days of her menses. During this time she was not expected to work and was treated as special by the other women, who would look after her and bring her food. This 'woman's bleeding' was considered to be a sacred process, a time of special woman power. Some anthropologists have interpreted the moon-lodge as a way of isolating the woman, away from society, as though she were sick or unclean. But this is to misinterpret the intention. In the Shamanic tradition, the menstruating woman is a goddess, deeply connected to moon energies and magical, mystical powers.

Marriage ceremonies were generally held at night, often at full moon when the sky was at its brightest and most powerful. The villagers, carrying torches of fire, would form a circle round the couple who were marrying, dancing round them as they chanted special incantations; the fire, symbolic of cleansing and purification, protected them from evil spirits. The fire dancing was accompanied by drums and rattles, singing and chanting, and the ceremony ended, of course, with the drinking of ayahuasca. Finally, the newly-weds would be accompanied in procession by the whole village to their new hut, where the spirits would be invoked to bring them blessings, fertility and joy.

Of all the rituals marking rites of passage within the Shamanic tradition, death is the most awesome. The ceremony generally lasts for three days, as Shamans believe that it takes that time for the soul completely to leave the body. So it is vital that the Shaman works with the soul all through this time, to guide it safely on its journey to its next home. Usually, only the family of the deceased will attend the ceremony to mark the death. The Shaman will start by drinking ayahuasca, to be closely in touch with the dead person's soul. He will burn special herbs and resins from the trees, and chant *icaros* to protect the soul on its journey, during which it may face many trials. At the same time, the Shaman acts as a link between the deceased's soul and his or her family, explaining to the relatives what the soul is going through at each stage of its journey. He would also pass on to the soul any messages from the relatives. These could be profound spiritual thoughts and blessings to help the soul on its way, or quite prosaic things that the family had forgotten to say during the soul's earthly incarnation.

Early one morning an important Elder died, an *Ayahuasquero* with whom Tony had worked closely. In fact, Tony had been with him the previous day. The Elder, a sprightly eighty-nine year old had told Tony that his 'time to move on' had come. And then he smiled to Tony a smile full of love, acceptance and peace.

A ceremony was planned for that night, the beginning of the three-day ritual. Tony spent the day, along with everyone else, preparing for the ceremony, collecting the special herbs and resins, and making small gifts to protect the Elder's soul from evil spirits on its journey. There was, of course, great sadness at the ceremony, but also great joy; Shamans have no concept of mourning the dead as we do in the West. The Shamanic ritual is both a celebration of the Elder's life, honouring his actions and great wisdom, and also a liberation of the soul from its earthly bonds as it starts its journey to the spirit world.

Tony was now attending ayahuasca rituals almost nightly, and the *Ayahuasqueros* were now ready to teach him about the more profound levels of their work.

The first task of ayahuasca, the 'sacred medicine', is to clean out the physical body. In the rain forest this needs to be done very frequently as, in the intense heat and humidity, parasites flourish in the human body all year round. And for Tony it was a real physical purge; during every ceremony, he vomited and had diarrhoea until there was nothing left inside him to eliminate. But only when the physical body has been thoroughly cleansed, can the real work of the ayahuasca begin.

The journey of ayahuasca is a portal into the realms of spirit, where the Shaman connects to his spirit guides and brings back their wisdom to use in his work in the physical world. But the core spiritual work of the Amazonian Shamans is their work on the astral level. The astral level is the dimension closest to our physical reality, through which every soul must pass when it leaves its earthly body, before journeying up through the many realms of the spirit world. It is a halfway house, a kind of 'clearing house' for souls.

The aim of the Shamans in cleaning the astral level is two-fold, though both tasks are interconnected and simultaneous. Their first job is to take the astral beings to a higher spiritual level, to help to move them along on their journey. They need to travel through the 'dark void' [the black hole] to the realms of the higher spiritual beings: the angels, fairies, nature spirits, and Shaman Masters.

The Shamans, through the ayahuasca ceremonies, accompany these souls on their spiritual journey and help to precipitate their ascendance.

The second task of the Shamans is perhaps more difficult. This is the work of cleansing the astral level, the depository of human negative energies, and so influencing life on earth. They believe that all human negativity is recreated on the astral level, which is a mirror of what is happening in the physical world. So the astral level is polluted with all the violence, wars, pain, suffering, oppression, destruction, disease, disharmony, that is being created on earth.

It is also polluted by human emotions – hatred, anger, envy, greed – and by negative thoughts: the residue of all destructive unfinished business on earth is mirrored on the astral level. Every angry thought or action of a human being creates a parallel angry being in the astral level, which in turn creates more anger among human beings: a vicious circle of harmful forces feeding, and feeding off, each other. The Shamans believe that these 'mirror beings' are alive and thriving, with a vested interest in remaining so; they flourish on the anger that created them, and so strive to create more anger, which in turn sustains them. In order to free the human world of all its sicknesses, they must first be cleansed from the astral level.

The mutual process that increases the forces of evil between the human world and the astral level has even more far-reaching effects. The residue of wars and oppression, violence and destruction, can be held on the astral plane for many years after the actual events have played themselves out. This residue of evil sits like a black cloud over the areas of the world in which the original events took place, and it continues to influence all human behaviour there. So it is that people living in these areas of the world will be more likely to behave intolerantly, act violently or commit crimes.

And they may do these things without knowing why; the astral spirits attach themselves to the unconscious level of human action, and so people may perform terrible acts without knowing what has driven them to do so. You have only to look at the unbearable tensions and aggressive behaviour that often exist in places where wars have recently been fought. This is why it is difficult to believe that political solutions can be found for any of the world's serious problems. It is impossible to eradicate evil using the same energy that has created it, no matter how noble the intentions of the people who try.

The spiritual work of the Shaman on the astral plane is undertaken on behalf of the whole of humanity and for the benefit of all.

Aided by this deeper knowledge of the work of the Shamans, Tony was able to pursue his own spiritual journey with greater effectiveness and more profound understanding.

Now, during ayahuasca ceremonies, he was intensely aware that his spirit would leave his body and would journey to other realms. He was conscious of watching his body as though from far off. In this 'out of body' state he could go wherever he wished: climbing trees, or a mountain; moving around the rain forest at will; visiting another country, or another period of time. He could hear the sound of a bird, and then be inside that sound, and then become the bird; he could merge with the spirit of a wild animal, and then become the animal itself. In the world of spirit, there are no limitations.

These 'spiritual acrobatics' were fascinating: visiting other worlds and being able to look down on his physical body and its environment from another place, another perspective. But there was a more serious purpose to it all. Tony was being called by Shamanic Masters to fulfil some predestined and profound spiritual design, beyond his choosing, beyond the limits of his imagination. All the guides who now visited him during his nightly ayahuasca encounters, were leading him inexorably towards an initiation into another realm of being; a spiritual dimension that was all encompassing, and would change forever the way he was in the physical world as well.

One night, during an ayahuasca ceremony, Tony suddenly felt driven to go alone deep into the forest. It was a stormy night and rain was lashing down through the canopy of trees. The Shamans would not allow him to go, saying that it was much too dangerous and he would never be able to find his way back. Disappointed, Tony lay in a tree close by and closed his eyes. As the storm raged, he was suddenly filled with foreboding, a sense that something terrifying and different from all his other experiences with ayahuasca was about to happen. In fact, the experience of that night was the most extraordinary and transformative of his life.

His soul began travelling through many different dimensions; it seemed to be visiting every aspect of Tony, through many lives. It was like watching a dream, yet his mind was fully engaged and he had never felt so alert. He was bombarded by thoughts, but they came so fast that he didn't have time to grasp them. Yet he was aware of thinking all the thoughts, with great clarity, simultaneously. Then suddenly he heard a strange sound, a piercing, wailing sound like no other; it was the sound of his soul. But he heard it not with his ears but with his whole body. And this was peculiar, because he couldn't feel his body at all.

Then he saw that his body was being dismembered and the flesh scraped from the bones. There was a loud bang, and then parts of his body started to fly off by themselves. He watched, stupefied: arms and legs and head and hands flying off into the ether, as though they each had a life and will of their own. In that moment, he knew that he was dying. Everything disintegrated around him. Then he saw flames surrounding his body, for although all his limbs had broken off and flown away, his body was somehow still intact. The flames grew higher, the heat fiercer, completely engulfing him; he was burning, suffocating, and there was no escape.

The light was now intense, brilliant, as though it were midday. Tony was enveloped by terror; this was nothing, nothing like any previous experience with ayahuasca. He saw his soul disintegrating, and was consumed with fright. He called out to the spirits for help, but his cries went unanswered. The spirits remained silent.

He saw the wind, and it was coming out of the mouth of a snake. It appeared to be a spiral of fierce lights whirling towards him, whole galaxies dancing and twirling towards him, all coming out of the snake's mouth. The wind became more and more ferocious, blown out of the snake's mouth with tremendous menacing force, hurtling towards him at great speed. He had an overwhelming sensation of wanting to scream, to wake up from the nightmare, but it wasn't a dream. Then suddenly he was swallowed up by the snake, and everything disappeared.

Tony was paralysed with fear. He couldn't move. He was dying, he knew, but he was still alive, and in agony. But as he forced himself to stay with it, inside it, the fear gradually began to dissipate, and he was enveloped by an intense feeling of calm.

He realized then that this had been his initiation, that he had come through it, and that his life had changed irrevocably and forever. He understood that his soul had died, and he had just witnessed the birth of a new soul. He realized that in coming to he rain forest and living and working with Shamans, he had been fulfilling his destiny; that for whatever reason he had been 'chosen' as part of some divine purpose, to become a Shaman, and that following and propagating Shamanic teachings would be his life's work.

All Shamanic initiation involves some form of death and rebirth, symbolizing the death of the body and the rebirth of the spirit. Death and resurrection, and with the rebirth of the soul, the acknowledgement of spiritual powers, of illumination; a transformation from human limitation to endless possibility in other realms of existence.

But although it is symbolic, it is also 'real' to the initiate experiencing it; he both experiences what is happening and, simultaneously, is aware of watching it happen. But the terror and the physical agony as the flesh and bones are chopped up and burnt, are real and have to be endured. Often the Shaman 'dies' in horrible agony. Enduring and coming through this terrifying ordeal, the Shaman earns his ticket into the spirit world and gains his magical powers. After his own initiation, Tony was told stories about Shamanic initiations that would make the latest horror films seem like nursery games.

Tony's initiation was similar to all classic Shamanic initiations of death and rebirth. But his period of 'apprenticeship' had been telescoped into several months rather than the usual many years. Although everything in his life, he now realized, had been leading up to this momentous experience. He understood that his recurring childhood illnesses, his severe suffering caused by his feelings of separateness and isolation, and also his mystical connection to other worlds were all, indeed, a part of his Shamanic 'apprenticeship'.

The initiation of a Shaman is the culmination of all this work, rather than its inception, and marks the readiness of the neophyte to take on the full responsibilities of a Shaman. It also marks his acceptance as a Shaman by the spirits. Before the initiation ceremony, there will be some form of purification: by fasting, by water, or through a fire ritual. This also happened in Tony's case, although his purification by fire had taken place many months before his initiation, in a different location, and with a very different group of Shamans. But now he realized that his fire walk, too, had been part of his Shamanic training, leading to his initiation.

Coming back into the world after his initiation, the Shaman is a changed being. The initiation marks a severing from everything that comprised his past life, but not from the way of life of his community, to which he is attached by deep roots and to which he will return and minister. Reducing him to just his bones represents the essential material of life that is not perishable. For from his bones, he would be resurrected and reborn.

This transfiguration marks the rebirth of the Shaman, and his acquisition of sacred knowledge. His ability to overcome the agonies of the flesh that he suffered during his initiation confers on him prodigious healing powers. He has met death and has returned; the successful outcome of this journey grants him great understanding and great power, acknowledged by the spirit world and the human community alike.

After his initiation, Tony spent many days doing very little, allowing the experience of that fateful night to sink into his bones, into his soul.

There was now no need to continue with the ayahuasca ceremonies. He felt that he had learnt everything that the *Ayahuasqueros* had to teach him: how to grow, pick and prepare the ayahuasca, and the secrets of its Spirit. He knew and understood the ceremonies, how to invoke the spirits and how to accompany an ayahuasca journey. The road that he had walked with the *Ayahuasqueros* was reaching its end.

He had lived with and become part of the local culture, but he wasn't bound by the fears and superstitions of the indigenous people. In fact, he was beginning to find them tiresome; they really had nothing to do with spirituality. He was struck more and more by the huge gulf that existed between the great spiritual wisdom of the *Ayahuasqueros* and their very primitive culture.

He needed to explore further his own spiritual path, which he now realized could not be fulfilled where he was. And it was clear, too, that the spirits were guiding him to undertake the next stage of his journey.

He was enormously grateful to the *Ayahuasqueros* for the experiences they had shared. But he knew that now he was ready to work alone. It was time to move on.

Chapter Five
The Andes Mountains: Bolivia and Southern Peru
The Quechua Shamans

The view from the plane as it began its descent into La Paz airport, Bolivia, was magnificent: from this height, it offered a spectacular and panoramic vista of the whole city and surrounding area. To Tony, as he peered through the aircraft window, his first sight of the city was unforgetable.

La Paz is Bolivia's largest city, home to over a million people and the centre of finance, commerce and industry. It was founded in 1548 by the Spanish on the site of an old Inca village, following the discovery of gold in the Rio Choqueyapu, and was originally called Nuestra Señora de La Paz ["Our Lady of Peace"]. But the gold rush didn't last long and the town fell into neglect. In 1835, to commemorate the decisive battle in the colony's wars of independence, it was renamed La Paz de Ayacucho. Since 1898 it has been the administrative capital of Bolivia, but it wasn't until the middle of the twentieth century, when peasant migration began in earnest from the countryside, that La Paz really began to expand into a major city.

One of South America's poorest countries, Bolivia was plagued by governmental instability for much of the 20th century. By the 1990s it had become one of the world's largest producers of coca, from which cocaine is derived. The government subsequently instituted a largely successful programme to eradicate the crop, although such efforts were resisted by the many poor farmers who depended on the coca plant to eke out their meagre existence.

The population of La Paz is mixed, reflecting that of Bolivia as a whole. The majority are Indians, descendants of the *Aymara* and the Quechua; some are Spanish and mixed-race Indian-Europeans; and there is a large community of *Mestizos*, heirs to Spanish and Indian blood intermingling in this part of South America during the last four hundred years. The culture is a curious mix of ancient tradition and modern invention, existing more or less harmoniously side by side.

From the airport, Tony moved up into the mountains on which the city is built. The world's highest capital, it stands over 12,000 feet above sea level, spreading out down the mountains to the city centre in a canyon formed by the La Paz River. Tony looked around and breathed deeply. After the incessant noise of the rain forest, the heat and humidity, the flies and mosquitoes, it was a pleasure to be here. He looked forward to enjoying the quiet and peace of the mountains, the gently warm days and cool nights.

La Paz is a very stratified society. Contrary, perhaps, to what one might expect, the upper classes, mostly Europeans, live at the bottom of the mountain, in large and beautifully appointed villas. The middle classes, mainly those of mixed race, live half way up the mountain, in pleasant but generally quite small homes. At the top of the mountain – with the best views and the freshest air – live the Indians, the poorest inhabitants of La Paz and definitely the lowest class.

Tony headed for the Indian quarter high up in the mountains and found a cheap room [ten dollars a month!] but with very basic facilities. The houses were made of mud brick; there was no running water, no sanitation, and of course no electricity. He had to share a primitive outside toilet and shower with several neighbours. But it was a pleasant room on the top floor of a four-storey mud brick building, with fabulous views over the whole of La Paz. After living for so long in the jungle that was the rain forest, it felt good to be back in a city.

The people living in the Indian quarter, especially the women, were truly wonderful; warm and generous and caring. The young daughter of Tony's neighbours took it upon herself to look after him, insisting on doing his washing and cleaning, for which she refused to accept any money. It transpired, though, that she did have an ulterior motive: very soon she declared her love and her desire to marry Tony. But even when he made it quite clear that this was out of the question, Rosa still insisted on looking after him. Here the women expect to do everything in the home; she would have been insulted had Tony refused her kind offers. Gracefully, he conceded to the macho culture – and certainly part of him enjoyed the convenience.

Rosa took complete charge of her new neighbour, taking him to the markets, showing him the best stalls at which to buy different goods, making sure that the vendors charged him the lowest prices. The fruit and vegetables here were abundant, delicious and very cheap: huge mangoes and papayas, and bananas that were red inside and cost about two pence a kilo. And wherever you bought food, the stall owner would give you a little gift, in the hope that you would return. Tony found it very enjoyable walking around the markets with someone who understood both the verbal and the hidden local languages. And it was certainly an added bonus to be in the company of a beautiful young Indian woman.

The Indians here are Quechua, and very proud of their ancient Quechua and Inca heritage. In the early fifteenth century, the Quechuas were conquered by the Chancas, who in turn were subdued by the Incas. Much of the traditional Quechua way of life continued under the Incas, and there was a lot of intermarriage. But everything changed drastically with the brutal sixteenth century conquest by the Spanish. Now, many of the traditional Quechuas are poor farmers living high up in the mountains, with wonderfully fresh air, but difficult land to farm.

Various waves of Christian missionaries to South America during the last several hundred years have converted the Quechua people to Christianity. They go to Church regularly and tell you that they believe in *Jesu Christo*. But if you look beneath these surperficial customs, you will discover that their Roman Catholicism is liberally infused with primitive ideas and pagan practices. They still follow their old ways, believing in evil spirits, taboos, stealing power, casting spells and black magic; and they remain highly superstitious. Even their 'churches' are full of artifacts not seen anywhere in the Christian world. They share the beliefs and culture of their Shamans.

The Indians that Tony met during his stay in La Paz lived in tight urban communities with strong family ties and a strong sense of communal responsibility. They lived mainly by trading. They would go to the edge of the rain forest – the tropical mountain rain forest was only thirty kilometres away – and bring back wonderful fruit and vegetables, which they would sell in the markets; and La Paz is full of markets. They would also sell pots and pans, T-shirts and Indian tops, hats, spare parts of cars, tools, beads and belts, brightly coloured cloths and rugs, amulets and crystals; in short, anything they could get hold of very cheaply and sell for a little more. Living in the Indian quarter among them, Tony found them warm and friendly; and blessed with the friendship of the indomitable Rosa, he was introduced to many interesting local people.

But enjoyable as all this was, Tony was here on a mission: to find the Quechua Shamans and discover what they had to teach him. He was curious to learn about their traditions and their culture, which he understood to be very different from the Shamanic practices of the rain forest. But the Quechua Shamans are very reserved and they do not like outsiders; they were extremely adept at eluding him. Eventually, however, through people that he met at one of the markets, Tony managed to make contact with them. Apparently, the Shamans had been observing him for some time, and finally, when they were ready, they 'allowed' him to find them.

The Quechua Shamans mostly act as 'medicine men' for the local community, and ceremonial guides for everyone – and here everything needs a ceremony. Nobody would dream of getting married, buying a car or making a business deal without the appropriate ceremony.

And the Shamans have a ready ritual for everything. If you buy a new car, they will paint it with strange signs and symbols, and throw 'holy water' from a church or sacred lagoon over it, to make sure that you don't have an accident. If you want to make a business deal, your first call will be to see the Shaman. He will usually send you off to the market to buy the special herbs and seeds you need; when you return with your purchases, he will prepare them in his special secret way, and then perform a ceremony for you. The Shamans may also give you amulets, special stones or crystals, shells, even tobacco, to protect you from evil spirits. Everything to them has symbolic meaning.

During Tony's stay in La Paz, a large building project was about to get underway. The architects' plans were completed, the builders had been hired, but no-one would start work until the appropriate ceremony had been conducted. Everybody gathered at the building site, dressed in their colourful best. Then the Shamans appeared, majestic in their ceremonial robes, blowing sacred smoke, drumming and rattling and making a great noise. They danced back and forth, criss-crossing the site many times, stamping their feet, wailing, and waving their arms around, to clean the land of evil forces before the foundations were dug. Then a llama was sacrificed to appease the gods and ensure that none of the workers was hurt while the building work was being carried out. Animal sacrifice was frequently used in rituals here, if the project were deemed important enough.

The Quechua Shamans are very different from the Shamans of the Amazon Rain Forest. They are very conservative and they don't like change, not at all like the open-minded and welcoming *Ayahuasqueros.* They have their own ways and a strong sense of their own culture and heritage, and their own language which they are doing their best to preserve. [The Kkechuwa language is still spoken by some twelve million people in southern Columbia, Ecuador and northern Argentina, as well as Bolivia. Tony even managed to grasp a smattering of Kkechuwa while he was in La Paz.] The Quechua Shamans consider themselves to be the 'purest' of the Andean population. They also have a strong sense of the suffering they incurred at the time of the Spanish conquest, which they seem to carry with them down the generations.

Their ceremonies, too, differ greatly from those of the *Ayahuasqueros*. They don't drink ayahuasca or have the same kind of spiritual experiences as the Shamans of the Amazon basin; although they do chew the leaves of the coca plant, which is sacred to them, and which also creates a mild state of altered consciousness. Their ceremonies are full of superstitions, much of their ritual an attempt to appease the gods and so forestall 'bad energy' being visited upon them. But they do use many 'classical' Shamanic artifacts, in common with Shamans across the world.

One of these was the Medicine Wheel, used by Shamans on all continents for their rituals and ceremonies. It gave them a way of tapping into hidden knowledge and power, access to all worlds, to all levels of consciousness, to all time. The Medicine Wheel acts as a bridge between the physical world and the world of spirit. It is an altar, a magnetic symbol, which both attracts and radiates spiritual power. It provides a physical focus for the work of the Shaman, and something visible and tangible that everyone participating in the rituals could see and relate to.

The Medicine Wheel is generally built in a place of sacred power where the Shamanic rituals of the community usually take place. Most Medicine Wheels follow some variation of the Stone Circle, made from a large circle of stones: four big stones to mark the four cardinal directions, and three smaller stones between each of the larger ones, representing the twelve moons of the year, would form the diameter of the circle. Still smaller stones would be used for the four spokes, placed from the centre of the circle out towards the four cardinal directions.

Sacred artifacts would be placed within the circle of the Wheel: crystals, feathers, stones believed to have special power, bones of animals or wise ancestors, birds' claws, animal paws, dried leaves and herbs; indeed, anything with which a particular Shaman felt a special power connection. The Medicine Wheels of the Quechua Shamans manifested their eclectic heritage: they often put pictures of Jesus or the Saints on their Wheels, as well as the more traditional Shamanic artifacts, and would call on them for their help, along with the Shamanic spirits and guides. Sometimes, they would place a small container with alcohol in the centre of the Wheel and light it; the ensuing flames would purify the Wheel and, symbolically, everyone participating in the ceremony.

Many of the Quechua Shamans also use the *Mesa*. This is a smaller version of the Medicine Wheel, the Shaman's personal Wheel that travels around with him and is used when he is working with just one or two people or perhaps a small group. Made from small stones and crystals, it would contain the personal artifacts of the individual Shaman. The whole Wheel would be small enough to fit into a pouch or bag that he would carry with him at all times, and could be set up easily whenever necessary. The Quechua Shamans carried their *Mesa*s in the most colourful and elaborately decorated bags.

Having finally been granted access to the Quechua Shamans, Tony was struck by the great showmanship they exhibited at their rituals. Their clothes were flamboyant, the objects that they placed on the Medicine Wheel often startling and the hybrid mix of ancient Shamanic lore with watered-down Catholicism was disconcerting. On the whole, he found the Quechua Shamanic practices to be more superstitious than spiritual. He could find no profound connection with them, such as he had found with the Egyptians or the Amazonian native people.

But in spite of this, Tony still wanted to use his time in La Paz to find out about their healing plants and learn from them all he could. When he had first appeared on the scene, the Quechua Shamans dismissed him as just another college kid come to gawp at 'the natives'. But with equal measures of patience and persistence – augmented no doubt by his impish smile and characteristic stubbornness – Tony was eventually able to connect to them in a meaningful way. Their shared point of reference was their profound love of *Pachamama* and their concern for her well-being. So, in the reverse order of his process with the Shamans of the rain forest, Tony was first invited to their rituals [in fact virtually anyone could attend] and only later did they agree to work with him.

When they finally got to know him and realized that he had much Shamanic knowledge, they began to trust him. They would tell him where the local herbs were most powerful, and eventually they were happy to swap 'recipes' with him. Once they opened up to him they became very friendly. Tony spent a lot of time with them after this, questioning them about their local plants and herbal remedies. He watched the gentle and special way in which they picked the herbs, safe-guarding the spirit of the plants. He watched the healing ceremonies they performed – much more in tune with his own spirituality than their more flamboyant rituals. And he was able to incorporate this growing knowledge more deeply into his own work.

Tony started travelling around some of the villages in the area, with his own potent herbal remedies. The local people, at first curious to see what this new Shaman could do, would come to 'try him out'. But as soon as he healed one person, others began to trust and came to be healed. News of this 'European' Shaman spread like wild fire, and often as he arrived in a new village, there was already a line of people and ailments waiting for his healing. He didn't take money but would happily accept food or shelter in exchange for his services; or nothing at all if the villagers had nothing to give. Sometimes, individuals were too poor to give him anything, but the village collectively would host and feed him.

Moving from village to village, he began to cover quite large distances. He was welcomed wherever he went as a fully-fledged Shaman, and his reputation for healing began to precede him. But as news of his success spread, it also became his downfall. In several of the larger villages, the indigenous doctors became jealous of his success. Tony was now healing people with quite serious illnesses, something that the local doctors had not always been able to do. In one place, they became so angered by his success that they convinced the local politicians to make his stay there 'difficult'. Tony moved on.

At about this time, a young Bolivian woman of ancient Spanish decent stumbled into his life. She was studying at the University of San Andrés in La Paz, and they became friends. She was a *Chapaco* [a resident of Tarija, her home town, near the Argentinian border]. The *Chapacos* are very proud of their ancestry and consider themselves more Spanish or Argentinian than Bolivian. Marillia was beautiful and educated and Tony found her and her mixed-heritage culture fascinating. Very soon, she, too, told him that she wanted to marry him. Perhaps much of the local interest in Tony was the unusual figure that he cut: a white-skinned long-haired European, who lived with the Indians, looked about sixteen and was a Shaman to boot! But he was also blessed with incredible good looks, which may have influenced, just a little, the young women he met.

Tony really liked Marillia but was not interested in marrying anybody at this time. And he did not want to have just a physical relationship with her; he felt that this would be taking advantage of her interest and vulnerability. Somehow they managed to overcome this imbalance of desires [or at an rate, she was able to put her deeper feelings for him on hold]. They established a really good friendship, and he enjoyed many pleasant weeks in her company.

When the university semester ended, she had to return home for the vacation. She invited Tony to go with her to Tarija, to see the town and meet her family. She tried to tempt him with the delights of a Mediterranean-style town in the heart of South America, with its wonderful architecture and famous fiestas and music. He said that he wouldn't go with her, but would visit her later. But after she left, he realized that this would be a distraction from his spiritual work, and he didn't go. [Echoes, perhaps, of his attraction to the young woman at Mount Baldy, and a similar renewal of spiritual dedication and his 'vow' of celibacy.] It was clear to him that if he were serious about pursuing his spiritual path, he would have to leave earthly pleasures to one side, at least for the moment.

Tony had learnt from several sources that the best 'medicine place' in this part of Bolivia was Lake Titicaca. The bus journey there from La Paz was very cheap; it was also very bumpy and very hot and very uncomfortable. And very long, as the roads were more like donkey tracks than modern highways.

Tony travelled the Bolivian way, on a bus crowded with local people, piled high with children and goods pushing him into less than half a seat. If you needed a toilet break, you shouted to the driver to stop, and then had to fight your way past the kids, the fat women, the sacks of vegetables from the market, the chickens, rabbits and guinea pigs, to get to the exit. No tourist bus, this! But an experience to be savoured in its memory, if not entirely enjoyed at the time.

The journey was also marked by an abrupt change of scenery. After the hustle and bustle of the city, the starkness of the countryside was quite a shock. There would be an occasional hamlet here or there, two or three families of herders living in a few isolated mud huts. And then suddenly, there was nothing: no villages, no outposts, no trees; just a few llamas, condors and flamingoes, proudly wandering the sparse landscape, unencumbered by humans. Here were strange rock formations, too, and sudden craters, like an eerie and lonely moonscape, or a scene of devastation after a nuclear explosion. The comfort of journey's end beckoned enticingly through the monotony of the scenery.

What greeted Tony, when the bus finally pulled in beside Lake Titicaca many hours later, was as unexpected as it was bizarre: a wonky street sign which read "UFOs frequently sited here". Intrigued, he questioned the local people, and was told stories of strange and mysterious lights flashing overhead. All the local Quechua had seen them, and were very scared; they feared that they might be abducted. Farmers, among the most down-to-earth people anywhere, told of unfamiliar objects they'd seen darting at great speed across the sky. Fishermen had seen lights bubbling up out of the lake, and then disappearing. They believed that the lake had magical powers, and they wouldn't fish at certain times.

The local people were very superstitious, but there did seem to be something behind all these sitings. Lake Titicaca is very high up and the air is cool and very pure, very thin. As there is so little oxygen, it is very easy for people to have 'strange' experiences. But Tony felt that there was more to it than that, and he looked forward to investigating. Strangely, or perhaps not so strangely, it was through his later visions of the past in altered states of consciousness, that he would come to understand these symbols of the future.

When he first arrived, he stayed in Copacabana, on the southern shore of the lake. It is an astonishingly beautiful place – all three streets of it! And it boasts a most wonderful, extravagant and very old cathedral. Apparently, miracles began happening here in the sixteenth century, after a statue of the Virgin of Candelaria was presented to the town. Since then, people from all over the country come on pilgrimages to Copacabana, to receive the Virgin's blessings.

Copacabana is a sleepy little town with very little to do. Again, Tony found cheap lodgings; but what he didn't pay in money, he more than made up for in health risks. He rented a tiny room in a mud hut, which contained almost nothing but the most uncomfortable straw mattress ever. He would wake up in pain every morning, and became convinced that many of his later back problems could be traced back to that mattress.

But the worst part was the bugs. The roofs of the mud huts were made from reeds, which were home to a particularly nasty little bug known as the 'kissing bug' because of its short sharp bites. The bugs would drop from the reed roofs at night, carrying with them a disease for which there is no known cure. This can incubate for up to ten years; then it attacks your heart muscle and you die. Tony stayed in this mud hut for many months…

In the West, Machu Picchu is thought to be the most sacred place in the Andes and hundreds of people on the 'spiritual trail' visit there every year. It is indeed a spectacular and magnetic place. But the most sacred place to the Andean people is Lake Titicaca.

The lake itself is magnificent: all shades of blue and green and violet that change with the changing light. It comprises a vast expanse of water, some 190 kilometres long and 80 wide. At nearly 4,000 meters above sea level, it is the world's highest navigable lake, and the second largest lake in South America. A narrow strait separates it into two bodies of water, which are scattered with forty-one islands, some densely populated. And it boasts one naval boat – the entire Bolivian navy – proudly flying its flag. This is a lake, remember; Bolivia must be the only land-locked country in the world with a navy, even if it does comprise only one boat!

Straddling the Peruvian/Bolivian border, Lake Titicaca is encircled by volcanic mountains, though so far they have never errupted. No-one has ever fathomed the bottom of the lake, which is so deep that it may even go down to sea level. The Lake is of great historical interest and the remains of one of the oldest known American civilizations have been found around its shores. And temple ruins on Titicaca Island mark the place where the first Inca priests worshipped. Its serene liquid beauty in the middle of the parched surroundings, together with the quality of light and the luminous blue of the sky over the lake, may also account in part for its mystical significance.

The local people believe that monsters live at the bottom of the lake, and fishermen have disappeared, 'swallowed by the spirits of the lake'. There is a feeling when you are on the water that you are being pulled down by some unseen force; even Tony, who is in no way superstitious, was aware of these feelings. There are also frequent lightning storms over the lake, when it seems as though the whole sky is firing at you, exploding just above your head, and it's easy to see why the local people feel that the gods are angry with them.

There are sacred sites, Inca and pre-Inca, all around the lake; or rather remnants of sites, for most have been almost completely destroyed. The whole landscape around Lake Titicaca is considered by the local Quechua people to be sacred. In the centre of the lake are two sacred islands, the Isla del Sol, the Island of the Sun, and the Isla de la Luna, the Island of the Moon. The Island of the Sun, the Quechua people's most sacred site, is much the larger of the two islands, and is reputedly the place where the sun itself was born. It is also believed to be the birthplace of the first Inca man, Manco Kapac, and the first Inca woman, his sister/wife Mama Huaca. The Quechua people who live around the lake now still accept these legends as history.

Tony visited the Island of the Sun many times. It is a very mountainous and barely habitable island, but there are a couple of tiny villages at the top of the mountain where it is possible to stay for a few days at a time. Tony came to the island to explore the Inca ruins, including the famous Pilko Kaimo and the Sacred Rock of the Inca creation. But there are many other ancient Inca ruins scattered about the island, and walking among them gave him a feeling of real connectedness to the Inca people and a strong desire to know more about their history.

The Quechua people living today are the direct descendants of the Incas. The Inca Empire originally stretched from what is now Chile, through Bolivia, Peru and Ecuador up to southern Colombia, before this vast land mass was divided into separate countries.

According to tradition – the Incas left no written records – the founder of the Inca dynasty led the tribe to Cuzco, which became their capital. Under the fourth emperor they began to expand, and under their eighth emperor they began a programme of permanent conquest by establishing garrisons among those they had conquered. By the early sixteenth century the Incas, having conquered or absorbed many other peoples, now ruled over some twelve million subjects.

At this time, the peak of the Inca Empire, it was the most advanced civilization in South America. Their architecture was highly developed, they had constructed a vast network of over twenty thousand kilometres of roads, a system of bridges and tunnels to link all parts of their empire, and the remains of their irrigation systems, palaces, temples and fortifications are still in evidence throughout the Andes, witness to their astonishing engineering skills. They also stationed fast relay runners every two kilometres across the Empire, and so could cover a distance of some 250 kilometres a day if they needed to deliver urgent messages.

As well as boasting such great feats of engineering, Inca society was highly sophisticated and stratified, and featured an aristocratic bureaucracy. But the ruling Inca also abolished private property and established a system of social security, unrivalled at the time, to take care of everyone's needs. Their pantheon, worshipped in a highly organized state religion, included a sun god, a creator god, and a rain god.

But everything was to change in 1532, when the Incas were invaded by the Spanish. Although there were only a few hundred Spanish soldiers and many millions of Incas, there was really no contest. The Spanish came on horseback, and the Incas had never seen horses; the Spanish had guns, but the Incas didn't understand what they were or how they worked. They saw the soldiers ride triumphantly through their cities on these strange animals; then they would hear a loud bang and people started to drop down dead. The Incas, superstitious and terrified, thought that they must be 'white gods' and put up no resistance.

The Spanish conquest was swift, vicious and wantonly cruel. The *conquistadors* demolished the healing schools in Cuzco, that had practised and taught the ancient sacred healing rites of the native Americans, inherited and zealously guarded by the Incas. The Incas saw their temples dismantled, their healing ceremonies outlawed, their spiritual teachings, dating back thousands of years, denigrated. The knowledge and spiritual wisdom and traditions of their ancestors was all but destroyed.

The Spanish captured Atahuallpa, the Inca emperor/god, believed to be a divine being in human form, and worshipped by the entire Inca people. The *conquistador*, Francisco Pizarro, met Atahuallpa just before the emperor's triumphal entry into Cuzco and invited him to a feast in his honour. When Atahuallpa and his unarmed retainers arrived, Pizarro ambushed them on horseback with cannons and guns, slaughtered thousands, and took Atahuallpa prisoner. In terror for his life, Atahuallpa tried to make a deal with Pizarro and offered him a ransom of a roomful of gold. Pizarro accepted and the Incas worked furiously day and night to bring gold to fill the designated room. But when he had received twenty-four tons of gold and silver, Pizarro reneged on the deal and ordered Atahuallpa to be burned at the stake. The sentence was changed to death by garrotte when Atahuallpa agreed to convert to Christianity.

With the capture and death of their emperor/god, the war was virtually over. But this was still not enough for the Spaniards. Originally coming on a mission as part of the Spanish Counter-Reformation to Christianize South America and its black inhabitants, whom they thought of as sub-human, they were now interested only in acquiring ever greater wealth and power.

They wanted more gold, and they started to search for the place where the gold had come from, the fabled city of Cuzco, the sacred heart of the Inca Empire. The Spanish soldiers found Cuzco, and gold in abundance. But not just gold; they found the most beautiful artifacts made in gold, ornaments and amulets, holy texts and drawings, and amazing calendars, detailed for centuries ahead, all inlaid and preserved in gold. They found ancient temples with rich carvings in gold, gold statues and pillars, ceilings encrusted with gold.

In their greed and their ignorance, the Spaniards melted down everything that could be melted, and then shipped the gold back to Spain. What they could neither melt nor destroy, they turned into magnificent palaces for themselves. Spain was now ruler of this vast land mass; what is now Bolivia, Columbia, Chile, Ecuador and Peru together, all became part of the Spanish Empire. The King of Spain was so delighted with his vast new wealth that he rewarded the soldiers by dividing up the land and making them viceroys or governors over huge areas. The Incas, with their emperor/god dead and their temples destroyed, simply disappeared. Centuries of a rich and glorious culture were lost forever.

Tony stayed in Copacabana for many months and started to work with local Shamans. They taught him about the indigenous plants and the secrets of the herbal remedies of the lakes and mountains, carefully guarded by native Shamans for millenia.

At first, they allowed him to work with them only on herbal remedies. Tony started to collect different artifacts from the sacred sites around Lake Titicaca: shells, crystals, rocks, stones, bits of remnants of old temples; anything that he thought might be useful in Shamanic work. He was practising now as a Shamanic healer, and there were always local people with ailments willing to try out someone new. He began to feel completely at home here and thought he would stay forever, although with his long hair and frayed jeans he still looked like an American college dropout.

The Shamans here spoke Spanish as well as Kketchuwa and so he managed to talk with them, although his Spanish was not yet good enough to communicate with them on a very deep level. After a while, he began to work with a well-known local Shaman, Don Augustin, and as he got to know Tony and accepted him, other Shamans followed suit. Eventually, they acknowledged his deep commitment to Shamanism and allowed him to work with them in different dimensions.

And so began Tony's work with the Shamans of Copacabana on the astral level. This work was largely focused on purifying himself, seeking further knowledge and cleaning the astral realm. The Shamans showed him many places of power and he would go from one power site to another, places of intense mystical beauty as well as powerful spiritual energy. Some sites were so magnetic that a compass would whirl out of control, spinning round and round in circles. Tony would sit and meditate for many hours in these places, feeling extraordinarily 'connected' and empowered.

Gradually, he developed his own ceremony for accessing the astral level. Sitting outside in a sacred space, he would prepare himself physically, mentally and spiritually. This would usually be in the late afternoon as it was too cold outside at night. He would breathe deeply and slowly, and enter a profoundly peaceful state of being. Then the visions would begin to come. [Today, he is able to enter the astral plane without any special preparations. When he gives retreats, he is in both the physical and the astral worlds, simultaneously, and now finds it very easy to move between worlds at will.]

On the astral level, he felt completely connected to all the Shamans he worked with [real physical beings] and to the spirit guides that visited him. He was again being bombarded with knowledge: where to go, what to do, which power sites would offer him particular insights. Often he would have a vision in the astral plane which would give him amazing information about a sacred site of which he had not even heard. Later, when he went to the museum to check it out, he discovered that everything he'd been told by spirit guides was documented there.

His work on the astral level was giving him profound knowledge about the world, about healing and about spirituality. It was teaching an ancient wisdom, held in sacred sites or places of power. It seemed that Tony had been chosen for some special task, for he was able to understand, instantaneously, everything that was shown to him, though this was knowledge that would normally have taken Shamans years of study and 'guided journeys' to acquire, and would have been beyond the reach of others altogether. He felt extraordinarily blessed, very grateful to the spirits, the universe and his 'guardian angels'. At the same time, he was journeying to 'the Underworld' – the deepest part of his own consciousness.

All this time, Tony was still living very much 'in the world', visiting the markets and talking with local people. He had no source of income and had to support himself; although it was very cheap to live in Copacabana, he still needed some money. Anticipating this, he had bought lots of goods very cheaply at the markets in La Paz, which he was able to sell in Copacabana for a little more, and then live off the profit. Or he would learn where to buy the cheapest things at one market, and sell them at another for a small mark-up.

A far cry from buying and selling shares in Oslo to support his Buddhist practices, but he was still a good businessman! [He also believes that taking responsibility for our own survival and creating abundance for ourseves, provided that we are coming from a place of highest integrity, is a basic part of spiritual work. As adults, we should not expect anyone to support us.] Sometimes he would swap things he had and didn't need for other things he wanted. And so he got by. He also spent lots of time with the local kids, who were much more open and friendly than the adults, and very savvy and street wise; they would tell him which were the best stalls at which to buy goods for selling on.

This was also a time of relaxation for Tony. Copacabana exudes a special languid ambience and he spent a lot of time on the beach, watching the fishermen out on their boats or hauling in their catches, or just sitting by the lake soaking up the atmosphere, and feeling that he never wanted to move from this place, ever. [Yes, Tony does seem to have a penchant for falling in love with places and wanting to stay forever! An extension, perhaps, of living in the moment in pure joy, wherever he finds himself.]

He also spent a great deal of time hanging around waiting for a boat to take him to the Island of the Sun, or to bring him back. Time here, like in the rain forest, does not exist as we know it in the West. A boat scheduled for ten o'clock in the morning may well turn up at three in the afternoon – if you were lucky. He was having to learn serious patience.

It was a time, too, for having fun. Two fiestas were held during Tony's stay in Copacabana and suddenly the whole sleepy place sprang to life. On the Good Friday festival, the town filled with pilgrims who held a candlelit procession at dusk, majestic and solemn and beautiful to watch. The Independence Day fiesta lasts a whole week, with parades, brass bands, Indian dancers performing traditional *Aymara* dances, fireworks and general mayhem; the whole town seemed to be out, making music, drinking and feasting.

There were other smaller celebrations too, local gatherings which he discovered by accident – or synchronicity – by being in the right place at the right time. One festival was to celebrate summer solstice; another, a special family occasion. Great music was played on wonderful instruments that he had not seen before [the *charango, tarka, quirquincho,* and *sikuri*] and everyone came along to sing and dance.

And drink; everybody here drinks a lot. The local drink is *chicha,* a very strong beer brewed from maze or corn; fermentation is started by someone spitting into the barrel. Tony decided not to try it. But, along with everyone else, he did chew coca leaves, which helps against altitude sickness, and gives you strength to walk in the harsh climate of the mountains. Other side effects were, of course, quite coincidental!

Copacabana is most famous for its reed boats. Thor Heyerdahl, the Norwegian ethnologist and adventurer, led the Kon-Tiki Expedition from South America to Polynesia in 1947 to demonstrate the possibility of ancient contact between the two cultures; and he had come to Lake Titicaca to have his reed boats built there. Tony was fascinated to see how the reed boats were made, and to discover that they have been made in exactly the same way for thousands of years; the same techniques are used here today as were used in ancient Egypt.

Heyerdahl had also sailed a reconstruction of an ancient Egyptian reed boat [the Ra] from Morocco to the Caribbean to show that Mediterranean peoples could have preceded Christopher Columbus to the New World. Clearly, there had been contact between them in ancient times. Tony has always felt a special affection for Egypt; it was his childhood, his roots, his earliest visions, and to find this connection to Egypt here by Lake Titicaca was extraordinary. Later, he would realize that this was also a sign, leading him in another direction, more deeply into his real self and what would become his life's work.

But before this, there was another discovery that Tony was to make, which would bring an additional dimension to his spiritual work: the Inca temples.

The ruins of old Inca temples are strewn all around Lake Titicaca and Tony became drawn to spending most of his time exploring these sacred sites. The local Shamans all knew where the temples were, but hardly visited them. This seemed strange to Tony, as they had all been built in places of great power. Most of them had been destroyed by the Spanish invasion, but remnants were scattered all around the sites: bits of walls and pillars, and huge rocks, too large for the Spanish to destroy. These had been exquisitely shaped and smoothed to fit perfectly together, without the use of cement or glue; you couldn't pass the thinnest sheet of paper between them.

How had the Incas managed to do this? And how had they managed to move the rocks to build the temples? They were enormous; a crane today would not be able to lift them. The Incas were a small and primitive people; they didn't have horses, or cutting tools of any kind. Sitting for hours among the ruins, feeling the extraordinary power and energy of these places, Tony would contemplate their mysteries. In later visions, answers to all these questions would be divulged.

Tony did not consciously set out to explore any particular temple. But now he was working a great deal in parallel worlds, and felt guided all the time. Sometimes, as he was walking around with no special intention, a bus would come along and he would take it to wherever it happened to be going. And when he arrived, he would find himself at the site of an ancient Inca temple.

One temple had a hot spring inside it and held tremendous energetic power. A few pieces of broken walls were still standing, and Tony took to visiting this site many times, sitting there for hours in the stillness of the night. The deep silence of the mountains [most of the temple sites were up in the mountains] forced him to listen to his own inner sounds: his feelings, his processes, his heart. It was like a deep silent meditation, alone, embraced by the mystical power of the place. He found himself living in some of his own past lives, which would illuminate particular aspects of his present life. He felt physically connected to the ground, as though power were seeping up from it into his body, and he was receiving wisdom and guidance directly from Mother Earth. The place itself vibrated with power, similar to that of the Pyramids.

He discovered the remnants of the Temple of the Gate, one of the most ancient Inca temples, and learnt its history. The main gate was made of two huge vertical boulders, with a horizontal one placed across the top. According to Inca legend, if you walked through the gate you would move into another dimension, and become invisible. Tony did walk through the gate, he did feel the power of the site very strongly, and found it easy to move into other realms; and as there was no-one there to see him, maybe he did become invisible!

One day, on the Island of the Sun, he came across some caves beside a tiny ruin and discovered the openings to huge tunnels that had been dug out by the Incas and reached all the way to the Pacific Ocean, hundreds of miles away. How had they managed to do this without any tools? The tunnels had been built as a 'quick route' to the sea, for buying salt and other goods. Walking through the tunnels [remember, the Incas had no horses] might have taken them a couple of weeks; but without the tunnels, they would have had to cross up and down the mountains, taking them many months. The tunnels may also have been used as an escape route in times of war, or perhaps to smuggle goods. The Incas had no written language, and our knowledge of their history is therefore sparse. But important Inca stories were woven into cloth and decorative hangings, and also handed down orally to their Quechua descendants.

As he visited more and more temple sites, Tony realized that he was being given sacred knowledge, which had been lost to civilization. His work with the Quechua Shamans was now waning as he spent more and more time by himself, engulfed in the mysteries of these ancient sites, transported to other worlds. He was being drawn along another, magical path, and he understood that now he needed to work alone; that something was being shown to him that would alter the direction of his journey. It was very clear that a huge amount of information is stored at these sites and that, in an altered state of consciousness, he was being given their secrets.

He saw detailed scenes of Inca life, the experiences that people had lived through in the Inca temples hundreds of years ago, and was able to tap into their thoughts and feelings. Priests, resplendent in colourful ceremonial robes, were conducting a ritual; the Inca gods with their huge feather head-dresses and brightly painted faces, were smiling down upon them from on high. Everything used in the ceremony was covered with gold, which represented the sun, the chief Inca god, to bring sun energy into the ritual. Then he saw the sun itself shining into the temple, reflecting on the gold artifacts, and a brilliant light emanated upwards, startling in its splendour. The whole ceremony unravelled gradually, like a movie. Time now appeared to stretch and change; after sitting at the site for ten minutes, Tony would feel that he had been there all day. Hours seemed like days, so much was being crammed into them.

These experiences were very different from those he had had while taking ayahuasca. Here, he didn't travel to the spirit world, but rather was transported into exotic worlds that had actually existed, in what we think of as reality, in the past. He felt deeply connected to the people, their lives and rituals, but unlike his previous journeys into other worlds, this was not about him. Here, he was watching historical scenes that were part of an ancient culture; and he was also actually there, with the Incas in the temple, at the time that these events were happening. Sitting with them in the temples as they had been in all their past splendour, he watched enthralled as the ceremonies unfolded.

The visions that he was having in the temple sites were extraordinary and overwhelming and he felt awed and humbled by the knowledge that was being vouchsafed to him. He knew that the next stage of his odyssey would be to visit all the temples of power in the area, and he set off to explore further afield.

Tony's journey took him to the ancient town of Cuzco, high up in the Andes mountains just across the Peruvian border, where there were many more Inca and pre-Inca temple sites. Cuzco had been at the hub of the Inca Empire and Tony was eager to discover its secrets.

Inca legend has it that Cuzco was founded in the twelfth century by the first Incas, who made it the capital of their vast empire, naming it the "City of the Sun.". And nearby ruins include an Inca fortress, the Temple of the Sun, and Machu Picchu, the ancient fortress city of the Incas. But archaeological discoveries show that it had been occupied by other cultures several centuries before the rise of the Inca. Its history shows many waves of conquest by different peoples, culminating with the Spanish conquest in the sixteenth century. Since its beginnings it has always been populated; in fact, it is the oldest continuously inhabited city in South America.

Many of its main streets today still boast the remnants of stone walls built by the Incas, which now form the foundations of modern buildings. Although it suffered a major earthquake in 1950, many of its ancient sites have since been restored. Its cathedral, built in 1654, and the university, founded in 1692, were largely unscathed. Several streets are for pedestrians only, and look as though they haven't changed in centuries. The population of some 300,000 are mainly Quechua, and very proud of their ancient heritage.

Tony found his perennial cheap accommodation, and then set about discovering what was left of the ancient Inca temples around Cuzco. He had no difficulty making contact with local Shamans, who were able to help him locate many of the temple sites; but they didn't seem to know much about them, or indeed show any particular interest in them. Yet he knew from the temples he had already visited around Lake Titicaca, that they were places of immense power, able to teach us many things.

The most famous of the Inca ruins was the *Coricancha,* the Golden Courtyard. In Inca times, the walls of the temple were covered with solid gold, reflected in the sunlight to create a golden aura around the temple. During rituals at the temple, life-size gold replicas of corn were 'planted' to encourage the gods to favour a good harvest. The Golden Courtyard also housed the mummified bodies of particularly important Incas, which were brought into the sunlight every day. They were offered food and drink, which was later ceremonially burnt.

Of particular fascination to Tony was the additional function of the *Coricancha:* it had been constructed as an observatory, which the Inca priests had used to track major celestial movements. One wall of the temple is still standing: a huge curved structure, about six metres high, perfectly fitted, that withstood the Spanish invasion as well as the later violent earthquakes that destroyed much of the city.

Tambo Machay, which boasts the ruins of another Inca temple just outside Cuzco, is the site of four underground rivers, which meet and surface in a spring in what would have been the grounds of the temple. Tony climbed to the top of a hill behind the temple, which offered an extraordinary vista of the whole area. Here he went into deep meditation, connecting to the four power animals of the Inca – the jaguar, the serpent, the condor and the eagle – and to the four streams of energy represented by the four rivers. He stayed there for many hours, studying the different animals, connecting to their spirits, their special energy and their wisdom.

In other temples around Cuzco, Tony began to learn about the power of sound. In one vision he saw around the inside walls of the temple, large, round, beautifully-carved rocks with thin holes bored through the centres. These formed a big circle, in the middle of which all the people were gathered. He watched in amazement as the Inca priests blew sound through the holes in the rocks – pure sound, not song – and the whole temple started to vibrate. It was as though the temple were filled with the loudest modern stereophonic sound, entirely surrounding everyone there in it. As the sound grew in intensity, the people in the centre began to levitate, carried upwards by the power of the sound. How had the priests managed to do this? It was awe-inspiring.

Tony stayed with this question and entered another vision, which demonstrated an alarming resolution to the riddle: the Incas had employed the power of pure sound to absorb the weight mass of the people, and so they were light enough to be raised off the ground. It also became clear that the Incas had used sound to cut through rocks; by 'blowing' sound at specific angles to the rocks, they could cut through them like a knife through butter and shape them in any way they wished, to fit perfectly together, as they had done in other temples.

In pursuit of his understanding of the power of sound, and the ways in which the Incas had used it, Tony was guided to another temple in the area. This temple had been constructed according to specific geometrical formulae, so that sound bounced off the walls in a specific pre-programmed way. And suddenly it all became abundantly clear, the amazing power of sound; knowledge that had been granted to the Incas hundreds of years ago. They had used sound to cut through stone and move huge rocks. They had also used sound to carry out medical operations.

In another vision, Tony saw them actually performing such operations. In some, they used sound for psychic surgery, carrying out the operation on the patient's aura. But in other's, they actually cut through flesh with sound, and then used it to heal the scar. The Incas had used the perfection of geometry to bounce sound off the walls of the specially constructed temples, they had used it to move and cut through enormous rocks, and they had used it to carry out operations and to heal. Hundreds of years ago. Where had their knowledge come from?

It struck Tony that he might be able to use the power of sound in his own healing work. He had seen the Incas operate with sound, use sound to mend broken bones, and heal burns and scars. He understood that sound could kill cancer cells and reinvigorate a weak immune system. Every cell in the body has its own vibration. Sound also vibrates and can be tuned in to the vibrations of the cancerous cells or an immune deficiency and so heal them. And the sound used in this vibrational healing may well be beyond the range of the human ear. [Compare the use of sonar sound by dolphins to communicate with each other over distances of hundreds of miles, or to heal humans, such as autistic children or pregnant women in difficulties. They are using sound frequencies beyond human hearing.]

Tony started to collect artifacts from the temples around Cuzco: crystals, rocks of all kinds, bones, soil, water; anything that might be impregnated with the resonance of pure sound. And he began to experiment with the use of sound in his own work. Later, he discovered that he could use sound to help certain plants grow in areas where they hadn't been able to grow before. [And recently, a brain surgeon who has been to several of his retreats has started, at Tony's suggestion, to incorporate the use of sound energy into his operations, with considerable success.]

Tony was now spending all his time in the temples, and was having extraordinary visions. He saw scenes of great Inca rituals: the temples were crowded with hundreds of people dressed in colourful flowing robes, and musicians playing many different ancient instruments were walking among the crowds, making majestic music. Special attendants carried flaming torches, which created wild fire dances as they moved slowly around in a cicle. The energy intensified and became almost frenzied. And then, the culmination of the ritual: a human sacrifice, made to the sun god to bless the temple and all those who worshipped there.

In Inca tradition, it was considered the greatest honour to be sacrificed, and only the highest among the Incas would be chosen. Although a barbaric custom, it had about it a kind of awesome and powerful beauty. The human sacrifice would be resplendent in special robes, and would be led in priestly procession, with fire torches, to the high point of the temple. As the sacrifice was made, the music and chanting would reach a crescendo, and it felt as though the energy in the temple could lift off the roof.

In his altered state of consciousness, Tony was being shown a world of ancient wisdom and he didn't want to leave it. He started to sleep in the temples, and his visions became ever more dramatic and powerful. He began to study the ancient statues and the postures of the carvings. He would stand beside a statue and adopt its posture, and then remain standing in that position for hours at a time. Gradually he came to understand that these were magic healing postures, initiation postures used by Shamans – in ancient Egypt! Again, a clear Shamanic connection to Egypt. Surely another sign?

Up to this point, Tony's journey had been fascinating. From living with different Shamanic communities, he had learnt great wisdom and a whole new world of natural healing. It had been through the Shamans that his spiritual journey had taken him into other realms and altered states of consciousness. But now, high up in the Andean mountains, his visions became filled with Shamanic connections to Egypt. He was embraced by memories of his childhood, by the visions he had had and the mystic connections that he had felt in Cairo. The Andes were energetically very similar to the Pyramids.

He was buzzing with energy and new awareness. He realized that he needed to go further, to explore the ancient roots of Shamanism, undiluted by tribal, cultural or psychological influences. It was clear that Shamanism was his way, but he hadn't yet reached the depths of it. It seemed that the deepest part of Shamanism had been lost in South America. And Tony knew that he would find it by going back to Egypt, to his roots.

But before this, there was one more area that he needed to visit.

Chapter Six
The Andes Mountains: Northern Peru
The *Huachuma* [San Pedro Shamans]

The mountains of northern Peru are one of the great natural wonders of the world. The highest peak of the range, Mount Huascarán, in the Cordillera Blanca, stands at 22,205 ft. As well as magnificent scenery, this part of the Andes boasts many Inca and pre-Inca temples, places of enormous power and great knowledge. Tony was eager to explore.

He broke his journey in Lima, and ended up staying there for several weeks. Nicknamed El Pulpo ["The Octopus"] because of its sprawling metropolitan area spreading over nearly four thousand square kilometres, Lima is the capital of Peru and the country's economic and cultural centre. Founded as a city by Francisco Pizarro in 1535 on the Feast of the Epiphany, prompted the name Ciudad de los Reyes ["City of the Kings"] but the name never really took hold. Later, it became the capital of the new vice-royalty of Peru. Its major historical sites include the cathedral, which was begun in the sixteenth century, and the National University of San Marcos, founded in 1551.

Tony found Lima fascinating in a grotesque sort of way, but certainly not a comfortable place to stay for any length of time. The centre of the town, which still boasts its old colonial buildings, has a lot of charm. But the rest of the city is overcrowded, noisy and very polluted. About a third of Peru's total population of over twenty-two million people now live in Lima. A migratory explosion into the capital from all over Peru began in the 1920s and was still erupting towards the end of the twentieth century. Mostly, those who come are the very poorest people, desperate for work and a chance to make something of their lives; to give their children an opportunity for a better future. But jobs are scarce, money scarcer. Large shanty-towns have grown up around the city, lacking the most basic facilities. With no electricity, clean water or sanitation, disease is rife, and hope all but extinct.

The climate, too, is dismal, with a thin grey mist perpetually hanging over the city, blotting out the sun. Tony decided that he would stay for just a few days in Lima, and headed to the beach to enjoy some 'time out'. But even this simple desire was blighted: large warning signs cautioned the public to keep away from the beaches as they were contaminated by untreated sewage. Apparently, all of Lima's waste products are deposited into the Pacific Ocean; the beaches that line the coast may look beautiful and inviting, but they present a very real danger to health.

Tony took a 'bicycle taxi' to the centre of the city, to find a clean [and of course cheap] Pension. But then, in the split second that it took him to get out of the taxi, his bag was stolen. Tony had everything in his bag: his passport, all his money, and the names of people to contact further along his journey. But Tony was not one to be outwitted, even though this was clearly a professional job. He summoned all his energy, which at this time was very strong, and gave chase to the thief.

The street, in a busy shopping centre, was crowded with people, pushing and shoving and hurrying about their daily business, certainly not caring about what anyone else was up to. But everyone was so struck that somebody was actually chasing the thief – robberies are so commonplace here that no-one usually pays them any attention – that they stopped what they were doing and joined in. Some began to chase the thief, others urged them on; eventually some people ahead of the thief managed to cut him off and apprehend him. When Tony caught up with him, he gave him a whack across the face, not hard, more to stun him than hurt him. Astonished – the thief had obviously never been chased before – he instantly dropped the bag and fled. The crowd seemed delighted with the show, and cheered Tony on as he happily retrieved his bag and walked back to the Pension. A little wiser, he reflected on the best and worst aspects of human nature that this city seems to draw out of people.

Lima boasts many marvellous museums, with much for the curious visitor to explore, and Tony decided to use his first days in Lima to see what its famous museums had to offer. They include some wonderful sacred pieces, made of solid gold, too heavy for the Spaniards to steal at the time of the invasion. The exhibits at the National Anthropology and Archaeological Museum trace thousands of years of Peruvian history, showing artifacts from the earliest archaeological sites to the arrival of the Spanish. He also visited museums that house ancient ceramics, pre-Colombian furniture and cooking utensils used by pre-Inca cultures, all fascinating to see.

The Museo de Armas, which reputedly houses one of the best collections in the world depicting history through its changing armaments, struck Tony as an odd view of history and a bizarre way of measuring 'progress'! Traditional folk art, colourful costumes from different periods, and stuffed animals depicting the fauna of Peru, all exhibited in different museums, were much more to his liking. He also discovered a wonderful collection of erotic pots at the Museo Rafael Larco Herrera, which depict in graphic detail the sexual practices of several ancient Peruvian cultures. But for Tony, the highlight of his museum-crawl was the collection of old Inca artifacts. Pieced together in Tony's mind as he looked at them, they painted a colourful canvas of Inca life hundreds of years before.

Coming out of one of the museums, Tony was surprised to see someone waiting for him: it was a street child, no more than six years old. Tony stopped and looked at him. The child looked back, holding Tony's gaze with huge dark eyes and a haunting sadness. Tony gave him a little money, probably more than the child had ever been given, for his thanks were so profuse. As the child disappeared, Tony thought of the little boy who had sold him sweets across the school fence in Cairo, and that haunting look of children who have nothing to lose but their lives.

Within minutes, the little boy was back – and with him was a group of his friends, all needy, all desperate, all looking up at Tony with big expectant eyes.

These kids were so poor, so exploited, tipped out onto the rubbish heap of humanity and left to rot. So like the street children of India, Tony thought. But here he felt a much stronger affinity with the kids. He has a real affection for the people of South America, as though he had known them before. And whereas he felt spiritually connected to India, it remains for him an exotic place, somewhere to visit, but not to live. South America felt like home.

The lives of these street kids were dire. And their stories were heart-rending: children being thrown out by their parents, too poor to feed them; others who had run away after terrible beatings for not bringing home enough money [from begging, stealing, or selling a few meagre goods]. Several of the little girls had been raped, often by members of their own families.

Some of the children managed to earn a few cents shining shoes, running errands or selling sweets or postcards or other knick-knacks to tourists. They slept mostly huddled together on the roadside, and the roads here are among the most polluted on the continent. There was also vicious warfare between rival street gangs, and kids often disappeared. To the *Limenos,* the street children are considered at best a nuisance, polluting their city: to the authorities they are 'vermin' that need to be periodically 'purged'. These kids had to be tough to survive at all.

Tony felt stirred to the core by the iniquitous circumstances in which these children existed, so he decided to stay in Lima for a while and see what he could do to help them. So few people pay them any sort of attention that it was easy to gain the kids' confidence. As always, Tony was living on a very limited budget and didn't have money to give away. But the awful conditions of these children…

He started to buy things from them, rather than just give them money, in order to preserve what little dignity they had left. Then usually, what he'd bought from kids in one place, he'd give to other kids, to resell. But as he helped the first little boy, and then his friends, ten others immediately appeared out of nowhere, and then fifty, scrambling all over him. Like India, it was a bottomless pit of harrowing human misery. But for as long as he was in Lima, he spent his days with the street children, sharing with them whatever money he had for that day's food.

And it provided a salutary lesson in active spirituality. It's easy to feel 'spiritual' when you're sitting atop a mountain, or on the shores of Lake Titicaca, with a full stomach, fresh air and glorious views of nature. It's not so easy in the grinding filth and poverty of a large city, with so much deprivation and suffering all around you. Many good people cannot cope with the distress of it and turn a blind eye. But this, of course, is the real test: to bring spirituality into our daily lives, wherever we are, whatever we are doing. To find in every situation a way of being actively compassionate. It was a reaffirmation that would inform Tony's future journey and teachings: for spirituality to have any value, it must include selfless service to others. Not giving or helping in a way that demeans the recipient, but serving – which enriches both giver and receiver, reinforcing the essential humanity of both.

Before leaving Lima, Tony went to the markets and stocked up with a variety of goods – as much as he could carry – to sell as he travelled north. Then he bought what he could from the street children, bade them farewell and left the city.

Tony's mission was to reach the north of Peru and find the *Huachuma* Shamans, to whom he'd been guided, both by spirits in his visions and by Shamans in Cuzco.

The *Huachuma* are not exactly a people in the sense that, say, the Quechua are. Rather, '*Huachuma*' describes the particular way in which they work as Shamans, just as '*Ayahuasqueros*' describes a certain group of Shamans in the rain forest; they are not a separate people. '*Huachuma*' is actually a Kketchuwa word, *hua* meaning 'spirit' and *chuma* meaning 'come to me'.

Today, the *Huachuma* live mostly in the more remote areas of northern Peru and Ecuador, mainly in the mountains. Most of them trace their ancestry and their traditional healing practices back to pre-Inca days. They were then absorbed by the Incas, and later by the Spanish; the remnants of their pre-Inca belief system is overlaid with strong resonances of Inca, Quechua, Spanish and other Christian practices.

Trujillo, the main town of northern Peru, was recommended to Tony as the best place to stay. And what a pleasure he found it after Lima! Though only five hundred and sixty kilometres to the north of Lima, it is a world away. Clean, uncrowded, with fresh air unpolluted by urban discharge, the stench of poverty or a ubiquitous grey mist. Like Lima, Trujillo was founded by the Spaniard, Francisco Pizarro, in the 1530s. Today, a town of three quarters of a million inhabitants, it still retains much of its old colonial splendour.

There were cheap places to stay on the beach, and Tony settled in. After his difficult experiences with the street children in Lima, it was time for a break, to wander round the streets of Trujillo, drinking in the local culture and exploring its rich heritage. And there was plenty to see. Tony, with his insatiable curiosity, lapped it all up. Impressive statues of the heroes of Peruvian Independence gazed down at him in the Plaza de Armas by the cathedral. Colonial architecture was evident everywhere, with many fine churches and colonial mansion houses dotted across the city. There were many museums, some quite small, offering collections of religious and colonial art and artifacts, and ancient pre-Inca pottery. And quite by chance [or not] Tony discovered the Museo Cassinelli, which boasts a magnificent archaeological exhibit in the basement of a petrol station!

The two cultures that have left the strongest mark on the area round Trujillo are the Moche and the Chimu. The Moche flourished in the first seven centuries of the Common Era, leaving the history of their people decorated on their ceramics;

there are no written records. Their greatest bequest to the world is the Moche Pyramids of the Sun and the Moon – Las Huacas del Sol y de la Luna – near Trujillo. These gigantic 1,500-year-old structures also held echoes of ancient Egypt for Tony. The Chimu period followed from about one thousand until the late fifteenth century. The ancient Chimu capital of Chan Chan was the largest pre-Columbian city in Peru, home to about fifty thousand people. It was conquered by the Incas and it is still possible to find ruins of Inca temples there.

Tony spent a fascinating few days absorbing all these discoveries; but he was here to work. His first port of call, as usual, was the markets: first, to sell a few things and make a little money, then to buy provisions; and then the real pleasure – to walk around imbibing the flavour of the place and talking with the local people. His Spanish by now was fairly fluent [he was even having occasional dreams in Spanish] and this made his life a lot easier.

As in most towns in the Andes, the markets here were the centre of life. Talking to people between the scores of vegetable and fruit stalls, Tony discovered that all the locals around Trujillo share the same background, belief systems and culture as the *Huachuma*, though only a few are initiated Shamans. It wasn't long before he discovered the stalls that supplied goods to the Shamans: amulets, stones, crystals, herbal remedies, etc. And it wasn't long after this that he made contact with the *Huachuma* Shamans in person.

The *Huachuma* Shamans are known for their deep commitment to caring for the natural world. We are living in an era of destruction of much that we know to be sacred. Water, mountains, forests, air, the soul of *Pachamama*, are being polluted by ignorance, greed and arrogance. The Shamans of the *Huachuma* tradition have become the guardians of the planet, and for centuries have taken it upon themselves to preserve the sacred wisdom contained in the heart of Mother Earth. Their reverence for this wisdom, their profound connection with *Pachamama*, is the heart of *Huachuma* Shamanism.

Tony began to work with the *Huachuma* on herbal remedies, the perennial starting point of his work, it seemed, with most new groups of Shamans. They taught him about the local plants and herbs, and went deeply into their own healing practices for his benefit. They were much more open and friendly than the Quechua Shamans had been, and quite soon Tony was invited to join their ceremonies.

And it was at his first ceremony with the *Huachuma* Shamans that Tony was introduced to San Pedro – a discovery that would have a huge impact on his work and change the course of his life. Their work with San Pedro is in fact what defines the *Huachuma* Shamans. A cactus plant that grows mainly in the mountains of northern Peru, San Pedro is nurtured by the *Huachuma*, and then picked and made into a powerful brew. It has mildly mind-altering properties, and when used in ceremony by the *Huachuma* Shamans, it is a gateway to wondrous worlds and visions, and can bring a deeper insight into ourselves.

When Tony took his first drink of San Pedro, he was surprised that the effects were so much milder than those of Ayahuasca. Whereas Ayahuasca bombards the system with extraordinary visions of other worlds, transporting the drinker to other realms, San Pedro is much more gentle. Tony was being given a different experience of himself; the San Pedro moved him not into other realms but more deeply into his own soul. He realized then that he needed to work as much as he could with San Pedro, and follow wherever it would lead him.

The *Huachuma* Shamans told Tony about the sacred places where it grew, and taught him how to pick and prepare it. If it is not picked at exactly the right time, it will lose its potency. The preparation is very much connected to the Spirit of San Pedro, and special ceremonies are held at every stage of the process. Anyone, of course, can buy the San Pedro plants in the local markets, but only the *Huachuma* know the correct way to prepare it and retain its spirit.

The San Pedro ceremonies held by the *Huachuma* were quite different from those of the Quechua Shamans and the *Ayahuasqueros.* For a start, they don't dress up in any special ritual robes; they would attend ceremonies wearing their ordinary clothes, usually a T-shirt and shorts. And the ceremonies were very informal. However, they did use a host of different artifacts: candles of all sizes and colours, totem animals, bones, herbs and seeds that had no medicinal properties, walking sticks decorated with strange carved symbols, bells and chimes and rattles – anything, it seemed, that looked colourful or made a noise. And swords, many swords, which they stuck into the ground at odd angles all around the ceremonial site. Everything that was used was to keep away evil spirits and protect the participants from bad energy.

To one side there was a large altar on which all the artifacts were placed, and many people would crowd around to be as near as possible to the altar. Some would sit or lie next to it, making sure that they were touching it with some part of their body. During the ritual, there was much chanting and a high-pitched, screeching sort of whistling, to call the spirits to the ceremony; but no musical instruments were used other than the small rattles. To Tony it all seemed rather 'showy' and lacking in depth.

The San Pedro ceremonies would be held once or twice a week, and all the local people would come. In summer, they were held outside, in the ruins of one of the old temples. But only during daylight hours; ceremonies were never held outside at night as robberies were endemic. Mostly they would be held indoors, usually in a specially large room in the Shaman's house, set aside for this purpose.

Most of the *Huachuma* Shamans worked for only a few years, often not more than five or six. Apparently, the work with San Pedro was so demanding that after a few years they would be worn out, physically and energetically. They also explained that to do their work was a gift of the spirits, and it didn't last forever. And everyone knew when a Shaman had lost his gift!

As their working lives were so short, the *Huachuma* charged relatively high prices for their services. It could be thought of as an investment for the future, rather like a football player, or a ballet dancer, whose active earning capacity may be high, but limited in time. They did have a sliding scale of charges, but it wasn't so much 'pay what you can' as 'pay for what you want to receive'. So if you paid five dollars, you would receive five dollars' worth of the Shaman's time and effort.

Many people with serious problems would give the Shaman three months' wages or more, so that he would exert his best efforts on their behalf. Although some of the *Huachuma* were undoubtedly materialistic – after all, the people who came to them were generally very poor – they did believe in what they were doing, they did solve problems and they did cure people, sometimes of serious diseases.

Most of the ceremonies held by the *Huachuma* Shamans were concerned with healing people, physically, emotionally and energetically. The *Huachuma* were considered to be the elite of the local indigenous population [though not of the educated middle classes] and were highly regarded by them. As well as being medicine men, they were also skilled psychologists, working with many emotionally troubled people. At the ceremonies, everyone would drink San Pedro, including the Shamans. The San Pedro, specially prepared and blessed, really opened people up to their higher selves, helped them to get in touch with their deeper feelings and confront the real problems that were facing them.

Tony witnessed many San Pedro ceremonies with the *Huachuma* while he was in Trujillo, but they were not really to his taste. They seemed to be based more on black magic and superstition than on deep spirituality. People would come to the ceremonies for what often seemed to him rather spurious reasons: one man said that someone had stolen his power and he wanted it back; another sought revenge on a man whom he thought was cheating on him with his wife; a third was faced with a business transaction and wanted advice from the spirits on how to secure the best deal and make the most money. It was all about the need to placate the evil spirits and 'make bargains' to invoke the protection of the good spirits. The way that the artifacts were chosen and used had more in common with sorcery and superstition than with spiritual growth. The Shamans clearly did possess psychic knowledge and could see into the future; but again, it didn't seem as though this facility were being used in a spiritually enhancing way.

Tony realized that the essential thing for him was to work with San Pedro itself and understand its true spiritual potential. He wanted to learn as much as he could from the *Huachuma* Shamans about the plant: how to grow it, when to pick it and how to prepare it so that the spirit of San Pedro remains within it and its potency was preserved. Once he had learnt this, he no longer felt the need to work with the Shamans in Trujillo.

Tony now understood that his life's journey, leading him through all his spiritual questing, had been guiding him to the *Huachuma* Shamans, and to working with San Pedro. His 'Holy Grail' had reached its culmination. He understood that using San Pedro would be a central part of his work in the future. Now it was time to trust his own intuition and the Spirits that were guiding him on his way.

Straddling the border of Peru and Ecuador are a number of sacred lagoons. The lagoons are breathtakingly beautiful, each one a different colour; together they create a picture that dances like a perpetually moving rainbow.

Several Shamans in Trujillo had suggested the lagoons as a good place for Tony to continue working with San Pedro. The lagoons are surrounded by great mystery, and for hundreds of years have been known as a place of exceptional power. Many *Huachuma* Shamans live scattered around the lagoons, attracted by their air of mystery and magic, and it wasn't difficult for Tony to find them.

The lagoons are surrounded by secrecy and can be visited only by invitation, either by someone who lives there, or by a Shaman. Tony, invited by local Shamans, was in for a big surprise when he met the people who lived there near the lakes. They were genetically totally different from the native people in the rest of the area. They themselves said that they were not native and that their ancestors hailed from Pharaoic times. They are absolutely certain of this, but have no idea how they came to be there. Anthropologists say they are descendants of pre-Incan people, but nobody knows for sure.

Tony wanted to see what more he could learn about San Pedro from the local Shamans. They were very friendly, and happy for Tony to work with them. Some of their healing work was very impressive: they were curing people of cancer, AIDS, tuberculosis, cholera and other serious diseases. But again, to Tony their work seemed to lack spiritual depth. He was very grateful that they had let him work with them and had been willing to share their 'secrets' of San Pedro. But, as with the *Huachuma* that he'd worked with in Trujillo, he didn't find with them the spirituality he was seeking. Now it was clear that it was time for him to work alone.

The San Pedro plants were grown locally and sold in the markets so it was quite easy to obtain them. Tony started to buy the plants and prepare them as he'd been shown. The area around the lagoons was energetically very powerful, and the plants growing round them would imbibe this power. So drinking the San Pedro here could have very potent effects. Tony would make his own ceremony, and then sit in a place of power near the lagoons, meditating for many hours, letting the power of the place and the essence of the San Pedro seep into him and transform him.

The local people thought that this was risky and warned Tony that it was dangerous to take San Pedro on his own. But he was an initiated Shaman, after all, and had undergone countless transformative journeys taking ayahuasca in the rain forest. He felt perfectly safe. San Pedro is very mild compared to ayahuasca, but it works in a more profound way. Ayahuasca is an Amazonian medicine, made from several wild plants. It is a very strong purgative, working firstly on the physical level, cleaning the body of parasites and other toxins and impurities. After drinking ayahuasca, you invariably vomit, and usually have diarrhoea; and this reaction is almost immediate. In contrast, San Pedro gives a more gentle body detoxification, nothing like as strong as ayahuasca.

On the spiritual level, ayahuasca is, in a sense, the same for everyone. That is, it takes you with it, wherever *it* is going; it doesn't take any account of where you are on your journey. San Pedro, on the other hand, 'tunes in' to where you are now; it mirrors your present reality and takes you forward, almost tenderly. It always deals with what is relevant and important to you at any given time, and so each person's experience of it is unique. Also with ayahuasca, you tend to lose touch with physical reality, which is not the case with San Pedro. If you are serious about spiritual work, you will realize that it is crucial to remain grounded when journeying to other realms. Most importantly, perhaps, San Pedro always serves a purpose beyond the individual, which ayahuasca does not necessarily do. Tony felt that San Pedro reached a deeper wisdom.

All this while, Tony was still exploring temple sites and discovered many Inca and pre-Inca temple ruins around the lagoons. Walking among the ruins, he would find places of particular power, and would hold his San Pedro ceremonies there. He felt totally in harmony with the drink and its process. It opened up vast areas of knowledge, difficult to put into words. It was as though the spirit of San Pedro were pouring out its ancient wisdom and showering it upon an eager recipient; bypassing his mind, so that he would access the teachings directly with his heart, his soul.

Tony began to take the San Pedro at whichever temple site he was exploring. If there was water there, he would make the San Pedro in the temple; this made the process of preparing it very special, connecting the sacredness of the site with the spiritual power of the drink. Otherwise, he would make it beforehand and bring it with him to the temple. Either way, he would accompany the preparation with special prayers and blessings, asking the spirit of San Pedro to remain within the drink, to be his guide and teacher.

The work that Tony did alone with San Pedro moved him along his spiritual path at great speed. It became clear that San Pedro was his 'sacred drink' and he would let it transport him wherever it wished to take him. He was again working on the astral level, and was visited by many spirit guides. It was a deep process, incorporating all the knowledge that he'd gained previously from his work with ayahuasca, and his experiences with the Quechua Shamans. For Tony, it became a portal to reaching a profound spiritual consciousness.

Sometimes, in sacred sites, the place itself seemed to be the source of knowledge. Sitting in meditation, Tony would begin to feel its essence slowly flowing into him, filling his whole being. He would know things about the place, without knowing where this knowledge had come from. Then, in a vision, he would see himself in the temple as it had been in the past: its history, its rituals, the wisdom that it held, would be revealed in stunning detail. And without knowing quite how, he suddenly understood everything, the meaning of the past and how it impacted upon the present; in fact, the whole relationship between past, present and future, which are not separate entities at all but exist in a timeless simultaneity.

Being able to work alone with San Pedro gave Tony great freedom and opened up infinite possibilities. He was no longer tied to any particular place, nor any special group of Shamans. He started to move round the Andes following a trail of temple ruins and sacred sites, seeking out places of particular power.

In each new place he arrived, Tony would explore the surrounding sites, visit the temples and hold San Pedro ceremonies for himself. Sometimes he would stay in a place for a while and do a little healing. If he spent more than a few days anywhere, people would start coming to him; word of mouth that a new Shaman was in the region spread with astonishing speed.

He was still driven by his insatiable curiosity to explore as many temple sites as possible. Partly he was guided by remarkable people whom he'd meet on the way, partly by spirits, and partly by his own intuition. He had many extraordinary visions in the temples, with and without the aid of San Pedro. And sometimes, just walking alone on the side of a mountain, he would feel amazing energy, and some inner voice would guide him to stay there and meditate.

In the course of his travels in northern Peru, Tony found himself in Cajamarca, about a hundred kilometres north east of Trujillo. A traditional and tranquil city, with a friendly population of about seventy thousand people, Cajamarca boasts impressive colonial architecture and some of the best Andean food in the region. This was the place where Atahuallpa, the last Inca god/king, was ambushed, captured and finally assassinated by the Spanish. There is only one Inca building still standing, El Cuarto del Rescate, the ransom chamber, where Atahuallpa was imprisoned, but not where the ransom was kept. And nearby, there are also pre-Inca caves, with channels that run for several kilometres across the mountains. But for Tony, being in Cajamarca became significant for another reason: high up in the mountains overlooking the town, he had one of the most powerful experiences of his life.

The Temple of the Pool exuded innate power and Tony decided that he did not need to take San Pedro here. Almost immediately on sitting down in the temple, he entered another realm. In his vision, he saw the past as it had been in all its monumental glory. The area of the temple was massive, like a small town, much larger than the site of the Pyramids. There were finely chiselled stone steps leading up and down, water channels that criss-crossed the area for miles, carved pillars covered in gold, huge rocks layered with gold and inlaid with jewels and precious stones. At one end of the temple, a magnificent golden gate faced the rising sun. At equinox, the sun shone directly through the centre of the gate, right through the temple. The whole scene shimmered; it was magical, like a child's vision of heaven.

Steps led down to what looked like a vast swimming pool but contained no water, with thousands of faces hewn out of the walls of the pool. Like an old army recruiting poster, wherever you looked, eyes were staring ineluctably at you. But what was most extraordinary was that many of the faces were not Inca faces at all. Some were African, yet the Incas had had no contact with Africa. Some were Viking, with beards, and the Incas never had beards. And other faces looked as we may imagine aliens to be, with strange, non-human features and eyes reflecting other worlds. Where had these faces come from?

In the centre of the pool was a large pillar, rather like a totem pole, with faces carved in each of the four directions. Tony was drawn to reach out and touch the faces in two particular places. Suddenly, energy ran through his body like an electric current and he was transported into a trance. He realized in a flash [almost literally!] that this temple had been constructed on this site because it was a place of tremendous power, and the totem pole was standing at the epicentre from which intense energy was emanating. He felt physically overcome, nauseous and dizzy. He didn't know what was happening.

The vision was overpowering. It seemed to be pouring knowledge into him, not into his mind but rather filling his whole body with a profound kind of wisdom, beyond the grasp of the mind. He understood that this was not just a place of supercharged energy, but that this 'totem pole' was actually a transmitter, encoded with ancient secrets, relaying information out across the universe. The ceremonies that were held here were calling to beings from other realms; the rituals that the priests performed were carried out in order to prepare themselves to go on a long journey. The 'totem pole' was the point of contact with people from other galaxies. Tony was stunned; yet it all made perfect sense to him.

[Compare the Nazca Lines, the huge ancient geometric markings carved in Nazca, in the southern desert of Peru, most of which had been made during the nine hundred years preceding the Common Era. Many people, including the highly respected German mathematician, Maria Reihe, dedicated their lives to studying these ancient symbols, which seemed to make sense only when seen from the air. They therefore concluded that they were some kind of landing fields for visitors from outer space. But Shamans claim that they are gigantic mandalas, created to bring balance to heaven and earth, part of a sacred geometry, long forgotten.]

It was already the middle of the night and very dark. Tony walked around, straining his eyes to make out the shapes of the shadows around him. Suddenly, bright coloured lights began pouring down over the whole temple site. It was like an explosion of fireworks, but focused, not random. And in an instant, everything became clear: the power of the Incas in all the temples across the Andes; how they had managed, without any tools, to lift enormous rocks into the temples, how they had smoothed and shaped the rocks to fit perfectly together, and how strange faces had been carved onto the walls of the pool. The Inca priests had received their astonishing knowledge by journeying to other dimensions.

Sitting in a different part of the temple site, Tony felt the ground start to 'buzz' and he became aware that physically this was a powerfully magnetic place, that the very stones seemed to be drawing him to them, as though they were magnetized. And then he knew, with absolute certainty, that the ancients had used magnetic force to travel, being pulled energetically towards their destinations. It was a mind-blowing revelation.

Tony stayed in the Temple of the Pool for many days, enraptured by the visions that were unfolding. He remained in a state of deep peace, just allowing his spirit to absorb the amazing knowledge that was being granted to him. He didn't eat and he wasn't hungry. After a while, sated with revelations, he left the temple and spent some quiet days in the cool mountain air reflecting on all the extraordinary things he had seen and experienced.

Over the next weeks, Tony started to move around, exploring other sacred sites in the area, taking San Pedro, meditating in the temples. And again, visions of ancient Egypt flooded over him. And suddenly, in one extraordinary vision, he saw the real connection of Shamanism to Egypt.

Thousands of years ago, a highly advanced civilization had flourished in Egypt. The high priests, like those of ancient Greece, had great esoteric and alchemical knowledge. They were medicine men, psychics, seers; they could interpret dreams and visions; they performed birth and death rites and understood the passage of the soul; they had advanced methods for embalming bodies and burying mummies; they performed surgery; they could foretell the future. They were, in fact, very similar to the ancient Shamans, though they didn't share the many Shamanic superstitions.

Towards the latter part of the Pharaonic period in Egypt, the priests foresaw that the time of the Pharaohs was coming to an end, and their demise would herald the death of their advanced civilization. They understood that their great knowledge, gathered and distilled over hundreds of years, was a treasury of deep wisdom, and realized that in a post-Pharaonic period it could not be preserved in Egypt. The Biblical 'seven fat years' were to be followed by the 'seven lean years'; only they weren't years, but eras of time. So the priests set about guarding the knowledge, by putting it into sacred vessels. Some of it was written on papyrus, some was carved onto gold plates; but mostly, the 'essence' of the knowledge was preserved energetically and sealed in the sacred containers. The priests knew that 'wise people' receiving the vessels in the future would understand how to access the knowledge.

The sealed containers were then shipped to seven different places around the world, selected for their strong energetic power. The priests knew that these places were great centres of spirituality, and would preserve their knowledge for humanity. The seven chosen places were: India, near the Himalayas; the native American Hopi tribal lands, in the South West of America; Lake Galilee, in northern Israel; the Caucasus Mountains that range across Russia, Georgia, Azerbaijan and Armenia; a site between Tahiti and Easter Island in Polynesia; the ancient continent of Atlantis [which no longer exists]; and South America, between the Amazon River in Brazil and the Andes Mountains.

The ancient Egyptians had brought the sacred vessels in ships from the temples of the Pharaohs, then taken a known route across the Mediteranean, through the Straits of Gibraltar, to the Canary Islands [which still boast remnants of Egyptian culture]. Then they would have followed the currents across the Atlantic Ocean to South America, and sailed up the Amazon River to the fabled Lost City, through Brazil and across the border into Peru and the Andes Mountains.

And suddenly, everything made perfect sense. Many people in the Andes Mountains talk about strange foreign-looking people sailing up the Amazon thousands of years ago. And there are carvings in the temples in the Andes depicting these events. Many of the carvings in the ancient Inca and pre-Inca temples are very different in style from the local designs, and have a strong Middle Eastern look about them. There are pyramids in the Andes decorated with hieroglyphics. The Andes is one of the rare places outside ancient Egypt that mummifies bodies. And then there are the reed boats, still made here, which are exact replicas of those used along the River Nile thousands of years ago. If further proof of a connection were needed, archaeologists have recovered objects that show the traditional healing of the Andes to be more than five thousand years old – and similar to practices prevalent in ancient Egypt.

Tony's visions now, in each of the different sacred sites, were all of ancient Egypt. In glorious technicolour, scene after magical scene unfolded before his astonished eyes. He saw the priests in the temples, magnificent in their ceremonial robes, performing majestic rituals; he saw them in the splendour of the great palaces offering wisdom and advice to the Pharaohs. And later, he watched as they sealed their wisdom in the sacred vessels, ready for transportation across the world.

The final piece of the puzzle jumped out from his vision with such force that it almost knocked him over. The key to everything was in the San Pedro! The energetic essence of the esoteric knowledge of the ancient Egyptians had been hidden in San Pedro. If you knew how to work deeply with San Pedro, you would be able to connect spiritually to this esoteric knowledge. By drinking San Pedro, Tony was able to see the threads leading back to Egypt, threads like beams of light travelling through distance and time. He saw the connections to this ancient knowledge and was granted access to the very heart of it.

The ancient Egyptian priests had understood that many centuries later, wise people in the Andes Mountains would be spiritually conscious, seeking the profound truths of the universe, and would come to know San Pedro. And so they had diffused their esoteric knowledge into the spirit of the San Pedro plants, which could be found in northern Peru. The knowledge spread across this area, and from here it trickled to other people across the world who were 'ready' to receive it. It also reached Brazil, through special sacred crystals; the ground in Brazil is filled with these crystals, all containing potent energy.

Tony had one more vision, very bright and very powerful, which completed the circle of his extraordinary experiences in the Andes. It seemed to have come specifically to emphasize the connection between the Inca and the ancient Egyptian civilization. The Pharaohs had had a strong connection to the sun, and held many sun festivals; the sun was the Inca god, and the centre of all their rituals. The temple carvings of both places were very similar to each other, yet unlike those found anywhere else. Then there are the pyramids in the Andes decorated with hieroglyphics. And the vision showed that the perfection of sound, used by the Incas to cut and move enormous rocks, might also have been used by the ancient Egyptians in building the Pyramids.

But most importantly, both cultures had had contact with 'luminous beings' from unknown dimensions. In his visions, Tony witnessed again and again scenes of the ancient peoples interacting with these other beings. How else was it possible for these ancient civilizations to have been so advanced? It was clear that both peoples had had access to a higher intelligence – philosophy, art, physics, medicine, alchemical and esoteric knowledge of all kinds – that had been vouchsafed to them on their journeys to other realms.

Tony realized that the essence of Shamanism traced its roots back to ancient Egypt; and that his future journeys would take him there. But these would not be physical journeys. His experiences across the Andes had been intense, remarkable, expansive, infinitely enriching. Now his external search here was coming to an end.

He thanked the South American Shamans for their wisdom, and particularly the *Huachuma* for introducing him to San Pedro and sharing their knowledge of it with him. His journeying with San Pedro had taken him to unimagined places, and was a hugely significant marker on his path towards Enlightenment. He realized now that the wisdom of San Pedro was to become a major part of his future work and teachings.

Chapter Seven
Moving On
The Caribbean/Australasia/Europe

The Amazonian Rain Forest, North Western Bolivia and the Andes Mountains in Peru had been home to Tony for some years now. His journey though the physical terrain of these countries, and his explorations through the spiritual depths of the different traditions of Shamanism that he'd encountered, had changed his life forever. He knew now that he had learnt everything that he needed to learn from the South American Shamans. It was time to take stock.

It was clear to Tony that the practice and teaching of Shamanism would be his life's work. He also realized that he was now able to work alone, and that this was what he needed to do. It was no longer necessary for him to be physically in any particular place; he was able to work anywhere. He felt enormously empowered, extraordinarily blessed, and truly free; free from any ties to anyone, and free to live wherever he chose. He knew that he wanted to live somewhere within easy access of South America, which he loved, and where he intended to continue travelling and working. And he knew that he would be 'guided' to the right place – which turned out to be the Caribbean. He decided to go and set up home there.

On the way he stopped for a while in Ecuador, and when he came to leave he had one of the scariest experiences of his life. When he arrived at passport control to board his flight out of Ecuador, he was stopped by a customs official who arrested him. He was locked up in a small room with no explanation and left to stew. He wracked his brain to think of what he could possibly have done to warrant his arrest, but could think of nothing. Then a more sinister thought crossed his mind: he had been apprehended because of what they thought he had done; this was truly scary. He needed all his spiritual wisdom to stay focused in the moment and not give space to his fear; he connected to his spiritual centre, knowing, profoundly, that if he stayed connected, nothing really awful would happen to him.

Eventually, an immigration police officer came into the room and began to question him. He was interrogated for several hours, as the suspicious police wanted to know exactly what he had been doing in Ecuador. He had a hard time explaining to a police officer who had to 'follow the rules' that he was a spiritual teacher and healer. They were not interested in Tony's story, and were convinced that he was lying. After several hours of questioning, it transpired that on his arrival in Ecuador the immigration official had stamped his visa with the wrong entry date and so when he came to leave, his visa had already expired and he was arrested for "outstaying his welcome" – obviously for sinister reasons. It troubled him greatly that people suffer so much hassle in this life due to other people's inflexibility and stupidity. Finally he was released and summarily bundled onto the next plane out.

He eventually arrived on the island of St. Barthelemy [known locally as 'St. Barts'] in the French West Indies, shaken, exhausted and somewhat sombre. He had been invited there by a young woman yoga teacher whom he'd met on his travels and who had been interested in his work. And he immediately fell in love – with the place, not the yoga teacher. He decided to stay… It was a great place to be, with beautiful beaches, laidback people and a wonderful climate. He stayed with the yoga teacher and her boyfriend for a few days, then found a small place on the beach to rent very cheaply. It was good to take some time out, just relaxing, meeting people and enjoying life.

The culture of the island greatly appealed to Tony: French, filtered through the more indolent ethos of the Caribbean. He loved the delicious tropical juices, and the food – French, spiced with African influences to create exotic and mouth-watering dishes. And he loved the local people, their relaxed lifestyle, their friendly and easy-going manner, their unhurried and accepting attitude to life. Work somehow got done, but it never seemed to be anyone's priority.

The original native population of the islands had been Indian, but they had been killed off hundreds of years before. Then Africans were brought over as slaves by the colonizing Europeans. Now Africans comprised about ten percent of the population, the rest being a mixed bag of Europeans. The way of life seemed to combine the best possible mix of its varied heritage.

Tony felt that he was in Paradise. He was living very simply and hardly spent any money; tropical fruits grew in abundance and could be picked and eaten at will. He allowed himself to spend some weeks enjoying the sun and the sea, rest and relaxation, and some pleasant company. But eventually, his money did run out. It was time to start work.

Everyone on the beach knew that Tony was a Shamanic healer, and word travelled fast on the island. When he was ready to start work, there was already a queue of people waiting to try out his Shamanic skills. By this time, he had gathered an impressive pharmacopoeia, consisting of herbal remedies that he had learnt from the different Shamans with whom he'd lived, in the Amazon Rain Forest and the Andes Mountains, and also many additional plants that he was discovering in the Caribbean through his own intuition and connectedness to the place. He made his medicines by combining herbs that he had brought with him with local healing herbs and plants.

Healing became the major focus of his work. Living on this idyllic island, making his own natural remedies and working as a healer, he felt that he had truly come home. The memory of his grandmother's medicines for his maladies as a child resonated strongly with him. In fact, growing out of the illnesses and suffering that had plagued his own childhood, he had started healing instinctively as a small child. Spending a lot of time in nature, he had often come across a small sick animal, or a bird that had broken its wing. He would hold the sick or injured creature in his hands and give it love. He knew that by connecting to its spirit in this spontaneous way he had been able to increase its own life force and so help it to heal. And he understood now that the most potent ingredient of this healing had been pure love. His own childhood forays into the world of plant and herbal healing had in fact been the early precursor of the work he was doing now.

What he had been doing, in fact, as a child, was energy healing, though of course he didn't know this at the time. What he did then was purely intuitive. Now he was able to use this same intuitive healing, together with the deep Shamanic knowledge that he had acquired, and his own unconditional love, in the service of the many people who came to him in need – tourists, local people, and many people who came to work on the island for short periods of time. In the most natural way, Tony was continuing a practice that had always been a part of his life.

Many Westerners started coming to Tony for healing, people with serious diseases such as cancer or AIDS, as well as those who were not physically ill but felt that their lives needed repairing in some way. He would start his healing sessions by diagnosing the sickness through a 'hands on' process: by entering into a meditative state and feeling over a person's body, he was able to detect which organs were not functioning properly. He would then treat the malfunctioning organs with herbal remedies, and also give the person hands on healing, breaking up energy blocks and increasing the flow of 'chi', life-energy, helping the muscles to relax and the person to let go of tension and stress. In this way, the blood would begin to flow freely again and so oxygenate the whole body, bringing renewed health and vitality to the patient. However if, during a healing session, he felt a serious malfunction in an organ, he would also suggest that the person see a qualified medical doctor.

Gradually, Tony started to talk to the patients about areas of their lives in which they might be 'stuck' and began to take them, if they were willing, on a spiritual journey. For this is really the beginning of all healing. Very gently, he would help them to see their lives with new eyes and open them up to new possibilities. He found that generally people would open up to him in ways that made it possible for him to give them guidance and help them to move on.

As his healing work began to expand, Tony also started to teach small groups of people. He was teaching the first steps into spiritual consciousness based on Shamanic principles, unlocking doorways for people who were keen to learn but who, perhaps, were not yet aware of their spiritual path.

As he worked with people and gained their trust, he was able to help them on their journey, showing them how to make contact with their own higher self, to trust their own intuition and wisdom, to connect more deeply to nature and open themselves up to receive the blessings of the universe; to begin to feel their own divinity within, as they connected to the Divine in the All That Is. Slowly and gently, Tony was beginning to change people's lives.

The framework that he used for his teaching was Shamanic ritual, and he taught what could loosely be defined as classical Shamanism. This incorporated the use of many Shamanic symbols and artifacts: the drum, the rattle, the use of smoke, sometimes animal and bird artifacts, crystals or special stones. But he wore no special robes, being quite happy to stick to jeans and a T-shirt, the unofficial 'uniform' of most people on the island. He followed traditional Shamanic practices and used their sacred drinks. This was distilled, of course, through the sieve of his own life experiences: the frequent physical suffering and spiritual questioning of his childhood, the intense influence of the two years that he'd spent in the Zen Buddhist monastery, and his years of work with the Shamans in South America.

Word of mouth spreads quickly in this part of the world, and his 'small groups' soon began to attract a lot of attention. He started to travel around the local area giving talks and holding workshops, as more and more people wanted to come and learn about Shamanism, spirituality, and a more 'connected' and joyous way of living. And so Tony began to 'open doors' and lead people to take their first tentative steps along their spiritual path.

Through the very efficient 'grapevine' that operated on St Bart's, it also became known that Tony was able to predict the future. Many people came to test this out, curious to see if it were true, and interested to know what they would be told about their own future lives. As he was able to tell them many things about their past experiences that they knew to be true – and that he could not possibly have known in the normal way – they began to trust his future predictions. As those who had seen him told their friends, and they told their friends, people began flocking to him from all around the area, and then from further afield.

But after a while, Tony discontinued this work. He felt that people had to experience their own journeys, and telling them what would happen in the future was counter-productive. It was not in the best interests of people's spiritual growth, where a core part of the lesson is to learn to trust, to accept what is and welcome the unknown without fear.

Along with his healing work and teaching, Tony now started to lead guided meditation workshops, taking people on a journey into their deepest selves. He used the Shamanic concepts of the cave and the tree as a portal to travel to the Underworld, the seat of the subconscious and a person's deepest level of understanding.

The tree is an archetypal image found in many traditions. The Evergreen Tree was a symbol of eternal life among the ancient Egyptians and Chinese. The Tree of Life, with its ten *Sefirot* [levels of Divine Essences] of the Kabbalah; the Cosmic Tree, connecting the celestial realms to the earth [Shamanism]; the origins of the Christmas Tree, traced to a German medieval play about Adam and Eve, suggesting a 'Paradise Tree'; these routes are all seen as ways of leading us to deeper knowledge. The World Tree of many mythologies connects heaven, earth and the underworld, symbolizing prophetic wisdom. The tree can be seen as an apt metaphor for spiritual journeying: with its roots extending beneath the ground, it takes us into the deepest, darkest part of ourselves; its branches, reaching up to the sky, draw light down through our whole being, enlightening the darkness deep within.

The cave provides another way of leading us into our own depths. Merlin's Cave, Aladdin's Cave, the Cave that Mohammed entered, and the Shamanic Cave, used as a portal to Shamanic 'journeying' since ancient times, are all symbolic of a doorway leading to the world of the subconscious. And Plato's Cave, of course, helping us to know what's real by showing us a shadow reality.

As word of Tony's work spread further around the Caribbean, the workshops on Shamanism rapidly began to expand; there seemed to be a great hunger among Westerners to learn about this ancient tradition. His workshops among small groups of people who mostly knew each other were growing exponentially, and as they grew they inevitably became more impersonal. They began to require a framework, organization, people to arrange the practicalities and take care of the details. Tony was becoming an institution.

And so a group of people sprang up spontaneously around him; they organized his schedule, planned his meetings and took care of all the arrangements. An 'inner circle' of devotees was formed, people who were hungry for spiritual guidance; and they saw in Tony a miracle teacher who could move them out of their 'stuck' lives and offer them spiritual succour. They were not paid, but in exchange for looking after the practical side of his life, they had the privilege of being close to Tony and his work and had ready access to his ear.

In fact, Tony probably spent more time giving his energy and care to the people 'helping' him than it would have taken him to organize his own life. But although he says that he in no way sees himself as a 'guru', people seem to attach themselves to him, and are happy to work for him for no material reward, as long as they can spend time in his presence, and perhaps feel 'special' by association with him.

So Tony continued to live on St Barthelemy, working as a Shamanic healer and teacher, learning more about local medicinal plants and healing, and moving ever more deeply into the realms of Shamanic wisdom. He taught Shamanism as it was practised by the indigenous people of the Andes, explaining it in such a way that Western people could understand it and incorporate its practices into their daily lives. He was working and living the life that he was meant to live. He would make forays to South America to work, perhaps for a few weeks at a time, and then return to the island to recoup, and continue his work there. He was deeply joyous, at peace with himself and the universe. He was living in a place that he loved, this magical mystical island, epicentre of spiritual power and Shamanic wisdom. He really intended to stay there forever.

But the universe had other plans for him. Gradually, Tony felt guided to travel more and more to South America, where his work continued to flourish.

As his reputation grew, word of the 'white-skinned Shaman' travelled far and fast, and he became much sought after, way beyond the borders of South America. Through his old connections to the university of New England in New South Wales, he was invited to work in Australia. On his way, he decided to spend some time on the Pacific Islands, and ended up on Morea, a tiny island next to Tahiti, the largest of the hundred and thirty islands that make up French Polynesia.

Tony visited many of the islands of the five archipelagos, working with local Shamans on each of them. He realized that the basic tenets of Shamanism were similar across the world, though of course there were variations based upon local customs and traditions, and very often on tribal superstitions as well. The local Shamans were happy to work with Tony, and this proved a most productive partnership for him. Ever curious, he expanded his knowledge of local herbs and medicinal plants, and was now frequently invited to work as a healer alongside native Shamans. He also continued to hold workshops of Shamanic teaching and guided meditations.

He arrived in Australia in the spring of 1993, established his base in Sydney and began to teach. At first he worked only with small groups and by invitation only; there was no advertising. Again, a small group of dedicated people grew up around him. Enthusiastically committed to his work, they wanted to spread his teachings and were happy to do anything for him that would help to promote his work. And like the small group that had formed around him on St. Barthelemy, the people here too were happy to work for him without remuneration, their reward being the inspiration of being close to him, one of the 'chosen few'. So they set about organizing his talks and workshops, meetings and healing sessions. Perhaps it would be more accurate to say that in their enthusiasm, they tried to organize *him*.

But Tony – as anyone who has ever tried to organize anything for him will ruefully attest – is 'unorganizable'; he is totally unpredictable and does not fit easily into anybody's plans. He works according to his own truth, as it manifests to him, moment by moment. At this time, going against the expansionist 'wisdom' of his organizers, he wanted to work one to one, or with very small groups. Occasionally, he would agree to hold a large workshop for which scores of people would sign up and then, on the day of the workshop, he might cancel: he felt that the energy was not propitious, or that someone who was ill needed him urgently for a healing session, or the spirits were telling him that this particular workshop was not in the highest good of everyone involved. In short, Tony was a free spirit – and an organizer's nightmare!

He lived, as he always had, very simply; everything that he owned in the world fitted easily into one small backpack. He was not interested in making a lot of money or becoming famous. His purpose in life was to spread the teachings of Shamanism, to move people forward on their spiritual journeys and open their eyes to a more conscious, more joyous, more fulfilling way of living.

But after he'd been working in Australia for a short while, word spread further afield and he was invited to teach in Singapore and Hong Kong. Tony did not want to go; there were plenty of people close by who needed his help. His organizers tried to persuade, cajole, badger him to accept the invitation. Their arguments ranged from "you owe it to the world to spread your teachings" to "we need the money to create a bigger and better organization". But Tony did his own thing – and stayed where he was.

At this time he was living in Queensland, in a part of the country with a tropical climate, which he loved. He felt at home. His neighbours were Aboriginal people, and he would spend time on their reservation, talking with them and getting to know their way of life. He continued to give one to one healing sessions, and work with small groups. But, for the moment at least, he decided to work without his 'organizers'. He wanted to be free, to come and go as he pleased, to do the work that felt right for him in the moment, to travel when and where the fancy took him.

And where the fancy took him was to Cairns in eastern Queensland, which then became his base. And it was here, one sunny afternoon, that Sylvia walked into one of his workshops – and into his life. Before meeting her in the flesh, Tony had 'seen her' in a vision, and knew that she would be his life partner. But when he met her, it was quite a surprise. She was working in the foreign exchange department of an old established bank, where she had an excellent and 'prestigious' job. She was well-paid, well-off, and well-satisfied with her life. She owned her own luxurious home with a swimming pool in a natural rain forest just outside the city. When Tony first saw it, he said it looked like an advertisement in a glamorous property magazine. She drove an up-market 'posh' car and wanted for nothing materially. She was also an aromatherapy masseuse and performed aerobics. She was svelte, dark and pretty, but hardly the personification of the life partner of a spiritual teacher.

Tony was patient. He knew that ultimately she would become his wife, and he was happy to bide his time and enjoy overseeing her transformation. He watched with gentle amusement as slowly, one by one, she began to relinquish the trappings of her successful lifestyle. Defying all the logic of her bright well-trained mind, she resigned from her job, sold her house, gave away her expensive clothes, and threw in her lot with Tony. When she was ready, they moved in together, and founded the Samara Foundation, a non-profit organization established to promulgate his teachings.

After spending a few months together in Australia, Tony decided to take her back to the Caribbean. He wanted to show her the islands where he had spent such happy times, and intended to continue living and working there for a while. Sylvia was excited to go, and share with Tony the place he loved so much. But when she got there, she found the tropical climate very difficult: she felt washed-out most of the time, unable to summon up the energy for even the simplest of tasks. And so they left and returned to Australia.

A few days after they left, the Caribbean suffered its worst hurricane for a hundred years. Boats out at sea were lifted like tiny toys and deposited on land, trees that had stood erect for hundreds of years were blown down like paper straws, houses were washed away. A friend of Tony's told him later that for days the noise of the destruction had been ear-splitting, sounding as though jet planes were flying through their heads. Tony's own little house at the top of a hill was completely destroyed. Thousands of people lost their property, many of them, their lives. Had Tony still been there... He blesses the synchronicity of the universe.

Tony re-established his base in Australia and continued his work there, teaching and healing. Now, with Sylvia by his side, he felt guided to travel more extensively; first criss-crossing Australia, then moving on to teach in Singapore, Bali, the United States [mainly California] and Canada. They went together to meet her parents in New Zealand, where Sylvia was born, and decided to marry. Tony did not believe that a marriage ceremony was important; what mattered was the way you lived and the inner commitment you made to the other person. But it was important to Sylvia's parents, and he wanted to do the right thing for her family.

They married on a beach in New Zealand, near where they were living, under a pohotukua tree. This tree, growing on rocks on the beach, provided a magnificent canopy of bright red flowers under which to hold the ceremony. It was a simple wedding: the legal side of it was performed by the Registrar of Weddings, a very correct, businesslike man who didn't hide his astonishment at the informality of the setting. Then they both signed the Register and he pronounced them legally to be husband and wife. Just two friends were there to witness their exchange of rings and their vows. Later in the day, they would go to Roturua for a private ceremony of their own.

Roturua is the birthplace of the Maori culture, very different from the rest of New Zealand, which is largely European. Sylvia had always felt a strong connection to this place, and believes that she may have Maori ancestors. Roturua, sacred to the Maoris, is a magical place: a volcanic site, the earth bubbles up with a continuous flow of hot mud and steam. The young couple stood transfixed, watching the molten eruptions rise and fall. Then, in a dramatic gesture, they threw their engagement rings into the mud and watched as they were accepted into the bubbling liquid, melting and becoming one with each other and with the earth.

Before the ceremony, they took a steam bath together. The Maoris had put a fence around a natural pool with steam coming out of the earth, and they sat in it for three hours, soaking up the steam and the magical atmosphere, transported to another world. Sitting there naked, at one with Creation, this was symbolic of their purification for one another and their connection to *Pachamama*. Then they cooked traditional Maori food – *taro* steamed with vegetables, which they cooked in a metal container with holes in it, which they put into the hot ground. In half an hour, they had a delicious meal, which they ate outside in the beauty of nature.

At dusk, it was time for the ceremony. Sylvia wore a long white Mexican dress with coloured embroidery around the neck and sleeves; Tony was dressed in a South American rainbow-coloured shirt and white trousers. Neither wore shoes, wanting to feel the earth beneath their bare feet. It was a beautiful ceremony, just the two of them, alone in the universe. They exchanged the wedding rings they had bought from the Maoris just before the ceremony – jade rings, known as *punamu* in Maori, which are believed to be stones of peace. Then, holding both hands, looking deeply into each other's eyes, into each other's souls, they asked for the blessings of Great Spirit to be with them always, as they made their vows of unconditional love and commitment to each other, forever.

They spent their wedding night up in the mountains of Roturua, under a canopy of stars, embraced by each other, by the abundant gifts of the universe and the All That Is. A sacred union, blessed by their love for one another and the love of the Divine.

After their marriage Tony and Sylvia continued to travel, wherever his work took him. His teaching 'circuit' now included Australia, Bali, Singapore, California, Canada, the islands of French Polynesia and the Caribbean. They also went to Bolivia and Peru, where Tony wanted to continue his work, and also show Sylvia the places that had been important landmarks on his journey before he met her.

Following a period of extensive travelling, they returned to New Zealand. Sylvia had had a lifelong love affair with the Polynesian people, the Maoris, and wanted to stay there for ever. Tony was happy to do this, and they set up home on Waihiki Island. Sylvia was offered a high-powered job remodulating the computer system of a large company, and Tony continued with his teaching and healing work. He was also enjoying teaching Sylvia about Shamanism and spirituality. In all ways, he felt that he had come home.

But again, the universe had other plans for him. He had a vision in which his guides told him that his work was more needed in Europe, where people were on the whole less connected to their spiritual roots. It was important, he was told, to reach out to these people; in Europe, he could make a real difference to people's lives.

The universe supported his decision to move with two synchronicitous events: his mother, who was now living in Spain, became ill and Tony, as the eldest son, felt that he needed to be there with her. And at the same time Sylvia became pregnant, and Spain seemed a good place to give birth. Spain also offered other advantages. Tony by this time was fluent in Spanish and so could begin to work immediately, without the need of translators. And the temperate climate suited them both.

They arrived in the Costa del Sol, Andalusia, in the spring of 1997, and moved in with Tony's mother. She had to undergo a serious back operation, after which she would need complete bed rest, and a great deal of looking after. Sylvia, pregnant with her first child, needed a lot of time and attention from Tony, as he wanted to prepare for the birth in a Shamanic way. This involved making special meals and keeping to a diet of foods rich in minerals, vitamins, enzymes and vibrant life force; spending as much time together as possible in nature, embracing the stillness and harmony of the natural world, letting it seep deep into Sylvia and her growing baby within; and performing Shamanic ceremonies, connecting to the spirit of the unborn child and preparing it for its earthly incarnation.

This was a time of 'karma yoga' for Tony, selfless service, as he took care of the two women at the centre of his life. He also continued his own Shamanic work, mainly one to one healing. He didn't charge a fee for this but asked for donations – not the soundest of economic decisions, but it felt right spiritually; although Sylvia had now stopped work, and Tony needed to earn money. Living his spiritual path, he knew that if we are open to life's own process, the universe always answers our needs, although not necessarily in a direct way, nor in a way that we might expect.

But in this instance, the answer was immediate and direct. One of Tony's next patients was a wealthy golfer with back problems that orthodox medicine had been unable to cure. Spending a large amount of money, chasing many doctors who, in the event, could not help her, had left her in a lot of pain and quite desperate for a cure. When Tony healed her, she and her husband, who together owned several restaurants in Andalusia, spread the good news. Very soon, a long line of people was knocking on Tony's door – often literally, and at all hours.

When his mother's health improved and she no longer needed his constant care, Tony and Sylvia moved from her home to a little beach house, and though they lived very simply, even simple living costs money. And so, as well as his one on one healing, Tony now began to teach small groups. Without advertising or marketing, people seemed to know about his work, and the small groups very soon grew into very large groups indeed.

As word spread of his work, Tony was invited to appear on a television programme in Gibraltar. This led to many invitations to participate in radio interviews in Spain. As a result of this, he was inundated with work, and too much of his time became taken up with organization. He wanted to teach and guide; he did not want to spend his time sorting out schedules and timetables, booking retreat centres and making travel arrangements.

Then into his life walked another synchronicity of the universe, in the person of Angelina: a Portuguese woman who, with her husband Gabriel, owned Monte Mariposa in the Algarve, Portugal. This was a Centre that they had recently built to house creative classes, workshops and retreats of all kinds. She was excited by Tony's work and wanted to learn more; and so she invited him to come and work at Monte Mariposa. Tony went to visit the Centre and loved it. Angelina and Gabriel, keen for Tony to work there, made him a proposition: they were ready to do all the organizing and marketing; Tony would be free just to teach.

Following the birth of their son, Sai, Tony and Sylvia left Spain and, after living for a while in England where Tony taught in Glastonbury, and where Shara, their second child, was born, they moved to Portugal. Angelina, Gabriel and Tony talked of their vision for Monte Mariposa. Until that time, it had been a Centre for cultural activities, such as music, art and pottery classes, and some 'alternative' therapies like yoga, Reiki and Thai massage. Now, their shared vision was the creation of a 'Spiritual Centre', where Angelina and Gabriel would organize and administrate, and Tony would teach.

As the owners of Monte Mariposa opened up more and more to their own spiritual paths, they committed themselves to creating a Centre of spiritual teaching and guidance. They built the Temple and accommodation down in the valley, in the grounds of Monte Mariposa, especially for Tony and his retreats. This is an idyllic setting for spiritual retreats, separate from the main building at the top of the hill, surrounded by untamed countryside and its own aura of tranquillity and peace.

Fired-up with excitement for his work, and backed by their keen business acumen, Angelina and Gabriel enthusiastically took on the responsibility of all the advertising and administration. For them, it was a way to manifest their dream of establishing a truly spiritual Centre and, with Tony's guidance, move further along their own spiritual paths. Angelina, especially, was a wizard at marketing, and within a short space of time, the Centre really took off and people started to come from all over the world to experience Tony's work.

But this was to be only the first of many Centres in which Tony would teach. He felt that his work was needed in many places in the world. His vision was to create Centres, or Ashrams, in different places, where people who want to work with him, and are committed to the spiritual way of life, would come and live. Others could come for short periods to practise 'karma yoga', or as an 'apprenticeship', to see if the spiritual life really suited them. The residents, as a community, would be responsible for running the Ashrams, and Tony would rotate among them, teaching and working with the people who live in them.

But all this was yet to happen; the vision would take time to materialize. Meanwhile, as a core group of people dedicated to his work formed around him in Portugal, Tony began looking at possible sites for an Ashram: in Portugal, and also in Brazil, Costa Rica and Slovenia – places where the energy felt good, and people were already waiting to work with him.

In the event, Tony established his first Ashram in the Algarve in Portugal, less than an hour's drive from Monte Mariposa. Some benefactors who supported his work generously donated the funds to buy a small piece of land up in the hills near Bouliquieme. The land was a wilderness: old trees, perhaps hundreds of years old, stood witness to the ravages of time. Stones and rocks and dried earth covered the rest of the ground in a carpet of neglect. An old stone ruin, long devoid of human habitation, stood in one corner, the only building there. How could this abandoned piece of land be turned into a habitable home? Trust, said Tony. Trust, yes; and a great deal of hard work.

Not far from the Ashram land was a large villa that was rented out at an exorbitant price to tourists in the summer, but was available for a reasonable rent during the winter. And so it was that a group of people closely involved with Tony's work moved into the Rainbow House to support the work of establishing the Ashram. Tony and Sylvia and their two children, six-year-old Sai and his sister Shara, now two, moved into a house nearby, on the other side of the Ashram land.

As the vision became clear, the people around Tony began to organize. Everyone in the Rainbow House was working in some way with Tony. Most of us were involved with working on the land; I was there to write this book, and this was accepted by everyone as my work. It was also accepted that I was ill [I still had M.E.] and I was not skiving off when I needed to rest. [Somehow, I always managed to do my turn of house cleaning!] Some days I would visit the Ashram, to have a break from my computer and connect with the land – the smell of the earth, the stillness of the air, the old trees watching and smiling on our labours. When I felt well enough, I would do a little gentle digging or weeding, although I believe that this was more of therapeutic benefit for me than a useful contribution to the project. But it gave me a feeling of being part of the communal endeavour, and connected me to the land.

Everyone else in the Rainbow House toiled long and hard on the land, the women as well as the men moving heavy stones or chopping dead branches from the trees. And a few people were even more intrepid: a couple of caravans appeared and a few people settled on the barren land to live and work. One marvellous couple from Lisbon, no longer in the first flush of youth, moved into a tiny wooden hut, with nothing in it but a bed and a table. At this stage, there was no electricity, gas or running water on the Ashram. Often during that long icy winter, one or other of the Ashram residents would make it up the hill to the Rainbow House for a hot shower, a bowl of soup, or a game of backgammon or chess; or just a warm place to be. We became a community. A family.

I had wondered how this rough piece of land could become an Ashram. But when at one stage I was quite ill and didn't visit for three weeks, the transformation that had taken place during that time was astonishing. A prefabricated wooden hut, which would eventually become the office, housed a makeshift kitchen and, under the most primitive conditions, still with no running water and with just one small gas burner, delicious hot food appeared at lunchtime, to keep up the energy and spirits of those working on the land. The old stone ruin was beginning to look more like a house than an abandoned orphan, and a sizeable tract of the land had been cleared for planting.

Plans were drawn up: for every useable space there was a vision of what it would become. Astonishingly to an outsider, perhaps, but in accordance with the spiritual values that hold that we, humans, are here as caretakers of the planet, to live in harmony with nature and not to exploit it, no tree was displaced as the foundations for eco-toilets, showers, yurts, wooden huts and vegetable and fruit gardens were laid. Everything that would come to be was woven through the spaces among the trees, and in the end it all became part of one magical organic whole. It was hard to remember how it had been before.

And so, through that hard but exhilarating winter, a pattern of shared living and working emerged. Tony would come up to the Rainbow House early every morning and lead us in meditation. Then there would be a discussion of what needed to be done that day on the Ashram, and each person would decide what they would do. Every job was voluntary, but difficult tasks were chosen as well as easier and pleasanter ones. No-one was paid; the rewards were the creation of a shared vision, and the opportunity to be close to Tony.

In the early spring of the following year, we held a celebratory dinner in which we ate the first fruits of our labours. Or, more accurately, the first vegetables: lettuces, cherry tomatoes, broccoli and basil shared our table with olives that had been picked and soaked during the previous months and were now ready to eat. We had a feast that both fed our bodies and nourished our souls; this was the result of the work of our own hands. My joy was infinite, though the real work had not been mine; but I was allowed to share in the celebrations.

From April, the Rainbow House would be rented out to tourists; it was time for us to move on. Most chose to move onto the Ashram, where there was now a choice of accommodation: a yurt, which could sleep six or seven, various sizes of tents or a caravan. I needed to return to England where I was scheduled to lead my own healing retreats. I had no idea where I would live when I returned to Portugal a couple of months later, though I had joked to one of the residents that 'a little wooden hut' on the Ashram would be a dream come true. In reality, I expected to rent a small flat somewhere close by.

When I arrived back on the Ashram to see Tony and the others, he greeted me with his inscrutable smile and a mysterious "Come with me". He took me to the far corner of the Ashram, where a small wooden hut, that hadn't been there when I left, stood ready to house me. It meant that I could live on the Ashram with the others and be part of the community. I felt that I was truly coming home.

But the romantic idyll of 'a little wooden cabin' didn't quite fit the reality. Actually, it was more a garden shed than a cabin in the woods; if I stood in the middle, I could almost touch all four walls. It was unbearably hot that summer and my little wooden home was like an oven. A fan, installed to alleviate the worst of the heat, merely moved around the hot air – and blew the pages of my manuscript in all directions. At night, I would wrap myself in towels soaked in cold water to try to relieve the worst of the heat that had built up, and get some sleep.

I stuck it out for six weeks, but I was feeling more and more ill; my M.E. was seriously aggravated by the heat. I could not go on living there. Then the universe stepped in: an opportunity arose for me to move into a small room in the old stone ruin that had been refurbished. And there I stayed.

Tony's vision for the Ashram was of a deeply spiritual community, living and working together for the highest good of all. He believes that community is the healthiest way to live for everyone, but is particularly pertinent to the spiritual life. There has to be discipline and rules, as in any community; but this is in order to stop people from becoming too wrapped up in mundane nonsense and free them to concentrate on what is really important – the spiritual journey.

Spirituality, of course, is not only about meditating or going on retreats. Spirituality is about the way we live, the way we relate to each other and other creatures; the way we care for the planet. It should inform every aspect of daily living: how we cook our food, tend the land or clean the toilets is all part of spirituality. Tony reminded us – frequently – that Zen Buddhist monks clean their own toilets, with joy!

And so the Ashram became established. A core group of about ten of us lived there and were responsible for running the Ashram. We worked and ate together, and made all decisions by a democratic process, though we opted for consensus rather than a vote. Other people came and went, wanting to have an experience of living a shared spiritual way of life. Some stayed for a day or a week to try it out; others returned again and again for short periods, and sometimes decided to stay for good. We welcomed everyone and journeyed together, along our own spiritual paths. Everyone who came to stay on the Ashram, for a few weeks or a few days, enriched our lives in some way.

Life on the Ashram is really about two things: 'karma yoga', selfless service, and 'bahkti yoga', the way of the heart. When new people came to the Ashram, Tony asked them to consider what they could give to the Ashram, not what they could get from it. Frequently, they would be given the least pleasant jobs to start with, to see if they were really committed to the idea of selfless service. 'Bahkti yoga' involves letting go of the outside world and the demands of the ego, and devotion to the higher self; letting the heart guide you to a place of compassion and unconditional love. It is about learning to love the divine within oneself, and so connect to the divine within everyone and everything else.

Tony believes that we need three things in order to realize our higher spiritual purpose: to live in nature and in harmony with all life, to live in a spiritual community, and to have a spiritual teacher. The Ashram was founded to fulfil these three conditions. It is important that everyone living in the community takes responsibility for themselves and for the smooth running of the community, and does not become dependent on Tony. He sees his role as spiritual teacher and guide, not manager or caretaker. Everyone working with Tony has their own path to walk, their own destiny to fulfil. Tony's role is simply to be a mirror for each person, showing them where they are on their journey, where they are 'stuck', and how they can move forward.

During this time, Tony continued his work as a Shamanic healer, and his spiritual teaching. Shamanism was the medium through which he worked, through which he manifested his spiritual questing; it had become the language of his teachings, the portal through which he was able to guide others along their journeys into their deepest, highest selves, to realize their own greatest potential. His journey through the deeper beliefs and practices of Shamanism was to take him to a place beyond, to a place where he would further develop his own philosophy of life, his own spirituality and teachings, though his work would remain deeply rooted in Shamanism.

The way that Tony teaches makes Shamanism accessible to people living in the West, in the twenty-first century. He demonstrates how this most ancient wisdom is relevant to our lives today, how it can enhance and enrich the way we live and help us to connect to our own most profound spiritual truth.

Chapter Eight
Shamanic Wisdom for our Age

In ancient times, those magical times when our ancestors first walked upon the earth, the human race recognized itself as part of the natural world, and acknowledged the natural world as part of itself. The unity and harmonious order of Creation was apparent to all. All creatures that walked the earth, on two or four or many legs, flew across its skies or swam in its oceans were understood by humans to be interconnected and interrelated. The ebb and flow of night and day, of seasonal differences, of the changing weather, held mystery as well as practical application. The life of dreams and of the waking world were interwoven; the physical and the metaphysical embraced one another without separation. Visible and invisible worlds were known to be entwined, and our ancestors walked the sacred path between the two. This was the world inhabited by the first Shamans…

Since time immemorial, Shamans have been able to inhabit other realities, deeper dimensions of consciousness, invisible worlds of spirit and mystery. They have been a link between the metaphysical world and the world that we perceive as physical reality. They have charted the interconnecting threads of the Web of Life, and served as a bridge between realms. They have known and carried spiritual truths down the centuries and across the world.

One of the great services that Shamanism renders to the world is the map that it draws for us, reconnecting human consciousness with nature and the hidden world of spirit. This Shamanic map webs the connection between all that is within us, unknown and unseen, and everything in the natural world that we do not perceive as part of our everyday reality. It awakens our sense of awe and wonder and our acceptance of the rightness of everything within the All That Is, as it is.

The world that the Shaman inhabits has come into being through balance. Balance is achieved through the interaction of the two polarities that exist within everything. Everything in creation is part of a duality: heaven and earth, day and night, sun and moon, masculine and feminine, life and death. But they are not seen as two opposing forces, for nothing in creation is separate from anything else; neither are they the two ends of a line, for nothing is linear. Rather, everything is interrelated and infinite, in constant circular motion. There are no beginnings and no ends. All 'opposites' are two aspects of a union, forces forever feeding into each other, which is their role in the harmony of the cosmos. And neither could exist without the other. When the Shaman enters his ecstatic state, he may be said to be sitting at the still centre of all existent dualities; dissolving all distinctions that separate matter, he embraces the mystery of totality, becoming part of the divine unity of the All That Is.

Shamanism has bequeathed to us a profound and lasting wisdom, the knowledge that everything within Creation is imbued with Spirit. Spirit is the life force that vibrates within every being and within every part of the natural world; and indeed within *Pachamama*, Mother Earth, herself. Spirituality is the invisible essence that infuses us with the power of imagination and creativity, intuition and spontaneity, curiosity and courage; it transcends the intellect and reaches into the deepest part of ourselves, our heart.

Spirit is the hidden power of our lives. Our physical body has the *appearance* of being, our spirit is what *is*, the spark of the Divine within us that breathes our life. Living within Spirit gives meaning and purpose to life, as we understand that nothing is chance or random or coincidence; everything happens for a reason, though we might not see or understand it. There is no longer the confusion of the mundane world, as we are able to direct our lives with focus and power. Living within spirit colours all our experiences, opening up new perceptions, new visions, giving us access to growing wisdom and untold joy.

The way of the Shaman is a sacred way. It personifies awareness of and harmony with the sacredness of all life. It offers a way of awakening consciousness to the perfection of the natural world and all life within it. It teaches acceptance of and gratitude for what is, and humility in the knowledge that we humans are a tiny part of the cosmos, not its rulers. No life form, including humans, is superior or inferior to any other.

Shamans believe that every life form has within it an awareness of itself and its own place in the universal scheme of things, and its connection in a circular never-ending flow of energy to the universal Web of which we are all a part. They believe in the immutable order of the universe and the understanding that the Earth, on which we are all dependent for our survival, is also a conscious, breathing and evolving being, subject to the laws of its own orderly existence.

Shamanism is the awakening, within each person, of the knowledge that we are mutually interdependent; just as the universe nourishes us, so we are here as guardians and caretakers of the planet. Within each person, Shamanism espouses the indivisibility of the physical, mental, emotional and spiritual, each feeding and nurturing every other aspect of the individual. If something is out of kilter in one element, it will affect all the others. The way of balance and harmony is achieved through our recognition of our interconnectedness with the energies of the natural world, and our connection to Spirit.

All spirituality talks of living in the moment. Shamanism teaches us a way of rooting ourselves in the present moment through its reverence for nature and the healing power of the natural world. Spending time silently in the beauty of nature helps us to connect more deeply to ourselves and experience joy in the moment. We are all part of nature and we need to remember this, especially when we are rushed off our feet in our bustling office, or busy with kids, cooking or cleaning in our high-rise city apartment.

If we open our hearts to the Shamanic tradition, it can show us a way of living our lives, in the West, in the twenty-first century, that will bring peace and love and harmony to us as individuals and can enhance and enrich all our relationships. Connecting experientially to the sacredness of life, brings us into a relationship of profound respect and rightness – with ourselves, with others and with the universe. In this way, Shamanism can lead us along the path towards our own individual spiritual development; a path of compassion, joy and deep love.

In the thousands of years since the first Shamans walked the earth, humanity has evolved and advanced, but not all development has been positive.

In the West, we have largely lost touch with our roots, with the sacredness of the natural world, and mostly with the spiritual realms of our own lives. We have forgotten how to seek out the unseen, the unknown, the unmanifest. We have become prisoners of a cultural trance, living within the narrow confines of a mundane reality that we ourselves have created, thinking that this is all there is, blindly inhabiting a tiny corner of the universe of possibilities.

Tony shares the Shamanic belief that all the misery and suffering and oppression in the world are caused by our disconnectedness from nature and the natural order; which means, of course, that we are also disconnected from ourselves: as individuals, as societies and as nations. The urbanization and industrialization of modern society has cut us off from the understanding of the natural laws of the universe. This has resulted in massive imbalance, disharmony and alienation for us in our individual lives, and this in turn has led to our wide-scale exploitation and abuse of the planet.

As a species, we humans have never before in our history been so destructive of all that has nurtured and sustained us. Global warming is already beginning to create havoc; climate changes, the melting of the polar ice caps in both the Arctic and the Antarctic and rising sea levels are already causing devastation. The balance of our ecology is in grave danger and the very life of our planet is being threatened. If this process of destruction is not halted very soon it will be irreversible. Rome is burning. Time *is* running out. And it affects us all.

The rain forests, the throbbing heart of Mother Earth, are being destroyed so fast that in Africa they are rapidly turning into desert. At the time of the Pharaohs, what is now the Sahara desert was green and lush and fertile. Now the desert is encroaching in all directions, and if this wanton destruction is not halted, now, the rain forests in Africa will soon disappear altogether. In Indonesia, Thailand, Malaysia, Burma, in fact in the whole of Southeast Asia, the rain forests are being cut down at such speed that in twenty years time there will hardly be a tree left standing.

When Tony was living with the Shamans in the Amazon, he witnessed the beginning of the destruction of the rain forest on a massive scale. Much of this was done to provide land for raising cattle to feed the American craze for hamburgers. Sometimes, whole areas of forest were *burnt* because felling the trees was considered too slow, and it was more profitable to clear the land quickly by burning it than to cut down the trees and sell the wood. There were parts of the rain forest that Tony visited where you could see – and smell – nothing but smoke for miles around. These pictures of burning trees are printed indelibly in his memory to this day.

But somehow the destruction of the Amazon Rain Forest – the largest single area of rain forest in the world – caught the attention of the media in the West and the popular imagination of the younger generation. Now, due to pressure groups across the Western world, the rate of destruction has begun to slow. But it needs to stop altogether. Now.

According to scientific research, the hole in the ozone layer has never been larger than it is today. In Argentina and Australia, which are closest to Antarctica where the damage is greatest, sheep are going blind and indigenous plants cannot survive because the UV factor is so strong. Farmers are worried that because of the UV factor, they won't be able to export their cereals. And Australia has the highest rate of skin cancer in the world.

Across the globe, oceans and rivers are violated with toxins. In some places they are so polluted with chemicals and hormones that little children are already reaching puberty. Whole species of animals and plants are becoming extinct. Nuclear waste, dumped into our seas, can take *two thousand* years to decompose. In the West, we are so out of touch with the natural world that we seem oblivious to the fact that in the eco-system everything is interdependent; if one element is seriously out of balance, the whole system will collapse like a pile of dominoes. We urgently need to consider the consequences of our actions.

In the name of profit and 'progress' our planet is being wantonly destroyed. We know this, and at last the world is beginning to take note. But even seemingly well-intentioned projects, based on a genuine concern to help people, can also cause serious damage if they are not undertaken in harmony with nature's purpose. There must be thousands of cases of this happening all over the world, motivated by people who are convinced that they're doing something worthwhile and beneficial. I'll cite just two examples.

In the old Soviet Union, huge areas of forest were cut down in order to create farmland for poor workers, and give them and their families a sustainable life. But when the forests were cut down, the rains washed away the soil, forever, and the lives of those workers' grandchildren were irredeemably blighted.

In Australia rabbits, not native to that part of the world, were brought in at a time of food shortages to feed people. But the rabbits multiplied so fast, and ate so ravenously, that they destroyed twenty per cent of the natural vegetation of the continent. When the plants that had held the soil together were eaten, the soil was blown away, and now land that was once fertile has become arid desert.

In both these cases, the planners were convinced of the justice of their cause, and acted out of noble intentions. But they were not listening to nature; they were listening to their own ideas of what they thought was important, without considering the ecological consequences. As human beings, we have to understand that we are a minute part of the cosmos, not its centre, and not its masters. And that it is incumbent upon us to behave in ways that are in harmony with the natural laws of being. We need to understand this now, and act upon this knowledge. For if we do not, our children will not inherit a world fit to inhabit.

We have been brainwashed by the huge advances in science and technology into thinking that they will give us the tools to rule over the universe: first the earth, and then space. What hubris! Our concept of reality is actually extremely limited; we consider reality to be only that which we can experience with our five senses, what is demonstrably provable, and what can be analyzed by rational thought. Our consciousness sees life in materialistic terms, assuming that our natural environment is hostile and so it is our right, even our duty, to subdue and conquer it.

Furthermore it presumes that all of nature has been created for our benefit and therefore is ours to use as we see fit. Our deity, if we believe in God at all, is something outside ourselves, to be obeyed without question, and worshipped from afar. This may also fuel our self-righteousness and lead to separatism and, indeed, extremist actions in the name of our separate identity. We need to open ourselves up to the possibility that our Western mind-set may not be the healthiest one, either for the planet – or for ourselves. By trying to fight against nature rather than working in harmony and cooperation with it for our mutual benefit, we are destroying both ourselves and the natural world in the process.

Our only hope of reversing this runaway destruction and saving the planet, and thereby ourselves, is to reconnect with nature and respect the laws of the natural world. In other words, to reconnect to our Shamanic roots, lost centuries ago in our relentless march towards 'civilization' and 'progress'. For the wisdom of Shamanism has never been more relevant to the human race than it is today, nor more urgently needed. Our spiritual journey, as Tony teaches, is not only about the way we each live with ourselves and with each other, but must include our own individual commitment to taking care of the planet.

The way of the Shaman shows us another way to live. A gentler, more ethical way. The way of Tony Samara. Tony shows us a way of healing ourselves and healing the planet; a way of getting back in touch with our ancient roots, of reconnecting to the power of nature, to the divinity within us and all around us. A way of living from the heart.

Long ago, humans and animals shared the earth and lived together in harmony. Our ancestors talked with animals, trees and plants; they listened to them and respected their wisdom. To Shamans, animals are still seen as "four-legged people", just as birds are "flying people" and trees are "standing people"; all are our relations. To the Shaman, every living being is part of the interconnected Web of Life, the infinite energy that breathes the universe.

This process of connecting to the natural world teaches us about spirituality and leads us more deeply into our own essential spiritual being. Think about it, where would you naturally feel more spiritual, more connected to the All That Is, more at peace: sitting on a mountainside looking up at a sky full of stars, or riding to work in the rush hour tube in London? Though of course, once we are in touch with our spiritual core, we can experience it wherever we are and discern the Divine within everything. But it is certainly easier to feel 'connected' and live spiritually when we are living in the heart of nature.

Shamanism is simply – and profoundly – a deep connection to nature. As we have said, it calls on us to respect all life and not to assume that we humans are lords and masters over any other life form. Accepting this will fundamentally change the way we live. If we respect all life, then we cannot kill or harm or behave violently towards any living being, be it human or animal. If we respect all life, then we must also respect ourselves and our place within the natural order.

Understanding this may give us the courage to start looking within, to see how our life may be unbalanced and what we may need to do to change it. Then we may begin to live in harmony with ourselves, uniting the disparate and often warring parts of ourselves, thus growing towards wholeness and maturity. This will lead us to live in harmony with others and with the universe, creating a life that will nourish and nurture us, as well as the planet. When we recognize that nature feeds us emotionally and spiritually, as well as physically, our whole worldview changes.

The cosmos communicates with us and teaches us in many ways: through other humans, spirit guides, animals, trees, plants, mountains, stones, birds, the weather. As we become more aware and alert, we start to see the messages that the universe sends us: the movement of cloud, a sudden storm, a dog crossing our path, a rock to which we feel strangely drawn, the wild call of a bird, a rainbow, a flower we had not noticed before, a feather dropped at our feet – all may have something to teach us. And these messages are all around us. We have only to open our eyes to see them. To open our hearts.

Letting go of old stereotypical ideas and the rigidity of inherited belief systems, creates space for new perception. And then, opening up to everything that is around us allows us to expand ourselves, to reach a deeper consciousness of our own wholeness. Understanding that what we perceive as outside us is also within us, brings us into deeper relationship with ourselves. When our consciousness is in harmony with nature, worlds of wisdom open up for us.

As we begin to feel ourselves an integrated part of the whole, able to open our hearts with love for all beings, we lose our sense of isolation and alienation from life and the concomitant miseries and suffering that this brings. Helping us to connect to "all our relations" is the earth's way of leading us more deeply into our own spirituality. It may seem paradoxical, but by becoming more grounded in physical reality, without the confusion and dramas that we create around us, we open a portal to spiritual awareness.

162

More than this, spirituality remains just an idea if we are not grounded in our own bodies. We don't lose our individual identity by acknowledging our oneness with the whole; rather, we see it mirrored in every being around us, and so it is reinforced. When we realize what we share with other life forms, we can also understand what makes us unique, as humans and as individuals. Expanding all our relationships helps us also to extend and deepen our relationship with ourselves.

In Shamanic consciousness everything has consequences, not only actions but also thoughts, beliefs, emotions, attitudes, fears, desires, the way we use our energies. And just as we are influenced by forces in nature, so, too, we influence the natural world around us. So it is our responsibility to think and act as impeccably as we can, for the effects of our thoughts and behaviour may be unforeseen, unknown to us and far-reaching.

Shamanism sees the polarization of the modern world, driven by ego desires, selfishness and greed, as the cause of all the ills and conflicts that are rampant today. We are each responsible – and we can each make a difference. We don't need to have political power, or be another Mother Theresa, to make our mark on the world. We can start to make a difference in our own lives, in our local communities and then further afield. Taking personal responsibility for the ways we use the planets' decreasing resources is one example. Cutting carbon emissions is another. We can all make a difference. There are many ways in which we can make our homes more energy efficient: having windows double-glazed; using solar heating to heat the air and water; unplugging appliances when they are not in use. We can buy long-lasting low-energy light bulbs, which use about 80% less energy. We can take showers instead of baths; turn off water taps while we brush our teeth, wash the dishes or soap ourselves in the shower. We can recycle most of our household rubbish. We could drive a smaller car, or share car space, or use public transport, or cycle, or walk.

There are homes that are so over-heated in the middle of winter that the occupants wear summer clothes. If we all turned our central heating down by just two or three degrees, we could save huge amounts of energy – not to mention money! We need to be aware of how we use energy, and raise our children with the same awareness. Through the values by which we live and the way we are in the world, by living with spiritual consciousness, by talking our truth, and walking our talk, we can be a shining light to others, making our own contribution to repairing and restoring the world, and inspiring others to do so too.

In order to make changes in the world, we need to make changes in human beings. And this means changes in ourselves, in each of us. This is not about 'them', this is about 'us'. About you. We each need to take responsibility; to understand and acknowledge that changes in the 'outside' world, can only come about through changing ourselves on the 'inside' first. Truth is within us and needs to be uncovered, recovered – not discovered outside ourselves. By changing our own individual consciousness, our way of seeing the world, we create radical changes within ourselves; this in turn is reflected in the new reality that we create around us and brings about real change in the world outside.

Think of it: if you are aware that you truly love the beauty of nature, how can you destroy it? If you see yourself as part of the cosmos which is flowing with unconditional love and compassion, how can you behave with rage, aggression, selfishness or greed? As each of us begins to change inside, we create a new reality on the outside. We radiate a new energy and sense of purpose outwards, which has repercussions for everyone and everything around us.

The ancient traditions of Shamanism can bring inner peace and balance to our lives, and can help us to live a harmonious life supported by the energy of Mother Earth. The practice of these Shamanic traditions can open our hearts to the spirit of nature, which in its infinite wisdom points the way for us all.

There are several ancient Shamanic practices that are relevant to us today and can help us in practical ways to [re]connect to our spiritual roots. They can help to remind us of truths we may have forgotten, and bring us back to a celebration of our Higher Self. When approaching them, we should be focused in right intention to use them with reverence for our highest good, with our hearts open to the wisdom that they offer. Through right relationship with them, rather than the tools themselves, comes transformation and power.

The Shamanic Medicine Wheel offers us a way of connecting to relationship within all elements of existence, within all dimensions, awakening us to a truly sacred expression of life. Used since ancient times in Shamanic rituals, it can show us signposts on our personal path, a way of aligning with the natural forces of the cosmos, bringing us into sacred relationship with all life, more fully engaged with Spirit, and so with our own spiritual essence.

The Medicine Wheel represents a sacred space of interlocking symbols that can act as a portal into ancient wisdom on our own spiritual journey, a guide to the way the universe works, a focus for working with Shamanic power and healing, for creating sacred ceremony. A remembrance of lost roots in the natural world, of wise ancestors, of a deep connection to Spirit and the All That Is, it can help to reconnect us to our own wholeness and draw us back to the sacred path of life. The Medicine Wheel is a mandala of consciousness, a web of the cosmos, calling into wakefulness those aspects of Spirit that are reflected within ourselves. It is a wheel of power. Working with the Medicine Wheel is both a journey into the Great Web of the cosmos, acknowledging the interconnectedness of all life, and also a journey inwards into our own deepest selves.

Making a Medicine Wheel can be a portal for moving into the sacred and connecting more deeply to our own lives. It is generally most practical to set up your Wheel in a fixed place in your home, though it could be out of doors if you live in a clement climate. Traditionally made of stones, the Medicine Wheel is very easy to construct. To collect the stones, it is a good idea to go on a 'medicine walk', a walk in nature with the express intention of finding stones for your Medicine Wheel.

Before you start, centre yourself in stillness and focus on your intention for your walk. This is the first step in the ritual: conscious intention. Then as you walk, stay focused in the moment, with full alertness, and notice everything you see. Nature has a way of guiding us towards what we need; notice any signs of help. Select your stones with reverence, making sure that they are willing to be moved from their place in the earth. If you approach them with respect and listen to them, you will know. The more ritualized your walk becomes, the more aware you will be of which stones to choose, and the more meaningful and rewarding the whole process will be.

Build your Medicine Wheel in a place that is quiet, where you feel centred and peaceful. Consecrate the place as you might an altar, perhaps laying out a beautiful cloth, creating a sacred space. To make the Wheel, form a large circle of stones: four big ones to mark the Four Directions, one big one for the centre, and three smaller stones placed between each of the larger ones on the circumference, representing the twelve moons of the year. Use smaller stones still for the four spokes, from the centre out towards the four cardinal directions. The Wheel can be any size, whatever feels right for you; we are each unique.

Smudge the stones and bless them as you make your Wheel, asking them in return to bless you with their guidance and wisdom. Smudging is a form of purification, done by burning sweet-smelling plants and fanning the smoke across the objects to be purified. This brings you and them into sacred relationship. When you create your Medicine Wheel, be aware that you are doing so with right intention and full attention. Honour the process. The more focused you are on this, the more the Wheel will yield up its wisdom.

When all your stones are laid, spend a few moments with your Wheel, reflecting on which other objects you might like to place within it. For example, you may choose crystals, small stones, gems, feathers, perhaps a rattle, pictures or photographs, a copy of a special prayer or poem; anything that is meaningful to you and helps to make your Medicine Wheel a personal expression of the Sacred. The more you create the Sacred with ceremony, the more it will awaken Spirit within you, and imbue every aspect of your life. When your Wheel is finished, invoke the energies that you would like to be present within the circle of the Wheel, and thank the spirits for their help.

The Four Cardinal Directions of the Medicine Wheel [east, south, west, north] represent a journey through consciousness, a way of integrating our own wholeness with the balance and harmony of everything in creation. Working with the Four Directions helps us to navigate our way through the immutable laws of nature and orientate our own lives accordingly. As we connect more deeply to the moon, the stars, trees, mountains, rivers, rocks, we also connect to those parts of ourselves that they call forth. Working with the Four Directions calls up those aspects of Spirit that are reflected within ourselves, helping us to become more aware and participate more fully in life.

The teachings of the Four Directions give us an orientation to which we can turn for guidance to help us release our limitations and integrate into wholeness. The Four Directions are both symbolic guides and a practical resource. Working in the different directions according to the cycles of the sun or the different planetary movements, gives a metaphorical and physical shape to our lives. As we work with the physical elements we become more grounded in the physical world. This roots us for our spiritual work. For spirituality is not some airy-fairy notion wafting around in the ethos; spirituality needs to be firmly grounded. Only when our feet walk the earth with sure steps, can our souls begin to soar.

Although the basic interpretations of the Four Directions are similar among all Shamanic traditions, there are some variations. The interpretations given below are those of the *Huachuma* Shamanic tradition, which Tony follows. In Shamanic lore, the Four Directions are also represented by different animals, and are related to the four basic elements, providing a 'map' for understanding physical, mental, emotional and spiritual realities.

The journey of the Four Directions starts in the East. Dawn, spring, the rising sun, brings representations of new beginnings, new growth. East represents the innocence of childhood, the awakening of consciousness, spiritual vision and revelation, birth and rebirth, inspiration and new possibilities. East is the Direction of seeing the familiar with new eyes, of uncovering new meanings in what we perceive, for seeing what has hitherto been invisible. The element associated with East is Earth, the body; the animals are the eagle and the hawk.

South, noon, summer, with the longest days, is the Direction of warmth, growth, movement, of letting go. It is the Direction of personal development, of testing the visions that were perceived in the East, of cultivating its inspiration and new ideas. South connects us to alliance and relationship, to our sexual and conceptual energies, to our courage to move forward. The element associated with South is Air, the mind; the animals are the snake and the lizard.

West, evening, autumn, the setting sun, is a place of reflection, contemplation, release and self-acceptance, of exploring what was planted in the East and nurtured in the South. West is a place of absorbing what we have already learnt, of putting things in order, of shifts in awareness, of connecting us more deeply to the consciousness of power through action. The element associated with West is Fire, the spirit; the animals are the jaguar, lion and phoenix.

North, the night, winter, darkness, is the direction of healing and wholeness, of knowledge, of gathering strength, of rest and renewal, of stillness and inner focus, the attainment of wisdom and understanding. The vision that was revealed in the East, nurtured in the South and explored in the West, is now manifest and realized in the North. The element associated with North is Water, the emotions; the animals are the owl and the dragon.

The non-cardinal Directions also have symbolic meaning. The South East represents the past, the ancestors; the South West, dreams and personal myths; the North West, rules and behaviour patterns; and the North East, different levels of energy.

So we move through East, South, West and North. And then again, on to the East; a new day dawns, a new beginning awaits us...

Work with the Medicine Wheel can be on a regular basis, daily or weekly, or when you feel a particular wish to use the different energies of each of the Directions to connect to your different needs. It is always a good idea to smudge yourself before commencing work with the Wheel. This marks your entrance into sacred space, leaving behind the mundane activities of your life and aligning you with Spirit. It is an act of both commitment and affirmation.

In Shamanic lore, you cannot relate directly to power; you need reference points, ports of entry. For example, to understand the power – physical and metaphysical – of the sun or the moon, we need to know how they each affect us emotionally, physically, spiritually. A full moon, for instance, creates very different energy from a new moon. Knowing this, we can work in the West or the East, at different times of the month, depending on our intention at the time.

Working with the Medicine Wheel gives a tangible focus to our spiritual work. It is a permanent altar, a place of prayer, of gratitude, reminding us of the sacred path we are walking. It brings remembrance of who we are on the deepest level, connecting us to our spiritual centre and the wisdom of other realms. It acts as a lodestar on days when we temporarily lose our way, or our courage.

If you are finding it a little difficult to relate to these ancient concepts of the Four Directions, just think of the 'modern' art of Feng Shui. In the West, small fortunes are regularly paid for consultations with Feng Shui experts, who will tell you in which direction to sleep, where to place your furniture and how to arrange your home, to get the full benefit of the different energies of the different Directions. Something that Shamans knew, and practised, millennia ago!

Animals are an integral part of the Shaman's universe. Totem animals have been Shamans' helpers since time immemorial. As well as animals, totems may be birds, insects, reptiles, trees, plants or minerals, that have a special relationship with a human, imbuing the human with their 'medicine power', thus helping to further his/her growth.

In Shamanic tradition, a totem animal represents our highest potential. The totem is not a specific animal, bird or plant, but rather is seen as the perfected spirit of the whole species, whose power is thus inexhaustible. And it is this power that is available to the human. Totems teach us about ourselves, as well about the universe. They can reveal our strengths and weaknesses, reinforce our positive traits and alert us to what we lack. They can awaken qualities within us that may have been lying dormant for years, and of which we may be unaware. They can bring us perspective, knowledge, revelation. They provide markers to help us gage our state of consciousness.

Being in alliance with a totem is a recognition of our mutuality, a focus for us to learn about right relationship, with ourselves, with others and with the universe. It is an opportunity for us to gain wisdom, and also to express gratitude, generosity and blessing. It offers a way of learning that teaches profound respect for the other, which is at the heart of real sharing.

Totems are a bridge between realms, providing teachings and insights beyond the human; a portal through which we are invited by the totem to enter other realms. They are points of reference on the compass of our consciousness. They awaken within us the qualities and wisdom that we most need to manifest. A totem is a mirror of who we are, of our essence, of what we would be if we were four-footed, winged or rooted. A totem offers us a gift for self-examination, for measuring our humanness and moving beyond it. It can bring us power and protection, knowledge and wisdom, clarity and insight. A totem is a friend for life, and we may have one or several.

We need to remember, when we are in alliance with a totem animal or plant, that all interaction with it must stem from our intention for the highest good of both ourselves and the totem. It is by creating a relationship of mutual respect and understanding that the human may gain new perspective and vision. Relationship with a totem brings with it knowledge *and* responsibility. Awareness opens us up to change. The first lesson of relationship with a totem guide is humility.

A totem can help us in many ways: by strengthening our bodies and helping to increase our resistance to physical illness; by fighting off intrusions of negativity from the outside world, by bringing us physical, emotional and spiritual energy, empowering us to have more clarity of vision and strength of purpose, more confidence and decisiveness. By sharing what we have in common, it also shows us our unique humanness. Above all, our totem can mirror to us where we are on our journey, showing us a reflection of our own humanity and enriching our communication with our spiritual self.

Totems can be a powerful tool in our lives, but they do not of themselves bring us power. It is our *relationship* with them that makes them into totems for us. Through this relationship, our investment in learning what they have to teach us, also becomes the process by which we will learn. It is this alliance with them, our ability to connect to their energy and align ourselves with their intrinsic 'beingness' that brings us power; the teachings of totems are woven along this thread of relatedness. By bringing their power into our consciousness, we make it accessible. It takes patience, awareness of our interconnectedness, focused intention; a letting go of ego and our feelings of human superiority.

Through engaging in relationship with a totem, we can improve the quality of all our relationships. It takes an open heart as well as an open mind.

Finding or encountering our totems may not be as difficult as you may think. But first we have to recognize what purpose we want the totem to fulfil in our life, which qualities in ourselves we would like it to awaken. Each animal brings with it the unique qualities of the spirit of its species, and has different lessons to impart, so it is important to recognize the characteristics you are looking for in a totem.

Are you, for example, looking for the introspection of Bear, the symbol of dreamtime, where the illusion of physical reality is overlaid with deeper levels of consciousness? Or would you choose Lion, who teaches us the qualities of leadership, integrity, remaining true to your own values, the uses and abuses of power? Or the farsightedness of Eagle, who can teach us to see from a higher perspective and show us the way of spiritual illumination and power?

When you have pondered these questions, you might like to consider the plants or animals with which you feel an instinctive affinity. What is it that draws you to them? Think back to your childhood, to the animals and plants that were part of that landscape. Childhood, when we are more closely attuned to our intuition and feelings, offers a good window into ourselves. Did you have pets, ride horses, paint or write or sing about particular animals? Did you enjoy nature walks, in forests, on mountains, in parks, by the sea? To which plants or trees were you specially drawn? Think of the childhood stories you were told: which animals intrigued, attracted or frightened you? [Something we fear often has the greatest lessons to teach us.] Which animals have you always loved? Why were you drawn to these particular plants or animals? And if you were an animal now, which animal would you like to be? Answers to these questions may be one way of being guided towards your totem.

Another way of connecting to totems is through dreams. Our dreams come to us as gifts; if we are able to tune in to them and learn how to interpret them spiritually, they can act as great messengers and teachers. Animals often appear in our dreams, bringing us friendly reminders of our path in this world. Every time we dream of an animal, we are touching its spirit. It might talk to us verbally, or communicate through the vision of the dream. Animals may send us messages telepathically, or convey images that appear in our mind's eye. They may communicate through symbols, which we will need to decipher. Shamans believe that if an animal talks to you in a dream, this is a sign of totemic alliance.

Our bodies can be another guide to our own animal totem. Our bodies hold the memory of the genetic make-up of the whole of our evolution: all the plants, fish, birds and animals that have preceded us. So, by going deeply into our body, we can access the power of a totem animal through our body. Just watch how a baby evolves: rolling over [a fish], starting to crawl [a lizard], then trying to balance [a deer]. If we really tune in to our bodies, they can become portals to alignment with a totem animal.

Meditation and visualization may also connect us to a totem. For example, close your eyes and visualize yourself somewhere out in nature, sit quietly and wait. You might see a particular tree or plant, or a certain animal may cross your path. Appearing in your visualization may be its way of seeking relationship with you. Focus in the moment, watch and wait and see what feelings emerge; they will help to guide you. According to Shamanic belief, if an animal crosses your path four times, it is a sign that it is willing to be your totem. Stay with the images and ponder their significance. But be patient; it might take a while. Finally, you may just feel a 'knowingness' that a certain animal or plant is your totem.

I discovered my first totem, Wolf, through Iron, the nearly blind husky dog, who turned up on my doorstep and 'adopted' me when I was living in Tertit's flat, early in my love affair with Portugal. My second totem came to me in a less dramatic way. It was not a sudden realization, but rather a steady drip drip effect into my life, until I got the message. When I was living on the Ashram, I would sit on the step of my room in the early morning and greet the dawn. I noticed that two butterflies would fly around me, every day. [I also noticed that one day, when I was feeling out of sorts and out of touch, no butterflies appeared.] When I went for walks, butterflies would always cross my path. I received two postcards from friends, both with pictures of butterflies on them. A friend gave me a present, a book wrapped in butterfly paper. I dreamt of flying on the back of a large white butterfly... Eventually, I understood: Butterfly was also my totem. A symbol of transformation...

The universe has many ways of guiding us to our totems. We simply need to be aware, alert and trusting. When we are ready, the totem will appear, and we will know.

Trees have always played a special role in the Shamanic world. Known to Shamans as 'standing people', they are the unmoveables with which humans have the closest affinity. We and they are both nourished and nurtured by the same sun and soil, sky and water. We both have our roots [feet] on the earth, but reach upwards towards heaven [spirit].

Trees are the guardians of the earth, teachers of humanity. Being rooted, they teach us about the power of stillness, the strength of rootedness and immutability, the spirit of place through the spirit of one place. They bring us the knowledge of endurance, the wisdom of age.

On the plane of physical reality, trees are crucially important. They provide shade, shelter and fuel. They are the guardians of the environment and protect it from excesses of carbon dioxide that would otherwise seriously pollute it. They emit oxygen, which enables us to breathe. They hold together not only the soil, preventing it from erosion; they also provide the balance of our whole eco-system. Without trees, the earth as we know it could not exist.

But trees also have magical and mystical properties. As well as bringing great majesty and beauty to the earth, they contribute special energy to the places in which they grow. To the Shaman, they represent protective forces, and are symbols of particular power. They have lived through time, oblivious to the fickleness of their two-legged relations. They exemplify strength and resilience, endurance in perpetuity. Shamans consider trees as our spiritual grandparents, offering us manifold blessings and wisdom, if we know how to acquire it.

In ancient Shamanic traditions, trees were seen as the connection between the physical and the spiritual realms. Rooted in the darkness of the earth, they stretched up to the sun, the symbol of light. Symbolically, they were the bridge between earth and sky, between limitation and possibility, between the fleeting and the eternal.

Shamans frequently spend a great deal of time talking with trees. When he talks to a tree, he is not talking to this particular tree but rather is communicating with the spirit of 'treeness' with which it is imbued. It is this spirit, embodied in the physical tree, that holds and bestows wisdom. [See also next section on Vision Quests.]

Spending time with trees is good for our physical health, and can also deeply enhance our spirituality. If you are looking for wisdom from a tree, approach it with respect and humility and greet it as you would an equal. Then sitting peacefully, without expectation, attune yourself to its 'beingness'; this will allow you to absorb something of its spirit. When you feel comfortable, the best way to contact its wisdom is to ask it to reveal something of its inner self. You may ask it if it will give you guidance. You may ask with words or silently. Be patient and open; an answer may come now or much later, and it may come in an entirely unexpected way. But if you are open to receive, an answer will come. Then, before you go, make sure that you thank it. Shamans would always leave a small offering in thanks.

All trees have significance in the Shamanic world. The scope of this book does not allow me to mention the hundreds of species of trees that exist. I have limited my choice to those that I think are the most helpful for us to relate to, and are most likely to be found in our environment: Ash, Beech, Birch, Cedar, Elm and Oak. By spending time with these trees, sitting by their roots or leaning against their trunks, we can begin to imbibe their wisdom and their strength.

Ash: Ash was the Cosmic Tree of the Druids, encompassing all realms and all times. It brings understanding of the interconnectedness of the spiritual and the physical, and of the unity of everything in creation. Ash can bring spiritual awareness, intuition, protection and resilience, and can help us to attain right relationship with the earth.

Beech: Beech is the tree in which to meet and greet your creative muse. The guardian of wisdom, it brings knowledge to those who seek it with love and humility. It also helps to guard against the repetition of mistakes. A gentle tree, good for sitting in and reflecting, Beech brings peace and well-being, companionship and abundance.

Birch: Birch is a magical tree; meditating beneath it is said to align you to the spirits of the woods. It brings protection, specially of babies, and cradles were often made of its wood. Birch can manifest healing, purification and Enlightenment.

Cedar: A magnificent tree, Cedar is considered to be one of the oldest and wisest of trees, and is one of Tony's favourites. It grows mainly in the Middle East and North Africa, and is sacred in Lebanon [the Cedars of Lebanon are mentioned in the Bible] and in Morocco. Cedar oil was used by the ancient Pharaohs for embalming. Sitting under a Cedar tree can help prevent infection, and offers purification and protection.

Elm: Elm is sacred to Tony, as his name Samara is Latin for Elm tree. Elm is a soothing tree, very good for stress and anxiety. Slippery elm is good for settling upset stomachs. Elm trees, often found in churchyards, bring calm, comfort and peacefulness.

Oak: Old and sturdy, Oak brings strength, power and fertility. Oak was sacred to the Druids and was central to many of their ceremonies. Growing slowly, Oak's special qualities are strength and endurance, and it is a good teacher of patience and diligence. Oak is a good tree to consult when difficulties arise, and when we are in danger of losing touch with our aspirations.

Connecting in this way with trees creates space for mutual recognition and affirmation. You expand and open yourself more fully to the sacred, deepening your feelings of connectedness and wholeness. Letting go of your sense of isolation and human superiority, you bring more sources of guidance into your life and greatly increase your wisdom and your power.

A Vision Quest is an ancient Shamanic practice for gaining personal revelation. Today, we may interpret it as a process of going into nature in order to break habitual patterns of thought, belief and behaviour, by setting specific tasks that help to take us beyond our limitations to the immutable truths of the natural world.

A Vision Quest embodies our yearning for something more, a longing to touch the heart, the essence, of the Great Beyond, a homesickness to reveal the sacred dream; a stirring to connect to something authentic and true, a bridge between our consciousness and the Source. It is a journey into our own soul, as well as into the heart of nature. That is where they meet.

Through a Vision Quest, we may discover our own personal medicine. [Remember, 'medicine' in the Shamanic sense is not something that is given to us when we're ill, but rather something we have when we're well and living in harmony; our own personal power.] By seeking new spiritual landscapes we may become aware of transformative alliances.

At its simplest, a Vision Quest is a walk alone in nature in order to connect with the spirits of nature. To do this, we need to open all our senses to what is around us, to be focused in intention, commitment and openness to receive whatever the universe will provide. We need to leave behind our preconceived ideas that trees and plants can't communicate with humans. Non-ordinary reality exists all around us. Seeing a rainbow, the movement of a cloud, a leaf fall from a tree, a butterfly or bird cross our path, may all be a way in which Great Spirit speaks to us. If we are not conscious, these signs will appear as random events, without significance; we may not even notice them. If we are conscious, we may perceive in them coherence, affirmation, a message that resonates with meaning.

The natural way of life of our Shamanic ancestors gave a context to their vision questing. They were attuned to the wildness of the elements, the rhythms of nature, the connectedness of the All That Is. They were nourished by their natural environment in a way that we generally are not. We seem to be full of confusion, of psychological baggage and personal doubts. So we need to be armed with clarity of purpose to dispel any vagueness, and an openness to experience something beyond the parameters of our daily lives.

Before you set out on your Vision Quest, it's a good idea to create a ceremony, to mark your going out in some way. You might smudge yourself, meditate on the purpose of your quest, or work with the Medicine Wheel and ask for guidance in directions. Then as you walk allow yourself simply to follow in whatever direction you are led. If you are focused in the moment, aware and alert with all your senses, you will almost certainly find that you are drawn towards a particular plant or tree. Trust your intuition, trust your feet. If you bring pure intention to the Vision Quest, you will be guided by your higher self towards a deeper connection with the cosmos, accompanied along your path towards spiritual realization.

Communing with trees and plants is a central part of a Vision Quest. [You may like to go back to the previous section on trees.]

Rocks and stones have been around since the beginning of time, and are considered by Shamans to be their "oldest relations". They were present to witness the birth of plants, animals and humans and so carry the wisdom of the ages. They deserve our reverence and respect in the same way that animals and plants do. When we understand that we share a common spiritual source with all the elements of the earth, we also understand the sacred relationship between us, and so open ourselves up to receive the teachings and wisdom that they bring.

When we call upon the help of the natural world, we are asking to be drawn into balance and harmony with the universe, with the higher good, through the power of the essence of animals, trees, rocks or plants. The lessons that they teach us are about being human, allowing ourselves to be open and vulnerable, as well as guiding us along a path towards wholeness with the All That Is. If we honour every living creature as a teacher, and approach it with humility, the process can be deeply healing and rewarding. The lessons are eternal; a gift offered to help us in our understanding of our connection to the Great Mystery, a pathway to power.

In most Shamanic communities, a regular form of purification ritual is an essential part of their way of life. And we, in our own lives, could benefit by incorporating this in some way into our own spiritual practice. [Many religions also advocate some form of ritual bathing as a means of purification, and many of us go to a sauna or Turkish baths.]

The most common form of purification ceremony among Shamanic communities is the Sweat Lodge. This is an ancient ritual that is practised today not only among Shamanic tribes, but among many North American native peoples as well, and indeed among Western followers of what has become a 'New Age' tradition. Used for purification of mind and soul as well as body, regular attendance at the Sweat Lodge is seen as a means of detoxifying the body and maintaining good physical health, while connecting more deeply with Great Spirit.

The Sweat Lodge is a sacred place, a place of ritual purification and rebirth. To understand the concept of a Sweat Lodge, imagine a communal sauna but with the emphasis on prayer, redemption and renewal; a place where people doff their masks, their worldly personas and their emotional baggage, together with their clothes.

Sweat Lodges vary in shape and size among different traditions. They may be round or oval or shaped like a beehive; usually they are made from the pliable branches of trees, which are planted in the ground and then arched over to form a dome. This is then covered with thick blankets, to keep in the heat. They are generally built to face east, the 'birthplace' of the sun, though not always. Sweat Lodges built in the West generally follow this ancient design.

The ceremony of the Sweat Lodge incorporates the four basic elements: air, earth, fire and water. These elements are all present physically, and also bring with them symbolic meaning. The earth of the lodge represents groundedness in physical reality; the fire of the heated rocks contains the power of transformation; the water poured onto the rocks brings purification; the air is filled with the steam from the water on the rocks, and carries the prayers. The Lodge itself represents the womb of Mother Earth.

At the beginning of the ceremony the Shaman, or whoever is leading the sweat, stands at the entrance to the Lodge and smudges each participant as they enter. His/ her assistant brings the white-hot stones from the fire nearby where they are being heated, places them in the centre of the circle where everyone is sitting and pours on the water. As more stones are brought and more water is poured on throughout the ceremony, the temperature continues to rise.

In the first stage, participants are often asked to express their own personal reasons for attending the ceremony and what they wish to obtain from it. Then the leader chants special prayers, songs and evocations, and invokes the powers of the Spirits to be present; participants often contribute their own prayers. The last part of the ceremony, when transformation takes place, is usually held in sacred silence.

The Sweat Lodge is entered naked and vulnerable, symbolic of the way we all enter the world; a perfect way to open up to its redemptive powers. For it's difficult to hold onto the games of the mind and the ego, to dignity, to masks and facades and the accessories of status, when you are naked and sweating profusely! Attending a Sweat Lodge offers an opportunity to let go of mind-limiting beliefs, of the need to control, of suffering and pain, of struggle, above all of ego. And through physically letting go, to go beyond the comfortable and venture into the unknown; to accept and embrace the spiritual forces that are present; to transcend fear.

Many of us living in the West have an abhorrence of being uncomfortable, undignified and not in control. Attending a Sweat Lodge forces us to move out of our comfort zone and confront our demons. If we have the courage to do this, the Sweat Lodge can be a powerful and intense experience and an important marker on our spiritual journey.

The Sweat Lodge, the womb of the earth, offers the possibility for anything to be born out of its ceremony. It is a place of intense discomfort and endurance, but also of mutual support, of expanding compassion and a pushing out of the boundaries of fear. The ceremony of the Sweat Lodge is an ancient tradition, and so each one is connected back by a sacred thread to the spirit of all Sweat Lodges. It is the combined power of all these energies, resonating through ceremony, that may bring about true physical, emotional and spiritual transformation.

All these Shamanic practices are a portal into spirituality. In themselves, they are just tools. What makes them important is our relationship to them, the time and energy we invest in their use, our commitment to following our own spiritual path. Then these tools may become a powerful vehicle of transformation.

Modern-day Shamanism is about tuning in to the energy of the natural world that is present all around us and connecting more deeply to our own life-force. As we begin to experience oneness with all of creation, embodying the essential qualities of aliveness and awareness, we begin to feel deep harmony, balance, unlimited energy and enthusiasm for life. As we choose to embrace life fully, the opportunities for growth become limitless, and we open up to experiencing deep love, joy and peace.

Shamanism is an approach to life, the way we live each moment, the consciousness we bring to fulfilling our life's purpose. It is neither a religion nor a science, a dogma nor a philosophy. It is a way of experiencing our own lives and the world, an understanding that true knowledge can only come through our own experience. It is a journey into our deepest selves, into truth.

Book Two
Teachings

"Why have a spiritual teacher? When a log that has just started to burn is placed next to one that is burning fiercely, that log will then start to burn more intensely. To be such a fire is the function of a spiritual teacher… "

Tony Samara

Contents

Introduction: How I almost came *not* to write this book   181

1   Introduction to the Teachings   187

2   Letting Go: Beliefs, Emotions, Fears   198

3   Mind and Ego   217

4   Will and Intention   233

5   God and Goddess: Relationships and How to Love   245

6   Dreams and Dreaming   263

7   The Body: Health and Healing   281

8   The Body: Food and Diet   295

9   Freedom   315

10   Exercising: Spiritual and Physical   324

11   The Path of the Heart: Healing Ourselves, Healing the Planet   348

Epilogue   356

Afterword: Tony's work today   357

Contributions from people who have worked with Tony   363

Introduction
How I almost came *not* to write this book

Tony had invited me to spend August with him in the Algarve, Portugal, to interview him about the book he had asked me to write about him. I went to his workshops, I talked to him in between, and I made copious notes. By the end of the month, I had fallen in love with the Algarve, and decided to return and write the book in Portugal.

And so began one of the most extraordinary journeys of my life. I returned to Portugal in the autumn, and over the next couple of years I lived in various and vastly different situations. Firstly, I lived entirely alone in a flat at the top of a hill, with panoramic views on all sides and only the trees and birds for company; then in a villa shared with eight other adults who were all working in some way with Tony, and a small child; and then on Tony's Ashram, where a core group of about ten of us lived together as we tried to create a spiritual community, and make a patch of rubble blossom with hard work, a wing and many prayers.

I spent my time writing, reading vociferously about Shamanism [I arrived in Portugal with very overweight luggage: jeans and a couple of sweaters – and half a suitcase full of books] attending Tony's workshops, and talking with him whenever I could find him. But when I had finished the first draft of Book One, I came to a decisive full stop. There seemed to be no way that I would be able to continue.

Book One was to be about Tony's life and work as I accompanied him – imaginatively and spiritually, if not physically – on his journey, from his first childhood memories and earliest visions of other realities, through the Zen Buddhist monastery, until he became an initiated Shaman, and beyond. It was to trace the arc of his journey as he moved through Shamanism and the teachings that grew out of his Shamanic knowledge and experiences, ultimately leading him to develop his own teachings.

Book Two was to be Tony's teachings. By the time I moved onto the Ashram, I had completed a full first draft of Book One and was ready to move on and tackle the teachings. But then, without warning, Tony 'disappeared'. Well, he didn't exactly disappear. He went to give retreats in Croatia and Slovenia, and other far-flung shores; but in Portugal he was not.

I had expected to interview him and talk about the teachings. As the days turned into weeks and there was no sign of Tony, and no-one could say with any certainty when he would return, my emotions swung from impatience to annoyance to anger. I had come to Portugal specifically to write this book about him – why wasn't he here? Finally I just gave up and worked on the novel I'd been writing before Tony 'interrupted' me. The writing went well, life on the Ashram was challenging and rewarding, I had made other friends locally and was enjoying spending time with them. I decided to forget about The Book and just go with the flow…

Weeks went by. The Book remained untouched. Perhaps I was not meant to write it after all? But something gnawed at me and I couldn't walk away. I set myself a course of studying Shamanism in greater depth, and read ever more avidly. I reworked Book One, weaving deeper levels of Shamanism into Tony's journey, as I came to understand it more profoundly.

Then, very gradually, I became aware of another feeling beginning to prick my consciousness. I reminded myself that nothing in life is random. Tony had asked me to write this book, so presumably he wanted me to finish it. And as he had asked *me* to write it, with my 'take' on his teachings, there was perhaps a deeper reason for this, even if I did not yet know or understand it.

I needed to look with new eyes at the situation surrounding the book, and ask myself what I was really doing on the Ashram. I needed to stop making assumptions and trying to fit everything neatly into a preconceived game plan. And I needed to remember that Tony is the "Shamanic trickster" *par excellence*. What was he up to?

I didn't imagine that Tony had 'disappeared' solely for my benefit, but I realized that it was intentional towards me as well. By leaving when he did, by not being there when I thought I needed to question him, he was actually giving me a very strong message – that I needed to do the work on my own and he was not going to help me. And in fact this proved to be the greatest blessing he could have given me. For it forced me not to rely on him, but to turn inward, and look in the mirror.

And then I realized exactly what he was telling me: before I could write a book of spiritual teachings, I would have to experience the journey for myself. There is no other way. For spiritual teaching is not a matter of learning facts or acquiring knowledge, but rather of relinquishing assumptions, certainties, the control of the mind and ego-based attachment to outcome, and of opening up perceptions, of experiencing truth with the heart. I needed to journey further along my own spiritual path; to move away from theories and ideas, assumptions and beliefs, into feeling, intuition and trust. I had to let go of the need to control, my own life and other people and, more relevantly perhaps, my need to control the material of this book. I needed to reach not so much an intellectual understanding as an experiential 'knowing' of spiritual truth.

And so I started to open myself up more and more to my own spiritual journey, to allow myself to be guided by intuition rather than intellect. I began to listen to my inner voice, to absorb with my heart; I began to make notes in an unstructured way of whatever came up. I realized that I had actually journeyed a long way since first meeting Tony, and that I had in fact been 'doing the work' all those months, even when I was kicking against it. Once the door was opened – and Tony had given it an almighty push – there was no going back. You cannot 'unknow' spiritual knowledge.

A realization formed. Tony wanted the second book to be *my* journey through his teachings – and I needed to do the work; not only as a writer, but also spiritually. It was clear that Tony would not help me in the ways that I had thought I needed. My only way forward would be to continue to journey along my own spiritual path, opening myself more and more to receive spiritual guidance and wisdom, however it appeared. At the same time, I would attend more of Tony's retreats and gather the 'raw material' for Book Two.

It is an illusion to think that any path taken will necessarily lead to the conclusion that we imagine at the outset. And so it was with my writing of this book. My own spiritual journey led me more deeply into Tony's teachings – and to another, and totally unexpected, full stop.

For the more I tried to work on Book Two: The Teachings, the more of a Sisyphean task it became. I felt like "Alice Through The Looking Glass": the more I knew, the less I understood. The more I got to know Tony, the more confused I became. The only thing, in fact, that I was sure of now was how well-nigh impossible it would be to explain the essence of Tony's teachings, and do justice to his work, in a book.

By this time I had participated in many of Tony's retreats and workshops. I had sat there along with everyone else and found myself nodding my head in agreement with everything he said. But when, later, I read verbatim transcripts of these retreats, his words made no sense at all. Any hope that writing this second book would be an easy ride, as I used these transcripts as a guide and restructured them into a book, was completely scuppered. Perhaps this full stop would be definitive!

I made no decisions, except to stay open to whatever would be. If I were not meant to write this book, I would know and accept it. If I were meant to continue, I would be guided.

I tuned in to what I knew, which was not a great comfort: I would not be able to use any of Tony's written material. For Tony's gift does not lie in words. His magic lies between the words, between the lines, in his presence, in the immediate non-verbal energetic communication of the moment. It lies in a direct communion of truth between the spiritual reality that he inhabits and that place of Spirit deep within us all. Spoken words remain within the limits of the mind; only communion can reach beyond the mind and take us to a place of silent stillness within. Tony said that he hoped one day to be able to sit together with everyone at his retreats and communicate without words, energetically, in a deep shared silence; a true communion of hearts. [Tony has now instigated Silent Retreats. For more information on these, please see the Afterword.]

But in a book, words are all we have. What to do? I was totally frustrated by Tony's complete illogicality, by the way he jumps around from one thing to another like a cat on a hot tin roof, with no apparent connection between one sentence and the next. I found his game-playing infuriating. I thought he was supposed to be a spiritual teacher; why was he wasting my time like this?

I stopped, and reflected. I began to realize that this was simply my instinctive reaction to having my buttons pressed. Tony was showing me that I clearly needed to get out of my 'intellectual writer mode' and allow myself to be in a place of uncertainty, of questioning, of not knowing; of not having anything to fall back on. Of trust. Then I would be able to write the teachings.

It took me a long time, and a lot of 'journeying', to overcome my own stubborn opposition to Tony's total lack of structure – which, of course, I now realize, was intentional on his part. This, in fact, is Tony's first teaching: to jump around in a seemingly random way, to shake us out of our logical thinking and our servitude to our minds. The more rational we are, the more illogical he will become. This was apparently exactly the lesson I needed to learn.

I realized that in fact I needed to take time out, to open myself up to my own spiritual journey and do the work, allowing it to lead me wherever it would. I needed to find my own way to connect to the Source, to ask for spiritual guidance, to allow myself to be a vessel through which the teachings might be revealed. And then, to wait for grace…

As my consciousness evolved, I was able more and more to observe my own processes. Gradually, I came to realize that I *would* find a way to continue writing this book, although it was not the way I had previously imagined. I came to accept that the truth of Tony's teachings does not lie in his words; and that my job would be to find other words, to reach the meaning beyond the meaning of the words he uses. And that I would be guided. So I have tried to create a language that reflects the truth of his teachings, although it is not Tony's words; to find my own way in and map my own path through the teachings that can be understood by people who have never met Tony. And at the same time, I hope, recreate something of Tony's gentle magic.

I have written in good faith what I believe is most important about Tony's work, and in a way that I hope will be accessible to others. Having gone the journey myself, I am perhaps able to guide you on your journey through the teachings; and if you lose your courage or lose your way, I can show you that it is possible to continue, and can help you to find your own way through.

I hope that the glass through which I have peered is clear and not distorted. As my own spiritual journey has evolved, I believe that the glass has become more transparent.

I have journeyed into my own truth, as well as Tony's; and, of course, they are the same. And in fact, by 'disappearing' when he did and allowing me to go on my own journey, Tony gave me a direct experience of his teachings and taught me the most important spiritual lesson of all: that the greatest gift is to know that truth and love and divinity reside within ourselves. Our journey is to look deep within ourselves and uncover them.

The journey has been a long one, and of course it still continues. It is a journey that we each have to make for ourselves, paving our own spiritual path by the way we live and the choices we make. There are no short cuts. It may not be easy, but it is infinitely rewarding. As we walk, the signposts appear. The tests and the hurdles that we meet on the way are the best opportunities we have for learning and growth.

I hope that my journey through Tony's teachings may act as a guide and support to you on your own journey through the teachings.

Writing this book has been a major part of my spiritual quest. Reading it, I hope, may be yours.

Chapter One
Introduction to the Teachings

Tony's spiritual teachings are deeply rooted in Shamanism, steeped in its knowledge and its wisdom. He is an initiated Shaman and Shamanic healer, who spent many years living and studying with Shamans in South America. The spirit of Shamanism has informed his life's journey and still informs the essence of his teaching.

But over the years that he has spent working, teaching and questing, first in South America, then in the Caribbean, and later in Australasia and Europe, as he has moved more deeply into Shamanic lore and practice, he has come to realize that some Shamanic traditions have become distorted by tribal culture or superstition, and he has moved away from teaching what is generally defined as classical Shamanism, with all its trimmings.

Before we move into the teachings, it would be helpful to clarify those Shamanic traditions with which Tony parts company, so that we may come to a deeper understanding of the profound connection between his teachings and the real essence of Shamanic wisdom, the foundation of his spiritual path. It is important to emphasize that Tony's points of departure are not with the immutable spiritual truths of Shamanism, but rather with some tribal beliefs and customs that have come to be associated with it. His main divergences centre around four specific practices, all of which are influenced, in Tony's eyes, by primitive tribal culture and superstition, and are nothing to do with the deep truths that are the heart of Shamanism.

Classical Shamanism believes that the spirits are 'outside' us, in the Upper World or the Lower World, according to their particular roles and functions, and need to be 'invoked'. Furthermore, this act of invocation can be carried out only by an initiated Shaman. But Spirit, the Sacred, is everywhere: breathing the wind, lighting the stars, growing the trees; everything within creation is filled with the essence of the Divine. And Spirit is also within each of us, as well as within every other life form. Our spirit within may need to be [re]awakened, revealed, acknowledged, but it is not a separate entity that exists outside us. It is the divine spark within, eternal and indestructible, which is connected to the universal Divine all around us.

The Shamanic concept that views the Underworld with its spirit population as a real physical place, to which Shamanic 'travel' can take you, now seems to Tony a simplistic concept, born of primitive culture. Rather, he sees it as a metaphor for the unconscious, travel to the Underworld as a way of connecting to the deepest, hidden part of ourselves. The experience that Shamans have with the spirits on their visits to the Underworld and the wisdom that they bring back with them, can be seen to equate with our own spirit talking to us when we have reached deeply enough inside ourselves to hear its voice.

Around the time of Tony's initiation, when he went on many Shamanic 'journeys', the purpose was to help him to know profound spiritual truths. He looks back on this as an experience that was necessary in the time and place in which he found himself, a stepping-stone that he needed then on his journey towards Enlightenment. But now he no longer feels the need to 'travel' in this way; nor does he see it as a necessary part of a spiritual journey for others. What he teaches is the essence of *Huachuma* Shamanism: spiritual consciousness, the interconnectedness of everything, a ceaseless movement of awakening to the sacred dance of life.

Tony's second point of departure is with the practice of 'black magic'. Stealing power or souls, fighting psychic battles in other realms, putting sorcerers' spells on enemies or shape-shifting in order to play tricks on others, may be a glossy Hollywood image of the spiritual life, but it is certainly not Tony's. To enter altered states of consciousness to show off feats of magic simply because the Shaman can, seems to him to be not only a waste of time but also a distortion of what spirituality really is.

In many Shamanic communities in South America, the practice of witchcraft is a common custom. Witchcraft is a kind of 'magic', involving a belief in both positive and negative energies, and the interplay of the currents between them. But having lived in many communities in which witchcraft is practised, Tony has come to see it as just another kind of game playing, manipulating people's gullibility for rather spurious ends. He does not believe, as the tenets of witchcraft maintain, that there is a force of negative energies in the universe, which have their own powers and can be invoked and [mis]used by witches and wizards for their own ends. Rather, his worldview holds that everything in creation is perfect, divine, and the Divine can contain within it no imperfection. Witchcraft, when we come down to it, is another form of 'black magic', another exploitation of power.

Thirdly, the way in which a sense of community is generally fostered among Shamanic societies seems to Tony rather rigid. The glue that holds the community together, like many 'closed' communities, is a common set of values and practices, a way of life accepted by all. While there is much to be said for living within a caring, sharing community, it also has limitations. There is no space within it for individual questioning, and any deviation is generally not tolerated. But the greatest limitation, in Tony's view, is that the concept of individual spiritual questing, of personal growth and transformation, is unknown. 'The community' practises a kind of collective spirituality, much of it vicariously through the person of the Shaman; individual spiritual evolvement is something outside their experience and their aspiration.

Tony's last divergence from classical Shamanism focuses on the superstition surrounding many Shamanic practices and rituals, which may be heavily influenced by local culture and are often expressions of the natives' fears. Tony now sees many Shamanic practices as symbolic rather than literal. Indeed, many of their elaborate rituals seem to him now like a great show, connected to the powers of a spirit world, but far removed from his concept of spirituality. While there is certainly a place in life for ritual and ceremony – indeed, in the West, the loss of shared rituals can be seen as detrimental to the health and cohesion of our society and perhaps a major cause of alienation and social breakdown – nonetheless, rituals should be an outward celebration of an inward journey, not an observance born of superstition or fear.

A number of years ago, Tony conducted retreats in Australia for people who were interested in Shamanism. But some of those attending the retreats became angry, because he did not follow what they considered to be true Shamanism. Apparently, some Native Americans had been there shortly before and they were teaching classical Shamanism, with all the 'show' that this involved. But what is important is not to copy a traditional way of doing things, that was born in another era, in another culture, but rather to find the intention within it of what is relevant to our own society today; to connect to our own spirit, rooted in our heritage, in our own sense of place; a historical and geographical connection that is authentic. This is what Tony's teachings are ultimately about. Otherwise, it becomes a meaningless show.

These points of departure with classical Shamanism are not connected in any way with the truths that are the core of Shamanism. It is essential to emphasize this. By letting go of some of the 'trimmings' of Shamanism, Tony believes that he has reduced his teachings to the pure and profound essence of Shamanism: a deep respect and reverence for nature and for all life forms; a recognition that everything and everyone is connected to everything and everyone else within the Great Web of life, and to the sacred which is manifest in all of Creation. He espouses a celebratory joy of being fully present in each moment, to oneself and the world, living one's life's purpose with consciousness, integrity and intention for the highest good of all.

As we saw in Chapter Eight of Book One, there are many ways in which we can connect to Shamanic wisdom: being in nature, finding harmony in the natural world and its rhythms, communicating with animals and trees and learning their wisdom, finding totem animals, using the Medicine Wheel and going on a Vision Quest. They are all pathways to the sacred. Following this path opens doorways to greater awareness, to clarity of purpose, to understanding the true nature of freedom, to wholeness, to the fulfilment of our true human potential as we connect to the All That Is.

The spirituality that Tony teaches today is born of the deepest truths of *Huachuma* Shamanism, which are universal and eternal. But he has moved beyond classical Shamanic rituals to what he believes is relevant to us today, in the West, in the twenty-first century. What he teaches now is both more and less than Shamanism, being paired down to its one immutable and simple truth, that spirituality is the manifestation in all things, in every moment, of divine and unconditional love.

The real purpose of all Shamanic practice is essentially to bring us back to our lost connection with nature, to live in balance and harmony with the laws of the natural world, and so be most truly ourselves.

Shamanism is not a religion, a science or a theory. It relies on no authority telling anyone what to do. There are no leaders and no followers; no priests, imams, rabbis, or other spiritual intermediaries. There is no hierarchy demanding devotion and obedience; no oath of allegiance is required. It has no creed, no dogma, no articles of faith; it is not a set of intellectual ideas, it propagates no doctrine. It owns no holy books, no tablets of stone, no code of laws.

In a sense, Shamanism is the antithesis of organized religion. It boasts no church, temple, synagogue or mosque, no sacred buildings of any kind. To a Shaman, all of Mother Earth is a 'sacred place', and Spirit is everywhere. The only thing that a Shaman will tell you to do is to go out into nature – to see, to listen, to be; to have and honour your own experience and learn from this. The essential truth of Shamanism can only be known through personal experience.

Shamanism personifies a deeply spiritual way of life. But if you ask a Shaman to explain his concept of God, he will almost certainly laugh – as Tony did, loudly and heartily, when I asked him! For 'God' to a Shaman is not a separate entity that can be described as some other all-powerful being. Certainly God is not an old man with a long white beard – or, indeed, anyone – sitting in some far-off place called Heaven. For "Heaven lies all around us… "

God is the Source of the universe, the instigating breath of the Great Mystery, the spirit of nature. God is the greatest and the tiniest; the Great Spirit which imbues every part of Creation and holds it all together in the Web of Life, and the tiny divine spark within each life. God for the Shaman is both nature and our connection to nature. God is the sacred within us and within the All That Is; and the connecting path between them. And in fact they are one.

Shamanism is the practice of spirituality, but it isn't some airy-fairy concept; it is based on thorough practical knowledge of how the natural world works and the Shamans' interaction with it. As a species, particularly in the West, we humans have lost our instinctive connection to the rhythms of nature and the mystery at the heart of the natural world. But nature is there to teach us, if only we will open our hearts and our sensitivity to receive the lessons and the gifts that she brings us.

Following these Shamanic principles of life, we realize that we are not alone, ever. That Mother Earth, the mother of us all, is always supporting us, whether we are aware of this or not. In fact, everything in the interlinked Web of Life and creation is supporting us at all times. As we begin to reawaken to the natural world, we reconnect more deeply to our own energies and power.

The essence of Shamanism that Tony teaches is expressed simply, a direct communion between him and each person he works with, with no 'show' to distract or entice us, or lull us into surrendering our journey to its power.

The power is within us; Tony's job is to awaken us. The work is ours to do.

What, then, are Tony's teachings? The job of a spiritual teacher is not, actually, to teach us anything in the usual meaning of the word. He is not here to give us knowledge, nor even to bring us wisdom. He is not here to teach us anything new, for everything we need in order to live the perfection of our life is already within us.

This is the first spiritual truth: *Everything we need in order to live the perfection of our life is already within us.* Tony's job is simply to give us the key with which we may open the door – to ourselves. He is here to help us move beyond the ego, beyond our own limitations, beyond the 'reality' that our mind creates. He is here to awaken us to our spiritual power, so that we may follow joyously our own magnificent path. He is here to show us what is possible, to remind us of what we already know but may have forgotten.

The process of moving into our spirituality is one of relinquishing our limitations and entrenched beliefs, of liberating our heart from the tyrannies of our mind. When the mind is thoroughly confused, this is the place where spiritual work can begin. Tony's job is, perhaps, to be an archaeologist, helping us to dig deeply inside ourselves to see what is really there, the essence of who we are. He offers us his hand, to lead us across the bridge from the world we perceive as reality, to the real world of wonder and miracles and infinite blessings beyond. The key to our spiritual path, as Tony repeats again and again, lies in our own heart.

And in our own experience. Spirituality is an approach to life, a way of inner knowing, experienced directly by each individual as we connect to the Divine. It is a looking inward, to that magical place of love and laughter, of trust and wisdom, of healing and miracles, of infinite potential, that resides deep within us all. It is the practice of what is in our heart; for truth, the sacred, Enlightenment, are all to be found deep inside us. Tony's role is to awaken us to that path, so that we may walk it with awareness, with joy, with love.

Walking our individual spiritual path is both the same for everyone, and also unique. The same, in that there is only one truth, one Divinity, one whole, for which every soul yearns to return; unique, in that we each experience our own journey towards the sacred in our own way. Nobody can experience another's journey nor do the spiritual work for anyone else. For the essence of spirituality is the way we live, with a heightened awareness of the sacred, imbuing all our attitudes, relationships and behaviour with it, bringing it into our daily lives and our most mundane activities.

Often, we become aware of our spiritual path only through some dramatic, and usually painful, life event: serious illness, the death of a loved one, an acrimonious divorce, being fired from a job. The universe nudges us in such a way that we have to sit up and take notice. If we don't, it will go on nudging us, creating more serious illness, more painful experiences, until we do respond. Or until we die. But perhaps we don't need to wait for such a dramatic and painful message. Perhaps Tony can be that nudge for us, shaking us out of our complacency, "stirring up" what may seem to us a comfortable life and helping us to re-examine the premises upon which that life has been built. Perhaps freeing us to live fully for the first time; showing us that there is another way. The way of beauty and bliss. The way of the heart.

The reference point for Tony's work is the Self. But today we are generally so out of touch with ourselves that we first need to find a starting point within the language that we understand.

In his retreats, Tony often comes across people leading busy and productive city lives, with beautiful homes and successful careers, who will yet attest to a restlessness of spirit that they can't quite articulate. Even high-flying city brokers, jetting round the world making small [or large] fortunes, will sometimes admit in a quiet moment that there is an emptiness at the centre of their lives; they know that making money can't be all there is. But they don't know what is missing.

Tony sees his job as tapping into people's malaise, finding our 'weak spot' and then using it as the starting point to open us up to our spirituality. Perhaps we often get sick, we feel uneasy without being able to put our finger on exactly why; we may have unaccountable bouts of unhappiness, anger or frustration; maybe underneath the fantastic job and the social whirl, we are depressed.

Once we begin to understand that we ourselves have created our problems by the way we are living, we can start to work. Once we can begin to reach the real person beneath the façades, we can start to make changes. Once we begin to connect to our roots and realize that we are not separate and isolated beings but are all part of the same Web of Life, connected to the Source and to each other, there is a real possibility that we will start to create a life that is dynamic, joyous, fulfilling and greatly enriched. Tony can act as a bridge to connect us from where we are 'stuck' to where we could gloriously be.

Tony emphasizes that it is our feelings of separateness and alienation from each other that are at the root of our unhappiness and the cause of all our conflicts. The universe is the manifestation of the perfection of Creation. Everything is interconnected and one. It is only when we separate ourselves from this oneness that we suffer. And we really suffer because we are alone in that suffering. Our greatest source of misery, in fact, is our separation from our divinity, from our true selves.

The Hopi Indians of North America have their own special ways of dealing with children's conflicts. If two kids are fighting over the same toy, for example, one of the adults will tell them to look up at the sky. Then he/she will ask, "Who owns the sky?" The children will answer that no-one owns the sky. If we didn't share the sky, we wouldn't be alive.

There are many ways of looking at life. People in different cultures have different perceptions, different views of reality. If we can accept this, and accept that it is only *our belief* that the material reality we have created is the sum total of the world, it should help us to loosen the bounds of any rigidity in our own beliefs, most of which will anyway have been inherited from parents, teachers, and our society at large. Once we accept that there are other ways of looking at life, change becomes possible. And with change, a new world opens up, of infinite possibility for a life lived in touch with our deepest selves, a life lived in peace and harmony, joy and love.

Tony's teachings are simplicity itself: that happiness doesn't live in the outside world, but rather within ourselves. And the way to find happiness is to free ourselves from all the attachments of the ego that we manifest in the outside world and from our beliefs of what happiness is.

The teachings are simple, but the work, at first, may appear to be difficult and painful. If we are ready to work with Tony, we will need to give up many things that are familiar to us, many props on which we have come to rely. These props include our beliefs, our certainties, our fears, our anger, our suffering, our guilt; our need to control our life and our environment; our need to find someone or something else to blame. We will have to surrender the domination that our ego has over our everyday life, the material ambitions of fame, money, or social position, that are dearly bought at the cost of the soul. What we are really giving up, of course, is only our suffering, our isolation and our fear.

Our spiritual journey starts with the recognition that something needs to change. And that the only way to bring about change in the outside world is to change ourselves on the inside first. Then we need to be willing to take risks, to have the courage to let go of the props that have been supporting us and leap, without waiting for a safety net to catch us. And of course, once we leap, the safety net will appear. Or we will realize that we don't need it; for the universe itself is there, waiting to welcome and support us.

And when you are ready to leap, you will have the courage. Everything inside you will push you towards this path and you will not be able to resist it. And this is not intellectual curiosity, but something for which your whole being seems to ache. A voice from deep within is calling you, and though your mind may think that this is crazy, you are ready to follow this voice. When you start to listen to this force inside you, it is amazing what happens. The whole universe embraces you and you feel safe and loved, perhaps really safe and really loved, unconditionally, for the first time since you were a baby; or maybe for the first time in your life.

Tony calls the journey that he takes us on "The Path of the Heart". And where will this journey take us? Ultimately, it is a quest for freedom. It takes us through the games and tricks of the mind, as he shows us how to relinquish our attachments to ego and the 'reality' and needs that it creates; how to examine our beliefs and let go of our emotions and fears; how to drive our lives with intention, the aspiration for the highest good of all, rather than seeking only personal gratification.

As we begin to open our heart and manifest more love, we journey into relationships, into the different energies of the god and goddess essence; how to live harmoniously in an intimate relationship and move along our spiritual path side by side with our chosen partner. We move into our dreams and look at the visions we have for our life, and also learn to interpret and understand the messages that our night dreams bring us. Our journey includes the recognition of the importance of our body in this incarnation; we'll learn how to listen to its needs, what to feed it and how to heal it.

Our quest for freedom moves through consciousness, which is the essence of spirituality: consciousness of living with love, with joy, fully awake, aware, alert, totally present to yourself and the life around you. This means bringing consciousness into each moment, being in harmony with yourself and with the All That Is. Spirituality, in fact all of life, can only ever be lived in the moment, in the now; being present in the moment, every moment, is all there is.

One special thing we need to remember about spirituality: that whatever is the goal, is also the way. So that consciousness, freedom, unconditional love, are all the essential goals of our spiritual journeying, but they are also the *way* in which we journey. The destination and the journey.

The spiritual path is one of seeking, questing, openness to receive. Wisdom comes not through our efforts to be wise, but rather when we let go of our certainties and make space to receive it. So, instead of looking for answers, we should rather allow the unknown, the mysterious, to find us; to welcome its unfolding in its own perfect way.

Accumulating answers can be dangerous. It may give us the false sense that we know, that we understand, that we are becoming wise. Answers lead to dogmas, to scriptures, to rules. They are not the path of spiritual knowing. This knowing comes through wonder, through surrender, through allowing Mystery to inhabit us without the need to understand it. By trying to reason, we lose touch with the transformative essence of spirituality. By trying to define it, we reduce it to something that the mind can understand; but it is no longer truth. Truth can be known, it can be experienced, it can be lived; but it cannot be defined.

So, as you come to read the teachings, try to bring to your reading an open heart that allows for recognition from deep within you. Put your clever logical mind on hold and absorb what you read with the wholeness of your intuitive insight, your imagination, your heart. Tune in to your inner wisdom and let the words resonate there, in the stillness that is the centre of your being. If this does not make sense to you at first, trust that in time it will, when you begin to put the teachings into practice.

Allow yourself to look in the mirror and see yourself as you really are. This is the first step: to go inside yourself, into that still silent place at the centre of your being; begin to recognize yourself and accept yourself with love. Tony can take you along the path, he can show you the well; it is your choice whether or not you drink.

This book is intended as a guide to show how we can implement these practices in our daily lives, and so vastly enrich all our experiences. It is meant as a series of reminders, of gentle prods, of signposts to help us along the journey; to bring us back to our path when we lose our way, to encourage us when we feel that the journey is difficult; to show us that the journey is possible, that we are never alone, but are loved and supported at all times by the universe and by the Divine.

Spirituality is wholeness, oneness, the interconnectedness of everything. When Tony darts from one thing to another in mid-sentence in his retreats, it is not only to shake us out of our comfort zone and get us moving. The truth is that all aspects of spirituality are interwoven, forming one web in which every thread touches every other thread, as well as touching the centre. Every aspect feeds into every other; and not only is each a part of the whole, but each seemingly separate aspect of spirituality also *includes* the whole.

But how can each aspect also include the whole? Well, let's take as an example unconditional love. Every aspect of spirituality is included within this. If you are living with unconditional love, you are also living in freedom, which means making choices that come from right intention, not personal will; you will be actively engaged in relinquishing the control of your ego mind and letting go of the domination of your beliefs and fears. If you are living with unconditional love, you will treat yourself, as well as others, with deep compassion, and so you will be nurturing your body and feeding it healthy food. Living with unconditional love means that you will be following your dreams. And, aware at all times of this love, you will be living in the moment, the essence of spirituality – which is also unconditional love.

A book demands structure, chapters, titles, headings. So, for simplicity and clarification as we begin our journey together, I have structured it around what may be called the 'key issues' of the spiritual path. They provide portals into spirituality, tools to help us as we begin to look inside ourselves: letting go of our beliefs, our emotions, our fears; the ego mind and its domination of our lives; the tyranny of time and learning to be in the present; will and intention and the difference between personal desire and acting for the highest good; relationships and how to love; dreams and dreaming; caring for our body and understanding its function in this life; exercising, body and soul; freedom and responsibility; healing ourselves and healing the planet.

But be aware as you read that structure, chapters, headings, are simply an aid for the journey; remember that each aspect of spirituality is enmeshed with every other aspect, and is also the whole. Each chapter also overlaps all the others. So, for instance, talking about being in the present moment also includes releasing the control of the ego mind; talking about letting go of the tyranny of the mind includes living in freedom, and the difference between will and intention; living with higher intention includes the way we connect to others, our relationships, our dreams. Emotions, fears, ego, perceptions of reality, responsibility for our lives, freedom, love, come into every chapter.

In many places in the text, references are given to other chapters, pointers to help us expand our capacity for inclusivity, for seeing connections in things that may appear to be separate and fragmented. This is not intended to make you hop around the book like a kangaroo on heat; it's just a reminder that spirituality is always a whole, that everything is a part of everything else, and to see it as separate bits is actually an illusion. This is intended just to simplify the way in, to give us markers on our journey, a guide to finding our path.

To aid the reading, pivotal points, or headings, are printed in bold. They are also there to give you time to breathe; time, if you wish, to ponder and reflect; to see how the text that you've just read resonates with you, before moving on. There are also spaces in the text denoting a change of gear, a new perspective or a new direction for the journey.

In many places in the book there are repetitions. At his retreats, Tony repeats himself, over and over, and over – until we get the message. When reading the book, if you 'get the message' quickly and the repetitions irritate you, pause and breathe. Then, instead of feeling annoyed, allow yourself to feel good that you are open and receptive and absorb things quickly; other people may take longer. Things also crop up again and again in the text, perhaps in different forms, as reminders, as gentle nudges, that spiritual practice is on-going and circular, and the work is never done.

And now we come to the choice: your choice. You may read this book as it were at arms' length, finding it interesting or fantastical, challenging or tame; a theoretical look at one person's journey into the spiritual teachings of a Shaman. But at best this will challenge your intellect; it will not enrich your life.

The other choice is to read the book and do the work. If this is your choice, you will allow it to push your buttons, to 'make you' angry, to challenge your beliefs, your defences and your self-righteousness, to open yourself up and confront your emotions and your fears. To stop apportioning blame and accept responsibility for creating your own reality. To let it eject you from your comfort zone and begin to confront the real issues of your life.

As this book has come into your life at this time, and nothing in life is random, the chances are that you are ready to do the work and face your real self. Only you will know. Only you can do it. But be warned! If you open the door to spiritual practice, there is no going back. In undertaking the spiritual life, there is no place for compromise; awakening to spirituality is not negotiable. We cannot choose to accept the bits that appeal to us and discard the rest. We cannot 'unknow' wisdom that we have gained, or pretend ignorance on days when we want to sink back under the coverlet of our comfort zone and don't feel like doing the work.

And even if we fully embrace the spiritual life, there are no bargains to be made. We walk our spiritual path for its own sake, for our own sake, without expectation of reward. There are no brownie points on offer for 'being spiritual'. The reward is the walking. We take it on trust, making a leap of faith and courage into the unknown.

If you make the second choice, to do the work, be compassionate with yourself. Treat yourself gently, as you would a close friend. Journey forwards with courage, but don't be judgemental of your 'lapses'. Don't constantly be measuring your 'progress' and finding yourself wanting. The path is circular, and though we are in continual movement forwards, we do not move in a straight line but rather in a spiral of ever-increasing breadth and depth. Try to live in the moment and do not judge.

Take time, breathe, enjoy the moment, move slowly. Have no expectations. If you work with right intention, you will get to where you need to be. And in fact, you are there already. The work that is left for you to do is to take off the masks that are hiding your essence, your love, your divinity, part the clouds of the illusion of reality in which you are living and inhabit your true self.

Our spiritual journey is a journey of looking inward, into the stillness that lives in the depths of our own being. As we move along our spiritual path, with all the challenges that meet us on the way, we need to remind ourselves, again and again, to return to that place of stillness within. This is the wellspring of spiritual practice, for our deepest selves reside in the stillness, in the silence, in perfect peace.

And one more thing. We need to take ourselves lightly… Moving along on our spiritual journey involves serious work, but it should not be earnest, not heavy-going. Bringing the light of Enlightenment into our lives also means bringing lightness into our lives. We should tread lightly, touch lightly, think of ourselves as becoming lightness, as well as light.

And we should not take ourselves too seriously. At his retreats, Tony laughs a lot and always has a mischievous twinkle in his eyes and a teasing smile on his lips. We need to be in touch with our sense of humour, our sense of fun, with the divine comedy of life. Spirituality is joyous; if we are truly inhabiting our spiritual selves, we will notice a smile in our eyes and a dance in our hearts.

And this dance of joy will happily connect us to our inner child; not a psychologically damaged being who may have grown up limited by parents or society at large, but the real inner child that we were born, full of curiosity and laughter and love. We need to tap into this inner child, to connect to its innate spontaneity and creativity, its sheer joy of being alive, in the moment. We need to give ourselves permission *not* to be sensible, to bring this child energy into our adult lives, to have fun, to splash in puddles and run with the wind, to paint and sing and dance the dance of life, to open up and live the wondrous being we were born to be.

Let the sunshine in; let the sun shine out.

It doesn't really matter which doorway we go through to start. The beginning of our journey is where we are, right now, this moment. The important thing is to begin…

Chapter Two
Letting Go
Beliefs, Emotions, Fears

"I'm not actually speaking mumbo jumbo. But you may think I am. I'm just speaking to a part of you that is not really the philosopher. I don't really care to make sense – if you don't understand I'm not in the least worried about it. I'm not here to make you feel good. What am I here to do? I'm here to speak to a part of you that is really very interesting. It's the part of you that is really you, that is hidden behind so many layers of the mask. So I hope you can be patient with me and understand that the work goes a little bit deeper than just pure logic."
Tony Samara

Tony is sitting cross-legged on cushions on the floor, wearing an Indian shirt and jeans, his dark shoulder-length curly hair framing his pale face and clear green eyes. A helper sits on one side of him, a translator on the other; a small microphone is in place at his feet to record his words for posterity. This is because he never knows beforehand what he will say; for the real work of the retreat happens in the moment, as he feels the needs of each person present.

Around him, a circle of some fifty pairs of eyes sit watching him in silent expectation. Tony speaks in a low soft voice [always] in English [always] – which is then translated into Portuguese, Croatian, Italian, or whatever language is the vernacular of the country he's in. He smiles and laughs a lot, although participants do not always find the situation amusing! But even the harshest things he says are delivered with charismatic gentleness, and a smile of infinite love. Living spiritually is profoundly joyous, but the process of opening up to our own journey may not be easy or comfortable. It is certainly not easy or comfortable working with Tony!

As he speaks, Tony bypasses the mind and speaks directly to the heart, where all spiritual movement takes place. What he is saying does often sound like "mumbo jumbo". It makes no sense if you listen only with your mind, for the mind is limited by the 'logic' of the physical world. But spiritual teachings lie in the realm of mystery, in the metaphysical, in the world that we don't see that is all around us, showering us with its blessings. They are accessible only to the deepest part of ourselves, the part that we cannot reach through the mind.

On the first day of a retreat with Tony, most participants will confess to not knowing what's going on; some will wonder what on earth they are doing there, and what they have let themselves in for. They are perplexed and confused, as he takes away their props and their certainties, and leaves them with nothing familiar to hang on to.

Tony spends a lot of time at the beginning of his retreats shaking participants out of their minds, helping them to let go and open up to a place of stillness, deep within. He does this by playing games with everyone. He jumps around enjoying verbal gymnastics, turning our ideas upside-out and inside-down, thoroughly confusing us. He will hop with lightening speed from one idea to another. He may start a sentence talking about balance between masculine and feminine energies, touch on the importance of nurturing the physical body, and finish the same sentence telling us about Higher Intention.

One day, for example, he told us that spirituality is a large white bird. He is very persuasive. When everyone believed him, he said, "What utter nonsense! How can you believe that spirituality is a large white bird?"

Confusing us is Tony's way of showing us the absurdity of holding on to rigid beliefs of any kind, of shaking us out of the certainties of our logical Western minds, of confounding us so utterly that we don't know any more what we think or what we believe. And the confusion, of course, is intentional. He likes, as he says, to "stir the soup", to throw in "a little of this, a little of that, the opposite of both", mix it all up and see what happens. And the mixture can be explosive!

Tony is a great Shamanic 'trickster', darting like quick-silver in and out of our consciousness, stirring up our comfortable lives and ordered existence, our conditioning and our prejudices, our intractable beliefs of what is real and what is truth. Pushing us out of our comfort zone without compassion. The more he "stirs the soup", the more confusion he sets up, the more he is helping us to look at who we are when we take off our masks, when we look beneath the self-image that we parade for the world, and have possibly even come to believe ourselves.

The purpose of shaking us up like this is not to give us new ideas to replace our old ones, but rather to help us to let go of *all* our beliefs about ourselves and the world, and open ourselves up to a new way of seeing our lives; to give us space in which we may allow ourselves not to know, to be uncertain, to begin to take risks. Again and again, in every retreat, Tony repeats this, like a mantra: we must allow ourselves not to know, to be uncertain, to take risks. To trust – him, and through trusting him to trust ourselves.

Many people come to Tony's retreats thinking that he will change their lives. Frequently he will, but not usually in the ways they expect. If you are still stuck in your ego mind, in the constant buzz of your beliefs and certainties, there is no way he can talk to you, for you will not hear him. That is like trying to create beautiful music on a piano that is out of tune. It's not possible.

But if we really want to open up to change, he will work with us. And he will do this by holding up a mirror to us, showing us who we really are, in essence, where we are on our journey and where our true path lies. And if we are not happy with what we see in our mirror, if what we see is conflict, defensiveness, confusion, that is the reality we have created. The mirror is not cracked; the trouble lies not in the mirror, but in ourselves. Tony is only reflecting back to us the truth of who we really are. This is the only place to start work.

At every retreat, the phrase that Tony uses more than any other is "Let go. Just let go." He says this in response to so many different issues, that it has became a kind of mantra. Just let go.

The beginning of all spiritual practice *is* letting go.

Our spiritual journey is first and foremost a journey of letting go. Letting go of everything that keeps us stuck, closed and afraid.

This means letting go of the past and everything in it that has defined and limited our lives and our relationships until now. Letting go of our conditioning, of rigid beliefs. Letting go of our emotions [not the same as feelings – see section on Emotions] and our fears that keep us trapped, reacting unconsciously as we live on automatic pilot. Letting go of our dogmatism, our self-righteousness, our judgementalness and blame. And letting go of a mind-set that looks for happiness and fulfilment in the outside world.

Our spiritual journey is not a journey of acquiring anything: not information, nor knowledge, nor new ideas or beliefs. It's simply a process of letting go of our certainties so that we may open ourselves up to a deeper truth. And it's a never-ending journey; there is always more to let go of.

In his retreats, Tony talks about "letting go of everything, in the moment, and going deeper into yourself". This may seem possible when he is there to guide us. But reading a book and then trying to do the work on your own may prove more difficult. So, to help with the process, this chapter is broken down into what may be seen as the 'main areas' in which we need to let go: beliefs, emotions and fears. Though, of course, fears are emotions, and emotions come from beliefs.

This 'separating out' is intended to bring focus and clarity to the work, and make the process of letting go more accessible. But remember, everything is connected to everything else, everything is really one whole. Looking at separate bits is just a way of to helping us get started.

Beliefs

Before we can let go of our beliefs, we need to see where they have come from, to question why we hold them, and understand the stranglehold they may have on our lives. For our beliefs play a major role in keeping us stuck. Though of course this has mainly been unconscious. And this is not about blaming ourselves and feeling guilty for our unconscious past! What was, was. Now, from this moment, we are ready to allow ourselves to begin to move forward into our conscious future.

Our beliefs dictate the way we experience our life.

Our beliefs dictate the way we experience our life. And these beliefs have been permeating our subconscious since our earliest childhood. They are the result of familial, tribal and cultural conditioning, which we have internalized. And this process is filtered through our own mind, which is also party to this conditioning, reaffirming our beliefs and colluding to keep us in a known and familiar environment. We absorb the ubiquitous message to fit in and do what is expected, not to rock the boat. Unquestioning, like everyone else, we belong to the group. We are approved of. We are safe.

But safe means limited. Safe means staying where we are. And bent on staying safe, we do not allow ourselves to take risks. And so we are not able to make changes, to move forward into the unknown and enrich our lives.

Questioning our beliefs and letting go of the ways in which they limit us is a first step on our spiritual path. This does not mean that our beliefs are wrong *per se;* only that they need to be questioned, examined, looked at in a new light, and the *control* that they have over our lives relinquished.

Our beliefs are just that, beliefs; they do not necessarily have any foundation in truth. After all, it was not so long ago in historical terms that everyone believed that the earth was flat. The fact that everyone believed it didn't make it so.

Our beliefs are the prism through which we see the world and interpret everything within it. They reaffirm our place in the world. They dictate the aspirations we allow ourselves; they curtail our expectations and limit the fulfilment of our potential. Our beliefs also provide us with the authority *not* to act in a way that would challenge or upset the *status quo* and force us to acknowledge the need for change. Hiding behind the shield of our beliefs protects us from having to see who we really are.

Our beliefs about the world dictate the way we experience reality.

According to our beliefs, so we live. If we see the world as dangerous, if we feel that we have to fight for our place within it, if we believe that someone else's success inevitably means our failure, if our world view is competitive and contentious, rather than cooperative and compassionate, that is how we will experience reality.

If we believe that there is never enough to go round – enough anything: money, material goods, or love and 'happiness' – and that if others have more that means there is less for us, we will always feel threatened by other people's abundance and success. We will always be chasing after more – and this will dictate the way we live.

Many of us may feel that we have questioned the beliefs of our childhood conditioning and moved away from parental or societal values. As teenagers, we probably rebelled against our parents, teachers, 'the system' that we saw as antediluvian, to become 'our own person'. But if this questioning and rebellion comes from the same place of ego mind, no matter how 'different' the ideas or beliefs or lifestyle that we embrace, if it does not take us into the realm of spiritual consciousness, we have not really changed in any way that matters. We have simply exchanged one set of beliefs for another.

If our beliefs create our experience of the reality in which we live, then it follows that they also prevent us from having any other view of reality. If what I believe is true, then any different belief must be false. And we should not forget where rigid beliefs may ultimately lead. All wars, and the devastation that they cause, have been fought in the name of beliefs – religious or nationalistic, or the lust for personal power.

So, if we can recognize that other people hold beliefs different from our own and so experience a different reality, we can begin to see the limitations that all belief systems impose. And this includes our beliefs about 'truth'. The best way to avoid truth is to have a belief about it! For then what you believe is the belief, but this is not truth. Truth cannot be defined or labeled; it can only be experienced, not through the belief of the mind, but through the knowing of the heart.

Our beliefs not only dictate the way we experience reality; they also *create* our reality.

Our beliefs do not come from our experiences, as many people may think; our experiences are created by our beliefs.

We create our own reality.

This is a fundamental spiritual truth, and one that we need to grasp firmly, wherever we are on our spiritual journey; for it defines the way we live and the way we evolve. We create our own reality.

The outer world is a mirror of our inner world.

The world around us is simply a mirror of everything that we believe and think and feel. So, if we believe that life is a struggle, that people are uncaring and we will never be able to do what we really want to do, we will invite into our lives people and situations that confirm these beliefs. Alternately, if we believe that life is joyous, full of beautiful, compassionate people, exciting challenges and abundance for everyone, *this* is what we invite into our lives.

The situations and people that we invite into our lives are simply a mirror of our beliefs.

Our beliefs create as well as colour everything that happens to us.

Our beliefs are responsible for everything that we experience; both *what* we experience, and *how* we experience it. We need to come back to this again and again. Understanding that we create our own reality totally changes the way we experience our lives.

We may believe that our problems are caused by our circumstances, our parents, our partner; or God. If we do, we will spend our lives blaming someone else for everything that goes wrong for us. If this is what we believe, we will always find someone else to blame. And we will continue to be frustrated, miserable, angry or envious of others.

But if all our problems were miraculously to disappear, we would simply recreate a new set of similar problems – as long as we were still stuck in the same belief system.

Our beliefs about life are self-fulfilling prophecies.

Reality manifests according to our beliefs and expectations. It is really important to understand this. Many of us have difficulty in taking this on board. But it is a fundamental spiritual truth. We resist it because to acknowledge it would mean that we have to take responsibility for our lives. There would be nobody else to blame. And this is scary. But this is our spiritual journey: becoming an adult and taking responsibility is what spirituality is about.

Our beliefs are self-fulfilling prophecies.

Whatever beliefs about life we hold, our mind will ensure that they are confirmed and reinforced over and over by our experience. That is the job of the mind; to reaffirm what we believe, to keep us in a familiar place, to sustain the reality that we create. So, if men always treat you badly, if you never have enough money or you cannot hold down a job, if you don't like the people around you and they don't seem to like you, you need to look inside yourself and see what within you is creating this reality.

Whatever situations we find ourselves in, we can change them only when we realize that our beliefs are responsible for creating them. When we accept this, we see that we have real choices, to create the circumstances we wish to inhabit. And then we need to take responsibility for our choices.

Tony follows the Buddhist teachings that the world of physical reality is *maya,* an illusion.

The world of physical reality is an illusion.

The physical world that we inhabit is a world of our own making. *We create our own reality.*

And we create our own suffering when we perceive the material world as reality. Often it is hard to see this when we are living in the middle of suffering. We may ask scoffingly how it can be that *we* have created a life-threatening illness, or how is it *our* responsibility that our partner has left us or we were fired from our job.

This is a profound question and a difficult spiritual lesson. Fully to comprehend this requires deep spiritual journeying, until we arrive at the place where we know this to be true. For the moment, if it doesn't resonate with you, try to hold it in your heart, on trust. As you journey further along your spiritual path, you may open yourself up to accepting the wisdom of many of Tony's teachings that do not make sense at the moment.

But the simple answer is that we did not consciously choose these things to happen; of course. But something in the way we were living was unbalanced, out of harmony with our true selves, with our deepest integrity. We needed a wake-up call to move us on to the life we were meant to be living. Our soul, in its wisdom, has known this and so has created a situation that would force us to sit up and take notice, to begin to examine our life and our beliefs.

The world of physical reality cannot bring us happiness. This can only come from within.

Happiness can only come from within. It is only our beliefs that lead us to think that our happiness can be found in the outside world. It is only our beliefs that create our need for external things, and are responsible for our concomitant unhappiness when we are not able to acquire them.

If we believe that material goods will buy us happiness, we will strive to acquire ever more possessions. For if money and possessions equal happiness, then obviously more money and more possessions equal more happiness. But it will never be enough. The Nissan Micra that was going to fill our life with joy, pales into insignificance next to the neighbour's shining new Rolls Royce. The little holiday flat in Marbella doesn't seem so fabulous when we hear about our friends' luxury villa in the Seychelles.

If we are caught on a treadmill of comparing and competing for more material goods, there will always be someone who has more. And you know something? They are not happy either if they are depending on their wealth to provide their happiness.

The "hungry ghost" is never satisfied.

Tony calls this endless search for more and more material acquisitions the hungry ghost.

For the hunger is never satisfied. Its eyes are large, its belly larger. The more it seeks nourishment in the illusion of finding happiness in material goods, the hungrier it becomes. The mind tells it that it needs to devour more and more of the fruits of illusion – more money, a new house, a bigger car, a new lover, lots of new lovers – all these will make us happy. Anything in the outside world will make us happy, as long as it protects us from the need to look within ourselves for truth.

The belief that money will solve all our problems is built on sand. Think, for example, of people winning vast amounts of money on the lottery or the football pools. This may radically change their lifestyle, but not their life. They may buy into material wealth: new homes, fast cars, exotic holidays. They may give up their jobs and begin to follow a hedonistic path. But if they are not blessed with spiritual consciousness along with their newfound riches, their life problems, their relationships and above all their real feelings about themselves will not have changed.

Money does not buy self-esteem, meaning or wisdom.

If we are still stuck in the same limiting belief pattern, we will continue to create our problems and our suffering and our pain in the same way we have always done. We would just be living out our dramas in more luxurious surroundings.

We only have to look at the fabulously wealthy lifestyles of some film stars or sports celebrities [not all, of course, but some] – whose lives are torn apart by too much money and too little consciousness; by drugs, drink or other addictions, by multiple relationships or promiscuous sex, by the futility and emptiness that often lie at the centre of their lives – to bear out the truth of the old saying that money can't buy happiness. I know that the adage continues "but it can make unhappiness a lot more comfortable". But why settle for 'comfortable unhappiness' when living in deep joy and contentment is possible?

We search for happiness outside ourselves only when we are unhappy – and we are unhappy precisely *because* we are searching for happiness outside ourselves.

We need to get off this treadmill of looking for our happiness in the outside world.

Everything we need for our happiness in this life is within us.

It is only by letting go of our belief that our happiness is to be found in the outside world – in material possessions, in worldly acclaim or in other people – that we may create the space to go inside. And this includes looking for salvation in an intimate relationship. [For more on this, see Chapter 5: God and Goddess – Relationships and How to Love.]

As we begin to look within, to let go of the beliefs and certainties that have run our life, and have the courage to begin to change on the inside, we will see that this is reflected in everything that we create in the world around us. As we become more conscious, more authentic, more loving, this is the world that we attract to ourselves; this is the wonderful world that we create and inhabit.

At one of Tony's retreats, a high-flying lawyer who had recently recovered from cancer said that before her illness she had always been interested in accumulating more and more expensive possessions to fill her beautiful home in an exclusive suburb of a major city, in an attempt to bring herself happiness. Her illness changed her beliefs and she started to look inwards. After her illness she realized that the more she acquired, the less it meant to her. As she put it so poignantly, "It took my illness to teach me that owning and experiencing are not the same. Now I have much less, but I experience and appreciate much more. And for the first time in my life, I am really happy."

When we look for happiness in the outside world, we try to control our environment in order to get what we want.

Trying to control life is alien to spiritual practice.

It's also a waste of time, as it's impossible!

We try to control our lives in order to make them fit in with our beliefs: this is how life should be, this is what we want. And in fact, we try to control our lives more and more, the more we feel them to be out of control. But as we begin to relinquish the dictatorship of our beliefs, we begin to feel more 'in control', and the need to try and control our lives and our environment diminishes accordingly. We realize that our lives will unfold in exactly the way they are meant to.

This does *not* mean that we do not have choices. On the contrary, the more we let go of our rigid beliefs of how our life ought to be, the more real choices we have. This is a spiritual paradox, one of many we shall encounter on our journey. But as our life begins to unfold and flow in a balanced and harmonious way, we see that more and more choices open up for us. Instead of trying to control life, and failing, we begin to understand that we have an abundance of real choices before us.

Our job, then, is not to try to control, but to make responsible choices coming from our place of highest integrity; from seeing our life as it really is, not from our fantasy projection of it. This is our journey. Not knowing what the future will bring opens us up to the life that is happening now, around us and within us.

It is the certainties framing our lives that limit our experiences.

If we live only with the certainties of our mind, we are asleep to the experiences of our heart. Our beliefs are a potent force for disguising the nature of truth and keeping us from experiencing our true selves.

This doesn't mean that we have to change our way of life overnight. Although the realization that our mind and our beliefs do not create true reality is instantaneous, a sudden cosmic shift of perception that comes to us as a flash of Enlightenment; but it may have taken us many years of journeying to reach this moment. Like an actor becoming an 'overnight success' after working hard for twenty years!

Though spiritual knowing always occurs in the moment, inhabiting our spirituality is an on-going process, a constant movement towards a new way of being, with ourselves and in the world. A way of accepting what is. Of simply being.

Emotions

Emotions and feelings are often confused, but they are not the same. Feelings are profound and enduring and flourish as an expression of who we are. They come from a deep place within us and are not attached to anyone or anything in the outside world. Feelings nourish our heart and soul, and both manifest and reaffirm our connectedness to the All That Is.

Emotions, on the other hand, come from our minds and are ephemeral as sudden rainfall and may pass as quickly as a summer storm. They are connected to the behaviour of other people and are a result of our unconscious way of living. Emotions detract and distract us from our spiritual journey and often overwhelm us and take over our lives. If we are not living with consciousness, we are living 'in' our emotions; we identify with them and we let them dictate our lives.

[Some confusion may arise from the fact that we have only one verb in English, the verb 'to feel', to describe both feelings and emotions. But I think the real difference is clear. Just be aware that when we are talking about 'feeling' angry or 'feeling' jealous, etc., we are talking about emotions.]

No-one can 'make us' feel anything.

Our emotions belong to us alone. No-one else can ever 'make us' feel anything; not resentful nor angry, jealous nor guilty; nor, for that matter, can anyone else 'make us' feel happy. This is a basic tenet of spirituality and we need to take it on board.

If we feel that someone is making us angry, for example, what they are doing is 'pressing our buttons'. And when someone presses our buttons and we feel angry, they are actually tapping into our anger. *The anger is already within us.* It is up to us whether we choose to *be* angry or not.

So, if someone invokes your anger, you need to look inside and see which buttons are being pressed. For instance, if friends exclude you from a particular activity and this sparks your anger, they may be tapping into deep-seated feelings of rejection that you experienced as a child. If you can look inwards and connect to the source of your anger and recognize what it is attached to, you may be able to release anger that has lived inside you and festered for many years.

Alternately, if we feel that someone else is 'making us' happy, we are projecting onto them both our emotions and our needs: in the myth that we are writing with our lives, we have decided that this person represents our happiness and is therefore responsible for 'making us' happy. In both cases, whether anger or happiness is evoked, we have given away our power to someone else and we are letting them dictate how we feel.

Remember, the anger [or any other negative emotion] is already within us, otherwise it could not be evoked. So, if someone behaves in a way that 'makes us' feel angry, we need to step back, assess the situation, look at our emotions and decide which emotions we want to express. We may feel angry. *It is our choice whether we react angrily or not.*

Understanding how our emotions arise is the first step to being able to let them go.

But letting go of our emotions may not seem so easy at first. People often say that they are ready to let go, they want to let go, but they don't know *how* to let go. They try and try, maybe they do some spiritual exercises and 'releasing' techniques, but still can't seem to let go. Then they feel disappointed or a failure and become disillusioned with the whole process.

So, the first step to releasing our emotions is to observe them.

If we feel that someone is making us angry, resentful, hurt, or anything else, we need to slow down, stop ourselves in our tracks, and breathe deeply for a few seconds. Then we can begin to observe our emotions. Observing our emotions is the first step to relinquishing them.

So, become the watcher. Observe yourself becoming angry. As you observe your emotion as something separate from you, you realize that you, the observer, are not angry, for you are *witnessing* the anger. The very act of witnessing your anger means that you are detached from it. You cannot be in it and outside it at the same time. If you are observing it, you are outside it; and this is the first step to being able to let it go.

The appropriate response to someone 'making us angry' is to acknowledge the emotion and let ourselves witness it. As adults, we do not have to 'act out' our emotions, getting caught up in the dramas that they create. This is simply repeating old patterns of behaviour, developed in childhood, and followed without awareness. As we begin to bring awareness into our lives, we may simply acknowledge the emotion and then release it. We do not have to give it energy.

Letting go of negative emotions is not suppressing them.

Letting go of negative emotions is, in fact, the opposite of suppressing them. Releasing anger for example, does not mean that we don't deal with it. On the contrary. If the person who has 'provoked' the anger has behaved in a way that we find unacceptable, the appropriate response, as an adult, is to confront the person involved, in a mature way, and deal with the issues that it raises. But the anger, the emotion, is ours.

If we are feeling strong anger, we may choose to release it in any number of ways: we might want to beat some cushions, go outside and scream, or do a shaking meditation. We may decide to paint, write or dance our anger and release it that way. We may want to sit quietly and do a visualization in which we see ourselves relinquishing the anger.

But whatever we choose, we need to recognize that *we 'own' our anger,* and the process of releasing it is a process between us and ourselves. It should never be something that we let out on someone else.

We choose the emotions that we have.

We need to recognize that we ourselves have created our emotions – no matter who or what has triggered them – and acknowledge that we have a choice: whether to give them energy or not. It is our decision. Our spiritual path is strewn with opportunities for us to connect to these emotions, examine them, realize that we no longer need to hold on to them, and then let them go.

Other people pressing our buttons is actually a positive experience, for they are offering us a golden opportunity for learning: learning to tap into long-buried emotions, to witness them, deal with them, and then release them. Our daily interactions with others provide us with myriad opportunities to learn and let go. Every time someone 'makes you' feel angry, hurt, outraged or unfairly treated, is a chance to witness the emotions that this sparks and learn from the experience. Observe it, stay with it, really try to 'inhabit' the emotion. And then try to trace it back within you to its source.

You will probably not reach the source the first time you try. But you will connect to some buried emotions, which you can observe and then release. As you do this, over and over again, you will connect to deeper layers of stored emotions, which you will then be able to observe and relinquish.

Think of your emotions as a railway line. The station nearest to you is the immediate past. As you trace your emotions back along the railway line, you connect first to the immediate past and then, moving back along the lines, you trace further and further back into the past. As this process becomes a regular part of your spiritual practice, your interactions with others will become more conscious and it will become progressively easier for you not to get caught up in emotional reactions and dramas.

We are responsible for our emotions.

We are responsible for our emotions; we choose to have the emotions we have. It is really important to understand this. If we do not accept responsibility for our emotions, we cannot move forward. Our emotions may seem random and beyond our control, but they are not. Becoming conscious means both realizing that we are indeed responsible for our emotions, and then taking that responsibility.

This process is an on-going part of our spiritual journey. Each time we learn from such an opportunity, the process becomes easier, and we move forward. Ultimately, it is a mark of our spiritual journeying that we can feel gratitude towards those people who push our buttons and 'make us' angry, for the opportunities for learning and growth that they provide.

A question that Tony is frequently asked at his retreats, concerns love: Isn't love an emotion? The word "love" is perhaps the most misused and abused word in any language; we need to define what we mean.

Real love is unconditional and independent of any love object.

Real love is unconditional and independent of any love object. Unconditional love is a state of being, the way we live, the way we are in the world; it is not a passing emotion for a particular person, object or situation. Unconditional love comes from our heart, from our deepest centre and is the manifestation of our wholeness, our integrity, our connectedness to the Sacred and to the All That Is.

Unconditional love is our portal to Enlightenment. In fact, it *is* Enlightenment.

On the other hand, what we frequently describe as love – when we mean a particular emotion for a particular person – is ephemeral, and dependent on something outside ourselves for its existence. This is not real love. Our emotions are conditional: we expect something in return for this love, at the very least that the object of this love will love us in return. If the object of our love were to change in some way, then the love that we have for it, her or him, may also change. [For more about love – dependent and dysfunctional, real and unconditional – see Chapter 5: God and Goddess – Relationships and How to Love.]

Suffering comes from our attachment to our emotions.

Suffering comes from the mind-set that tells us that our emotions are real. But they are not.

Nothing that appears to fulfil us from the outside only, is real. Nothing that is real can be lost; whatever can be lost is just an illusion. What is true truly belongs to us: not our emotions, but our feelings.

Our emotions are the mind's way of both responding to and reinforcing the dramas that we are constantly inventing in our lives. And, like everything created by our minds, they are related to time.

Living our spirituality means living in the moment. And living in the dramas that our emotions create is one of the biggest obstacles to living in the moment. But as we begin to let go of our emotions and our dramas, we begin to live in the present. For every act of letting go, of witnessing, is a conscious act, and consciousness exists only in the present moment. [See also next chapter: Mind and Ego, and the tyranny of time.]

Letting go is an on-going process.

We need to be constantly vigilant, to remind ourselves over and over to be the witness of our emotions, to watch ourselves and the ways we react to other people's behaviour.

A middle-aged woman at one of Tony's retreats complained that she always had something wrong with her, although physically she was as strong as an ox. But she was holding so much anger and resentment in her body, such conviction that the world had 'done her wrong', that she was constantly feeling ill. When Tony gently suggested that it might help her if she were to let go of her anger, she shouted back at him, offended and outraged, "I've let go of everything there is to let go of!"

Sometimes our anger so overwhelms us that we are blind to it. Sometimes, we prefer to remain in familiar pain than risk living in unfamiliar freedom and joy.

Letting go is a process of detachment: detachment from our beliefs and our emotions.

Detachment does *not* mean being uninvolved with life. Many people think that being detached means not participating fully in life. But the contrary is true. Detachment is a state of being deeply engaged with life, involved in everything around us, intensely aware of our feelings, but at the same time observing our involvement, our feelings, as we might observe another person.

We do not deny our feelings. We feel them passionately, as they are, but without an agenda; without any attachment to outcome. We do not deny our emotions either. We observe them, we may try to see how they have arisen, what they are attached to, what we can learn from them. And then we let them go. *As adults, we do not need to act them out.*

Detachment from emotional dependence is part of our spiritual journey. And the process of detaching from our emotions is on-going. It continues until we reach Enlightenment, or until we die; whichever comes first.

Perhaps the hardest process of all is detaching ourselves from being emotionally needy: of other people's approval, time, energy, love, attention. I'm not talking about the healthy interdependence of autonomous and mature people, who can give freely of their time, their energy, their love, but do not *need* to receive these things in order to feel good about themselves.

Detaching ourselves emotionally is an act of becoming conscious, so that we don't just react like Pavlov's dog, with a series of preconditioned responses when the bell is rung. It means that we interact with others from our heart, from a place of love, because that is who we are, not because we want something in return, either emotional or material. We *act* out of our own integrity; we do not *react* to the situation unconsciously.

Our detachment from emotional dependence means that our feelings of self-esteem come from our recognition that our true worth is to be found within ourselves and is not dependent on anyone else.

Spirituality recognizes that our true worth comes from within.

Most of us seem to suffer in some way from feelings of low self-esteem; from feeling, perhaps, that 'we are not good enough' and 'do not deserve' better. These emotions generally start in early childhood, when we are not 'recognized' as the beautiful unique being that we are, and are reinforced throughout our lives by the self-perpetuating prophecies of our beliefs. This may lead us to be timid and fearful, or to false arrogance and bravado as a means of self-defence. But either way, we will be looking for our self-esteem in the outside world; for other people to approve of us and 'make us' feel good about ourselves.

Becoming emotionally detached means freeing ourselves from being at the end of someone else's yoyo string, and reacting or behaving according to what others think of us, or the buttons that they press. Becoming emotionally detached means that other people's opinions of us do not influence how we feel about ourselves. Whether they praise or blame us.

To be equally unmoved by praise or blame is to move towards spiritual Enlightenment.

Becoming emotionally detached means that we move into a place where we can be equally unmoved by praise or blame, criticism or compliment, spitefulness or kindness, judgementalness or compassion. This frees us from the influence of other people's opinions. This is a great step forward on our spiritual journey.

We can do this by bringing awareness into every situation in which someone praises or blames us, observe how we feel, and then detach ourselves emotionally. And if you are able to do this, to be equally unmoved by whatever others think of you – not to feel you have to justify yourself in any way on the one hand, nor feign false modesty on the other – you have taken a huge leap into spiritual consciousness.

To be equally unmoved by praise or blame. How liberating is that!

Emotional detachment means being in touch with our own centre, acknowledging what we really feel, from the heart, without the baggage of conditioned responses, or any expectations – our own or other people's. It means understanding the difference between ephemeral emotions, which are connected to the mind, and deep feelings, which live in the heart.

As we detach ourselves from our emotions, we move away from our minds into our hearts. Our heart is the home of our true feelings. And our heart is the home of trust.

Trust is an essential element of spirituality.

Learning to trust is a huge part of our spiritual journey; we will come back to this again and again. Trusting ourselves, trusting others, trusting the All That Is. In fact, our ability to trust is the measure of our spiritual consciousness.

Trust is *not* the same as gullibility. We are gullible only when we don't see a situation as it really is. Trust thrives as we see more and more clearly what is, with growing emotional detachment.

And trust is not passive. It is always a deliberate choice, both a result and a tool of our consciousness.

As we begin to detach ourselves from our emotions, we begin to trust. And the more we trust, the easier it is to let go of emotions. We create a virtuous circle – trust and detachment feeding into each other, nourishing each other, nourishing us. Trusting the innate goodness and perfection of the universe, trusting that we are loved and embraced by God/Spirit, trusting our own deep wisdom and intuition – all take us forward on our journey.

Trust is the opposite of control.

When we try to control the universe, we are actually saying that it is imperfect as it is, and we need to improve it. Trusting is accepting that the universe and all of creation is perfect as it is, even if we may not know its purpose. And that when we trust in the Great Creator, our lives will unfold as a manifestation of this perfection.

When you trust someone completely, you open your heart – to them, to the universe and to yourself. All spiritual work requires this deep trust, for it is the work of the heart. And you cannot do it half-heartedly! You cannot trust a little bit, but take out an insurance policy just in case it doesn't work. You have to give one hundred per cent.

And when you take the first step towards the Divine, It will take ten steps towards you. You have to start the process, make a conscious decision to make the first move, and then ask for guidance from the universe. Ask, and you shall be given. And when you trust the Divine, you trust the work, and you also begin to trust that deepest part of yourself, the divine perfection within.

Fears

The other major factor that keeps us stuck in our ego illusions of reality and prevents us from following our spiritual path is fear. And this is really a major factor!

Fear is an emotion, and our emotions are born of our beliefs, of how we think things are and how they are supposed to be. But because our fears have such an overwhelming impact on our lives, it is helpful to look at them separately, to see if we can begin to unravel them. And actually, when we trace back our beliefs and our emotions, behind them we always find there is fear.

We all have fears.

If we don't think we have fears we are either truly enlightened, or our fears are so deeply buried that we're not aware of them. With our beliefs and our other emotions, even if at first we are not conscious of their roles in our lives, we are at least aware that we *have* beliefs and emotions. With our fears, the situation is much more complex; they may be so suppressed that we do not even know we have fears.

We may hide our fears behind many other labels.

Most of us are very good at pretending to ourselves that we don't really have fears by finding other labels for them. Somehow, calling them doubt, worry, inhibition, scepticism, shyness, suspicion, lack of trust, seems easier to deal with than the idea that we may have fears. It doesn't matter what we call it; behind all these labels lies fear.

We all have fears, though we may think that we are the only ones.

We may compare ourselves to others and think that only we have fears. On the surface, the lives of those around us may seem successful, exciting, full of interesting things to do and wonderful people to be with. We may feel that only we are stuck or fearful, unable to venture out of our shells. But ours is the only life we see from the inside. We see others' lives from the outside, and we mistake the gloss for the substance. This compounds the problem and increases our sense of isolation, and our fear.

But the people around us are afraid too. Indeed, for most of us our lives are actually dominated by our fears, though we are probably unaware of this. But unconsciously, we act out of fear.

We act out of fear because we are scared to look within.

We are afraid of being with ourselves, alone in that deep still place within. So we create full and busy lives to protect ourselves, to craft a self-image that reflects a happy and successful person back to us; to make sure that we have no time to spend with ourselves, no unaccounted for moments, just 'to be'. We create noise all around us: the television, the radio, loud music, constant aimless chatter, anything to avoid inhabiting that silent place within. For we are afraid of being alone with ourselves in the silence, with no distractions, no means of escape. We are afraid of what we might find, deep within ourselves; of what we might not find.

Our fears may be so deeply buried that many of us ridicule the very idea that we have fears at all. We may cover our fear with bravado, with actions that seem daring and exciting.

A woman that Tony met in Slovenia told him that when she was younger she had spent a year hitchhiking alone across South America. How brave, said her friends, how thrilling, possibly with a twitch of envy. But in truth, her decision came from fear. Travelling catapulted her into a world of excitement and adventure; it reinforced her self-image as intrepid and different from the run of the mill people who spent their lives working in offices. But really it was an escape, because she was afraid of making a decision to follow her dream and become an actress. She was terrified of rejection, of failure, of not being as good as she thought she was. As long as she didn't do it, she could go on dreaming that one day she would, and when she did, she would be a great actress...

Twenty years on, she's still dreaming, still running away. [See also Chapter 6: Dreams...]

But we can let go of our fears. Not all at once; don't panic. Slowly, gradually. But we need to start – now.

The first thing we need to do is name our fears.

Naming our fears makes them real to us. It is an act of recognizing and acknowledging that we have fears. We cannot relinquish something amorphous and vague. Naming our fears gives us something tangible to work with. It is the first step in the process of letting them go.

We start by looking inside. Let's try a simple exercise. Close your eyes, breathe deeply, and relax. Focus on being inside your body. Let go of all thought, all expectation, and just allow your body to feel what it feels. Don't judge; allow. The process is not one of 'trying to accomplish', but rather one of letting whatever is there surface so that you can deal with it.

As you stay in your body, you may begin to connect to one of your fears. Remember, our fears are held in every cell of our body. As we allow ourselves to let go of the fear of the fear, we allow our fears to surface. Nothing may surface for you the first time; or the second. Just continue to practise, and allow. Eventually, if you stay consciously in your body, you will begin to connect to your fears. For all our fears live in our body.

As you begin to connect, see if you can name any of your fears. Just one to start with. Perhaps, for example, it is fear of rejection? Ask yourself what might lie behind this fear. Don't analyze it, and don't judge. Try to feel the fear in your body. [See also Chapter 7: The Body – Health and Healing.] You may discover that behind this fear is the fear of not being good enough, of being worthless. And that behind this fear is the fear of abandonment. And that behind this fear…

Like all spiritual practice, letting go of our fears is an on-going process. As we move more deeply into ourselves, we will discover that behind the fear that we can connect to, lies another fear, and behind that, another.

Naming our fears is the first step to releasing them.

Fear is almost certainly present when we begin our spiritual journey.

We may be terrified that if we open up to our spiritual journey, we will have to let go of old comfortable habits and embark on a new, and scary, way of living. We may have fear, perhaps, that if we change we may lose our friends or threaten our primary relationship. Fear that if we embrace a new way of living, our 'comfort zone' will be jeopardized and we won't be able to cope. We may be afraid of being loved or afraid of being unloved; afraid of failure or afraid of success. Afraid of exposing ourselves and being 'found out' and found wanting. Afraid of intimacy. We may be afraid that if we finally find the courage to look inside, we will find nothing there.

Fear is a fearsome taskmaster and to some extent it enslaves us all.

We live in a culture of fear.

This fear, although unconscious and unacknowledged, is wittingly and unwittingly spread by society, and individually reinforced. Unconsciously, we collude with the prevailing attitudes, values and norms of our culture. We think we are making free choices. But actually, much of the time we make choices that come from a place of unconscious fear.

Our consumer societies tempt us with round the clock distractions – spectator sports, shopping, television, pubs, pop music, action and often violent movies. And of course the Internet, where we can now live 'virtual lives' without having to leave the security of our own homes. These all-pervasive distractions provide us with ubiquitous escape routes and keep us from looking inside, from questioning, from living conscious lives. We are 'too busy' to look at what is really happening inside us.

We are not afraid because the world is a terrifying place; the world is a terrifying place because our fears have created it that way.

The world out there is only a mirror of the reality that we have created. If it is a frightening place, it is because it reflects our fears. We need to remind ourselves that *we create the reality in which we live.* And this reality is created by our beliefs – and by our fears.

If we see reality as a world of suffering, greed, poverty, hatred, violence, oppression, we need to look in the mirror and see what it is about ourselves – our imbalance, our disharmony, our attitudes and beliefs, our perceptions and presumptions, our prejudices and our fears – that has contributed to this.

Of course, we have not individually created this world, but on some level we are part of the collective endeavour; for if we do nothing consciously to change this world, we are colluding in perpetuating the *status quo.* So, we need to look in our own mirror, to see what 'out there' reflects what 'in here', and then take responsibility for it. And of course we also create the way we see reality.

It is important to emphasize that our fears are mostly not conscious.

But although we are not conscious of them, our fears are the constantly fertilized ground out of which our limitations grow. They are the place where our boundaries are mapped, our aspirations reigned in, our potential thwarted.

And out of our fears, we create our dramas.

Usually, we get so caught up in our dramas that it is difficult to extricate ourselves. Spiritual practise helps us to let go of the fears and detach ourselves from our dramas, from our suffering. It enables us to stand back and observe, to be a witness, to step back from being emotionally involved.

If we can become detached and not allow ourselves to get caught up in the drama of the suffering we create, if we can see it as something objective, not personal, then it will obviously be easier to let go of it; easier to create the circumstances in which letting go can happen.

Fear is an illusion that we create.

As Tony says, "You don't need to spend twenty years on a psychiatrist's couch analyzing everything that is wrong with your life. What a waste of time that is!"

This is not the way to deal with your fears, your anxieties, your suffering, your sickness, your malfunctioning relationships; what your parents did to you when you were a child, or what your partner is doing to you now. You simply need to stop the busy whirl of your life, to breathe deeply, and then allow yourself to go inside and begin to look at your fears.

Of course, this is easier said than done. But if we can recognize that our fears are actually more frightening than the things we are afraid of, if we can begin to understand how our fears are created and where they come from, we can begin the process of releasing them. Yes!

Our fears are created by the mind.

Fear is another tool of the mind to keep us 'safe'. And safe means stuck. [See also next chapter: Mind and Ego.] Our fear of change and of the unknown, is created by our mind to stop us from getting hurt. Our mind creates fear to prevent us from taking risks. In its efforts to keep us in the safe and familiar world we know and prevent us from being harmed, our mind keeps us stuck in a world dominated by fear.

By bringing our awareness out of our mind and into the present moment, we are able to bring our fears into our consciousness and so begin to release them. And if we were to do this every moment, in the moment, we would have no fear. For fear is always projected onto the future; it does not, cannot, exist in the present. [I am talking here of psychological fear which has probably accompanied us all our life, and is divorced from any real danger; not the physical fear you would feel if you were suddenly confronted by a hungry tiger or a person with a gun.]

There is a story about a village priest who was out walking one day, when he met Death. Death informed him that there would shortly be a plague of cholera in his village, and that it would claim five hundred lives. The villagers were terrified and stayed in their houses. But as they came out to bury their dead, the death toll mounted, and nearly a thousand people lost their lives. Some time later, the priest was again out walking, and again met Death. He was pleased at the opportunity to confront him. "You told me that five hundred people in my village would die of cholera, but nearly one thousand people died." Death looked at him and smiled. "My friend, the plague claimed five hundred lives, as I told you it would," Death answered him. "The rest died of fear."

We need to remind ourselves that what we believe about our life becomes the way we live it. And we may be as wounded by our perceptions and fears of a difficult situation as by the situation itself. Our beliefs can be our greatest prison, our fears the prison guard.

At the heart of all fear is the perceived threat of 'the other'.

We are afraid because we perceive 'the other' as threatening. This 'other', we believe, invades our space and takes what is rightfully ours.

But this fear comes from our perception of ourselves as separate beings. When we realize that we are all part of the same oneness, created by the same Divinity, and that we are all interconnected with each other, we understand that there is no 'other'. And then our fear begins to disintegrate. We realize that we, ourselves, have created our fears, and they are, indeed, an illusion.

Chapter Three
Mind and Ego

"The mind can be a very good trickster. I call it the "monkey mind". And this monkey mind will make you believe that your reality is so important, so real that you won't see the simplicity in life. Where is simplicity? It is not in your mind. You have to let go of everything that occupies your mind. But the ego says I'm real and puts all the energy into the mind. The energy needs to be in your heart. This is where the real love is."

Tony Samara.

There is a famous Buddhist story about a man who spent his whole life searching for Truth. He left his home and his family, and journeyed far and wide. He travelled for many months, many years. He met a large number of people and gained many different views of life. He read uncountable numbers of books in numerous languages and acquired a great deal of learning. And all the while he journeyed, he was supported by his belief that he was getting ever closer to finding Truth, to reaching Enlightenment.

One day, when he was already quite old, he heard about a famous Indian Spiritual Master, who was renowned for his deep knowledge of Truth. The man travelled for many weeks to reach the home of the venerated Indian, the last few days trekking through difficult terrain on foot. He arrived exhausted, but full of hope: his life's quest, to learn the Truth, was about to be fulfilled. He was greeted on his arrival by followers of the Great Master, shown into the courtyard and asked to wait there. He waited, all that day and all night, unable to conceal his impatience. At dawn the next day, he was ushered into the small inner chamber where the Indian Master sat in deep silence on a mat on the floor.

The man was very excited to meet the Spiritual Master, and spent many hours telling him enthusiastically about his long years of travelling, across many countries, and how much he had learnt in his extensive search for Enlightenment and Truth. When he had finished, the Indian sat and stared at him in silence for a long while. Then he got up and poured him a cup of tea. The cup became full and overflowed, but the Master kept on pouring. "What are you doing?" asked the man in surprise. "Can't you see that the cup is full." The Indian Master looked at him and replied quietly, "Yes, my friend. Just like your mind. Where is there room for truth when it is so full already?"

Where is there room for truth when our minds are so full? And our minds are always full! Thinking, wondering, speculating, projecting, reminiscing, going over and over things that have already happened or rehearsing things that we want to do; stressing about the past and worrying about the future. Our mind is always full.

We need to empty our mind of its ceaseless clutter.

If we are serious about embracing our spiritual path, we need to empty our minds and begin to make space, for silence, for stillness.

The process starts when we recognize the compulsive thinking that so fully occupies our mind. For our minds are on duty all our waking hours, endlessly churning out thoughts and ideas, buzzing with plans for next week or next year, regurgitating what we did yesterday, or what we ought to have done, planning our agenda for tomorrow, or running alternative dialogues for future conversations; an unstoppable barrage of information.

Once we recognize what is happening in our mind, we can begin to step back from the noise and clutter that fills it. Because it is just this noise and clutter that stops us from hearing the silence of the sacred within. Truth can be experienced only through silence, through stillness, in a state of serenity; not through the busyness of thoughts and ideas. The road to Enlightenment begins in the silence of the heart, not the excitement of the mind.

Our teacup has been filling up for many many years! It is time to empty it.

The trouble is, most of us find the mind a comfortable place in which to live; for it is a place of certainties, of facts, of reliable information; a place where we feel secure and in control of our lives. It is the safe, familiar territory in which we have always lived, the place that directs our will, drives our ambition, oils the wheels of our success in the world and reaffirms our self-image, to ourselves and to others. It is, in fact, probably the only place we have ever lived.

The mind is not the enemy.

We need to be clear about this: our mind is not our enemy. Every human facet that we have, has been given to us as part of the divine purpose for us in this life. Our mind is an essential component of our humanness. It is the seat of our reason, our discernment, our ideas, our cognitive power, our store of factual knowledge, our logical questioning, our intellectual acuity and curiosity. It provides a framework for our creativity. Most importantly, the mind is the bridge from our inner selves to the outer world. It is to be respected. It is to be valued.

The problem arises when our mind rules our lives.

The problem starts when we allow our mind to take over and rule our lives; when we are trapped in our mind, automatically wrapped up in the constant stream of thinking, quite unconscious of the control that our mind has over us and the way that it dominates our lives.

The mind is not our enemy. Thinking has its rightful place in the human scheme of things. The problem arises when, instead of serving us as a useful tool, we have allowed it to see itself as commander-in-chief, dictating our actions and dominating our lives. The useful servant has become a tyrannical master.

So the first thing we need to do is acknowledge that our mind is in control of our lives, and see how it entraps and enslaves us. And how its constant bombardment of thoughts and ideas, its noise and chatter, happens without our willing it. We seem to be living on automatic pilot, and our mind is in charge.

If you are not convinced, try this short exercise. Close your eyes and try not to think for ten seconds. As soon as the first thought comes into your mind, open your eyes. How long did you manage to keep your eyes closed? Three seconds? Four? Maybe five or six? Very few of us will reach ten seconds the first time we try. Or the second…

Our minds are programmed to be compulsively busy. So, what should we do?

The first step is to recognize what is going on in our mind, and bring consciousness into the process. As Tony repeats, again and again, spirituality is consciousness. When we begin to bring consciousness into our lives, we can start to see the non-stop busyness of our minds. Our minds, in fact, are an escape from consciousness, the place we stay so as *not* to have to be conscious and see what is really going on. The place we live, willy nilly, when we are not conscious.

If we are living without consciousness, we assume that we *are* our mind.

It doesn't occur to us that we are not our mind. It probably doesn't occur to us to think about it all; for if we are not living consciously, we are not aware of any other possibility; we do not know that it is possible *not* to live in our minds. We do not know there is an "I" outside our thinking mind.

So our next task is to see how our mind works, what lives in our mind and how we identify with it; and how, unknowingly, we allow it to dominate our lives.

We need to understand what our mind creates and how it dominates our lives.

What our mind creates, as well as the constant buzz of our thoughts and a running commentary on our every action, are the certainties that run our lives, our fixed ideas of the way things are and the way they ought to be, our prejudices and pre-programmed responses to every situation and circumstance.

Our mind is the centre of our judgementalness and criticism, competitiveness and self-centred desires, comparison and blame, self-righteousness and justification. It creates our emotions of suffering and pain, separateness and alienation, guilt and low self-esteem.

What lives in our mind is our belief system and our perceptions of the world, our self-defence mechanism, our resistance to change, our refusal to open up, to move forward. Above all, our mind is the home of our fears: our fears of change, of taking risks, our fears of the unknown.

Our mind creates our identity.

The root of the problem is the way we let our mind create our identity; when we not only live in our minds, but think that we *are* our minds. That our minds are us.

Once we become aware of this, we can begin the process of dissociating our sense of self from our mind. Our mind creates a warped sense of our own identity. For the mind is only a small part of who we are and sees only a tiny part of the picture. This reality is blinkered, a tunnel vision of all our possibilities. And from this limited view, it creates the reality in which we live.

If we live only in our mind, we live in a small place, isolated from each other and from our true selves, limited by the reality we have let our mind create. We are not just our minds!

The great reinforcer of our self-identity, created by our mind, is the ego.

The mind is the kingdom of the ego.

When we live in our minds, we derive our self-image from the activity of our minds; there, our self-identity blossoms and flourishes. This is the dominion of the ego.

Based on our past conditioning, reinforced behaviour patterns and fears of real change, this ego self tells us who we are and creates the self that we present to the world. But this self, centred in its own ego demands, needs and perceptions of reality, lives in a world of fragmentation and separation. As we see ourselves as separate from others and from the universe, we become isolated and may feel deeply alone, even if we are surrounded by family and friends.

If we do not connect from the heart, from our wholeness, we do not really connect at all. And as long as our self-identify is wrapped up in the workings of our mind, of our ego, we will never be able to free ourselves from its control.

So, what exactly is ego? The ego is the self that seeks constant and immediate gratification, the self that sees its happiness and salvation in the outside world. It is the self that is constantly battling in the world of physical reality to attain more, obtain more, achieve more; the self that defines itself in relation to money, success, power, status, popularity and sexual desirability. This is the self that is never satisfied.

The ego, in fact, is the *mind* thinking that it is the *self*.

The mind, thinking that it is the self, creates the ego. And this false self keeps us from inhabiting our true self, from fulfilling our true potential, from living fully in our hearts. It is the self that is not conscious.

As long as we derive our sense of self from our ego mind, there is no way we can let go of its domination. For who would we be if we let go of our mind? We find our sense of who we are in the dramas and problems that our ego mind creates; in the pain and suffering that seem to be our lot in life.

So we moan, we grumble, we bathe in self-pity; we crave sympathy and attention; but *we do not actually want our problems to be solved*. In fact, we may even become quite angry if solutions are offered, for this would destroy the foundation of our fragile identity. We are comfortable with what we know, however limited or painful this might be. We do not want to venture out of our comfort zone; it is too scary.

It seems that many of us would prefer to live in pain, in anxiety, in misery, rather than begin to question the domination of our lives by our ego mind. Again, it's important to stress that all these ego games are not conscious. That is the problem. If we were living consciously, we would be able to see what was really going on and so begin to bring about change.

But fear of losing the identity we know creates very strong resistance. Letting go of the control of our ego may seem such an impossible task that we deny its importance. Indeed, we may deny its control. In fact, we are often quite unaware of its domination, or how it works. So we need to understand the machinations of the ego mind and realize what its job is.

The primary job of our ego mind is to keep us safe.

Keeping us safe means keeping us in a known environment where there can be no surprises, and we will not get hurt. This may sound laudable; we are being looked after, protected.

But keeping us safe means preventing us from taking risks and moving forward; keeping us safe means keeping us perpetually stuck in past patterns of behaviour, because change means moving out of our comfort zone, and the future is unknown and frightening.

In order to keep us safe the ego creates 'needs'.

The ego creates our 'needs'. And the greatest of these 'needs' is to find our happiness in the outside world; our belief that someone or something in the external world will 'make us' happy, if only we can find it. For as long as we are busy trying to fulfil our needs in the outside world, we will not be looking within; we will not be moving towards consciousness. We will remain the plaything of our ego. [Ego relationships are one of the greatest sources of misery in the world today. This is dealt with at length in Chapter 5: God and Goddess – Relationships and How to Love.]

The other great offender is our attachment to material goods, possessions and money. I'm not talking about real survival needs here, but acquisitiveness. Do we really need a bigger house, more clothes, more money in the bank? Or are these things, perhaps, compensation for feelings of inadequacy or unhappiness or our failure to find real fulfilment?

Letting go of material 'need' is a huge liberator. When we can free ourselves from the *idée fixe* that tells us that we *need* to own a bigger car, a holiday home in the south of France or a state- of-the-art computer system, we can also free ourselves from the need to be enslaved to the job that would pay for them. And working at a possibly boring job in order to earn money so that one day we will be able to afford to buy these extraneous goods or do what we really want to do, is a nonsense.

Life is for living; there is no interest returned for investing your life in a Swiss bank account!

It is not only the belief that we need all these material possessions that keeps us stuck in our ego; actually owning so much stuff can also be a burden. The more possessions we have, the less free we are to follow our spiritual path. For our fabulous home is no more than a beautiful prison, if we are tied to it in order to take care of it and all the expensive possessions with which we have filled it. We cannot leave, for someone may break in and steal them. We cannot leave, because our home represents who we are, our position, our status, our success. We cannot leave because we have no identity without it.

An elderly woman at one of Tony's retreats said that she couldn't move because her husband refused to leave their home. Their four children were now grown and their large house was too big for her to take care of. But her husband was so attached to all their beautiful possessions bought so carefully for this house, that he would not move. Possessions can imprison us.

The way that the ego keeps us safe is by creating needs that will keep us constantly busy trying to fulfil them. These 'needs' are our ego desires and, being created by the ego, they are centred in our wish for our personal gratification. The ego is not concerned with other people, with altruism or the higher good of anybody, not even of ourselves.

The ego is concerned only with the 'us' that it can dominate. It wants to protect us, keep us in a known environment, so it holds us in a vice-like grip of past stuck patterns. It absolves us from having to take risks and acknowledge the need for change. Even if we are hurt, suffering, in pain, the ego will do its best to keep us there, for at least it is familiar; the unknown could always be worse.

The ego, keeping us happily under its thumb, is responsible for most of the pain created in this life. Spiritual teachings talk of pain as an illusion, created by the ego mind that depends for its existence on constant replenishment from the outside world.

The ego mind tells us that we are all separate beings.

This, of course, is the way the ego mind controls us; the ego's own brand of 'divide and rule'. For if we were not separate and unconnected with each other, we would have no need of ego. So we buy into this, and it causes us to live in conflict, fear, suffering, pain.

Pain is the gap between what our ego tells us we need and what we are unable to attain.

And this pain is cumulative. From the time we are babies, the pain we experience is stored in our body and in our mind. Our first feelings towards life and the way we function are formed as a baby. Often our entrance into the world is violent and traumatic, and these negative experiences will colour our attitudes to life evermore. They become imprinted in our bodies and are reinforced by our mind at every step as we grow older, so that this becomes our permanent way of seeing the world. They act like a magnet, attracting experiences and perceptions that help to reinforce this reality.

If we do not deal with the pain, there it remains, to fester and harm us. It is no wonder, then, that if we live in our minds, if we think that we *are* our minds, we will be living in pain. And creating more pain, because that is what our mind has programmed us to do.

So how can we unlock this powerful grip of the ego?

The first step is to recognize how we collude in keeping our ego alive and thriving. How do we allow it to dominate our lives? How does its survival depend on our unconscious collusion with it? How does our deep-seated fear of confronting the pain it creates keep it alive and vigorous?

And how can we release its control?

Consciousness is the key.

It is only our non-conscious self that gives the ego mind its power.

People often say that you cannot live without the ego; indeed, that it is a positive force. After all, the ego drives us to create, produce, accomplish, work, contribute, procreate; it pushes us to help reduce suffering and repair and restore the world.

Well, it is not the drive for these things that is wrong; on the contrary, this drive in itself is noble. But if it comes from the ego, it will be goal-oriented and fuelled by personal ambition. It will be attached to outcome and personal achievement, and is ultimately looking for self-glory, recognition and enhanced reputation, no matter how well it is disguised, nor how honourable we think our intention to be. For real creativity, in any form, the desire to relieve suffering, to serve, to restore the world, do not come from the ego, but from the heart.

As we accept that the reality our ego mind creates is not the true reality, it follows that all the 'needs' it creates are also false, created by the ego to keep us in its power. When we acknowledge this it is obvious that we will no longer need to be ruled by them, chasing our tails to fulfil phantom needs, enslaved to the dramas and suffering that our ego mind creates.

But of course, knowing this intellectually is not the same as being able to put it into practice. But it is the first step. And like everything on our spiritual journey, it is an on-going process. It takes practise, commitment, awareness; and time. Don't judge yourself when it doesn't happen overnight.

The important thing is to make a start. And we start by bringing our awareness into the way we look at our ego, the way we come to understand the function it plays in our life.

The process is not a 'smooth run'. We may experience it as long, circuitous, and with many surprise turns. We need to stop, breathe, and remind ourselves that we move forward by bringing ourselves back again and again to focus on our awareness. This is the key. And we need to remember to be compassionate with ourselves, not continually judging ourselves and measuring our progress.

As we bring awareness into the process, we may begin to recognize that the ego mind does not have the answers. We realize that the ego mind, experiencing separateness and fragmentation, cannot understand wholeness and union, and so creates pain and suffering. We realize that struggling and suffering are created by the ego and are a waste of time. We do not have to indulge them.

And so we move more into consciousness. And then we understand that we have a choice; a choice to continue living in pain and suffering, or to see that this is all created by our ego mind, and that we can choose not to live there any longer.

And then a new attitude to ourselves emerges, a new way of experiencing life, rising like a Phoenix from the ashes. We are ready to turn off the noise of our ego mind and tune in to the music of the universe. We are ready for a new beginning.

But how exactly do we put this into practice? How do we turn off the continuous busyness of our mind and move into the knowing of our heart?

The first step is to stand back and observe our mind: the thoughts, the plans, the worries, the non-stop stream of chatter that the mind continuously emits. Just as we began to observe our emotions and our fears, we need to observe our mind. By standing back and observing, we become detached. And then we realize something amazing!

The 'I' that observes the mind cannot *be* the mind.

The 'I' that observes the mind cannot *be* the mind. So immediately we realize that we have an existence outside our mind. We have another self, the self that is doing the observing. If we are observing our thoughts, the 'we' that is observing is not wrapped up in the thoughts. So it must be a separate entity, watching, listening. Realizing this is to make a giant leap into consciousness.

As we observe the activity of our mind, we can acknowledge it as another *part* of ourselves, but it is *not us*. Witnessing this, we can begin to release the power that our mind has over us. Then we can start to redress the balance, to put our mind in its proper place as a wonderful servant of clarity and discernment, *but not the master of our lives.*

Through this process of observing, we can see that we are not our minds.

But don't take my word for it. Try it for yourself. Start to observe your thoughts, your reactions. Don't get caught up in analyzing or judging – that is still being involved in mind stuff. Just watch and notice. The very act of observing takes you out of the control zone of your mind into a quiet place within. Detaching ourselves from our thoughts in this way is the first step towards letting go of the power of our mind.

Our mind is not our enemy.

As we have said, it is not *our mind* that we need to relinquish, but the *control* that our mind has over our lives, and the false reality that it creates.

It is important to emphasize this. We need to let go of the *dictatorship* of our mind.

As we begin to observe this non-stop activity of our mind, we can detach ourselves from its power and begin to be present to ourselves and to the moment. *To be present to the self that is not our mind.*

Many people find it difficult when they start this process. You sit comfortably in a quiet place to be alone with yourself and focus on being in the moment, perhaps to meditate, and what happens? Within seconds the mind intrudes, busy with its thoughts, its endless games, playing the same old records. We think we are present, and then we catch ourselves in that moment of stillness and realize that we have actually been somewhere else, lost – again! – in our thoughts; our mind has taken over.

But don't be put off; this is a good sign!

Being aware that we have not been present is *being present now*. The challenge is to let go of our thoughts and bring ourselves back to the moment, over and over, reminding ourselves just to watch and witness; to bring awareness into our observation, again and again, as our mind fights for control.

And we need to do this without judgement. We need to be compassionate with ourselves and not see ourselves as failures when we slip away from being present, as we will. As you become aware that you have not been present, just bring your focus back into the moment. Again, and again.

As you do this, as you bring consciousness into the ordinary pursuits of your life, the process becomes easier. Each time you slip and come back to the present, is another moment reclaimed. Next time it will be easier. You begin to have more moments of being present than being lost in your mind. The spaces between your moments of presence begin to shrink. And gradually, you will find that you are moving quite naturally out of the control of your ego mind and into being present in your heart.

Spirituality is not an intellectual idea. It is an experiential way of living. Every moment.

The essence of all spirituality is living in the moment.

Being in the moment, each moment, is all there is. Everything else is an illusion. Understanding this is the first portal into our spiritual self.

The ego mind cannot live in the present.

The ego mind cannot live in the present. Realizing this is the second portal into our spirituality.

All thoughts are a product of time; they are always connected either to the past or the future. It is important to understand this: our thoughts are *always* busy either regurgitating past events, as they were or as we would like them to have been, or they are rehearsing imaginary scenes and dialogues for the future.

Let's try another simple exercise. Close your eyes for a moment and try to think 'in the present'. It is not possible; your thoughts will always be connected in some way to the past or the future. In order to be in the present, we need to get out of our busy minds.

We can only ever live in the present.

It is sometimes said of certain people that they are living in the past, often older people whose past may seem more interesting than their present lives. But you cannot *live* in the past; you can only, ever, live in the present. What they are doing is dwelling in their *thoughts and memories* of the past: past events, past pain and suffering, or the past seen through rose-tinted glasses. [Compensation, perhaps, for the suffering of the present, or the unconscious refusal to live in the moment.] They may be longing for some 'remembered' happiness, or busy rewriting history. But they are not *living* at all: not in the past, which is impossible, and not in the present, which they are squandering in their thoughts of the past.

Similarly, if we are wrapped up in projections about the future, imagining how it will be or how we would like it to be, endlessly writing film scripts in our head, we are equally not living: not in the future which is impossible, and not in the present which we are wasting on fantasizing about the future.

We can only ever live in the present.

The past is a country we have left behind; what lingers is our memories, or our fabrications of what did, or did not, happen. The future is a fantasy kingdom we can visit only in our imagination. We all know this; it is so clear, so obvious, so simple in fact. But we need to remind ourselves, again and again, so that we can begin to manifest this knowledge in the way we live.

This is a great gift, knowing that our real lives take place in the present moment. We often forget. We get lost in the busyness of our daily lives, lost in our work, our judgements, our ambitions. But if we feel lost or disconnected, we can tap into this gift. It is always there for us to use.

So, if you are feeling fragmented or confused, stop and breathe. Bring your awareness back into the present moment. Your heart rate will slow, your body will relax, and the work opens up once again, as your focus returns to the gift of living in the present moment.

We can only ever live in the present.

The way to liberate ourselves from our problems, our suffering and our pain, is to detach ourselves from the control of our mind and inhabit the present. Being in the present, living fully in the present moment, allows us to release the control that our ego mind has over us. And if the present moment is all we have, we might as well live it well.

Time is an illusion created by the mind in order to control us.

Of course, the mind cannot grasp this knowledge because it is programmed to run on time. That is like expecting turkeys to celebrate Christmas! We need to sense it with our inner knowing, not with cleverness but with wisdom. We need to allow it to seep into the essence of our being.

The ego mind cannot live in the present. By bringing our attention back into the moment, we deprive the ego of the fuel it needs to survive.

When we accept the truth of this, there is a shift in perception, in consciousness. When we can truly acknowledge that time is an illusion created by the mind, then we are ready to open ourselves up to life as it unfolds in the present. For this is all there is: this moment, and we need to treasure it. If we squander it, it will not return. Everything else is memory or projection. It is not life.

Imagine the following scenario: You are driving along a winding road in pouring rain. You are late for an important business meeting and you have a lot on your mind. In your rush to be on time you accelerate, as you review in your mind your strategies for this meeting, planning, perhaps, for many years ahead as you map out your successful future with this company. Now you are driving very fast; the rain is bucketing down and you are fully occupied in your head. And then you splash into a puddle of water and the car skids and you lose control and the car crashes into a wall and – bang! The car is finished. Kaput. And so, perhaps, are you.

Living in the moment, with full awareness of where you were and what you were doing, instead of being wrapped up in your future plans that were chattering away in your mind, may have been a better option!

Being focused in the moment is often a tool of physical survival [imagine living in the jungle and not being aware every moment of what was happening around you] as well as of spiritual Enlightenment. Instead of enjoying the moment and living within its reality, you were too busy thinking of all the important things you needed to do, later, or tomorrow, or next year.

But tomorrow will never come; it is an illusion.

We only have now, this moment. Are you going to live it or let it pass you by? If you are looking for tomorrow you will never find it and you will be running for the rest of your life.

What Tony calls the 'monkey mind' is always there, ready with an endless supply of excuses to 'help us' avoid the process of looking into our hearts and embracing our spiritual selves; of being in the moment. 'I am too busy,' 'It's my mother's birthday,' 'I have a plane to catch,' 'If I don't do all this overtime, I'll lose my job,' 'My partner is not well,' 'My son is truanting from school'. I am worried about this and confused about that. There is always something more important to do than be with ourselves, be in the moment, just be; now.

And so we postpone our lives.

We postpone our lives, and we do not really live at all. "Getting and spending we lay waste our powers... "

If we are honest with ourselves, we will acknowledge that there is some discontentedness at the centre of our lives. Perhaps we feel that there has to be more to life than struggling to pay the mortgage, doing a job that perhaps brings us little satisfaction, and not having time for our kids. There must be more to life than playing golf, attending bridge parties or holidaying in the South of France.

If we are serious about embarking on our spiritual path, we need to begin the process of change right now, this very moment. There is no time to waste. And we need to start – by stopping!

Stop, now, breathe deeply and bring your focus into being in the present moment. Without thought, without worry or anxiety. Just being, present to yourself, present to life. Present to this moment. Breathe.

Another way in which many of us are enslaved to our ego mind is through our addictions.

Most of us will not think of ourselves as addicts. But there are many kinds of addiction: the obvious ones, such as alcohol, tobacco, coffee, chocolate, drugs, gambling, food. And the more hidden addictions, those that perhaps are easier to disguise; easier to ignore. These include things that most of us would not categorize as addictions: work, personal dramas, material acquisitiveness, control of others, 'victimhood', sexual promiscuity, destructive or abusive relationships. But they can become addictions. And these addictions, mostly without our awareness and almost certainly without our acknowledgement, keep many of us stuck.

Addictions are created by our ego minds.

Our minds create addictions as some form of compensation. Different people adopt different kinds of addictive behaviour, for different reasons. So take a look at the above list and see if any of the items resonate with you. Be honest! This exercise is just for you.

Begin to question in which areas of your life your behaviour may be driven, which of your 'choices' may really be masking fears; in which ways you might be addicted. If the word 'addict' puts you off, use another word. But as part of our spiritual journey, we need to look at what may be compulsive behaviour, and how it can dominate our lives.

Addiction is an escape.

Addiction – any kind of addiction – is an escape from facing ourselves; an escape from the disconnectedness and discontentedness of our lives, from our feelings of separateness and isolation from each other; from the pressures to perform and conform.

Addictions come from a sense of powerlessness, from being out of control with our lives, from not being able to engage in a healthy way with our circumstances and the people around us. They come from a sense of victimhood, of not being able to make our mark, of not being noticed, of feeling inadequate, worthless or invisible. And generally, we are unaware of the causes of our addictions; although we may feel a sense of futility and meaninglessness about our lives.

Addiction is an escape route, an attempt to numb pain and suffering and hurt. Above all, addiction is an escape from fear – the fear of having to look within and face our truth; an escape from the fear of living in the reality we have created.

Through our addictions we create a comfort zone, a place where we can escape from everything that frightens us, everything that we don't want to confront, and indulge in our choice of 'drug' that satisfies our hunger or strokes our ego.

Addiction is a desperate cry for love or attention.

Desperately needing the love, attention and approval that we don't seem able to get, and perhaps feel we don't deserve, we turn to our 'drug' of choice. We think that the hurt, trauma, lack of love or low self-esteem that we feel will be resolved through the chosen 'drug'; and if not resolved, at least numbed for the duration. And the 'drug' may be anything: alcohol or gambling, overdosing on work or control-freakery.

Addiction is the small child within, lacking nurturing, loving relationship, crying out for help. It is the whimper of the wounded heart that has not been healed.

Many of us are addicted to being a victim; even if we are seemingly confidant and successful, we may feel like a victim underneath. Some of us hang on to our fears, our wounds, our suffering, with almost gleeful determination not to let go.

Our wounds give us legitimacy for staying a victim.

Being a victim is a way to gain sympathy. Being a victim may give us an identity: "He can't be expected to do this – look what a dreadful childhood he had." It gives us a justification for being needy, for being the centre of attention.

It is also a way of manipulating other people. It releases us from having to take responsibility for our lives, as we have other people constantly flapping around us, and use them to get our needs met. Victims destroy their own lives and then punish others through their uncanny knack of making everyone else feel guilty.

Our addictions offer us a respite from having to face the world, and ourselves. They both deaden our feelings of inadequacy and also give us a false sense of power. Being drunk, drugged, or abusing our partner, may make us feel very powerful – short-term. But then, when we sober up or stop the abuse, we generally feel worse than we did before, and so need greater and greater doses of our 'drug' to keep us going.

Abusive or exploitative relationships must be one of the more 'popular' addictions in Western society. Many of us are so disconnected from our true selves and from each other that much of the time we feel isolated, alienated, anxious, miserable or depressed. We seem to live on automatic pilot, our life running by us; the more we try to control it, the more it seems beyond our influence. Many people feel so inadequate in their lives that the only way they can feel any power is to control someone else. When control no longer compensates for their feelings of impotence, they often turn to abuse. Mostly this is psychological, but it may become physical. [For more about relationships – again! – destructive, abusive, healthy, holy and liberating – see Chapter 5: God and Goddess – Relationships and How to Love.]

If the addicted person has the courage to face the real cause of the addiction, and is blessed with people around who really care about them, then it can be resolved, and the person can be healed and become free. Otherwise, caught up in enslavement to an addiction, freedom to make real adult choices and move on in our lives remains an illusion. [See also food/drink addictions in Chapter 8.]

Sometimes, we seem to be attracted to spirituality, but are actually caught up in 'the idea of spirituality', and are still firmly locked in our ego mind.

'Ego spirituality' is a false god.

We need to be aware of the false 'spirituality' of the ego. When we first become aware of our spiritual journey and take our first steps towards living consciously, the mind becomes afraid. If we start to live consciously, the mind will no longer be able to control us, and it doesn't want to lose its power. So it starts to use 'spiritual language', to con us into believing that it really wants to help us, if only we will stay in its power. This is a mind trap, and we need to beware of its tricks. 'Spiritualizing' the ego is not the same as opening up to spirituality.

A woman whom Tony met some years ago is a perfect illustration of this 'ego mind spirituality'. She was a rich woman, used to 'buying' her own way in all things. She sat in front of Tony wearing her expectations like a suit of armour, believing that she was so powerful she could always get whatever she wanted. She asked Tony for an immediate private consultation. He looked at her, smiled his Mona Lisa smile and told her that it was not possible to have a private consultation with him. She stared at him in disbelief, shocked and angry. "But I will pay handsomely for a private session," she retorted. Tony asked her innocently why she wanted a consultation; sometimes he enjoys playing a little dumb. "I want to heal something." Tony looked deeply into her eyes and told her this was wonderful; she could come to a retreat where he would be happy to help her heal. She replied angrily that she had "no time to waste in a group with so many other people," and she stalked off in a rage.

This story has a happy ending. Five years later, she did attend a retreat. And she did heal. A pity that in those five years she had not been able to find the time for healing; just five days of time. But time, of course, was not the real issue.

You cannot 'buy' spirituality. You cannot demand of the light that it be there when you click your fingers. Spiritual practice takes commitment. It is slow, measured, gentle. We peel off our false selves layer by layer, like onion skins. And, like peeling onions, we may shed many tears on the way.

If you are serious about healing, your journey is to let go of what feeds the ego; to come back, again and again, as you catch yourself playing 'ego games', to that place of awareness within you. Each time you bring consciousness to bear, you transcend the ego a little more. Each time you bring consciousness into the way you live, you experience healing taking place within you a little more. Each time, a little more…

If we spent half as much time and energy on living as most of us do on making excuses why we cannot live fully in the moment, our lives would be transformed. The choice is yours.

As you re-awaken the life of your heart and your soul, reclaiming their energy and intuition, their wisdom and joy, you re-align the balance of your life and move into a place of harmony within. For true reality, as we know, is not to be found in the busyness of our minds, but rather in the stillness of our hearts. It is in this stillness that we find our path towards truth and self-realization.

Spirituality teaches us that we can only ever live now, in this moment – everything else is a fiction of the mind. Whether we do this consciously or not is the difference that defines our life.

Tony often tells stories in his retreats when participants seem to be going round in circles. Stories and allegories can help us to get out of our habit of trying to understand things with our busy logical mind and move us into the knowing of our heart, in a way that continued discussion often cannot.

This is a tale from the old Ottoman Empire, about a good and wise king. He loved his empire and he loved his people. One day, he decided to dress up as a poor man to see how his subjects were living. As he was walking along in the market, he heard a voice saying over and over, "If it's blocked, it's blocked!" Thinking there was something wrong with the plumbing, he went to check it out. Inside the shop, a wise man was saying to a poor man sitting in front of him, "If it's blocked, it's blocked!"

The king, whom no-one of course knew was the king, asked what was going on. The poor man explained that he'd had a dream in which a hundred thousand fountains were all working perfectly, except for one. He was standing in front of this fountain, which was trickling pathetically, knowing that he had to fix it. He tried to unblock it with his stick, but the stick broke and got stuck in the fountain and so it stopped even trickling. But the man knew that he had to fix it and didn't know what to do.

The wise man looked at him and said simply, "If it's blocked, it's blocked." The king felt sorry for this poor man so he decided to help him, and asked him what he needed. The man said that he was very poor and had a wife and five children to feed. So the king gave him a bag of gold, and wished him well. The man thanked him profusely, delighted by his good luck, and went off happily, sure that this gift would solve all his problems. He rushed home with his bag of gold, put it for safe keeping in a pair of old trousers at the back of the wardrobe and went back to the market.

While he was out, his wife heard a man in the street crying, "Old clothes, I will pay money for old clothes." She rushed out and gave the man her husband's old trousers with the gold hidden in them, happy to have a little money. When her husband came home from the market and his wife told him what she had done, he shouted at her in fury: "You stupid woman! My gold was in my old trousers!"

So the poor man went back to see the wise man and the wise man looked at him and said simply, "If it's blocked, it's blocked." Just then, the king happened to be walking by again and heard; now he knew that it had nothing to do with the plumbing. So he went inside and still feeling sorry for the poor man, he decided to help him once again.

He took the poor man outside and said, "I own all this land. Throw this stick as far as you can and the land between you and the stick will be yours." So the poor man lifted the stick and with all his strength threw it as far as he could. He threw it a long way, but the stick hit a tree in the distance and boomeranged off it, flying straight back into the poor man's eye and pulling his eye out. The king saw what was happening and said simply, "If it's blocked, it's blocked!"

If it's blocked, it's blocked. And it can only become unblocked from the inside. The fountain flows; it only becomes blocked when you interfere with it, when you see life as broken, as needing to be controlled and fixed. The fountain is the divine aspect of yourself, that place of sanctuary within; the water flowing out of the fountain is the flow of love through your spiritual heart.

Let go of the blockages and allow the waters of life to flow freely, unhindered; let the fountain sparkle, unencumbered, joyously. Dance in its waters in the stillness of your heart, the divinity of your soul.

Chapter Four
Will and Intention

"Willpower is the normal way of functioning for most people. Usually, the reasons why we do certain things in our lives are because the willpower inside us says, 'I want this' or 'I want that', and 'When I get this, I will be happy and free from suffering'. Willpower is the way we see the world when we feel separate from each other."

Tony Samara

When Tony first went to the Mount Baldy Monastery in Los Angeles, and saw the monks cleaning the toilets with such joy, he wondered how this was possible. How can you clean toilets joyfully, day in, day out, week after week, month after month? But the joy is not in cleaning the toilets *per se;* the joy is in doing *whatever you are doing* with your full presence, with total awareness, with Intention.

Intention and Will [or what Tony often calls willpower] are the engines that drive all our actions. They appear to be very similar in meaning and, in common parlance, are often used interchangeably. But they are not the same. The difference, in fact, is profound, and lies in the impetus that drives them.

Will may be seen as a subjective desire for a particular outcome and is personally driven; Intention, as an objective wish for the higher good to prevail. Will comes from the need to control one's own life, situations and other people; Intention is born of an acceptance of what is, a trust in the perfection of the All That Is. Will is driven by the stubbornness and self-interest of the ego mind; Intention lives in the openness and compassion of the heart. Will comes from unevolved individual perception; Intention from the expansion of spiritual growth.

Let's start by looking at Will, the place where most of us live, and then move on to Intention, the place that we would like to get to.

Will is the expression of the ego.

Will is determination masquerading as strength, but in fact is not strong; and because it is weak it tries to dominate our lives. The more out of control we feel our lives to be, the more we use Will to try and control them, to impose order on what seems to be chaotic. But it is *because* we come from a place of Will that our lives are chaotic, that they just 'seem to happen' to us, randomly, without cohesion.

Will lives in our ego mind, the faculty with which we think we are making choices. But Will drives the life that is not conscious; and so the 'choices' that we make coming from Will, are also not conscious. This is because Will sees only a tiny part of the picture. It is as though we were fish trying to order the relationship among sky and earth, as well as the sea. We are, literally, out of our depth.

Will is ego manifest in action.

As we saw in the last chapter, when ego creates our reality it controls our thinking, our perceptions, and our desires – all of which come from our beliefs about ourselves and the world. So we really believe that we *need* to gain everyone's approval, ruthlessly pursue career ambitions, work out at the gym three times a week and have a perfect body, change our partner, buy a bigger car, win the golf tournament and make a lot of money. And if only we could fulfil these needs, we would be happy.

This is the mind-set to which most of us have been conditioned. This is the mind-set of Will: if I do this, I will get that, and that is what I want. When we live from Will, our lives probably have high levels of stress, frustration, maybe sickness, perhaps a feeling of constantly chasing something that is always just beyond reach; certainly this merry-go-round will not bring us real happiness.

Will is the tool we use to try to obtain happiness from the outside world.

Will, caught up in the demands of the ego, is narrow, self-centred, and actually self-limiting, for it busies itself trying to fulfil illusory needs; needs which, even if fulfilled, would not make us happy.

We have been taught to think that our happiness will come from the material world, from something, or someone, outside ourselves, and we have bought into this belief system big-time. Stemming from the ego mind, our beliefs, emotions and fears are what drives this ambition. Will is the expression of this desire in action.

Will, like everything created by the mind, is also a child of time: it is driven by the past and projects into the future. And armed with all our 'baggage' from the past, it is also taken over by the emotions that come from the ego. And so Will acts out the jealousies, the anger, the frustrations of the ego, reinforcing a vicious circle of fears, doubts and resentment.

Will, born out of conditioned responses and reinforced by our repetitious behaviour patterns, creates a world of darkness, doubts and delusion, taking us away from our real self, which is connected to joy, love and light.

Will is born out of a sense of isolation.

We act out of Will because we feel a sense of disconnectedness from others and from our Higher Self, a sense of separateness and fragmentation. We harbour emotions of isolation and alienation. We feel the world to be a hostile place, and so our life becomes a battle against others, to get what we want.

If we felt connected to others, understanding that we're all part of the same oneness, coming from the same Source, how could we ever think of enhancing our own lives at the expense of someone else?

Will comes from an arrogance born of insecurity.

People often exhibit arrogance as a cover for their insecurities.

If we are not seen as successful, as strong, dynamic individuals, controlling every aspect of our lives and getting what we want, we feel that we are failures.

We pursue money, position and social status in the erroneous belief that this will give us greater power over our own lives and so we will not have to submit to other people's agendas or authority, or choices made for us by others. It is Will, expressing our insecurities, that drives us to try to control our environment.

Will becomes a tool of manipulation to get what we want.

Will is the dictate of *I want* or *I must have.* Acting out of Will, we are determined to get what we want, whatever the price. Will does not consider the cost, not to anyone else, and not to ourselves either.

Perhaps we can better understand the concept of Will, if we think of 'wilful' – literally, full of Will. The image that this conjures up is that of a young person – usually a small child or a stroppy teenager [or a very immature adult] – wrapped up in his/her own needs to the exclusion of everyone and everything else, demanding that these needs be met, immediately. Wilful is the stamped foot, the temper tantrum, the scream for attention, *now* – metaphorically, if not literally. Wilful is the spoilt child who hasn't grown up.

Living driven by Will is living without consciousness.

And living without consciousness has profound effects upon us as individuals, and upon the world we create. It is not an exaggeration to say that living without consciousness is the primary cause of all the ills of the modern world. All the ills.

It starts on a personal level – one individual acting out of Will behaves selfishly. Then, living on 'automatic pilot', this kind of behaviour becomes routine. As there is no aware questioning of motivation, and Will acts out of selfish ego 'needs', this self-centred behaviour becomes entrenched. With time, this leads to wanting more – more material possessions, more admiration, more power. We become greedy, ruthless, as we need to satisfy our desires at all costs. But we don't notice, because everyone seems to be pushing for the same things. So it becomes the normal behaviour of the group, then of the community, then of the nation. Then it begins to influence international relations.

People acting out of personal Will are ultimately responsible for the worst ravages of materialism, for personal and corporate greed, for vaulting ambition which builds one person's success on another's failure. *And we are all responsible;* for each group or organization of people is made up of individuals. Wars, oppression and the abuse of human rights, can all be traced back to their source – overweening greed and hunger for power at all costs: the manifestation of ego Will run wild.

As individuals, we may feel helpless to change anything, our personal power subsumed by the group or nation to which we belong. But we still share responsibility. Ordinary people can do unspeakably evil things if circumstances allow. And evil spreads because good people stand by and do nothing.

There is another way to live: with Intention.

Intention is the expression of our Higher Self.

Intention is living with consciousness, the consciousness that all benefit to our own lives is inextricably bound up with the good of all. It is living with the awareness that we do not have ultimate control over our lives. Intention is driven by the desire to flow with the natural movement of life, not to fight it nor try to control it. Intention takes account of the highest good of everyone involved, in every situation, and is not just concerned with 'what we personally want'.

When we are living with Intention, we are living consciously. When we are living consciously, we are living with Intention. You cannot have one without the other. Intention, in fact, is consciousness in action.

Intention is the manifestation of consciousness in action.

Whereas Will unconsciously tries to exert control over everything and everyone, Intention consciously relinquishes personal control and puts trust in the way things are. Intention is born by first accepting what is, then bringing clarity of purpose to fuel every thought, every deed, every activity. It is informed by the still strength of being completely focused in the moment, motivated by acting for the higher good of all.

Intention comes from a place of strength, harnessing our own energy to the natural forces of the universe; this is a formidable combination. As we become attuned to acting out of Intention, we may have a sudden flash of recognition: that although we are not trying to gain personal power [as we are when we act out of Will] when we come from a place of pure Intention, we actually become very powerful indeed.

Intention is the manifestation of compassion.

Directing our lives by Intention, we live with compassion in its profoundest expression: compassion for other people, for all sentient beings, for Mother Earth and for the planet.

And, of course, compassion for ourselves. Intention is the expression of our knowing that we are all interconnected and a part of each other, and a part of the same whole. What we do, what we say and what we feel *matter*. It is not arrogance to think this; this is just the way things are. Thoughts, too, carry energy out into the universe, and have consequences. Wherever our thoughts go, our energy goes too.

So, ponder for a moment: are you acting out of Intention? If your actions bring benefit and joy and blessing to the universe, if your thoughts spread light and love and inspiration, increasing the higher good of all, you are indeed acting out of Intention.

Tony quotes a simple example that can illustrate the difference between Will and Intention in action. An industrious gardener is becoming increasingly frustrated because his garden is overrun with slugs, which are destroying his carefully nurtured plants. He may try to control the situation and act out of Will by killing the slugs with powerful chemicals and pesticides, thereby also slowly poisoning the soil and rendering it infertile for future generations. Or he may act out of Intention and listen to the spirit of nature, which always creates balance. Then he will see that blackbirds love to eat slugs. He simply needs to dismantle his scarecrow and stop shooing away the blackbirds. Then everyone is happy.

A good way for us to understand Intention in action is to look at the way in which it is used in indigenous Shamanic communities.

Shamanism is the manifestation of Intention in action.

Shamans believe that we in the West are living in an illusion, a limited physical reality that we have created, and don't see the world as it really is. They do not understand our concept of personal Will, which simply doesn't exist in Shamanism. One person gaining benefit to the detriment of another doesn't make sense to them. If we are all interconnected, part of the same divinity, how can we think of harming another being?

The Shaman's world is built on cooperation, care and compassion for everyone in the community. Every activity is undertaken for the highest good of all. The Shaman has a simple way of looking at life: "How can I win if you lose?" And the 'you' includes all other beings: two-legged, four-legged, winged, gilled and rooted [except, of course, for essential food, which is generally vegetarian]. If we are all part of the same oneness, *then causing another person to suffer is actually harming part of ourselves,* upsetting the balance and harmony of our own life.

To the Shaman, Intention is the focus behind the communal desire to carry out the tasks of their daily lives, their way of walking the sacred path. It informs every action, every purpose: the way canoes are built, the way food is gathered and cooked, the way the children are raised. Intention motivates the planting and cultivating of sacred plants, the blessing of the process, the drive behind their harvesting. It informs the heightened consciousness created at ceremonies, the energies with which the Shaman carries out his healing and places his skill, knowledge and awareness in the patient's service.

The Shaman recognizes that Intention comes from the stillness at the centre of his being, whether he is inert or moving. It is connected to Spirit and guided by the All That Is, linked to the greater purpose of the universe. It will take account of the rhythms of nature, of the environment, of the ebb and flow of the natural world; of the changing seasons and the time of day. He will consider not only the benefit of his actions to his community, but will also think of the higher good of the animal and plant kingdoms, all the beings that make up the natural world.

For example, when a Shaman needs to cut down a tree to make a canoe or build a shelter, he will come to the tree focused in Intention and ask its permission to fell it. Perhaps this is not the right time for this tree to be felled; perhaps at this moment it is more propitious to cut down another tree. When the Shaman has been guided by the 'spirit of tree' to his correct course of action, the actual felling of the tree will be blessed and a small offering left beside the stump in thanksgiving. So, coming from the Shaman's Intention, nature has not been violated and the Shaman has his wood.

Intention is a *sine qua non* of life in a Shamanic community, binding everyone together in common endeavour and mutual support. It is the unfolding in action of the Shaman's interconnected and harmonious way of living. It is sacred.

Tony's first Ashram was established on Shamanic principles of unconditional love and the highest good of all. Intention was the guiding force that drove the life of the Ashram community, binding its members together in common endeavour and mutual support. Without Intention, this way of life would have been meaningless and would actually have collapsed. The Ashram was the manifestation in practice of Tony's teaching of Intention, where everyone was responding to universal energy, rather than to the individual Will of the ego.

Intention. Imagine a community where everyone acted out of compassion and love instead of selfishness, competitiveness and greed. Imagine a world where political leaders acted for the higher good of all, across nations and internationally, instead of out of self-interest, hunger for power and political manipulation. Imagine, in other words, a world guided by Intention. Our world and our lives would be totally transformed.

There are only two ways to live: consciously or unconsciously. There are only two ways to behave: with Will or with Intention.

If we are living unconsciously, we will be acting out of Will, out of our ego desires, acting in ways that we think will fulfil our needs and bring us happiness. If we are living consciously, we will be acting out of Intention, focused clearly in the moment, each action concerned with the higher good of all.

We all have a choice: to act out of Will or to act out of Intention.

As our consciousness evolves, this choice becomes more apparent. And more urgent.

To help clarify the choice, there are three questions you can ask yourself: what motivates your actions, who will benefit from your actions and how do you carry them out?

If you are not conscious of what motivates you – the why and the how of your behaviour – you need to switch off the 'automatic pilot' lever in your mind, step back and begin to observe yourself. [You might like to go back to 'witnessing' the mind in the last chapter for reinforcement.] Sit quietly and take a few deep breaths. Observe one action closely; stay with it and see what lies behind it.

Practise examining your thoughts and actions in this way, observing, questioning, reflecting, being in the moment. If you are motivated by personal desire, if you *react* to what is around you rather than *acting* from your own integrity, if you, solely or primarily, will be the beneficiary, then obviously you are acting out of Will. If, on the other hand, you consider how your actions will affect others, if you carry out your actions with awareness of their impact on everyone involved, if all those touched by your behaviour benefit, then clearly you are acting out of Intention.

We need to recognize that Will is a trap.

If we are acting out of Will, we are actually trapped in playing the role of victim. For if we are not living consciously, we are living as a victim of our unconscious drives. As we become the conscious observer of how we allow our ego to dominate us, we begin to move out of our victimhood. As we let go of our victimhood, we can move out of the trap; out of Will and into Intention.

Moving from Will to Intention is a process. And the process starts, like all spiritual movement, by bringing awareness into our thoughts and actions. By recognizing and acknowledging that we are acting out of Will, and bringing consciousness into the moment, we can begin to move from Will to Intention.

The answer lies in observing the process by which we move.

Sometimes, we are pushed by circumstances. However rich or successful or powerful we may be, we may reach a point when something goes wrong, something happens that we cannot control, and we realize that our personal power is limited. We may feel incomplete or empty, and begin to recognize that other forces are at work in our lives. When our lives seem most out of control, when disaster strikes, or illness or loss overwhelm us, this is often the catalyst that helps us to be receptive to guidance from 'another source'. A growing awareness of our own limitations may be just the push we need to open us up to a new way of looking at life; to moving from Will into Intention.

And sometimes, it is our own inner guidance that leads us to question the way we are living, and to wonder whether perhaps there isn't more to life. We begin to recognize the origins of Will, and the possibilities of Intention. We see that Will, self-centred, competitive and goal-oriented, is created by our ego, by our sense of separation from others, by our feelings of fragmentation and alienation from our environment, which then need to be compensated for. It is fed by externals and so becomes a self-perpetuating vicious circle.

And we begin to recognize that Intention, on the other hand, comes from a place of connectedness to our deepest selves, to others, to the universe and to the sacred; it grows from a place of belonging, of knowing that we are an indispensable part of the whole.

Will limits us to a physical 'reality' that is not real; Intention expands the heart and connects us to the All That Is.

We reinforce this process of movement from Will to Intention by allowing ourselves to be guided by the spirit of service, not by personal neediness; by the right course of action to take in any given situation, not by determination to achieve a personal outcome or objective. Unlike Will, Intention is not measured in terms of success or failure to reach a particular goal, but rather by how well it nurtures the well-being of all.

Intention means letting go of control, and trust.

Intention is a process, a direction, a relinquishing of certainties and the need to control; it is an acceptance of the way things are. It is reinforced by our growing trust in the All That Is, and trust in our own Higher Self to lead us towards rightness of action. It is a movement towards letting go of control and welcoming the unknown.

As we move along this path, we move into right relationship with ourselves, and hence with others and the universe. By doing so, we honour our deepest desires, those that nourish our spirit, and benefit the world around us as well.

239

Acting with Intention creates a virtuous circle. By acting with Intention, we move from our heads into our hearts; by opening our hearts and coming from a place of love, we reinforce our pure Intention.

Tony teaches the Buddhist practice of Mindfulness, which can be a great help in moving us towards living with Intention.

Mindfulness is the practice of focused Intention in every action, in every moment.

A good way to begin practising Mindfulness is to start off your day, first thing in the morning, by reminding yourself that you have awakened to a new day of living with awareness. Then bring this awareness into each action that you perform, especially those mundane actions that you perform every day; for unconsciousness lives most happily in repeated routine activity.

So be conscious of the way you get out of bed, the way you brush your teeth, shower, dress; the way you prepare and eat your breakfast. You could make a conscious choice to do things slightly differently: for example, put your left sock on first instead of your right, lay things on the table in a different order. This will start to break the unconscious routine, and frustrate the 'automatic pilot' in your head.

We can follow the practice of Mindfulness by consciously naming each action as we carry it out; and it is helpful to do this out loud. So you might say, "Now I am brushing my teeth with full consciousness, coming from a place of pure love"; "Now I am washing my face with full consciousness, coming from a place of pure love"; "Now I am preparing my breakfast with full consciousness, coming from a place of pure love." Naming our actions is a powerful tool for bringing our attention back into the moment; into Mindfulness.

Now ask yourself: how often in this short space of time has your mind wandered? What thoughts have you been wrapped up in, in the past or in the future? Where has your mind taken you? If thoughts come, as they will in the beginning of your practice, observe them and then let them go. Don't judge them, don't get involved with them, don't even try to chase them away; just acknowledge them and let them dissolve. Then refocus your attention on your breathing and come back into the silent stillness within.

Mindfulness helps us to live in the present moment.

Continue to practise Mindfulness throughout the day. You can do this by asking yourself, for example, are you bringing awareness into the way you wash the floor, make the beds or tidy your house? Where is your attention when you are travelling to work or doing the shopping? When you wash the dishes, are you involved in washing the dishes, being in the moment, solely involved in the task of washing the dishes? Or are you thinking about how much you have to do in the house, how little time you have, how you want to finish the chores quickly so you can sit down with a cup of tea and put your feet up?

In this case, you are not present to washing the dishes. Your mind is occupied with other things and you are not living in the joy of the moment. Then when you are drinking your cup of tea, you may be thinking about what to make for dinner, what your friend told you on the telephone, or the television programme you saw last night. You will not be present in the moment then either.

If we cannot be present while carrying out the simplest of tasks, we will never be present to life at all. And if we are not present to life, not in the moment, we are not living with Intention; in fact, we are not *living* at all. For the present moment is all there is; we need to remind ourselves.

So, for instance, if you bring Intention to the way you wash the floor, you will concentrate your whole being on washing the floor, because that is the task in hand. You are fully present, you are aware of your breath, breathing deeply and rhythmically, you are aware of how the mop moves over the surface of the floor, and your mind is not buzzing with clutter to distract you; you are simply washing the floor. And while you are washing the floor, you are not even focusing on how clean the floor will be. You are simply fully present to what you are doing: washing the floor in order to wash the floor.

How you wash the floor may seem like a trivial and unimportant matter. You may wonder what this has to do with spirituality. But it is not a trivial matter. For if you cannot bring awareness into the simple tasks of daily living, how will you be able to bring it into more profound activities, such as meditation?

Spirituality is actually *about* the way we wash the floor.

Spirituality is about the way we perform every task, no matter how simple or mundane, just as much as it is about the way we meditate or pray. So be aware each moment of the task in hand.

The motive that informs our actions is the key to the quality of our life.

If you have the radio on, or music playing in the background, ask yourself: are you listening to the radio or the music, or are you washing the floor? If your answer is that you are doing both, then you are doing neither with full attention. You are not focused in Intention.

This is not to say that you can't weave music into your washing of the floor. But then do it with Intention. Then it becomes a dance, a meditation in movement; the music feeds into your washing the floor. Just be aware of whether the music is enriching the moment, or whether you have it on in the background to avoid being with yourself in the silence, to take your attention away from washing the floor.

Aiding the practice of Mindfulness.

If you think that living with Mindfulness is a daunting process, start by limiting yourself to a specific time. You could try, say, half a day, a couple of hours, twenty minutes. Set yourself a limited time frame – and stick to it. The point is to start. As this becomes the way you live for half an hour, for a few hours, a whole day, as you become aware of the difference that this makes in your life, it will gradually become the way you live every day, every hour, every moment.

Watch your actions, move slowly and in a measured and relaxed way. Practise being connected to your still centre, even when you are moving. Shamans talk of "moving in stillness": the centre remains still through all movement. Breathe deeply and be aware of your breath. Watch your actions. Give each task you set yourself your full attention. Don't do anything in a hurry in order to get it finished; do it for the sake of doing it.

Practise doing what you are doing in silence.

Silence is a very powerful instrument of spiritual evolvement. Noise is a distraction, a device to keep us from being alone with ourselves in the silence. Remember that it is not the silence that is frightening, but the being alone with yourself, with no distractions; the fear of going within. The fear of 'just being'. If this strikes you with terror, remind yourself that the *fear* of anything is always more scary than the thing we're afraid of.

If your mind is working on overdrive, a good way to quieten it and tune into your still centre, is to spend time just sitting with yourself, not doing anything, just being; not reading, not watching television or listening to music. Just tuning in to your own inner space. Bring your awareness into your breath. Stay with it.

When you are ready, focus your attention on the task you want to do. If you want to eat, for example, prepare your meal slowly, lovingly, with awareness. When you are eating, eat your meal in order to eat your meal, with joy: don't do anything else at the same time. Be in the eating. Eat slowly, chew every mouthful thoroughly, be aware of the different tastes, smells, colours, textures of your food. Simply be conscious of eating your meal.

Every task can be joyous if it is done with Intention.

Remember, every task can be joyous, even cleaning toilets!

When anyone wanted to join the Ashram, Tony would first give him or her the job of cleaning out the toilets. And we are not talking about wiping out a porcelain bowl with a long-handled brush! These were ecological toilets, which collect human waste in huge containers beneath the bowl. They needed to be emptied into other larger containers, where the excrement would spend some time incubating before becoming safe enough to put onto the land. Then they needed to have their contents emptied onto the land by hand as part of a fertilization programme. And then the containers needed to be thoroughly cleaned. A dirty, nasty, smelly job!

If people felt that they were too grand or too delicate to do this, Tony would suggest that perhaps they were not yet ready to embrace the spiritual life.

Intention is the action of bringing full consciousness into the moment, whatever you are doing: whether you are contemplating God, or wiping your baby's bottom.

The practice of Intention is at the heart of all spiritual practice.

No action is more or less important than any other. When we let go of judgementalness, we realize the truth of this; each task is simply the task to be done in the moment. Spirituality is concerned less with *what* we do, and more with *how* we do it. The way we perform each task is part of our spiritual journey.

So remind yourself throughout the day to be aware of what you are doing, each moment. When you are walking, drinking a cup of tea, playing with your children, going to work, is your full awareness focused in what you are doing? Is your attention fully committed to the task in hand, or is it something that you're trying to finish as quickly as possible so that you can get on with something 'more important' or 'more interesting'? Or is the task accompanied by a script you are writing in your head, rehashing the past or projecting into the future? What are you thinking about?

Observe how you are doing whatever you are doing. As you observe, this brings your awareness into the task in hand. If you are walking, be in the walking; if you are playing with your children, be in the playing; if you are cleaning, be in the cleaning. So you are able to infuse each action with consciousness and joy.

Being aware that you have lost focus is a good sign!

Each time you become aware that you have lost your focus in the moment, this is actually a good sign; for being aware that you have lost your focus means you *are aware now.* Then try to stay focused by breathing deeply and concentrating only on the specific task in hand. And nothing else.

Again and again, as your mind wanders and fills up with thoughts, bring your awareness back into the moment. Breathe into the moment, into the task you are performing. Again, and again. As you practise, more and more moments will become imbued with consciousness, Mindfulness, Intention, joy. As you practise, you will let go of the clutter of your mind and restore yourself to wholeness and peace, and the joy of being fully alive.

Stay rooted in Intention wherever you are.

So far, we have talked about acting with Intention when you are alone. But of course we should also practise Intention when we are with other people. If you feel that you are fully aware in the moment, but other people are distracting or disturbing you, you need to reconnect to your Mindfulness of where you are and what you are doing.

Observe the situation and the input of others, and then let go of their agendas for you. If you are stuck in a traffic jam, being pushed and shoved by the crowds in the supermarket, or worn down by the madness of the rush hour tube, stay centred in your Intention. Don't let yourself be blown about by other people's negative energies. You can also put an etheric shield around yourself, to prevent outside disturbance from penetrating your space. It will not only help you on your journey, it will also have a positive influence on those around you. Whenever you are centred in your spiritual Intention, you are also spreading light and joy to others.

Intention is both the purpose and the way of achieving it.

Intention is the way in which we journey as our life unfolds, not the destination. It is both the sacred path we tread as we walk towards wisdom, and the gateway to experiential knowing.

When Intention becomes an expression of who we are and how we live, the universe always answers us. There is a law of attraction; like attracts like. If you are negative, judgemental, fearful, that is what you will attract into your life. If you are loving, giving, trusting, *that* is what you will attract into your life. Whatever you put out into the universe, whatever you give to others, you bring to yourself.

And this works on the most profound level of spiritual nourishment, and the most mundane level of material comfort. As we give, so we receive. We may not see a direct 'cause and effect' connection between one specific action and another; but, as the saying goes, "What goes around, comes around".

Tony tells the story told of a Buddhist monk who had spent many years meditating silently all day in a Buddhist monastery. He was the most conscientious of monks, totally dedicated to spiritual practice. One day, he felt that he was ready to become a Master himself. So he undertook the long journey to visit an enlightened Buddhist Master who would tell him if indeed this was so. He was shown into the presence of the Master, who was sitting silently on the floor and gestured him to sit with him. The Master looked at the visitor in silence for a while, and then said: "My friend, it was raining when you arrived. No doubt you brought an umbrella with you? In the entrance hall there is a statue of the Buddha. On which side of the statue did you place your umbrella?" The visitor, mortified, could not answer. The Master told him to return in five years' time. Perhaps then he would be focused in Intention, ready to become a Master.

Intention is more than the impetus that drives us forward and directs our life towards fulfilling its higher purpose. It is where we live when we are spiritually conscious; the sacred centre out of which all things flow. It is the manifestation of love, for ourselves and for the universe. As Intention becomes the way we live, as all our actions come from our heart, filled with love and compassion for all, so we attract to ourselves an abundance of blessings, and the universe showers us with infinite joy and love.

Chapter Five
God and Goddess
Sexuality, Relationships and How to Love

"The divine philosophy of the man/woman relationship can become a magnificent initiation of discovering who you are, your spiritual qualities and virtues, your weaknesses and futile habits. A relationship is a dynamic interplay of your masculine and feminine principles made conscious through trust, courage and mutual respect. By honouring the masculine god and the feminine goddess within, we are able to deeply transform a relationship to a new level of spirituality, fulfilment, love and energy."

Tony Samara

We are all divine in our essence. Created in the image of the one divine God, we are each endowed with the spark of divinity that lives in our deepest selves, which is both god and goddess energy.

Each of us has within us the perfection of both god and goddess; the god within is the perfection of male energy, the goddess within us, the perfection of female energy. They are the two halves of pure love, fusing into each other to become the divine spark of love at the centre of our being; the love out of which everything else may blossom and grow.

When we are living consciously, these divine energies are balanced and manifest in all aspects of our lives, influencing our thoughts, our actions, our interactions with others and our relationship with the Sacred. We are in harmony with ourselves and with the world.

The god and goddess within us have a vital role to play in our spiritual work. They offer us a way of tuning in to our deepest selves, integrating the different parts of us, aligning ourselves with the balance and harmony of the All That Is. These male and female energies feed each other and together constitute the wholeness and perfection of each individual. If our god and goddess energy is balanced, our lives will be directed by a deep sense of rightness, wholeness and equilibrium.

Now, let's talk about love.

Love is one of the most abused words in any language, debased by frivolous or careless usage in a pop culture bent on instant gratification. It is bandied about in meaningless ways, such as in the phrase, 'I love going to football matches', or fancy-dress parties, or train-spotting, or Christmas, or whatever it is that gives you a buzz.

The word 'love' is used to cover a multitude of sins, often masking manipulative or abusive relationships, both sexual relationships between two adults, and those between parents and children, and indeed among other family members; and sometimes between [mainly male] bosses and [mainly female] employees. And how often in personal relationships, do we say 'I love you', when what we really mean is 'I want to have sex with you', or 'I want you to love me'.

The word 'love' is misused, too, in some New Age cults, where it is often applied to mask total obedience, and sometimes the donation of large sums of money, to a guru.

Tony uses the word love in its spiritual sense, to mean unconditional love for the All That Is and everything within it. We can see this, perhaps, in the adoring love that a mother may feel for her newborn baby, the total love that a very young child has for its parents, the love that an enlightened being has for Great Spirit, for the universe, for all life. The love towards which our spiritual journey is evolving.

Unconditional love is the bedrock of spirituality.

As we live our spirituality, love will infuse every aspect of our lives, and particularly our relationships with others. An intimate relationship provides the most fertile ground for deep spiritual work and should be treasured. It offers a way of engaging most intensely with life, living it at its most profound level. It affords a safe and secure setting in which to look within, to let go of the mind games and the tricks of the ego, and enter the sacred space of the heart.

Living in intimate relationship holds up to us the truest mirror of who we really are, without masks to hide behind. In an intimate relationship we are naked and all is revealed: it offers us a place where we can allow ourselves to be vulnerable, and so find real strength; to find the courage to reveal ourselves 'warts and all'. Then our relationship becomes a manifestation of divine love.

An intimate relationship also offers us the greatest opportunity to expand and express our delight, our deepest joy, our sense of wonder at being alive; our laughter, our passion, the vitality of our life force. We have probably never felt so alive, so open, so expansive. We feel our heart beating together with the heartbeat of the universe, as our whole being flows with the dance of life.

As we fully honour our god and goddess within, we open up to the beauty of our partner – and of ourselves. We mirror back to each other the possibility of touching perfection. And see that real love is opening our heart to our partner and allowing his/her light to shine through, illuminating their divinity, and ours.

When we truly love our partner, making love is the most exquisite human experience there is, as we share our wholeness, our vulnerability; as we open up to the magic and mystery of sexual union. Our bodies become the instrument through which our souls make love. We are truly one flesh, one soul. We are living in paradise, in bliss.

So, why are we not all living in this perfect bliss? Why are we not living in a paradise of perfect love? One of the most basic things that prevents us from inhabiting our most joyous and expansive selves, is our beliefs.

Our beliefs about sexuality seep into every aspect of our lives.

Just as our beliefs about everything else both create and colour our experiences, so too do our beliefs about sexuality. What we believe about sex and about our bodies, influences every aspect of our lives. Our sexuality is expressed not only in our intimate relationships, but also in our creativity, in the way we interact with everyone around us, in the energy and passion with which we invest our lives.

Sexuality has physical, emotional and spiritual components, which of course are all inter-related. In order to be connected to all of them, to integrate them and live them fully, we need to look at our beliefs about sex and sexuality. They are often deeply ingrained and not conscious; we need to begin to bring them into our consciousness.

We could start by questioning the belief system that we have inherited, examining the ways in which we uphold these beliefs, or indeed react strongly against them and go to the other extreme, also not a healthy adult choice. [You could look again at Letting Go of Beliefs in Chapter 2 to remind you.]

Our beliefs about sexuality create our experience of sex.

This cannot be overstated: our beliefs about sexuality create our experience of sex. Our beliefs create the role sex plays in our life, and how we experience it. And remember, our ego mind will reinforce these beliefs and 'help us' to manifest them.

If we are living consciously, beyond the control of our ego mind, our sexuality will be joyous and expansive, an expression of our wholeness, our integrity and our spirituality.

On the other hand, if we are stuck in rigid beliefs, 'religious' morality of sin and punishment, or are indulging in promiscuous sex to prove how free we are, we are not inhabiting our spirituality. Indeed, if we are using sex to prove anything at all, we are not coming from a place of highest integrity. Then sexual activity becomes mechanical, devoid of meaning and cut off from the soul.

Sexuality within an intimate relationship is, of course, about much more than the act of sexual intercourse. It is about sharing and communication, about giving joy and being open to receive; about touching and hugging and stroking and kissing. It may also create a spiritual bond that awakens the life energy, bringing the masculine and feminine aspects of a relationship into balance and completion. In a most profound way, the union of being intimate with the intention of sharing unconditional love, can teach us what it means to be both a human being in the physical sense and also a truly spiritual being. This is real intimacy.

If the sex act is just about physical release, then when it's over, it's over, and nothing remains. Indeed, the illusion of intimacy may leave us afterwards feeling more separate and alone than ever. We become disconnected from our true self, from our body; and then neuroses may set in.

This way of cutting ourselves off from our bodies often happens so early in life that it becomes entrenched. And every repression gets stuck in the body. Then one day you fall in love with someone and you think you are having a beautiful relationship; but in fact you are just sharing your neuroses with each other.

A person can be married for forty years, and still be sexually repressed. And having a new partner every week has more to do with the challenge of the chase than with expressing sexuality in a healthy way. Often, sexual activity does not translate into real intimacy. Indeed, a frequent change of sexual partners is often an expression of a deep fear of intimacy; there is safety in numbers and you don't get too close to anyone. And no-one gets close to you.

Behind our beliefs lie our fears.

Examining our beliefs means having the courage to see what lies behind them: to recognize that behind rigid beliefs always lie fears; and then confront them. [Chapter 2…]

So, what are we so afraid of? What is the fear lurking behind our fear of intimacy? Our real fear is of exposing ourselves. Our real fear is that as we get closer to our partner, as we become more vulnerable, he/she will see the 'real me' behind the masks and we will not live up to their expectations.

What our partner does is hold up a mirror to us, reflecting back to us who we really are. And it is this that we are afraid of. We are afraid of acknowledging parts of ourselves that we do not like, that we would prefer to keep hidden. Our greatest fear, in fact, is of looking inside and seeing who we really are, and having to confront this.

So, we may choose not to be in an intimate relationship at all. Or we may 'choose' someone who will not get close to us, someone with whom we can avoid real intimacy, someone with whom we can pretend we are living a life based on love, but actually it is based on fear. And so we pass up the greatest opportunity we have as human beings to explore our spirituality and live in real joy.

Our beliefs about what an intimate relationship is, dictate our experiences of it.

What we believe an intimate relationship is for, will define our attitude towards it and govern our 'choice' of what we bring to it: whether we will live with love and grace and compassion, or are still swamped by fears and doubts and prejudices; whether we fill our relationship with love, blessing and gratitude, or with judgement, criticism and blame; whether our interaction with our partner is determined by the demands of our ego or by the gentle knowing of our heart.

And whatever we are manifesting will be mirrored back to us by our partner.

Honest questioning is called for. And honest answers!

If you are living in an intimate relationship, it is helpful to ask yourself some questions – and to answer them as truthfully as you can. This is a process for you, just between you and yourself. No-one else needs to know the questions you ask, nor the answers you give. So be as honest as you can. This is not a test, or a way of 'evaluating' your behaviour. It is simply to show you where you are. Be compassionate with yourself, and don't judge.

So, how far are you able to give unconditional love and support to your partner, valuing their struggles, honouring their weaknesses, watching their journey with compassion, but not trying to mould it or limit it? How far do you accept them, *as they are,* without judgement or criticism or blame? How far are you able to mirror back lovingly to your partner the beauty and divinity that are their essence, their essential humanness? Are you connected by deep love and respect for them, by integrity and compassion, laughter and playfulness, sharing a sacred bond and vision of your life's unfolding path?*

Remember, this is a process, a direction that we move towards in our relationships, as we become more conscious. It is about *our relationship with ourselves* as well as with our partner. As our relationship with ourselves opens out and becomes deeper, more aware, so we are able to look at our relationship with our partner in a more honest and open way; to see them and the relationship as they really are, without 'smudging'. And so we may begin to manifest our relationship in all its glory.

However, sometimes we are not able to live this way. Then we may feel 'stuck' in our relationship, bored, resentful, angry, 'cheated', wondering where all the love has gone, but feel unable to leave. A lack of awareness may lead us to live in a pattern of serial destructive relationships, falling in love with one unsuitable partner after another, repeating over and over the same dysfunctional, unhealthy behaviour. If this is so, you might want to consider what is it about you that causes you to repeat this pattern. Why you continue to invite into your life partners who are not able to nurture and value you.

And then consider in which ways your choice of partner[s] reflects your own feelings of inadequacy, limited self-worth or self-destructive tendencies, or the myth that you cannot take care of yourself alone. Remember, we create our own reality!

What in the relationship is *your* responsibility?

If you feel that you are stagnating in your relationship, you might think of leaving. But before you do, ask yourself, what is *your* responsibility in the state of the relationship. Remember, we always project our dissatisfaction with ourselves onto others. And an intimate relationship, where we are used to each other and feel 'safe', often magnifies this projection.

So ask yourself, are your negative emotions about your relationship due specifically and personally to your partner, or are they your own 'stuff' that you are projecting onto them? This is always a difficult question: how much the problems you are having in your relationship are due to your partner, and how

---

* To obviate the constant use of he/she, him/her, his/hers, I will use the plural form, they, them or their when referring to a partner. Not grammatically correct, I know, but much less clumsy; until we invent unisex pronouns in English, I claim poetic license!

much they are the mirror of your own problems that your partner is reflecting back to you. Usually, of course, they are a mixture of the two, but try to see if you can where the 'weight' of the problems lies.

If they are the latter, this will be stuff that you will bring to every relationship, and it is not particularly related to your current partner. If this is so, you will repeat the pattern in every relationship until you begin to look at your issues and deal with them. So you might as well examine this now, and work through it with your current partner.

As you bring consciousness into the way you live, it will help to illuminate what is really going on in your relationship. Start to look at what your partner is mirroring back to you. And try to communicate honestly with your partner, without judgement, criticism or blame. And without expectation, attachment to outcome or an 'agenda'.

You might like to reread and reflect on the last paragraph, the last two sentences. They are all *huge* issues. Doing the work of this book may not be easy, but it's ultimately rewarding. Keep going!

Having seriously mulled over this, if you feel that your journey with your partner is irrevocably over and you can no longer grow by staying together, it may be time for you to gather your courage and move on.

Spirituality means living from our highest integrity.

Living our spirituality is a process of moving towards our highest integrity, and manifesting it in everything we do.

If you suppress your integrity in order to stay in a relationship – for whatever reason – you suppress your life force, your creative energy and your spiritual growth. You need to ask yourself, what are your real motives for staying in the relationship? What *really* lies behind your staying together "for the sake of the children"? And remember, living a lie is seldom in the best interest of children. Look inside and examine your doubts and fears, your ego 'needs' and insecurities, your hidden agenda and your 'payoffs'.

Similar honest and courageous questioning is called for if you are not in a relationship and would like to be. Ask yourself, what are the fears that hold you back – and it is always fear, behind whatever else you think is the reason. Most often this is expressed as fear of losing your independence; but this may mask a fear of intimacy, a fear of exposing yourself or a fear of feeling vulnerable. To say that you haven't yet met the right person may be a cop out! [Although many older women do have difficulty finding suitable men.]

In a profound sense, it doesn't matter who your partner is. There is not necessarily just one perfect 'soul mate' for each of us. You don't have to wait for Mr /Ms right to come along in order to live a beautiful joyous partnership. The important thing is to be in a committed relationship, working together through your spiritual journeys, sharing joy and compassion, supporting each other as together you walk your spiritual paths.

How, then, can we connect to this divine energy, to our own perfect centre, to our sexuality?

Sexuality is an integral part of spirituality.

Sexuality is an integral part of being human. So it is also an integral part of spirituality. It is a divine gift that we are born with. It is to be lived and enjoyed and nourished, not with license, but as an expression and sharing of our life force, our deepest, purest, most joyous selves.

In order to inhabit our spirituality fully, we need to connect to every aspect of ourselves; and this includes our sexuality. The integrity with which we express our sexuality is part of our spiritual practice. If we suppress our sexuality, our sexual energy, we cut ourselves off from our spirituality, which then diminishes and withers.

How then can we access our god/goddess energy and connect to our sexuality?

Like all aspects of our divinity, our god and goddess live in the stillness of our hearts. But they are also connected to our physical body, and to our sexuality. One simple way to awaken our dormant god/goddess, is by freeing up our hips.

Often at the beginning of his retreats, Tony will ask everyone to stand up and move their hips [definitely not in a genteel way!] – to shake them up as though their life depended on it, gyrating, leaping, dancing, wriggling, jumping, rotating as though they were twirling a hoop, or belly-dancing. People who haven't worked with Tony before usually think he's crazy – is this guy a spiritual teacher or some wild hippy gym instructor?

But after half an hour of hip rotating in a room of forty or fifty people, as they drop to the floor panting with exhaustion, they suddenly realize that they have moved the lower part of their body in a way that perhaps they have never done before, and have connected with their sexuality in a truly liberating way. And then, as Tony leads a breathing meditation in which they breathe deeply into their hips, into their sex, they start really to connect to their god/goddess energy.

Afterwards, everyone seems to move in a different way; they are more confident, more joyous, more aware of their bodies, inhabiting them in a way that they hadn't before. And interacting with others in a different way, too, looking into people's eyes, smiling, really connecting. A miracle. Try it!

Tony's interest in our sexuality is as an expression of our wholeness.

He is concerned with the ways we experience our sexuality as part of our spiritual journey.

While he was living in different Shamanic communities in South America, Tony had a front row seat into the ways they organized their intimate relationships. There was great sexual freedom among the young people, with no stigma attached to experimenting with several partners before marriage. And within marriage [and virtually everyone married] sex was accepted as a natural and fulfilling part of life. There was no sexual repression, no hypocrisy, and therefore no need of sexual games, manipulation, coyness or cheating; extra-marital affairs were frowned upon, but not hidden. Sex was an accepted part of life, as natural as swimming in the rivers or dancing at ceremonies.

The way people lived and worked and moved with their whole bodies reflected their easy sensuality. Perhaps, as we have lost touch with our ancient Shamanic roots, we have also lost touch with our own 'primitive' sensuality. In the West, we live primarily in our heads, not in our hearts; and not really in our bodies either.

We are all fascinated by sex; we gossip about it endlessly, our conversations are often spiced with sexual innuendo, or the sexual shenanigans of friends or colleagues. Flirting is a frequent form of interaction between the sexes. Stories of sexual, often prurient, interest adorn the front pages [and much of the inside] of the tabloid press, on a daily basis. Advertisements in all the media blare out titillating images of sex to sell anything from cars to shampoo to jeans to alcoholic drinks of all kinds.

But we do not easily talk about sex in a way that communicates anything real or mature. We may all be familiar with the writings of Freud and Jung, or even Kinsey, and so feel that we are knowledgeable about sex. But actually, what we know is *concepts about* sex, psychological interpretations of sexual feelings, drives and indeed neuroses; we may even indulge in frequent sexual activity, but have little experience of the divinity of sex itself. We have created so many myths around sexuality, so many distortions, that we have become separated from our own true sexual natures.

More nonsense is written and spoken about sex and sexuality than any other subject; perhaps religion comes a close second. In our liberal democracies sex is flaunted, but sexuality is repressed. We see our sexuality as a separate part of ourselves, something private that we indulge in, with varying degrees of frequency and satisfaction, but very rarely inhabit.

The West is dominated by aggressive male energy and excess testosterone.

When talking about the god and goddess within at his retreats, Tony frequently dwells more on the goddess than the god, although we each, of course, have both god and goddess energy within us. He says this is not just a personal choice [although he admits to finding women much more fascinating than men!]. It is also because female energy, in the West, has become swamped by aggressive male energy and buried beneath layers of dogma and cant.

We have bought into the concept that it is 'masculine' values that are important: worldly success, money, status, power, fame; and what are seen as masculine characteristics: ambition, competitiveness, ruthlessness. And we all seem to glorify these concepts, not only men. Women, too, seem to be striving for the same material goals, the same career success, the same power. Many women, too, are colluding in the domination of our society by these values, accepting 'masculine' definitions of success and priorities of what is important, wanting to be seen as just as tough as men.

In a culture dominated by 'male' values, we all need to find the goddess within. She lives deep inside each of us, in our hearts.

Our sexuality expresses our basic attitudes to all aspects of our life.

Expressing our sexuality does not mean being promiscuous. Sexual freedom is not sexual license, and certainly not licentiousness.

Sexual freedom is about directing our sexual energy into expressing the essence of our being. This is not confined to specifically sexual activity, but is also expressed in the way we move, the way we use our creativity, the way we relate to other people and the universe.

Sexuality is the manifestation of our essential life force, expressed in joyous, loving relationship with the world around us. It is about sharing real intimacy with one other person, allowing ourselves to open up on the deepest level, in all our vulnerability and weakness and insecurity. In all our glory.

Sexuality is an expression of the way we live and has nothing to do with age or physical beauty. A woman of fifty, fully inhabiting her body, imbued with her god and goddess energy, truly loving herself, can be extraordinarily sexual, in a way that a skinny twenty-five-year-old model, half starved to fit a certain public 'image' of what beauty should be, may not be.

For men and women sexuality is about honouring the god/goddess power within, taking a risk and opening yourself up, to yourself, and then to the world, loving with all of yourself, holding nothing back. Then, fully connected to your sexuality, you are the most desirable person in the world.

Most of us grew up on fairy stories in which, after many tests and trials and tribulations, love finally triumphs. The prince and princess fall in love and, with fairy-tale ending, "… live happily ever after."

And so, we think, shall we. We buy into the myth, we collude with the fantasy, and fall in love with the man/woman of our dreams. We are 'in love' and so we know that we shall have the perfect relationship, living happily together until "death do us part".

The myth of romantic love is powerfully ingrained in the ethos of our culture.

We have been conditioned to believe that romantic love holds out the promise of a magic wand that can be waved over all our deep-seated fears and negative emotions, and overnight will cause any anger, resentment or jealousy that we hold magically to disappear. Our feelings of low self-worth, inadequacy and incompleteness belong to another life, before we were 'in love'. Now, we are walking on air, we are ten feet tall and the world knows that we are 'special'.

What we are really looking for when we 'fall in love' is salvation.

We are all looking for salvation. When we fall in love, our unconscious need is often for someone to save us from ourselves; someone who will grant us our identity, our sense of self, and save us from feeling fragmented and separate in a cold, uncaring world. Our relationship will provide heaven on earth, creating excitement, safety and lifelong happiness. A fairy tale, in fact.

If we are not living consciously, our relationships will be based on ego love. And if our relationship is coming from a place of ego love, we will be bringing into it all our neediness, our fears, our insecurities and feelings of inadequacy and low self-worth. These aspects of ourselves will tyrannize the kind of relationship we create.

We enter the relationship full of expectations – which our partner is expected to fulfil. Suddenly, our partner has become responsible for our happiness, our self-esteem, our identity; for everything we need to make us feel good about ourselves and our lives. All the 'baggage' we've been carrying all our life – the pain, the anger, the confusion, the guilt – will magically be swept away in the arms of our lover. They will bring us comfort and joy and will make us feel secure, cherished and complete – forever. Salvation is at hand! We think.

But then, a few months, or a few years, down the line – depending on how long we are able to keep wearing the blindfold – this dream of lifelong happiness begins to dissipate, and we see that our partner is not actually able to offer us salvation. When we realize this, we become resentful, angry, hurt: if they loved us enough, they would fulfil all our needs. If they loved us enough, everything would still be as perfect as it was on our honeymoon. So, clearly they don't love us enough; or they are not the same person that we married.

And, of course, at the same time, we have become responsible for fulfilling the similar unconscious expectations that our partner has of us. They will then feel as angry, hurt, bitter and let down as we do. A clear recipe for disaster!

And so the arguments begin. They can be about money [there are always arguments about money, today's symbol *par excellence* of our control over our partner], or whose turn it is to wash the dishes [or even load the dishwasher], fold the laundry or supervise the kids' homework. You start to become irritated with your partner because he always leaves his dirty socks strewn across the bedroom floor, or she leaves hairs all over the bathroom basin, or s/he forgets your birthday, or – sin of sins – your wedding anniversary.

But the arguments are only the symptoms of discord; they are not the cause. The cause is our own false expectations, built on our unacknowledged neediness and the illusion of 'love equals salvation' that we have bought into.

And so, the irritation starts. Irritation becomes resentment, resentment turns to anger, anger turns to rage, as little arguments grow into full-scale battles. Small conflicts expand into confrontational no-holds-barred rows; gradually, manipulation, a cold shoulder, emotional abuse, psychological [and sometimes physical] violence, may take root. The anger, the pain, the hurt begin. The suffering.

And then the 'dramas' set in. Many couples actually become addicted to this pattern of behaviour, and get a buzz out of the dramas they create. It makes them feel alive, it is an 'exciting' interregnum, perhaps, in an otherwise dull and unfulfilled relationship. Often, furious rows will end in heightened and passionate sex, which may bring physical gratification, perhaps emotional release, but does not resolve the issues. It wasn't meant to be like this.

So what has happened to this perfect love, this blissful relationship? How has the love that once ignited the world changed into resentment and anger, or a state of bored disinterest?

The answer is that it hasn't changed, for it was never real love.

Relationships based on ego illusions of love cannot be truly fulfilling.

What we usually identify as love is an emotion created by the ego, to satisfy the needs that the ego creates. This is a phantom love, an illusion. For nothing created by the ego is real. We know this. [Ego, Chapter 3...]

Nevertheless, these emotions can be very intense; they come intensely, and usually go just as intensely, too. 'Love' that has withered, very easily turns to hatred, as many a divorced person will attest. For hatred is the ego's answer to failed love.

Then the relationship oscillates between love and hate, pleasure and pain, depending on which particular mirrors you are reflecting for each other at any given moment, which 'buttons' you are pressing, which bits of your partner's baggage – or your own – you are tapping into. Your ego is in control. And as long as it is, nothing will change.

And then you start to dwell on the 'if only's': if only my partner would work harder, or not always stay so late at the office; be more demonstrative, or stop pawing me all the time; cook more enticing meals, or not waste so much time in the kitchen; be more interested in my work, or not continually interrogate me about it. If only they were not so stubborn, so self-righteous, so critical, so lazy, so demanding; if only they would be more loving, more sympathetic, more understanding of *me*. If only I could change just a few things about my partner, the relationship would be perfect!

But of course you cannot change your partner.

And it wouldn't make any difference if you could; other traits and behaviour patterns would rise up soon enough to annoy and anger you. This is always the way when you project onto your partner your own ego expectations. This is always the way when you see only the 'clothes' of your partner, and not the divine essence within.

Everything created by the ego, as we have seen over and over again, is an illusion, and what it creates is limited, conditional and judgemental. Ego traps us into thinking of love as a commodity, a bargaining chip, something to be coerced or manipulated, parcelled out in bits for other things we want.

As long as we are living with expectations of finding our happiness in another person, we will not be happy. As long as we are living in our ego, we will continue to create dramas, conflicts and feelings of separateness, in order to keep real love at bay. For the ego is afraid of real love. If we really love, unconditionally, we will be beyond its control, and the ego does not want to relinquish its power.

As long as we continue to expect our partner to fulfil our needs and validate our life, the divine joke of life will keep laughing in our face.

So, what is this madness that drives us to live this way, in suffering, in pain, disconnected from our heart, from the essence of our being?

It is because we are looking for someone else to make us happy that we are miserable.

We are miserable as long as we don't let go of our beliefs that happiness and fulfilment can be found in the outside world, that making changes in our environment or circumstances will change our lives. We are miserable as long as we continue to believe that 'falling in love' and living with our 'perfect' partner will make us happy forever. We are miserable as long as we believe it is our partner's job to make us happy. We are miserable as long as we refuse to let go of the demands of our ego, and listen instead to the still voice of our heart.

We are miserable because of our reluctance to look within. And we do not look within because of our fears. Our fears of being vulnerable, fears of exposing ourselves, fears of revealing our weaknesses. But most of all, our fear of looking inside and seeing who we really are, and having to deal with this.

And so we continue to look for happiness in the outside world.

And as long as our identity is wrapped up in externals – our material possessions, our social status, our success in the world, our physical appearance – we will always be seeking more from the outside world and we will never be satisfied.

As long as you are looking for your happiness and fulfilment in another person, your relationship is doomed. And because nothing is ever enough to fill the needs created by the ego your struggle for fulfilment becomes ever more driven, more manic, more despairing. Your relationship deteriorates; it brings you disappointment, frustration and anger. And so you start, perhaps, to look elsewhere for another 'perfect love… ' [Go back to 'fears' in Chapter 2: Letting Go… Each time you reread, you may gain further insights, 'clicks' that now you understand something that you didn't understand before.]

And then, a 'miracle' happens. Along comes that special person, with a smile that lights up your world, and you feel that all your prayers have been answered. The sun shines out of your beloved's eyes and you feel thrillingly alive, throbbing with vitality and energy. Your new love makes you feel whole, complete, perfect. Your life now has meaning, content, happiness. The underlying fears, fragmentation and lack of self worth that create all the dramas of the ego, seem to have melted away. Life is beautiful!

But after a while, little things about your partner begin to irritate you. You are still 'in love', of course, for that is the myth you are writing together. But as well as moments of possibly great tenderness and passion, you now also feel inexplicable surges of anger, hatred or violence towards your partner. What is happening is that all your fears, pain, feelings of inadequacy, that were buried by this 'magical love' are beginning to resurface. And you think that it's all your partner's fault.

But your partner is not the cause of your unhappiness.

It is not your partner that is causing your unhappiness. Please reread this sentence. You are simply projecting onto your partner all your own fears, guilt, unresolved issues and accumulated pain, blaming them for everything that is wrong with your life. And it is *this projection* that causes so much grief and unhappiness in intimate relationships.

Relationships do not cause the pain.

It is supremely important to understand this. Relationships are not the cause of our pain. Our relationships *bring out the pain that is already within us* and reflect it back to us, often with a magnifying mirror.

And then what happens? As you project your own fears and pain onto your partner, you will inevitably begin to attack them; and they may attack you back, for they are also probably reacting out of their ego fears and confusion, and therefore will be going through a similar process. And so you create the dramas, the pain, the suffering, the blame, the guilt. The recriminations. The same familiar scenario. You may even become addicted to this way of relating, and so stay within a destructive or abusive relationship, in some way thriving on the dramas that it creates.

Or, if it all gets too much, you may leave. And then you look around for a new partner. And after a while, a 'miracle' happens. Along comes that special person, with a smile that lights up your world, and you feel that all your prayers have been answered… Back to square one!

I am going round in circles. Intentionally.

Going round in circles is exactly what most of us seem to be doing most of the time. Frustrating, isn't it? The collapse of our expectations. The road to nowhere!

This is the pattern: the person of our dreams falls into our lives. They are everything we imagined the perfect partner to be. We fall in love and, unbelievably, they fall in love with us. We start the 'perfect' relationship. But a few months or years down the line, when the first flush of being 'in love' wears off, we see that our partner is not fulfilling the expectations that we had, is not meeting our needs or making us happy… Got it?

Living within our ego 'needs' can never bring us happiness.

When we live inside our ego mind, which is responsible for creating our emotional needs, we try to fulfil them by buying into the belief that our happiness lies in the arms of the perfect partner.

Then we suffer because, at best, these needs are not being met; at worst, we may feel that our neediness is exposed, exploited and abused. And so we try even harder to get more of the 'riches' – material and emotional – of the outside world; but this does not fulfil our needs. And so we live in pain, discontent, suffering, despair.

It is only when we realize that living in the dramas created by our ego, that expecting any other person to fill what is lacking in us, to make us whole, is utterly futile; when we accept that happiness can never come from anything or anyone outside us – only then is change possible. [Please read this paragraph again.] Only then is change possible. Only then.

As we evolve and move along our spiritual path, we realize that nothing real can be given to us by the outside world. That everything we need for our happiness is within us. We realize that the answers, *all* the answers, lie within ourselves.

All the answers lie within *you*.

When you fully accept this, that all the answers that can lead to a meaningful, fulfilled and deeply joyous life lie within you, and you take responsibility for your life; when you begin to look within, and have the courage and commitment to start to change on the inside; then this is reflected in everything that you create in the world around you.

Paradoxically, when we stop looking for a partner to fulfil our dreams and 'make us' happy, we may find someone with whom we can share real love and happiness.

What we give out to the universe, we attract to ourselves.

As we become more conscious, more authentic, more loving, this is the world that we attract to ourselves. This is the world that we create. As we let go of the control of our ego mind with all its tricks, and enter that deep space within our hearts, we see that infinite grace and joy and love are waiting to greet us.

The essential ingredient in any relationship is trust.

Love actually *is* trust; without trust, there can be no real love.

This means, firstly, trusting yourself; trusting your own intuition, your own wisdom, trusting that your own inner voice is your best guide. Trusting your deepest integrity and following its dictates. Trusting yourself enough to allow yourself to be vulnerable, to reveal the normally hidden parts of you, your dark side, your fear.

This means trusting your partner enough to be open and honest with them and not play games. And it means allowing yourself to be vulnerable to your partner. This takes great courage. Being vulnerable is not being weak; on the contrary, it is being strong enough to expose the 'real you' to your partner, with all your human frailties. If we do not allow ourselves to be vulnerable, we are not relating with the whole of ourselves to our partner.

When you really trust yourself, you will be able to trust your partner. And with trust comes total acceptance of your partner *as they are*. You do not try to alter anything about them, not their character and not their annoying little habits, which invariably surface with time. That is not your job. Your job is simply to hold up a mirror to them, and support them as they look into this mirror. And you do this not in judgementalness or criticism, but in total love, reflecting back to them their deepest self – and still smile to them.

And if your partner can do this for you, too, then you can help each other to grow in the most marvellous and profoundly fulfilling way. The process may not be easy, it may not be comfortable. It brings with it a kind of 'creative insecurity'. But by letting go and trusting whatever will come, we open ourselves up to our full potential, to share with our partner the magic and grace and joy of our lives. And as we share these blessings, they multiply.

When talking about relationships in his retreats – and often when talking about something totally different – Tony often tells the story of a young woman whom he met when he was living on the Pacific Island of Moorea.

This woman lived with her lover, with whom she was besotted. But he treated her very badly; he humiliated her in front of others, he was abusive to her, and he would often hit her. One day she met Tony and told him that she was really suffering and she had to get out of the relationship. She was covered in bruises, to say nothing of her psychological scars. Tony offered her his help. He didn't have much money but he gave her what he could so she could buy a ticket to get off the island and find safety, away from this man.

This actually created a difficult situation for Tony because all the man's anger and violence was then directed towards him. Violent people always need to create an outlet for their violence; someone else is always to blame for it. Tony had taken away his lover and so he became the target. Rumours reached Tony through the grapevine on the island that this man was 'out to get him'. Though he knew that the 'universe' would protect him, it was definitely not a comfortable position to be in.

But this isn't the end of the story. A week or so after this woman had left the island, Tony was taking a walk along the beach. Everything was beautiful: coconut trees, white sand, people swimming and laughing and playing. And then, as he continued walking, he saw the young woman walking along the beach towards him, holding her lover's hand, smiling to him as though nothing had happened. Tony wondered at first if he were not seeing a mirage. But no, there she was in physical form, gazing up at her man in adoration.

Tony stared at her in disbelief. What was she playing at? Why did she return again and again to live with a man who abused her?

Why do people stay in abusive relationships?
The behaviour of abused women frequently follows a similar destructive pattern. [There are cases of men being abused by women, but the vast majority of cases of abuse between adults are of women by men.] If the relationship does finally end, the victim tends very quickly to find another self-destructive relationship, and then another, and another. The world outside is frightening and hostile. The victim is terrified that she won't be able to survive on her own. She has no self-esteem and feels worthless. She is used to being a victim. This is all she knows. The trade-off in an abusive relationship is 'security' against the terror

of being alone; of being too inadequate ever to find someone else. And it may be strangely comforting, for it is familiar. Better the devil you know…

The woman has so deeply internalized her feelings of worthlessness, and the repeated taunts of her lover[s] that she is ugly/stupid/useless, that she comes to believe that she brings the abuse on herself. If only she were a better wife, mother, cook, cleaner; if only she were prettier or not so stupid, he wouldn't abuse her. She vows to try harder. And harder. And many abused women have said of physically abusive partners, "It shows he loves me; he's not indifferent.". Often an abusive partner will say afterwards how sorry he is, he couldn't control himself, he loves her really. He promises he will change. And she, caught up in the dramas of her own helplessness, buys into this reassurance. Again. And again.

When you are addicted you are addicted. When you are blocked you are blocked. When you are living inside a destructive relationship, it is not easy to see that you can change; to see that you have choices. And a destructive relationship doesn't just mean physical violence, but includes psychological abuse, exploitation and constant undermining.

Our karma follows us from one life to another until we deal with it.

Why do we repeat patterns of destructive behaviour? Again and again. What karma have we brought with us into this life that we are refusing to deal with?

The doctrine of karma originated as a Hindu belief, that our actions and behaviour in previous lives influence each subsequent reincarnation. Karma is now accepted as an essential part of most spiritual traditions. Everything that we haven't worked through in previous lifetimes is brought with us into this life. And this 'baggage' can become exceedingly heavy! If we don't work through in this lifetime the emotional dramas and ego nonsense that we create, we will be born again, and again, and we will repeat the same experiences, over and over, through many lifetimes, until we confront them and deal with the issues they present.

The first step is to acknowledge that in some way you are addicted to this kind of relationship. This does *not* mean that a woman who gets beaten up by her partner is 'asking for it'; the violence is *his agenda* and is *in no way* her fault. But the adult victim of this kind of relationship is playing out some deep-seated drama of her own, and so attracts someone who will reinforce her own self-destructiveness and feelings of low self worth. Of course this is not conscious. That is the problem. If she were living consciously, she would not be in a destructive relationship.

And no, this is *not* about blaming yourself for not leaving. This is about taking stock, raising consciousness, understanding that no matter how you have behaved in the past, or how you have allowed yourself to be treated, you *can* move away from abusive behaviour.

This is about opening doors, giving you the opportunity to see that there is another place, another reality; and you can get there from where you are – whether you are in a seriously destructive relationship, or in one that is in some way manipulative, exploitative, or simply takes you away from living with your highest integrity.

Consciousness manifests choices and power.

The first step is to recognize and acknowledge that your unconscious self has colluded in creating whatever situation you are in, and to take responsibility for this. And then, as you bring consciousness into the situation, you begin to change.

Once there is consciousness, you realize that you just cannot stay in a dysfunctional relationship. Once there is consciousness, you begin to see the way out. Once there is consciousness, you begin to realize your own self worth, your strength, your determination, your bravery.

Once there is consciousness, you begin to see that you have choices. And along with choices comes the strength and courage to act upon them. No matter how scared you are to leave, or how bleak the future looks at the moment, evolving consciousness will empower you to break the pattern, and you will no longer allow anyone to treat you badly.

There are two steps: firstly to see the situation as it really is and acknowledge your part in creating it. And then to move forward with Intention; you really have to want to change. And you have to accept that change means changing on the inside first.

Once you accept this, you recognize that you have a choice: either to stay in your situation in suffering and pain, which will go on repeating itself over and over; or to take your courage in both hands and move out. And move on. Once you take the first step, however difficult the path forward, the universe always lights your way.

Tony teaches the Path of the Heart. The path of the heart is love: loving ourselves, loving others, loving the All That Is.

Love is independent of any object or person.

Real love is not an emotion, which is transient. Real love is not about loving a particular person, or being 'in love'. It is much deeper than that. It doesn't depend on any external circumstance or any other person for its existence.

Real love is expansive and inclusive of everyone, while ego love is exclusive and possessive, wanting the love object only for itself.

Real love exists beyond form, in the All That Is. And also deep within us. In our heart.

Love, in fact, is simply what we are.

Love is a state of being.

Real love is a state of being, a way of existing in the world, a way of relating to all beings and to the All That Is. It is unaffected by the way other people behave towards us. It lives deep in the stillness within us; it informs our presence. It simply is.

Real love is a direction, a movement forwards, forever flowing, in motion and in stillness. It is our essence. It is born of our consciousness, not of our ego. It is how we are. It is who we are.

Love is the opposite of fear.

Love is the antidote to fear, swallowing up all criticism, blame, guilt, doubts. Love is compassionate and forgiving. It doesn't question, it doesn't judge. It simply accepts.

We do not create love, for we *are* love.

Love already exists within each of us, the divine spark in our centre. And we do not need to *deserve* love, for we *are* love. We manifest it, through consciousness.

Real love is consciousness made manifest.

The process of awakening to consciousness is the process of awakening to love. As we connect to the divine love within us, we also begin to love ourselves unconditionally. Loving ourselves is our connection to the divine love within us, and the manifestation of this love in every aspect of our lives. It embraces loving the perfection of the universe and everything within it.

And then we are able to bring this unconditional love into our intimate relationships. Recognizing and mirroring the divine love within our partner, we are truly blessed. Then our journey becomes magical, joyous, blissful, as we begin to live in the perfection of unconditional love.

Unconditional love transforms unconditionally.

When we have the courage to trust our hearts, to inhabit our deepest sacred space and love unconditionally, everything is possible. Everything is.

Chapter Six
Dreams and Dreaming

"When you start listening to your dreams then something fantastic happens. You connect to the pure harmony of the universe and everything falls into place. Everything here is to help you, not to stop you. If you listen to that part of yourself that accepts help, that is, your dream, then there is no problem. The problem is only in your mind."

Tony Samara

Our life's journey towards self-determination starts with a dream, a vision of how we want our life to be. We are all here to live our dreams; this is our soul's purpose in this life – to follow our dreams wherever they may lead.

In order to follow our dreams, we first have to recognize them – often the most difficult step – then to acknowledge them, then to believe in them, then to believe that we are worthy of living them, and then to believe that we are capable of manifesting them.

Every great movement for change has started with a dream. Usually, it has taken one person of immense vision, courage and dedication to articulate the dream of a whole people or nation, and inspire the struggle for its implementation. Tony often quotes Martin Luther King's famous "I have a dream" speech, which was delivered on the steps of the Lincoln Memorial in Washington DC in 1963. At the time, racial discrimination and unrest were rampant, and King was told that his dream was just a pipe dream, a fantasy impossible to fulfil. But he believed in his dream of racial integration and equality and freedom for all, and his faith galvanized the entire Black American community and changed the history of America forever. And now America has a black president.

The drive for individual change also starts with a dream.

The dreams we have for our lives are brought with us into this world by our soul. These dreams are incarnated with us and live in our earliest infancy, before we have words to express them. Before parents and the environment have set our course and perhaps limited our vision. Before our adventurous spirit, our curiosity, our wild imagination and innate delight in the moment have been curbed. Before our creativity and spontaneity have perhaps been quashed and we have started to feel that there is no point in trying to do what we really want to do, because we won't be allowed to do it, or we will be ridiculed, or we won't succeed. Somewhere, our dreams become buried…

Following our dreams is a spiritual imperative.

One of our major tasks, as we move into consciousness, is to discover, uncover, recover, our dreams. By living our dreams, the visions for our life held in our hearts, we reveal the unfolding meaning of our lives; its sacred purpose.

Everything starts with a dream. Our dreams are the essence of who we are, when we take off our masks and see the truth at the centre of our being. If we do not follow them, our soul begins to wither, our heart closes up, our lives become limited. We begin to live in unconscious fear.

There will always be people telling you that your dreams are impossible to fulfil. You have to get on in life, establish yourself, build a career, earn a living; be sensible. You can't just go off and do what you want. Who do you think you are? But that is exactly what you are here for – to be who you are, to do what you want to do, what you dream of doing.

At the end of your life when the time comes for you to meet your Maker and He asks you how you spent your life, what do you think will please Him more? That you spent your life pushing paper in an office because you were afraid to live your dreams? Or that you followed your heart and went to help street children in Mexico, or created a farm, or made music, or opened a bakery, or became an inspired teacher or painter or gardener or healer? What will please you more?

It is only our fear that prevents us from living our dreams.

Remember fear, that old false friend we've started to let go of? We need to be constantly vigilant, for fear is always waiting in the wings, ready to move centre stage if we are not on guard.

And behind the fear that we let go of, lurks another fear… There is always a deeper level of work to do. What stops us from following our dreams – behind all the reasons that we think are true, and all the excuses we may give ourselves – is always fear.

Do not allow other people's fears to connect to your own fear.

Letting other people's fears connect to yours is a recipe for a limited and impoverished life. Other people's fears simply reinforce our own. And remember, if other people tell us that we cannot go off and live our dreams, they are talking out of their own fear. For it can be very threatening for people to see others who have the courage to follow their dreams; it mirrors back to them their own lack of courage in not following *their* dreams.

Why are we all so afraid? Most of us, if we are honest with ourselves, have feelings of low self-worth, usually stemming from our childhood, when parents may have shaped us into a certain mould, not allowing us to be the unique being that we are. Often this has been reinforced by teachers and others later on. We learnt to do as we were told; to behave according to others' expectations and agendas for us. We did not do as we wanted to do. Somewhere in the process, our dreams got lost. And we buried our connection to them.

It is always easy to rationalize why we cannot follow our dreams. We fully intend to, of course, but we can't, not yet. We will follow our dreams – when we've made enough money, when we're successful, when the children are grown, when we retire. And one day we wake up, and we are fifty or sixty or seventy years old, and we wonder where our life has gone. We may have a nagging feeling that life has just 'happened' to us, and we never really lived it.

We have come to accept that growing up is about making sensible choices. Who are we to go off and live some crazy dream, just because we want to? Who are you not to? Life here on this earth is short. You are here to live your dreams. There is no time to waste.

So start by acknowledging your dreams and then give yourself permission to begin to open up to them. Remind yourself that this is why you are here: to live your dreams. Ask yourself, if you had no commitments, no financial constraints, if you could just wave a magic wand, what would you really like to do? Allow yourself to acknowledge this dream. Then go back and see how your commitments and your finances could fit into manifesting this dream.

Your soul's journey is to fulfil your dreams, and you are worthy of fulfilling them. When you have the courage to start following your dreams, the universe always helps. The practicalities get sorted. The obstacles that seemed insurmountable shrivel. We cannot know where our dreams will lead us; all we can do is follow, wherever they take us, and watch in gratitude the miraculous way they unfold our life.

So be brave! At this moment, you have only to take the first step – to acknowledge that you have dreams and to allow yourself to see what they are… Name them. As we begin to recognize and nurture our dreams, as we give them energy and bring Intention into fulfilling them, so they manifest.

Do you still think it's impossible to make your dreams come true? It's not! Take a leap of faith… Are you ready to stand opposite the fear and risk everything you have to follow your heart? Are you ready to stand in the centre of the fire, with arms outstretched, and shout "Yes!"? Then, watch your dreams begin to come true…

Our highest Intention is the magic that fuels our dreams.

The dreams that drive our unfolding journey through life are also connected to the dreams that pass through our subconscious as we sleep. They are both 'dreaming', and the link between them is more than just linguistic.

The dreams that we have at night bring us messages that are connected to our deepest selves. They are a blessing, a gift to us, even if we don't remember them. They allow us to enter a magical, mystical world, a world without limitations where everything is possible; where people can shape-shift, where animals can talk, trees can walk – and we can fly.

In the twenty-first century in the West, we have become largely separated from the world of dreams; our over-active egos and 'logical' minds keep us rooted in the world of physical reality. But in other times and other places, this has not been so.

Ancient dream wisdom has much to teach us.

Ancient societies were much more in touch with their dreams than we are today. The world of dreams was not something separate from their waking reality; they understood the significance and relevance of dreams to their lives.

In ancient Egypt, for example, people would go to the Temples and consult the oracles for information about their dreams before making any major decisions. In ancient Greece, there were special 'Dream Temples', where people would go and sleep for a few days if they had problems, in the hope of being blessed with profound dreams, which they would work through with an interpreter who sat in the temple for this purpose. Then they would be guided by their dreams in choosing which course of action to follow.

In Shamanic tribes, dreams are an essential part of everyday life. They believe that our dreams come from our Spirit Guides, bringing us deep knowledge and counsel for our waking lives. Traditional Shamanic communities gather each day at dawn to honour the wisdom of their dreams. Each person tells their dreams: men, women, children, everyone; and each person is listened to. Then the community discusses and interprets the dreams, not psychologically, but guided by the sacred knowledge of the Shaman and the intuitive understanding of the heart.

'Dreamtime' in a Shamanic community is often the most important part of the day. Revisiting their dreams together, the tribe would uncover the hidden wisdom of the unconscious that comes symbolically through dreams. In this way, they are always listening to the deepest part of themselves, opening their hearts to what their dreams have come to teach them. Only after allowing the teachings of the dreams to guide them, would they shape the activities for that day.

Understanding the process of Shamanic 'dreamtime' and the way they interpret the messages of dreams, may give us insight into our own dreams and help us to look at them in a new light.

'Nature dreams' can be very healing.

Living so closely with nature, Shamans find it plays a prominent role in their dreams. Though our lives are very different from those of Shamanic tribes, nature dreams can be significant for us, too.

Nature connects us to our own Higher Being, and teaches us that our relationship with Mother Earth and the cosmos can lead us back to the Source. With 'civilization's' compulsion to control nature and our environment, we have forgotten that by acknowledging the role of nature in our lives, we embrace a deep part of ourselves. Connecting to nature in our dreams can help us to regain the balance and harmony of the natural world and reclaim our lost connection with the universe.

Animals appearing in dreams have their own symbology, and can connect us to the Spirit of the animal. When we dream of a particular animal, we are connecting to the essence of ourselves that it represents. So, for example, dreaming of a lion will connect us to our fierceness and courage; a jaguar, to our power and strength; an eagle will connect us to our farsightedness, our ability to see from a higher perspective.

Our dreams are a gift from our unconscious and come to guide us on our way.

Our dreams are divine messages, signposts along our path towards self-knowledge and wisdom. If we listen, our dreams can show us where we are on our journey, where we are stuck and how we can move forward.

Our dreams are a mirror of our unconscious selves, but because they unfold in a non-linear, non-logical, way, we think they are complex, and often find them difficult to understand. But actually they are very simple; to unlock their secrets, we need simply to experience them with our hearts.

Listening to our dreams is an important part of spiritual practice.

By listening to our dreams, by interpreting them – not giving them a psychological interpretation, personal or archetypal, in which a stopped clock means this, or an air crash means that – but by listening with our heart, we can access their meaning and guidance.

To allow our dreams to guide us, we need to stay with them, try to recapture them as soon as we wake. Above all, we need to honour them as an important part of our lives, giving them time and energy, acknowledging that they come from within us and are not separate from our waking lives.

Honouring our dreams is a way of honouring ourselves and our spiritual process.

When Tony was a teenager, he had a very powerful dream that had life-changing repercussions for him.

In the dream he saw a brilliant light shining on the top of a mountain. It was an intense gold light and seemed to be beckoning to him; he felt driven to see what it was. As he climbed the mountain he started to get scared. The mountain was very high and as he climbed it the light seemed to be moving further and further away from him, but it was still beckoning to him to draw close. He felt impelled to go on. He continued climbing, his fear growing along with his curiosity. Then he saw what it was and he became very scared indeed. On the top of the mountain was a golden chair, which was reflecting the intense gold light. There was no-one sitting on it. Tony stood and stared at the chair, perched perilously on the top of the mountain. He thought how beautiful it was, and at the same time how frightened he was to get any closer. He woke up feeling scared but didn't understand why, as he was also aware of feeling simultaneously that the dream had been very beautiful and in some way very significant.

He stayed with the dream for a long time. Slowly, as he worked through it, it became clear to him that he had to sit on this chair; then many important truths would be revealed to him. He understood that the chair represented his spiritual self, and that by sitting on it – or rather in it, for it was very deep and he seemed to sink right into it – he would connect profoundly to his spirituality. Then he started to cry; crying as he let go of his deep fear, and also crying with joy, for at last he had found the thing for which he had been searching all his life.

This dream was a powerful marker on Tony's spiritual journey. Looking back on it now, he understands the depth of the dream. At the time, he was so frightened by it that he did not at first recognize that it was what he had been looking for. But when he plucked up the courage and sat in the chair, it all became clear. Then he recognized this part of himself, his deep spiritual longing, and understood his journey. Sitting in the chair, he was able to learn its lessons and apply them in a practical way in his everyday life.

This powerful dream helped Tony to understand the importance of dreams, and started him on his journey of interpreting dreams as an expression of our unconscious spiritual longings.

Working with dreams has become an integral part of Tony's work as a spiritual teacher, and is very popular among people who come to his retreats. Frequently, he is asked if dreams are 'true', something that perhaps we all wonder about.

Dreams are not necessarily factually correct, but they are profoundly true.

They are not 'true' in the sense that Jim, who pushed you off the Eiffel Tower in your dream last night, is planning to kill you this way in real life. Or that your Auntie Annie, who abducted your child in your dream, is actually intending to do this tomorrow.

But our dreams are profoundly true in the sense that they represent a true part of us; coming from our unconscious, they mirror what is happening on the deepest level. So, in your dream, Jim may represent your fear of leaving safe territory and 'flying off' into the unknown. Your aunt may be a symbol of your fear that your child is growing up and moving away from you.

Our dreams are gifts that come to illuminate our lives.

Our dreams come to remind us of our journey towards wholeness. They show us the self that we do not usually see in our waking lives. They are connected to our deepest yearnings, the longings of our heart and the wisdom of our soul.

They are also connected to our shadow side: the fears and anxieties that keep us from fulfilling our dreams. Frequently, they mirror our most entrenched fears. This inner voice speaking to us through our dreams brings into our consciousness many parts of ourselves that are deeply buried. Our dreams are a gift from our soul, showing us the work we need to do, guiding us along our journey. All we have to do is to listen to them with our heart and be open to receive the gift.

Everyone and everything in our dreams represents some part of ourselves.

Tony interprets dreams in the Shamanic way that sees everyone and everything in our dreams as representing some part of ourselves.

So, for example, if you dream about your child, your crippled uncle, a car chase, your seventh grade geography teacher, an airport full of terrorists, or making love to your best friend's partner, you need to ask yourself which part of yourself each of these represents. Don't try to analyze them [though a psychiatrist might have a field day!]. Try to feel the experience of being each person in the dream. Don't think about it; just feel each part, each person, from the inside. Ask yourself what it feels like to be your child, your crippled uncle, your seventh grade teacher, a terrorist, your best friend's partner.

And also, each object: what does it feel like to be the car and the airport? Stay with your feelings; interesting insights are likely to surface.

Bad dreams or nightmares are also a gift.

All dreams have something to teach us and can be an enriching experience. We usually dismiss bad dreams or nightmares because they are so frightening. But these dreams bring us profound messages, for they touch our deepest fears. Dreaming of something that reflects a certain fear is, in fact, a good sign, for it means that in some way we connecting to the fear. The dream is showing us that we are ready to deal with this, and provides a wonderful opportunity for us to do the work.

If we can accept that our dreams are not random but come to teach us profound truths, they can guide our journey through life in amazing ways. Our dreams can show us our limitations, where we are stuck, and how we can move forward. They can guide us towards the right priorities in our lives and show us what is really important. They can also guide us in more mundane ways, suggesting, for example, that we eat, or don't eat, certain foods, showing us that a particular activity would be in our best interest, or not.

But our dreams do more than this. They express not only the yearnings of our soul, but also its purpose in this life, of which we are not aware. Our dreams help to bring into consciousness many things that are hidden, and show us our deepest selves.

In his retreats, Tony often gives the example of 'the tiger dream' as a way of showing us how we can look at our dreams and connect to the profound truths they come to teach us.

The dream that a wild animal is chasing us is a dream that many of us have in early childhood. Small children are just beginning to make sense of the world and are often fearful. One night the child falls asleep and has a nightmare that a hungry tiger is chasing him and has come to gobble him up. The child wakes up terrified and screaming. The parent comes in to pacify him, and tells the child that there is nothing to be afraid of, it's only a dream. The tiger doesn't really exist.

But the tiger does exist. The tiger chasing us is our fears.

If a child dreams of a tiger, she is dreaming of that part of herself that is represented by the tiger: her deepest fears. Dreams that connect us to our fears are a profound gift; they bring the fears to the surface, showing us that they exist and that we can confront them and overcome them.

When we sleep, the ego sleeps too. So our dreams come directly from our unconscious, without being coloured by the 'agenda' of our ego and the turmoil it creates for us in our waking lives. Our dreams are messengers from our deepest purest selves; bypassing our ego, they are our profoundest teachers and guides.

But we may have become used to dismissing our dreams, very often having been encouraged to do so since early childhood. We have a frightening dream, our parent comforts us and tells us that there's nothing to be afraid of, that the monster doesn't exist and it was just a silly dream. And so, trusting our parents, we learn that dreams are not real, and we should just forget about them [though we may make a quick check under the bed just to make sure that there is really no monster there!].

And so instead of being encouraged to express our fears and deal with them in a safe and loving environment, we learn to suppress them. We learn that this part of ourselves is silly, childish, not real; just a dream. So we start the process of separating off from this part of ourselves, from the deepest, truest part. And as this programming is reinforced during our childhood, and we are encouraged to suppress everything that comes to us from the mysterious world of dreams, our feelings of separation and isolation can become entrenched.

Shamanic societies have very different ways of dealing with dreams.

A small child who dreamt of a tiger chasing her, would have her dream acknowledged and honoured by the tribe in early morning 'Dreamtime'. What our Western child may have been tempted to run away from, the Shaman befriends. The Shamanic child would be encouraged to accept the tiger as real; she would be invited to make friends with it, to understand the gifts that it was bringing her and accept them with gratitude. She would be encouraged to voice her fears, which would be listened to with respect; then she would be helped to understand and face them.

Our Western child is learning to run away from its fears and live with fragmentation; the Shamanic child is learning to deal with its fears and experience wholeness. In both cases these attitudes, fostered in early childhood, are likely to last a lifetime. And so, when our little child grows up, she may wonder why she seems to be out of touch with part of herself, why she is often unhappy for no apparent reason. She may look for this lost part of herself in the external world, possibly searching for it in relationships, money, excitement, maybe drugs or alcohol – anything except being still and looking inside her own being for the answers. For these gifts of introspection may have become buried along with the tiger of her childhood dreams.

If a Shaman were to meet our little child as a grown-up, he would probably suggest performing a ceremony as a way of re-aligning her with the 'tiger' that she lost touch with all those years ago. In the ceremony, the Shaman would invoke the spirit of Tiger, and bring its power to help the woman to reconnect to her early tiger dream. He would take her back through her life, connecting her to the many situations in which she has run away from 'the tiger', from her fears and anxieties, showing her the repeated patterns of her behaviour and helping her to let go of entrenched attitudes and beliefs, deal with her fears and move on.

We can transform the future by healing the past.

By revisiting old dreams that have traumatized us, and making different choices, we can heal the past and so transform the future.

In the case of the little girl and the tiger dream, the Shaman would bring her back to face her original choice in her dream: the choice between trust and fear. Then, as a child, she was encouraged to belittle the power of the dream, to 'choose' fear and run away. Now, as an adult, she can choose trust and openness. Choosing trust means accepting the energy of the tiger, being ready to receive its courage and its power, and using them to confront and deal with her own fears.

Then the tiger can become a true friend, perhaps the woman's animal totem. Welcoming this powerful animal ally can be transformative. Then, in every situation that evokes fear for her, she can call upon Tiger to inspire her with trust and courage. As she trusts herself enough to go back and reclaim the lessons and gifts of her childhood dreams, to welcome the 'tiger' within, she connects to the spirit of Tiger. And so she may lay to rest forever her fear of dealing with her fears.

When we honour our dreams and the process of interpreting their meaning, we honour our own higher self and its wisdom. The teachings that our dreams bring us come from within us; if we are open to them, they may change our life.

At his retreats, Tony shows us how to look at our own dreams and interpret their messages. He does this by encouraging us to stay within the experience of the dream, to *feel* the dream rather than think about it, and to connect to the feelings that it arouses within us, both during the dreaming and on waking.

Remember, everyone and everything in our dreams represents part of ourselves.

This is the basis of a spiritual understanding of our dreams. Often, our dreams represent some aspect of ourselves that we may not want to face. Connecting to all the different parts of ourselves portrayed in the dream can help us to access parts of ourselves that may so far have remained hidden, and then face them in our waking life.

To give us a sense of how we can begin to look at our own dreams, here below are several examples of dreams that Tony has discussed during some recent retreats. He works with the person who has had the dream, guiding them, through his questions, to come to their own understanding of what the dream means and what it has come to teach them. His interpretation is always led by the feelings and responses of the dreamer.

Each dream is different, and each dreamer is different. So, all interpretations are personal. As you will see, some people are more in touch with their dreams than others, more open to looking within and facing what they find.

R, an older woman on her first retreat with Tony, tells of a frightening dream that she has had many times. "All the heating in my house is turned off, the fireplace is blocked, and I am freezing. A huge terrifying monster is coming towards me. I call out to my husband [who is actually dead] but get no answer. The monster is getting closer and closer and is about to swallow me up. And then I wake up, petrified. I have no idea what it all means."

Tony suggests that she go back into the room, into the dream. How does she feel? She's very frightened. She speaks in a very soft, tentative voice throughout.

Tony: I think this dream is about fear. Your fear of opening up to your suffering.

R: I feel guilty that I didn't do more for my husband before he died. And sadness, too, at his suffering, his death.

Tony: Don't try to understand it. Just stay with the feelings.

R: I feel guilty because I always like to help everyone, and I feel I never do enough.

Tony: And what gets put aside?

R: Me, I suppose.

Tony: You do everything for everyone – your husband, your children, your parents. And then you give yourself a hard time for not doing more!

R: I suppose I do.

Tony: So what might your husband be trying to tell you in the dream?

R: That I should have more time for myself?

Tony: Exactly. You have no time for yourself. I think your husband is telling you that now it's time for you to invest in yourself. You have to free yourself from the past. It's time to light *your* fire. But you can't do it in the house you're living in. The fire there is blocked; there's no heating. It's a cold place, it doesn't nurture you. Perhaps the dream is telling you that you need to move.

R: It's the house where my children grew up.

Tony: They're grown up now. They don't live in the house; they don't need it. The dream is telling you that you need to move on, emotionally and physically. If you stay where you are, the 'monster' will get you. You will be 'eaten up' by your fears, your guilt. You are just repeating old patterns. You need to move.

R: Yes. As a matter of fact, I've been thinking of moving for a while…

Here there are appreciative smiles and grunts from people listening.

Tony: So? Are you going to move?

R: Yes. I'm going to leave London and move into the countryside.

Tony: When?

R: After the retreat, when I get back home, I'm going to put my house on the market.

Tony: Good. How do you feel now?

R: [Smiling] Better…

S, a middle-aged woman who has been to many of Tony's retreats, told a very short but very scary dream: "I was a very plain woman of about forty, short, plump with dark curly hair. [In fact, she has long fair hair and is very attractive.] I had sixteen children. And I was eating them, one by one. Sometimes, I was 'kind' and I killed them before I ate them. Sometimes I just hacked off limbs and ate them while they were still alive. I woke up terrified."

Tony: I think this dream relates to your body. Think back to when you were forty. Did you like your body?

S: No. I hated my body. I thought I was the ugliest thing on two legs.

Tony: And so, you were not very good to your body. You didn't respect it, you didn't treat it well. You created an unhealthy environment for your body, which allowed for your ill health to set in later in life. Does it make sense so far?

S: Yes. But why was I eating my children?

Tony: I think your children symbolically represent different parts of your body. After all, your children start by growing inside your body. In your dream, the children are parts of your body that are being damaged by you and maybe even energetically killed off. Think back to when you were forty. Did something particular happen in relation to your body?

S: I'd recently broken up with my long-time partner. And I remember on my fortieth birthday looking into the mirror and seeing wrinkles and feeling that now I was getting old. From now on it would be downhill all the way. And no man would ever want me again.

Tony: I think the dream has come now because you are ready to look at yourself and your body in a new light. It is showing you very graphically the damage you were doing to your body by not loving it. You were killing it off bit by bit. But now, if you begin to love and respect your body and treat it well, you can reverse the damage and start to heal yourself. Does this make sense?

S: Yes, I guess it does.

J, a young man attending his first retreat with Tony, told the following dream: "I had a weird dream about my landlady, Jo. We're in a large place together, like a warehouse. She tells me, if you give pills to someone, you must also give them money. Then she walks away from me and I say if you walk away I can't hear you. She turns round but doesn't come back, and repeats what she said about the pills and money. I say it doesn't make sense, even spiritually. If someone gives you pills and it makes you well, they are giving you the greatest gift, health. No? Why should they also give you money?

"Then the scene changes and we are in a large alcove with a big fridge, which Jo is carrying for her elderly parents. I am holding a two-year-old boy [who lives in the flat above mine in real life] and I ask him why we keep food in a fridge. I want to teach him. He doesn't know, so I ask him if it keeps food hot or cold. He says cold. I explain that keeping it cold makes it last longer. Then he disappears and Jo's father, a big man who looks about fifty, is there and he wants a different fridge. He

273

has a row of fridges on a bed. Only they are all flat, like the tops of coffee tables. He puts them into flat cartons. Then he grinned at me and I woke up."

There is general laughter when he finishes telling the dream, as it seems so bizarre and nothing makes any sense to anyone. Except, perhaps, to Tony.

Tony: Do you have any ideas about what it might mean?

J: Not a clue.

Tony: Go into the warehouse. What's it like? Can you describe it?

J: It's very dark.

Tony: And... ? What do you feel there?

J: Nothing.

Tony: O.K. What is a warehouse for?

J: For storing things.

Tony: Right. It's a place where you store things that are not of use to you at the moment. So perhaps it represents that aspect of yourself where things are stored. Maybe lots of clutter from your life that you don't need.

J: What about the pills and having to give money as well?

Tony: Any ideas?

J: Nope.

Tony: Part of yourself, represented by your landlady – the person who houses you, that is, your body – is trying to get well.

J: I'm not ill.

Laughter from some of the audience.

Tony: Wellness is wholeness. And we all have work to do to become whole. So, she is giving you pills, but tells you that's not enough, you also have to 'invest' more in yourself. The money in the dream represents the energy, the commitment, that you are not giving yourself. The investment. She explains this to you but you are not able to hear as this part of you 'walks away'.

J: I still don't understand about needing to give money. If someone gives you pills and that makes you well, why must they also give money?

Tony: This is the crux of the dream, and you don't understand. You even hide behind the word 'spiritual'. Your mind justifies the problem with a clever dialogue where you say you're giving the greatest gift of health with the pills. What you don't understand is that health and wholeness don't come from the pills, but from investing in yourself. You don't understand the deeper meaning of money in the dream. You see it just in its mundane aspect, which is actually just a reflection of how society sees it. In the dream, money is symbolic of an investment – of energy and time in yourself. When you're able to hear this, and do it, you'll heal, become whole.

J. is not convinced.

J: What about the fridge? And the little boy?

Tony: What do we keep in a fridge?

J: Ice-cream! Beer!

There is more general laughter.

Tony: Anything else?

J: Food, I suppose.

Tony: Ah, food. And what might food represent?

J: Don't know.

There is something almost defiant about J.'s answers, as though he is 'testing' Tony, and relishing not understanding.

Tony: Food represents nourishment. And the fear you had when you were little that there was never enough food, that is, never enough nourishment. The dream understands that it needs to show you things in a different way. Remember, everyone and everything in the dream is a part of you. So, it takes you back to when you were two years old. The little boy lives upstairs – upstairs being symbolic of your higher consciousness, which is trying to get through to you. You want to teach the little boy, to show him that we can preserve food. But this comes from your fear that there will never be enough, enough nourishment, so you always have to preserve the little that there is.

J: And what about Jo's father?

Tony: He is symbolic of your own father, and again, his concern with fridges, with preserving food, is about hanging on to the little nourishment that he was able to give you. The fact that he appeared in the dream suggests that you have issues with your father that you have not resolved.

J: What about the fridges becoming flat?

Tony looks at J. questioningly. J. just shrugs.

Tony: I think this is the saddest part of the dream. The fridges, where nourishment was stored, collapse; that is, any nourishment that there was has evaporated. I think the message of the dream is clear. That you need to make a serious commitment to invest in yourself – time, love, energy, and not rely on externals given to you by others: pills, food, or anything else. The fact that your inner two-year-old and your father appear symbolically, shows the continuation of the old pattern of fear that has been programmed into you and that you need to change. So, you've plenty of work to do here. Any questions?

J. shakes his head, looking confused, and still defiant.

Tony: If you want me to go into more detail, we could do that privately.

N, a writer, told the following dream: "I am in Africa, researching a book on native customs. I am in a mud hut with an old couple, 'the grandparents' of the dream. They look more Indian than African: small, wiry, very old. I understand that before the dream begins, they have been through the whole life cycle with me, explaining all their customs, and their relevance to each stage of life. Then they say, now we've come full circle. Now we're back to birth. And then two newborn babies appear, a boy and a girl. I am holding one in each arm, but they also seem to be suspended in space in front of me. The old couple explain that when a baby is born, its umbilical cord is cut very long. Only the cord isn't flesh, but made out of a kind of fine straw, which is plaited, and it's about a foot long. And the umbilical cords don't come out of the babies' navels, but out of their genitals. Then the old people tell me that when the cord is cut, it's buried in a special ceremony. And when the baby grows up and marries, the cord of the bride and the cord of the groom are plaited together and worked into the foundation of their new home together."

Some dream! Tony asks N. if she understands it.

N: No, not really.

T: Why Africa?

N: Well, maybe it represents the primitive side of me? Back to roots. Perhaps a place without the veneer of sophistication, culture.

Tony: Yes. And a place for getting out of… ?

N: My mind !!

Tony: You got it. Letting go of your mind. Your entrenched beliefs. Allowing yourself space to look at your life differently. What about the umbilical cords?

N: I suppose that's connected to my own child. It's a long cord. Perhaps it's about letting go of him too. But I feel that I really have/am letting go.

Tony: Yes, you have, and you are. But there's more to do. You've given everything to your child. You've been his mother and his father. You've had sole responsibility for him. In good times and very hard times. You've been everything for him. How does that make you feel?

N: Empowered. Drained.

Tony: How does your body feel?

N: Full of pain. Exhausted.

Tony: So, it's about letting go. Not doing so much for your son. He's doing fine on his own journey.

N: Yes.

Tony: What about the two babies? Any ideas?

N: I'm not sure. A boy and a girl… Maybe they represent my masculine and feminine side?

Tony: Exactly. It's about recognizing both aspects of yourself. God and goddess. Bringing balance between them. Integrating your masculine and feminine energies.

N: Yes…

Tony: And letting go, for you. Letting go of the umbilical cord that keeps you joined to your old life, your old ways, old habits. It's also about you giving birth – to a new you. Are you ready to take the risk? To jump?

N: Yes I am.

Tony: Of course you are. Otherwise you wouldn't have had the dream. Does it make sense?

N: Absolutely.

Dreams are a precious gift to us, a gateway to the mysterious world of our unconscious. Our dreams exist untroubled and untrammelled by our ego, our limitations, or the logical confines of the 'real' world. They are the medium through which our inner guides talk to us and teach us.

Our dreams offer us the truth of who we are, holding a mirror to our deepest inner selves. If we learn to understand their messages, our dreams can change our sense of ourselves and how we see the world around us. They can influence the way we relate to others and the way we shape and interact with our destiny. They can even give us practical advice.

So how can we connect more deeply to our dreams?

If we want to improve the quality of our dreaming, and of our remembering, and connect more deeply to the messages of our dreams, there are many things we can do to help ourselves.

Firstly, we can create a sacred sleeping place, which is quiet and peaceful, and undisturbed by the turmoil and turbulence of the day. You might like to have a small altar in your bedroom, where you can put crystals, stones, feathers, incense, angel cards, or anything else that helps you to create a gentle, sacred space. Some people also hang a dream-catcher over their bed.

You can also set up a Medicine Wheel, a Mesa, and work with the Four Directions. This can provide keys for us to work with our dreams. If, for example, you have a powerful dream that connects to the fear of change and you feel stuck, you can work in the Direction South, which is the Direction of air and wind. Air is the element of change, so working in this Direction can help us to let go of our emotions and the fear of change.

Ideally, a bedroom should be for sleeping only and should not contain television sets or computers, but in the small spaces in which many of us live today this may not be possible. If you have to have any electromagnetic objects in your bedroom, make sure that they are not only turned off but also unplugged before you go to bed. Remove telephones and clocks that flicker with a red light or illuminated hands. All electronic devices drain energy out of you.

If you have pictures on your bedroom walls, make sure that they are of peaceful scenes, preferably of nature. It is also good to have one or two plants in the bedroom, especially plants that have colour, like the spider plant. And peruviana and other cactus plants are beneficial as they eat up electromagnetic energy.

Some people in England use an electric blanket, which can be wonderfully warming and comforting on cold nights. But if you knew what it was doing to your energetic body, you would get rid of it immediately. Tony recalls that he once stayed in a bed and breakfast which had an electric blanket on the bed and his whole system was affected by it: he had strange dreams, and then experienced electricity buzzing through his body and was very sick. Don't use an electric blanket! Try a hot water bottle instead; or a lover.

The position of the bed is also important. If you live in the Northern Hemisphere, the natural position to sleep in is from north to south, that is, your head facing north and your feet facing south. This position allows the energy to move from the earth while you are sleeping, from the top of your head to your feet and circulate around your whole body. But if you are living in a place close to a prominent mountain, you should place your head in the direction of the mountain. If you are sick, the direction that is most helpful is from east to west.

You can create a sacred space around your bed. You can do this physically by placing a screen around the bed; or ritually by encircling the bed with your finger, or with a feather or other object from nature, or smudging a circle round it. [Smudging is a form of purification, done by burning sweet-smelling plants and fanning the smoke across the room.] Always do this in a clockwise direction and, as you do, be conscious that you are creating a sacred sleeping sanctuary into which to invite your dreams.

Make sure that your sleeping sanctuary is clean and uncluttered. You may wish to light a candle, burn some incense or play soft music. Do nothing else before you go to sleep. Avoid watching television just before going to bed, listening to the radio, or having an argument with your partner.

In fact avoid any heightened intellectual conversation. We need to relax the mind and create a stress-free environment as we prepare to enter the dream state.

Our state of mind and body when we go to sleep will influence our dreams.

If you are feeling angry, hurt, resentful, sorry for yourself or judgemental of others, this may all be reflected in your dreams. So when you get into bed it is helpful to practise relaxation; quieten your mind and let go of any stressful emotions.

You can go through a process of consciously tensing and then relaxing each part of your body, naming it as you do. ["I am tensing and relaxing my toes... ", etc.] You can do a breathing exercise, breathing in slowly and deeply, and on the out-breath letting go of any stress and negative emotions. You can also meditate before going to sleep. [For further details, see chapter 10: Exercising – Physical and Spiritual.]

This is time for you, your 'dream-time', eight hours of rest, deep sleep and rejuvenation. It is also important to try to finish eating at least two hours before going to sleep, so the body is not busy digesting food and can relax deeply.

Performing a ritual can help us connect to our dreams.

Performing a ritual half an hour before going to sleep is a good way to connect more deeply to your dreams, and also help you remember them. A ritual marks a transition from the daily routines of work and the mundane activities of the material world to a place of calm and quiet, stillness and peace. Remind yourself that you are now entering your sacred sanctuary. Just as your body is the temple of your soul, so your sleeping sanctuary is the temple of your dreams.

This is the place where your Higher Self, your spirit guides, will find you, for they talk to us through our dreams. By connecting to your Higher Self, you may invite these beings to bless your sleep and guide your dreams. You may consciously ask for their help; if a particular challenge is facing you, you can ask them to bring you guidance in a dream.

Recording our dreams can help us to remember and understand them.

A good way to decodify the messages of our dreams is to record them as soon as we wake. Recording dreams immediately upon waking, when we are still 'between realms' helps us to remember the feelings as well as the images of the dreams. For our dreams are a bridge between the mystical world of our soul and our everyday lives, a fleeting vision of possibilities that wafts away if we do not capture it immediately.

So, either write down your dreams, or speak them into a tape-recorder. Have paper and pen or tape-recorder next to your bed, so that you disturb the atmosphere of the dream as little as possible. A tape-recorder is the better option as you can record with your eyes closed, while still seeing the images of the dream. Record everything that comes to mind, however absurd it may seem, for these 'absurdities' are often the keys to a deeper connection with our unconscious. Coming back to them later, we may find that they resonate with us in different ways. As we connect to our dreams, we connect to the deepest part of ourselves, to our unconscious.

Sometimes when we wake, we know that we have been dreaming but cannot remember our dreams. If we want to help ourselves to remember our dreams, we should try to record whatever we can as soon we wake, when the gateway to our dreams is still open and we are most connected to them. If you can remember nothing of your dream, record your first feelings on waking, and anything else that comes to mind in those first few moments, a symbol, or a fleeting image; later, this may have meaning for you. Return to what you have recorded later in the day; it may be a key to jog your dream memory. As we honour the process, we validate the importance of our dreams, and then the dream often emerges.

By recording our dreams and returning to them later, we help to bring their energy into our waking consciousness and so aid the process of interpreting their meaning. This is also an act of honouring ourselves, having time just for ourselves. We can also paint, draw or write our dreams, sing or dance them, recreating their energy and the feelings they invoke in us.

Our dreams are blessings from our inner guides.

Our dreams are a reflection of our unconscious, steering us towards greater truth. They offer us a portal into the realms of magic and mystery and miracles. They remind us that our essence, our soul, is free, with limitless possibilities.

Our dreams belong to the dream world. But so do we. The more we work with our dreams, the more we come to understand their symbols and language, the more their meaning seeps into our consciousness, and the more aware we become of the knowledge and wisdom residing deep within us.

When we listen to our dreams, miracles begin to happen. If we honour our dreams and allow ourselves to inhabit them, they will show us that our lives in the world of physical reality can also be free, unbounded, magical and strewn with miracles. That in this life, too, we can soar...

Chapter Seven
The Body
Health and Healing

"We have to change our ideas about sickness. The body is the perfect instrument for healing and whatever the symptoms in the body they are not to be suppressed. If you have a headache, it is the easy way to take an aspirin to stop getting the headache, but what is underneath the headache? When you take the aspirin, the headache will go away but the energy of that sickness will not go away, it is still in the body. We have to deal with the causes of the sickness."

Tony Samara

Tony often talks about the body as the temple of the soul. It is our physical house in this incarnation. It needs to be nurtured and nourished, treated with love and respect, as the healthy home of our soul. A healthy soul cannot blossom in a sick body.

But our body also needs to be taken care of for its own sake; to be honoured and cherished and celebrated as a vital part of us, providing a healthy environment in which we can grow and flourish. Our body in its own right is an essential part of the unique person that we each are. The body, too, is a gift to us from the Divine.

Spiritual practice must be grounded in the body.

Many people who think of themselves as spiritual, are not really living their spirituality because they are not living in their body. Letting go of all that keeps us from following our spiritual path is not a mental exercise. Growth and movement take place in the body, as well as in the heart.

Working with our body is an integral part of the spiritual process. If we are not grounded in our body, our spirituality is not centred. The body is what grounds us, keeps us rooted in this world, not as a prison for our soul, but as its temple and its workroom.

Our body is a portal into spiritual consciousness.

Spiritual consciousness, as we have seen, is about being in the moment. We cannot be truly in the moment if we are not aware of our body. And conversely, bringing awareness into our body forces us to be focused in the moment.

The body is not inferior to the soul, something that we often forget in the first flush of excitement as we commit to the spiritual path. Indeed, in this lifetime, the body is not separate from the soul, but part of the same oneness that makes us whole.

In every incarnation, we are blessed only with what we need for that realm of existence. So, if we are given bodies in this incarnation, it is for a purpose. The main purpose is to ground us in the world of material reality, to enable us to experience physical being and work through our karma. The body also provides us with the opportunity of learning how to integrate the work of the physical world with the work of the soul. And for this work, we need to be grounded in a healthy body.

There is a crucial connection between spiritual consciousness and a healthy body.

As we become more spiritually aware, more committed to spiritual work, we realize the truth of this. In fact, we cannot move forward on our spiritual path without taking care of our body.

Caring for our body means trusting its intelligence to know what it needs, trusting our own journey enough to open ourselves up to face what our body is trying to teach us, trusting our spiritual process enough to let go of rigid beliefs that cause us to try to 'cure' the sick bits of our body without looking at the causes of our sickness. There is a healthy way to be ill!

There is also a healthy way to be well. We need to remember that good health is not just an absence of illness. We may not be ill, but we are not really well if we are feeling lethargic, run down or out of sorts. Wellness is living every moment with vibrant health and energy.

But the way many of us live is not conducive to a healthy life. Mostly we lead rushed and hectic lives, frantically trying to accommodate work, family, friends and personal interests; trying desperately to juggle too many balls. We do not have quality time to nurture ourselves; to nurture our bodies.

Our materialistic view of reality defines our attitudes towards sickness and health.

In the West, we generally perceive good health as an absence of illness; and illness as something random that just happens to us, perhaps because we were in the wrong place at the wrong time. It is something inflicted upon us by the outside world. It is nothing to do with us, and certainly we cannot be held responsible for it.

Our beliefs about health and healing are themselves the cause of much ill health.

If we see ourselves as fragmented and the world made up of separate disconnected bits, we are not likely to see the connection between the way we live and illness. Rather, we see illness at best as a nuisance, an inconvenience that needs to be fought and overcome; at worst, as something that meaninglessly debilitates us and takes over our life. We are simply 'unlucky'.

But if we could let go of these limited perceptions and see the interconnectedness of mind, body and spirit, humans as holistic beings, and health as harmony and wholeness, we could begin to understand the causes of illness and so become infinitely more healthy, as individuals and as nations.

282

We saw in Chapter 2 [Letting go of our beliefs...] how our beliefs limit our worldview and create our reality; and how letting go of them is a first step on our spiritual journey. In order to live healthy lives, we need to examine the beliefs that we hold about health and healing, and see how they may be the cause of less than vibrant health.

What we believe is what we manifest.

We need to remember this. [Our spiritual journey is all about reminding ourselves of things we already know.] It is as true of our beliefs about health and illness as it is of all our other beliefs. So let's look at these beliefs and see how they might be sabotaging our health.

As a society, our widely-held beliefs about health and healing do not encourage us to lead healthy balanced lives, physically, emotionally or spiritually. Our diet often consists of hurried 'fast food' lunches and pre-packed ready dinners that we pop into the microwave when we have no time to cook. Many of us, leading sedentary lives, do little exercise; maybe we walk to the car and back, or perhaps to the bus stop or train station. Most of us live with a lot of stress and have no time to nurture ourselves, no time to invest in healthy living.

We live out of touch with nature and alienated from our deepest spiritual selves. Most of us do not stop long enough from our busy lives to look inside and find out who we really are. The constant stress and tension, the endless struggle to keep going, to make a living, to keep up with the buzz of our mind and the demands of our ego, leave us little time to relax, to enjoy being with our families and friends; to spend time in silence, in stillness; just being. And this has a negative impact on our health.

Our society holds that it is the job of 'experts' to keep us healthy; we do not take responsibility for our own health and well-being. Nor do we take responsibility for our illnesses. We are still looking for 'salvation' in the outside world.

So, when we feel unwell we run to a doctor, the 'expert' whom we expect to heal us. But the most that s/he will be able to do is cure the sick bits of our body, but not address the underlying causes of our illness. This may not be the fault of the individual doctor, who is frequently a concerned and caring human being, but of the system with its rigid rules and time constraints. Often, an over-stressed and time-bound family doctor will prescribe medicine or pills because s/he has no time or training to do anything else; and because this may well be their understanding of what the practice of medicine is.

Western medicine largely suppresses the causes of illness.

Abdicating our responsibility for our health we put our trust in the doctor, the system, and like good children, we do what we are told. But the medicine we receive, though it may well relieve the symptoms of our illness, also suppresses its causes and gradually weakens the body's innate ability to heal itself.

Having no time or inclination to stop and look at the real causes of our sickness, we dose ourselves up with painkillers and antibiotics, and think we are curing the illness. We guzzle millions or billions of anti-depressants every year when our crazy lifestyle gets too much for us and we cannot cope. We drink trillions of gallons of coffee and other stimulants to keep ourselves going; then take more pills to relax us when we can't sleep. Everything becomes a search for a quick fix, an instant cure. We have no time to be ill.

So we numb the pain, we take care of the symptoms, and run away from everything that could help us to look inside ourselves and confront the cause of our sickness. Taking huge amounts of pain-killers and antibiotics is symptomatic of our modern technologically advanced society. We don't trust or respect our bodies, we don't look at what is happening within us, we don't honour the healing process. And then we wonder why we are sick!

Dealing with the physical symptoms of illness alone can never heal your body.

Curing the physical symptoms of illness can never heal the body; much less the heart or soul. The symptoms of disease are a warning that something within us is out of balance and needs to be looked at; they are a tool for learning, not an enemy to be vanquished. [Of course, if we have a serious illness we may also want to contact a medical specialist and seek his/her advice. But we should do this within the context of holistic healing rather than seeking cures for the sick bits of us.]

If you have a headache and immediately take an aspirin, the headache will subside, but the sick energy that was causing the headache remains in the body. So your headaches recur, you take more aspirin, and further suppress the cause of the headaches. Then you get a sore throat and feel really unwell, so you take antibiotics. But antibiotics suppress the healthy working of the immune system, pushing the energy of the sickness still deeper into your body, filling it with chemicals that disable its proper functioning. Gradually, the immune system forgets how to heal itself.

Consider the following scenario: you suffer from constant backache, but do not deal with the suppressed anger that is causing it. You take painkillers. The anger buries itself more deeply in your body. Then you get rheumatism and you can't move your joints. You still don't listen to what your body is trying to tell you. The pain gets worse and the painkillers you have been taking are no longer effective. You are given stronger medication, such as cortisone, which is really harmful for the body. But you are in so much pain, you don't care. You take more and more cortisone, and eventually it gives you cancer. The cancerous lumps are cut out of your body; but the cancer returns. Then you are given chemotherapy or radiation treatment. And one fine morning, the doctor walks into your ward and notes that the cancer is cured – but the patient is dead!

There is another way to look at health and healing: the holistic way, the way that considers a human being to be whole, an integration of mind, body, heart and soul. The Shamanic way.

The Shamanic way of health and healing has much to teach us.

If we really want to heal ourselves and become whole – and everyone has room for some kind of healing and growth towards wholeness – we could help ourselves by taking a closer look at the Shamanic view of health and healing.

These 'primitive' Shamanic ideas are very different from those of orthodox Western medicine, but nevertheless they have much to teach our civilization and can be a huge inspiration to us as we begin to examine our own beliefs about health. Indeed, many of the concepts that fuel the 'alternative medicine' that is gathering force in the West, come originally from ancient Shamanic wisdom.

Good health to Shamans is synonymous with balance and harmony among body, mind and spirit. It is the perfect balance of the life force, a state of grace and wholeness into which we are born. It is the integration of all parts of ourselves, living in tune with the harmony of the natural world. It expresses the orderly ebb and flow of life among the one, the many, the whole.

Good health to a Shaman is not an absence of illness, but rather a way of life; the holistic picture painted by each of us by the way we live. It encompasses the way we attune ourselves each moment to the harmony of the natural world and the will of the Divine. Illness is something that we bring upon ourselves by living out of touch with this balance and harmony, out of touch with our true selves.

The Shaman sees physical illness as the result of emotional or spiritual imbalance, being out of kilter with our true selves or out of harmony with the natural world. Shamans find our perception of physical illness as a disease of the body that needs to be cured by a doctor, quite bizarre. They simply do not understand our concept of the separation of body, heart and soul.

Shamanic medicine is actually power.

Just as Shamanic healing is something very different from our concept of healing in the West, so, too, the Shamanic concept of medicine is very different from ours. As we saw in Book One: Journeys, medicine to a Shaman is not something you take when you are ill, but rather something you have when you are well. Your 'medicine' is your personal power, your life force. It cannot be owned, given or taken away; it can only be engaged with, harnessed for rightful alignment with the universe and with Spirit.

This 'medicine power' is not power as we generally understand the term in the West. Shamanic medicine power means the power within, coming from Spirit, and is manifest in the way we relate to others, to everything within the natural world and to the Divine. This power has nothing to do with becoming personally powerful, a desire to have power, trying to hold onto power, or having power over others. Rather, it is an acceptance of the way things are, the acquiescence of a person's rightful place within the great Mystery. When we stop fighting the forces around us and align ourselves with universal harmony, we also share in universal power.

According to Shamans, it is the loss of medicine power which creates ill health. This loss of power is caused by disharmony or turbulence within, by internal conflict or the festering of negative emotions that have not been released. And if being ill is a matter of losing personal power, then healing will come about when we start to regain this power.

In Shamanic lore, illness is also something that the soul invites into our lives, a gift to show us something within that needs healing; a wake-up call when nothing else will alert us to what we need to see; an opportunity for learning lessons that we need to learn. The physical sickness is a warning light turned on by the body; it represents only the symptoms of emotional or spiritual imbalance. What needs to be treated is the cause.

As Tony was told by a Shaman in the Amazon Rain Forest, "White man's medicine may cure illness and bring the patient back to where he was before he was sick. Shamanic medicine heals the whole person, helps him to learn the lessons of his illness and leaves him further along on his journey than he was before he became sick; wiser and more enlightened. That is the purpose of illness."

This may turn our beliefs about illness upside down, but accepting the Shamanic concept that illness is not an enemy to be drugged, suppressed and conquered, but rather a gift to be welcomed for its teaching, may not only vastly improve our health and vitality, but may also radically change our lives.

Our mind may contain angry, jealous or fearful thoughts, blame, judgementalness or guilt. And our body holds onto the emotion behind the thoughts and the judgements.

Our body holds all our emotions.

Our body holds all our emotions; if we have not allowed ourselves to acknowledge and release them, they remain trapped in our body. All our emotional and psychological pain that has not been dealt with and released, is held in our bodies. *All* our emotional and psychological pain, from our earliest childhood onwards. This is an awesome amount of pain to hold in one body. And these emotions will have been festering in our bodies for years and years, gathering not dust but toxins. No wonder we are often tired, dejected, miserable, depressed, full of aches and pains, and ultimately become sick!

The unity of body and mind has been part of Eastern spiritual knowledge for thousands of years, but it is a relatively new concept in the West. But it is beginning to be accepted here, too, that emotional pain is often expressed as physical pain, and frequently leads to illness. If we are living cut off from our emotions, they will eventually make themselves felt as physical symptoms that have to be dealt with. As the toxicity of all our unreleased emotions builds up in the body, the body will eventually react and become sick.

Suppressed emotion is one of the major causes of illness.

Smiling when we are angry, pretending to be fine when we are hurt, and all the myriad emotions that we suppress in our unconscious way of living, damage our body as well as our heart. It is important to stress this, for becoming aware of this knowledge may radically change our attitudes towards health and healing. Anger and resentment, the most commonly suppressed of all emotions, may turn up first, perhaps, as chronic backache, later on as cancer. Suppressed love or a dysfunctional relationship may eventually manifest as heart disease. Severe headaches are usually an expression of unresolved inner conflict and tension.

This does *not* mean that if you have cancer or heart problems you should also be feeling guilty about it and start blaming yourself! But we do need to look at our emotions and the ways in which we express or suppress them – and what this does to our body.

The body has its own intelligence and wants us to heal emotionally.

Our body wants us to heal. And it knows that in order for us to heal we have to deal with what we have suppressed. And so it will go on creating more and more severe physical symptoms until we take note and deal with the causes.

Research has shown that powerful emotions can even lead to changes in the biochemical make-up of the body. A simple example of this is the huge adrenalin rush that accompanies the flight mechanism when we face immediate physical danger. Not to mention all the physical reactions to being 'in love'.

But help is at hand! Nature always provides the remedy as well as the signals: our emotions, as well as being held in the body, can also be released through the body. Our body holds all the answers!

Our body is a map of our psychological and emotional state of health.

We need to consult our body map and pay attention to what it is showing us.

Different organs are associated with different emotions. When we understand this, we can look at the pain or discomfort in a particular part of our body and begin to connect to the underlying emotional cause. The liver, for example, holds stress and anger, grief becomes lodged in the kidneys, the bladder may be 'weeping' for a loss, fear can be held in all our muscles and joints. Connecting the symptoms to the emotion that is held there, we may begin to heal our physical pain, and our heart as well.

To do this, we need to go inside our body. Let's try. Sit or lie quietly and watch your breathing. Relax your body, then focus on slowing your breath and breathing deeply. Go into the pain and see where it lives in your body. Then see if you can connect to the emotion stored in this part of your body. Stay with the symptoms, with the emotions.

This is a process. The lessons of the symptoms will reveal themselves to you, in time, if you continue to look inward and stay in your body. Maybe not immediately, but if you stay with the emotions, what you need to learn will be revealed. Ask yourself: what is its message, its meaning, its metaphor. Seek answers in your body, not your head! According to metaphysics, even terminal illnesses can be healed if we deal with the emotional blocks that have created them.

As we start to look inwards, we need to pay great attention to what is happening in our body; and the effect that connecting to suppressed emotions may have on our body. For instance, as the liver beginsto release anger, your skin may suddenly erupt in a nasty angry red rash; you might get eczema, itchy or dry skin, or dry hair. Don't try to suppress the symptoms – learn from them! On some level you have anger in your body, and this is creating the sickness. As you rid your body of the anger, the rash and dryness will disappear. Stay with the symptoms – they are only symptoms; trust your intuition, trust the intelligence of your body and deal with the cause.

We need to remember that our own body is the perfect instrument for healing. It provides us with a map. If we learn how to read the road signs, we may discover not only that our liver is diseased, but that the anger that has taken up residence there is left-over baggage from our childhood, that has not been claimed and 'owned'. By looking beyond the physical symptoms of disease to its cause, we heal our emotions and spirit as well as our body.

Owning our emotions is a first step towards healing.

Allowing ourselves to own and then acknowledge our emotions, is the first step towards releasing them, and healing. As you allow yourself to feel these emotions and give them attention, you are also accepting them, as they are; acknowledging that it's all right for you to own them. Don't think about them, don't judge them, just feel them.

Remember, no-one can 'make us' feel anything. [You might want to check back to Chapter 2: Letting go of emotions… No-one can 'make us' feel anything.] *We alone are responsible for our emotions.* It is crucial to take this on board. If we are feeling angry, rejected, resentful or jealous now, the person who has triggered these emotions *is not the cause of them.*

Another person may be the catalyst for our emotions, but they are not the cause.

If we feel that someone is 'making us' angry, what they are doing is 'pushing our buttons', causing us to tap into past anger, jealousy, etc. that is already held in our body and has not been dealt with. [This explains why, for instance, we sometimes feel hugely exaggerated anger over trivial things.] And so, every time someone comes along and pushes your buttons, this gives you a first-hand opportunity to connect with these emotions, examine them, learn from them and then let them go.

How other people behave towards us is *their* agenda.

We've talked about this, but we need to remind ourselves: other people behave towards us because of who *they* are, not because of who *we* are. We are *not* responsible for their behaviour towards us. We *are* responsible for our responses.

So, if we can stand back from our emotions and recognize this, we may actually become grateful to the person who has 'made us' angry, for the opportunity they are giving us to deal with past anger and let it go. And by the way, observing our anger, or other negative emotions, does not mean that we don't feel it. We may feel it intensely; then we need to go inside it, confront it, and finally release it.

This is an inner process between us and ourselves, not connected to anyone else. Then, as we let go of the anger, we will begin to release the physical pain that it has been causing.

Illness can be a great blessing.

When nothing else seems to wake us up, illness is often the nudge that the universe gives us to force us to look at our lives and see what is out of kilter, what is behind the symptoms of the illness. As we accept the disease for the lessons it has come to teach us, we may begin to understand what changes we need to make in our lives. As we let go of the limitations of our beliefs that perceive the world as random and illness as 'unlucky', and start to see the interconnectedness of mind, body and spirit, ourselves as holistic beings, and health as harmony and wholeness, we can really begin to heal. And as we heal the illness, we also heal our lives.

The ancient art of Shamanic healing is very relevant for our age too, and has much to teach us. Indeed, it was never more urgently needed. Tony is trained as a Shamanic healer, and advocates and practises Shamanic healing to this day.

If you were to visit a Shaman for healing the first thing he would do, before he examined your body, would be to look at your lifestyle, the way you were living with yourself and interacting with the world around you. He would examine which parts of you were out of sync, where you were unbalanced, how you were out of harmony with yourself or with your environment. He would take account of your moods and your general outlook on life.

Then he would watch the way you breathed: was it deep, conscious, engaging with life in each breath, or was it shallow, unconscious and automatic. He would observe your levels of tension and stress and where you held them in your body. All this information would help him to locate the source of your sickness. Then he would work with you to release the emotional or spiritual cause.

Tony uses similar diagnostic techniques to those used by Shamans. First he will examine all aspects of the patient's make-up: physical, emotional and spiritual. The headache, the sore throat, the back pain, is a physical symptom, but the underlying cause is emotional or spiritual. Tony will look at what is causing the disease or pain, usually by examining the patient on the energetic plane as well as talking with him/her. He does this by running his hands over the patient's ethereal body, several centimetres above the physical body. In this way, he can determine which organ is harbouring the sickness, and this in turn will tell him which emotions he has to deal with.

Then he will embark on a healing journey, *together with the patient.* He is always a co-healer with the patient, acknowledging the patient's responsibility for her/his own health, and the wisdom of his/her body. Simultaneously, he will treat the symptoms naturally, using herbal remedies, similar to those used by Shamans for thousands of years.

Shamanic herbal remedies help the body to heal itself.

Herbal remedies do not 'cure' in the way that Western medicines do; rather, they help the body to experience the pain or the sickness, and then release it. Often the symptoms may become temporarily worse during the process of releasing the sickness from the body. This is because herbal remedies bring out the sickness, they do not suppress it. Natural remedies not only counteract the physical symptoms of illness and pain, they also assist the healing process by strengthening the immune system and helping the body to heal itself.

Herbal remedies are used by Shamans for anything, from a mild tummy ache to a raging toothache, to cancer. For those of you who are still sceptical, Shamans have great success in treating cancer with the Chuchuhuassa plant, a powerful herbal remedy. The spirit of Chuchuhuassa is seen as fiery, young and very strong. When prepared in the correct way, this remedy is given to people with cancer, and 'miracles' happen. Its fame has spread far and wide, and people come from across the world to be healed by Shamans.

But Shamanic healing has to be understood and practised in a Shamanic way. The herbs have to be planted, nurtured, picked and prepared in a loving way with Intention, that respects the Spirit of the plant, which is the essence of its healing.

Tony tells of an incident that was told to him by a Shaman when he was living in the rain forest. The Amazon forests were 'invaded' by large numbers of scientists, sent by several big pharmaceutical companies from Switzerland and America to test the Chuchuhuassa plant and other Shamanic herbal remedies, to see if they really could cure cancer and other serious diseases.

The scientists came and saw the patients with large cancerous lumps. Then they saw the Shamans working 'miracles' with herbal remedies: the cancerous lumps disappeared, and the patients were healed. But when they took the same plants back to their laboratories, they found nothing there. This is because they did not understand Shamanic medicine: that plants cannot be taken like drugs that simply suppress the symptoms of disease. They had not learnt how to work with these plants. They did not treat the plants with love or respect; on the contrary, they tried to control them for their own ends. And so the spirit of the plants eluded them, and the plants were rendered ineffective.

There are hundreds of herbal remedies used by Shamans for healing.

It is beyond the scope of this book to list them all or go into details about them. What is important is that we understand the principles, and allow them into our healing. In Shamanic wisdom, illness is perceived as a gift that provides an opportunity for learning and growth. The more difficult the experience, the greater is the opportunity it presents for learning. And we have a choice: either we remain stuck – and become sick, and sicker; or we learn from these experiences, heal ourselves and move on.

There are many everyday conditions that we can easily heal ourselves by using herbal remedies. To give just one example: the common wart, which often drives people to distraction. People try everything, but the unsightly little growth stubbornly refuses to budge. If you have a wart, you need to ask yourself why it's there. It's not random; it's an expression of something happening inside you that you are not dealing with.

You have a choice: you can burn away the wart, burn away that part of yourself that is not being dealt with, just as cancer is burnt away with radiation. Or you can take herbal remedies that allow you to work more deeply with the issues that are causing the wart to grow. In South America, they use a plant called Maticau, which supports the inner process. When this is dealt with, the wart disappears.

This process is similar for any number of conditions, from a wart to cancer. There are many amazing herbal remedies, but the remedy will not cure you. It will help you to work with the causes of the disease, to go more deeply into your process, and to heal inside. Then the symptoms will disappear.

Another wonderful remedy used by Shamans is a plant called Maca. In the West, it has become fashionable for menopausal women to be given Hormone Replacement Therapy [HRT]. But the hormones that are used in HRT come from pigs. So millions of women are regularly putting tablets containing pig hormones into their bodies. Who would want to do that? In South America, native menopausal women use Maca. This supports the body naturally as it goes through the changes of this time of life, and these women don't suffer with any of the usual symptoms that we associate with the menopause.

Many parents who happily take responsibility for their own health and use natural remedies if they become ill, panic when their children get sick. As soon as a child gets a fever of 40 degrees, your fear overtakes you; you don't trust the process, you rush to the doctor and happily accept the antibiotics or pain-killers. But by doing this you actually harm the child, because you are not respecting its own healing process. The fever is helping to heal the body by eliminating the poisons. Suppressing the fever means that you are pushing the poison further into the body and suppressing its own healing process.

Of course you are not going to let a child burn with fever, but there are many ways of dealing with it. There is a variety of herbs that can cool the body and bring down fever, such as mint oil, or even vinegar. By using natural herbs, instead of suppressing the life energy of the child you are listening to its body, taking the fever from the head to the feet and then out of the body so that the whole body can heal. At the same time, you are validating the wisdom of your own intuition, gaining strength from this and reinforcing your own spiritual process.

This in fact is what health and healing is about; taking responsibility for our own body and the holistic healing of ourselves and our children. Bringing consciousness into all our choices, not rushing to be 'saved' by someone in the outside world, but trusting our own inner wisdom and the sacred guidance of our own heart.

Healing with herbal remedies is a spiritual as well as a physical process.
When we are involved with spiritual work, using natural herbal remedies becomes increasingly important as we begin to open up and connect to old painful emotions that are trapped inside the body. Remember, as you embark upon your journey towards vibrant health, that you may temporarily feel physically much sicker, as your body brings to the surface all the painful memories that were contained in the cells of the different organs.

So, for example, if you are opening up to anger, you are opening up to the physical aspect of the liver; if you are opening up to grief, you are opening up to the physical aspect of the kidneys. And so all the memories that are contained in the liver and the kidneys also open up. You become vulnerable, raw, exposed, and your body may react with many symptoms of sickness and pain.

These are all good signs. Stay with the process; the body is helping you to release toxins and let go of old negative emotions. Remember, negative emotions that are held in the body are toxic.

Herbal remedies can enhance spiritual work and help the integration of the physical and the spiritual. For example, there are plants that help to open the heart. The rose is one, associated with love since time immemorial. The Damascus Rose, which Tony uses, is a very powerful remedy. The water is drawn off the rose at a specific time, and the remedy is prepared and used homeopathically; the intelligence of the plant speaks to the heart and you open up. So instead of suppressing your emotions, causing all kinds of physical problems later on, you deal with your situation now. The body becomes stronger, the process becomes deeper and you find yourself able to give unconditional love.

Tony has also created his own herbal brew, Theriaca, as an antidote for all ills. This can be particularly helpful in dealing with the intensity of these transformational times. [See Index, note 1, for more information.]

Herbal remedies can be hugely beneficial not only when we are sick. They can also help in dealing with many aspects of our daily lives; for example, in our living and working environments.

If you are spending a lot of time in an atmosphere where you are constantly being bombarded by the lower vibrations, be it from disharmony, friction, frustration or anger, or from radiation from computers or mobile phones, your body is constantly being weakened energetically. Then you need to remind yourself that you are a human being, not a machine.

You should take frequent short breaks from your workplace [it *is* possible; lots of people take many toilet or cigarette breaks!] and go outside. Try to connect to the harmony and balance of nature. If you can, go and sit by a pine tree. Pine trees have many small antenna-like needles, which absorb radiation from the body and open the lungs. Breathing deeply next to a pine tree cleans out your body and fills it with healthy energy.

Another natural remedy to help offset the damage of computer radiation is a cactus plant called peruviana. It comes from South America where it lives four or five thousand metres above sea level, where the radiation is very strong. It has lots of long spikes, which function as antennae, similar to pine trees. Through these antennae, it absorbs the radiation, drawing it deep into itself, and flourishes on it! So, if you put the cactus close to your computer, the cactus is happy and your body stays healthy. If you can't get hold of a peruviana, or as a stopgap measure, a bowl of water placed in front of your computer screen will absorb some of the radiation.

Shamans discover their herbal remedies by observing nature and animal behaviour in different situations. This was how they discovered the beneficial properties of lichen. Lichen is another remedy for radiation. It doesn't actually block radiation, but it teaches the body, through it's own intelligence, how to survive in an environment of high radiation.

During a solar flare [the sun releasing parts of itself] the radiation that reaches the earth is very powerful and affects us strongly. Shamans noticed that the vicunas, very clever wild deer, could sense the solar flare before it happened, and would go to the rocks where lichen grew in profusion. They had never eaten this plant before, but now they consumed great quantities of it, to prepare their bodies for the physical and energetic changes of the solar flare. Shamans, observing this, made a remedy out of the lichen to protect their community from radiation sickness.

In Japan, the healing properties of lichen have been known about for centuries. After the explosion of the atomic bombs in Hiroshima and Nagasaki at the end of the Second World War, many people in Japan ingested large quantities of lichen. Those who did suffered measurably less damage than the devastating symptoms of those who did not. So, if you spend hours sitting in front of a computer, or talking on a mobile phone, it is a good idea to take lichen. If you spend hours sitting in front of the television – don't!

The lotus is another wonderful plant that can be helpful to us when we are not sick. The lotus flower represents deep spirituality and is especially beneficial before meditating, particularly to people who have a hard job calming their mind and being in the stillness of the moment. The lotus plant opens up the crown chakra, thus helping the process of moving more deeply into the meditation and experiencing the deep silence and spirituality within.

In the West, we have been conditioned to think of our body as a servant, and our mind as master. But this is to malign our bodies, and give destructive power to our minds.

Living a life of health and harmony is a life lived with consciousness of our bodies.

Our body is a true representation of who we are. Whereas the mind has its own agenda for controlling our lives, the body truly reflects our state of being. So, if we are feeling out of touch with ourselves, we should look to our body for guidance, rather than our mind. Our body, if we only let it, is here to support us in this lifetime. It has its own profound intelligence and can teach us many things. We need to listen to its messages and nurture its needs.

These needs include physical work of some kind; gardening, working on an allotment, or other work in nature is a wonderful way of combining physical work with being centred in the moment, in our spirituality. And some kind of regular physical exercise is absolutely essential. Correct breathing is also crucial. Breathing deeply fills the lungs with clean air, oxygenates the blood and invigorates the whole body. [For more on exercise and breathing, see Chapter 10: Exercising – Physical and Spiritual.]

Rest and relaxation, and enough quality sleep, are also an integral part of a healthy regime. The sleep that we have before midnight is thought to be twice as beneficial as sleep after midnight. And play is also an important ingredient of a healthy lifestyle, something which as 'sensible' adults we often forget. Doing things for fun, just because they bring us joy, is a vital component of a healthy life. We need to let out the little child inside us and give it free reign!

Taking care of our body means being aware of what we put into it [healthy food and drink] and what we don't put into it [unhealthy food, and also alcohol, drugs, etc.]. Periodic fasting cleanses the body of toxins and helps us to loosen our addiction to food. It is also a way of cleaning out the poisons of suppressed emotions that are festering in the body. [For more on diet, food and fasting, see next chapter]

And lastly – and firstly – some form of spiritual practice is essential to a harmonious and balanced life. This can be just a few minutes of prayer or gratitude when we wake up in the morning; it can be meditation or sacred dance; any ritual, in fact, that brings us into relationship with the All That Is, and connects us to our own sacred centre.

Chapter Eight
The Body
Food and Diet

"Let food be your medicine and medicine be your food."
Hippocrates, frequently quoted by Tony

As we have seen in the last chapter, the loving attention that we give our body has repercussions not only for our physical health, but also for our emotional and spiritual well-being.

Food, and our attitude towards what we put into our bodies, also has far-reaching implications, and does much more than feed and nurture the physical body. Our diet is a reflection of our conditioning, our upbringing, our beliefs and values, our awareness and spiritual development, and is both effect and cause of our lifestyle and our state of health: physical, emotional and spiritual.

Food is a yardstick by which we can gage both our psychological health and our spiritual growth. It not only nourishes the body; food also contains emotional and spiritual energy, which we imbibe as we eat. What we feed our body expresses our attitude towards our body, our soul, our self. Eating is a spiritual practice as well as a physical necessity. As we bring spiritual consciousness into all aspects of our lives, we also bring it into our attitudes towards food and diet. The food we eat, and the way in which we prepare and eat it, mirror our spiritual development.

Spiritual consciousness leads us to a natural diet.

The dietary choices that we make are an expression of our relationship with ourselves and with the universe; a manifestation of our psychological health and our attitudes towards our body. They are also a reflection of our level of consciousness.

As we grow in consciousness, we become more attuned to the natural world, more in harmony with the All That Is, more balanced within ourselves. And so we will inevitably be drawn to a natural diet. This will include eating the fruits of the earth, in season, as they grow on the fertile soil that nature provides; eating foods that are organic, unprocessed, in which neither soil nor foods have been chemically 'enhanced' or otherwise modified.

Spiritual consciousness leads us to a vegetarian diet.

As we evolve spiritually, and feel ourselves more and more a part of the oneness of Creation, we also awaken to our connectedness with our animal "relations"; and this includes birds and fish. When we connect with them, we feel their pain and suffering; our sensitivity then dictates that eating them is no longer a viable option for us. Unless it is a matter of survival, eating meat must be seen as incompatible with walking the spiritual path. Vegetarianism then both becomes a powerful element in our process of spiritual evolution, and also reinforces it.

We should remind ourselves that animals are not placed on earth solely for our benefit, but have a life and purpose and soul of their own. So next time you fancy a steak, remember that meat is dead animals, creatures that not so long ago were walking this earth and breathing the same air as you and I; our four-legged "relations".

If we had to kill the animals ourselves, most of us would not do it. We eat meat only when we are not brought face to face with the killing. Tony suggests that if you still feel that you cannot live without meat, you should go and kill the animal yourself. Or at the very least, visit a slaughterhouse and see for yourself what goes on there. This may be enough to put you off eating meat for a while!

When choosing our diet, we should be driven by our compassion and Intention for the highest good of all, guided by the principle of 'greatest harmlessness'. The less sentient the life form, the less pain it will experience. People often scoff at vegetarians, saying that if they were logical, they would not eat plants either, for they too are alive and feel pain. Yes, they are and they do. But fruit and vegetables reproduce themselves: if you pick an orange from a tree, another will grow in its place. If you do not pick it, it will fall off the tree anyway when it is ripe, and rot. Animals do not reproduce in this way; if you kill an animal, it's dead.

Living by the principle of greatest harmlessness in all aspects of our lives is a powerful spiritual marker.

Eating should be a celebration of life and our connection with it, a joyous expression of who we are and where we are on our spiritual journey.

Spiritual practice is about celebrating life with joy in every moment.

Preparing our food with reverence, gratitude and joy is part of spiritual practice. It connects us with Mother Earth, with the rhythms of nature, with the abundance of the All That Is.

In the Shamanic tradition, the growing and preparation of food is seen as an expression of the spiritual life of the community. Eating with consciousness connects Shamanic tribes on a daily basis to the abundance and sacredness of the gifts of nature. Everything connected with food is a celebration.

In the many years that Tony spent living among Shamans in South America, he was struck by the vitality and life-force of people in their eighties and nineties, who sparkled with the energy of people half their age in the West. They rarely became ill, and many lived to be over a hundred – old, but still in vibrant health. They all testified to the fact that not only do they eat the healthiest food, but eating for them is also a celebration of life and the community.

The way that we eat clearly impacts upon our health.

It is obvious that taking time and love to prepare nutritious food is a healthier choice than a rushed ready-made take-away, gobbled out of a cardboard box between other 'more important' things. But to many of us, our diet often consists of hurried 'fast food' lunches and TV dinners. We buy pre-packed prepared meals that we pop into the microwave, and in three minutes we have a 'delicious' meal. But nutritious it is not. We eat frozen or tinned vegetables and mountains of hamburgers and chips. We have no time to prepare fresh, nutritious food, no time to invest in being healthy. The wonder is that we are not sick more of the time.

Many of us live alone and use this as an excuse not to spend time preparing nutritious food. After all, it's only for ourselves. Indeed! It's really important that we take the time to prepare our food even when we're on our own. By nurturing ourselves in this way, we reinforce to ourselves that we are worth it. And while we eat, we should eat, with the Intention of eating, bringing all our awareness into the eating, and not doing anything else – not watching television, reading the papers, listening to the radio, or doing a crossword or sudoku.

Most important of all, of course, is *what* we eat.

All food that has life force within it is sacred, and connects us to the spirit of the earth, to the harmony and healing rhythms of the natural world. So, are we eating sacred natural foods, full of life force? Or do we make do with 'quick-fix' junk food sitting in front of the television? Do we eat nourishing foods because we are hungry, or do we run to the cookie jar or the brandy bottle when we are feeling low, and drown our discontent, our frustration or our anger with chocolate, caffeine or alcohol?

Eating should be a joyous and nurturing experience. When we take the time to eat nourishing food in a relaxed manner and enjoy what we are eating, we naturally absorb more life force and enliven and vitalize our whole being. Eating 'comfort food', on the other hand, does not nourish our body and is a way of numbing ourselves to pain, a way of not dealing with suppressed emotions or spiritual challenges. At the same time, we are poisoning our bodies with all the toxins contained in the comfort food.

Our bodies have an in-built intelligence, which knows what is beneficial for our well-being – and what is not. We need to listen to what our body needs, not to what our mind wants or our mouth craves! Taking care of our body means being aware of what we put into it [healthy, life-giving foods and drinks, all in moderate quantities] and what we *don't* put into it [alcohol, drugs, tobacco, unhealthy and processed foods]. Our physical health, our psychological and emotional well-being, and our spiritual evolvement, are all affected by this.

What follows is a *very* brief look at the major components of healthy eating, which sustain the body, nurture the heart and nourish the soul. This is intended as a guide, not a dogma. If your diet is very different from this, change it gradually, as a sudden change may release more toxins than your body can easily cope with at any one time.

Do your best, but don't punish yourself for occasional indulgences! And don't become a fanatic either, turning nutrition into a rigid set of rules divorced from the spirit of the food and from the joy of eating.

As your diet becomes healthier, you will gradually realize that you no longer have cravings for foods that are harmful. By following these guidelines, you open yourself up to the fountain of health that is your birthright, and which it is possible to achieve at any stage of life. No matter how unhealthy your diet has been in the past, it is never too late to change. The healing capacity of the body is miraculous. Bon Appetit!

Tony's Pyramid of Health Diet is an excellent guide to healthy eating.

The Pyramid of Health is what Tony calls the diet that he proposes. This is a diet rich in natural vitamins, minerals and enzymes, which strengthen and energize the body, enhancing the functions of both the nervous system and the immune system, while filling our whole being with the vitality of their life force. It is also essential to drink plenty of water [purified, or at least filtered] – between one and two litres per day is recommended. This helps to rehydrate the body, cleanse it of toxins and keep everything in the system flowing freely [but beware of becoming fanatical about drinking too much water and over-loading the body's systems].

Tony's Pyramid of Health Diet outlines the general principles of healthy eating and gives the main categories of foods and some examples on each level. Foods on the first level of the Pyramid, the foundation of the temple, may be eaten in abundance. As we move up the Pyramid, foods should be eaten in smaller and smaller quantities. Foods at the top of the Pyramid should be totally avoided. [See the Pyramid of Health Chart on page 299]

The first level, the base of the Pyramid.

This is the level of raw living foods of all kinds. Fresh fruits and vegetables, preferably organic and locally grown, not sprayed with chemicals and pesticides, and certainly not GM modified, are the staple foods of this level. Vegetable and fruit juices, which should be organic and freshly made, are highly nutritious as well as delicious, and are a wonderful start to the day. Freshly juiced wheat grass and barley grass are among the healthiest of all foods, although they are highly concentrated and so should be taken in very small quantities [and the taste may take a bit of getting used to!]. All organic fresh fruits, vegetables and juices, help to eliminate toxins.

More than this. Fresh fruits and vegetables are so steeped in sunlight that they become a condensed form of light. Eating these foods, bringing this concentrated light into all parts of our body, also helps to invigorate our life force and bring us into balance and harmony. The more we bring light into our physical body, the more we become light, and radiate light out into the world. [For more detailed information on food and light, see Index, note 2.]

Tony's Food Pyramid of Health – Basic Principles and Foods

avoid
meat
chicken : fish : eggs
tea : coffee : sugar
all processed food
white bread, rice, pasta
tinned and frozen foods
margarine and animal fats
alcohol : chocolate : gluten
artificial colours and flavours
these foods are highly toxic
eat if you must
[very small quantities]
salt
vegetable oils
all dairy produce
these foods are usually full
of hormones and antibiotics
eat in small quantities
soy milk
nuts : beans : honey : syrups
dried fruit : tofu : mushrooms
highly energizing and concentrated
proteins and sugars – a little is enough
eat in fair quantities
rice milk, almond milk
tomatoes : citrus : carrots
potatoes : turnips : sweet potatoes
strongly connected to the earth
these foods are very grounding
eat in large quantities
brown rice : lentils : buckwheat
wholegrain cereals, grains, pulses
rye, corn, spelt and hemp seed bread
oats : quinoa : corn : millet : amaranth
goat's and sheep's milk, cheese and yoghurt
these foods are rich in minerals and
help to strengthen and nurture the body
eat in unlimited quantities
olive oil, virgin cold pressed if possible
vegetable and fruit juices – freshly made
all sprouted grains, seeds, nuts, beans, pulses
fermented [live] yogurt, miso, tempeh and kefir
raw fruits and vegetables, avocado – organic if possible
these are cleansing foods and help to eliminate toxins

Sprouted foods – nuts, seeds, pulses, beans and grains – are the foods richest in nutrients. Sprouting is a simple way of bringing extra life force to these foods, creating a huge release of enzymes, thus adding greatly to their nutritional value and making them more easily digestible. Almost all foods in these categories can be sprouted: simply soak them overnight [two desertspoonsful in a glass of pure water] then place them in a sprouter, or anything with fine holes through which water may drip, run pure water over them twice a day and let the water drain out. They will sprout in three to four days, less in hotter weather. This is also a very cheap way of eating very healthily, as sprouts are cheap to buy and the sprouted volume is much greater than the original bought seeds or grains. A little goes a very long way.

Live [fermented] foods, such as tempeh, lichen, kefir and yoghurt, are also excellent sources of nutrition, but make sure that the yoghurt is live; fermentation brings these foods to life, helping them to play a central role in health and healing. We should add to this list the sea vegetables, such as kelp and algae, especially spirulina, which are essential for pregnant or lactating women, and very healthy for everyone. All these foods – sprouted and live – contain an abundance of vitamins and minerals and are teeming with enzymes, which provide our life force, energizing and revitalizing every cell in our body.

The foods on the first level of the Pyramid are cleansing and help to eliminate toxins, keeping the body clean and congestion free. Eating plenty of these life-rich foods nourishes us on all levels, helping to transform our body into our temple of light and support the changes that we may be making on other levels.

The second level of the Pyramid.

This level includes foods such as cereals, seeds and grains, which should be wholegrain: oats, brown rice, amaranth, quinoa, corn, buckwheat and millet, and unsprouted seeds [sprouted seeds are included on the first level] such as pumpkin, sunflower and sesame, are all highly nutritious. These foods contain many essential minerals, which build up the stamina of the body. Seeds, nuts and grains are among the healthiest foods because we eat what is actually planted, the seeds. They can also be stored for a long time without losing their life force. Fresh fruits growing from seeds, are very nutritious, but should be eaten soon after being picked as their life force is quickly depleted. Also on this level are goat's and sheep's milk, cheese and yoghurt

The foods on this level are especially important for growing children and for people engaged in vigorous physical work. And they are invaluable after illness, during convalescence, or during pregnancy or lactation, when they strengthen and help to rebuild the body. These foods, when combined with fresh vegetables, provide an ideal source of protein. As a general rule, they should be eaten in good quantities, but a little less than the foods on the first level.

The third level of the Pyramid.

This level includes the tubers and the root vegetables [anything that grows underground] such as carrots, turnips, potatoes and sweet potatoes. They are helpful in grounding us in our body when we are involved in spiritual work. These foods are particularly important during the winter months, as they warm and sustain the body. Like seeds and grains, these vegetables are very healthy as they grow from themselves and we eat what is planted in the earth. They are not included lower down the Pyramid, however, as they are quite heavy on the body. All these foods should be eaten in fair amounts, but in smaller quantities than the foods on the second level.

The fourth level of the Pyramid.

As we move up the Pyramid to the fourth level, we come to foods that are very concentrated and high in protein, salt and sugar. Foods on this level include beans, dried fruit, especially dates and raisins, tofu [though this should be fermented with kombucha or another live ferment], honey, corn and maple syrup, mushrooms, very salty varieties of algae, and soy milk. These foods are very healthy, but a little is enough, and more than a little is too much! So they should be eaten sparingly, except at times of strong physical exertion or if you are feeling physically depleted, when a little more is fine.

The fifth level of the Pyramid.

Climbing up to the fifth level, we reach foods that are best avoided, but may be eaten in very small amounts, perhaps as part of a transition programme as you move from your old eating habits towards the Pyramid of Health diet. [In this context only, a little fish may be eaten.] Foods on this level include all dairy produce [milk, cheeses and yoghurt] except fermented yoghurt and kefir, which live on the first level; and vegetable oils. Salt also belongs on this level, although a little salt is necessary in very hot weather.

The sixth level, the top of the Pyramid.

At the top of the Pyramid are foods that should be avoided at all costs! And at the head of the list is meat. If spiritual reasons don't convince you to give up meat, perhaps physical reasons will. Read on!

Meat – dead animals – is just about the deadest food there is! Not only does it not provide us with nutrients, it is also harmful to our bodies. It is heavy on our system, both physically and energetically. It is an irritant to the intestines, is very acidic and is depleting to the body. Unless it is organic, it is full of hormones, pesticides, antibiotics and dyes – in other words, poisons! Meat also produces excess mucus, and is very hard to digest, requiring a great deal more hydrochloric acid to break it down than is needed to break down a good vegetarian diet. And most people are already deficient in hydrochloric acid. Red meat has been linked to coronary and digestive diseases, and contains high levels of saturated fat, which is damaging to the whole system.

Other foods to be avoided include chicken, fish and eggs, all processed foods such as white bread, white rice, white pasta, and all tinned and frozen foods. These foods may appear to be appetizing but no longer contain anything of nutritious value. Tea, coffee, sugar, fizzy drinks, alcohol, crisps, chocolate, sweets, ice-cream, gluten, and all artificial colours, flavourings and sweeteners all live at the top of the Pyramid and should not be consumed. [Decaffeinated tea and coffee, though not as harmful as the caffeinated variety, are still unhealthy as they are full of chemical alternatives.] Saturated fats [those fats which become hard at room temperature] and hydrogenated oils are damaging to the body and should always be avoided.

Eating according to Tony's Pyramid of Health diet has an added advantage: if you are overweight [as over *one third* – and rising – of adults in the Western world are] you will gradually lose the excess weight, and keep it off; unlike 'fad' diets, which tend to cause a great increase in weight as soon as the diet is stopped, and often wildly fluctuating weight thereafter. Remember, fad diets are a business and have little to do with healthy eating.

If looking at the Pyramid of Health Chart is bringing on feelings of deprivation, don't be alarmed. There are many delicious as well as healthy alternatives to many 'forbidden' foods. Goat's and sheep's milk, cheeses and yoghurts, for example, rice, almond and soy milk and desserts, are all delicious alternatives to dairy foods. Almonds, sesame seeds, seaweed, tahina and green leafy vegetables all provide a rich source of calcium. Breads made from seeds and grains, such as oats, corn, rye, buckwheat and millet are all highly nutritious and an excellent alternative to white or even wholewheat bread [which is often white bread dyed brown, and anyway is not good as it contains wheat which is high in gluten]. Spelt bread, while containing wheat, is made from the original ancient recipe, which neutralizes its harmful effects and is a healthy and tasty alternative.

Freshly made fruit and vegetable juices and 'smoothies' are a delicious alternative to soft drinks which are either full of sugar, or sugar-substitutes, which are often worse. Regular coffee and tea can be traded for fresh organic herbal teas, dandelion root coffee, barley cup and caro. There are healthy options for snacks that are full of goodness and taste great. Just try your local health shop, or better still, make your own. Remember, eating healthily is not about denial. Eating should be joyous, creative, nourishing – and fun.

An increasingly popular choice of diet by people who are becoming more aware of their spiritual journey, is a raw food diet.

A raw food diet is one of the healthiest diets there is.

The more we eat healthy fresh food teeming with life force – that is, raw food – the less appetite we will have for dead, devitalized foods.

All the raw foods on the first level of the Pyramid contain abundant vitamins, minerals, enzymes and fibre, and have a high water content. They rehydrate and revitalize the body, making a major contribution to vibrant health. Enzymes, abundant in raw foods, are essential in maintaining internal cleanliness, health and strength. They are even more important to our health than vitamins, minerals and amino acids, and play a vital role in helping us to digest our foods, fight disease and break down foreign matter. Cooked foods may contain vitamins, minerals and proteins, but they all depend on enzymes to do their work efficiently, and enzymes are largely destroyed in the cooking process.

Good health depends on having balanced intestinal flora. Most raw foods, especially those with chlorophyll, feed the friendly bacteria in our intestines. Cooked and processed foods, on the other hand, feed the harmful bacteria. It is possible to implant friendly bacteria into the intestines with lactobifidus and streptococcus supplements. But acidophilus, marketed as the best friendly bacteria to buy, will only implant in the intestines if we also eat live yoghurt, otherwise it dies before it can do much good. Always check that the brand of yoghurt you buy is reputable, as many brands are not live. Or make your own.

The mainstay of a raw diet is plenty of raw fruit and vegetables.

Raw fruit and vegetables provide the body with an excellent source of nutrients, without adding excess calories, and a fair amount of good roughage, which keeps the system well-oiled and prevents constipation.

There is an abundance of raw foods with which you can experiment and be creative. Breakfasting on fresh fruit is an excellent choice as it cleans out the system and is easily digested on an empty stomach. Fresh fruit, by the way, is much healthier than dried fruit, which contains high levels of sugar and should be eaten more sparingly. An even better way to start the day is to drink a large glass of freshly made fruit or vegetable juice. Alternatively, start your day with freshly squeezed lemon juice in a glass of pure water to alkalinise your stomach, and then wait half an hour before eating.

Fruits and vegetables should be organic if possible, grown on fertile soil which has not been chemically treated and not contaminated with pesticides, herbicides or hormones, all of which are toxic and harmful. Natural, organically grown food has a much higher nutrient and energy content than commercially grown food, promoting vibrant health and helping to build up resistance to disease. If you cannot find organic produce [although it is becoming available in more and more places – ask in your local library, health food shop, or try the internet] the next best thing is locally grown food, which will have been freshly picked and therefore is more alive. Your local farmers' market is also far less likely to have products with as much contamination as those found in large supermarkets.

Eating local products also creates less pollution as they don't have far to travel, thus benefiting the planet. Flying strawberries half way round the world out of season to impress dinner-party guests is not an environmentally friendly action. We should also remember that we are helping to sustain the countryside by supporting local and organic farmers who generally have an intrinsic love of their land and are not motivated solely by profit.

Sprouts, nuts and seeds are all living foods and constitute an intrinsic part of a healthy raw diet. Sprouts, such as mung bean, alfalfa, lentil, buckwheat, humus and radish are easy to grow at home and provide an excellent fresh, organic, nutrient-rich food source. Seeds, such as sunflower, sesame and pumpkin, can also be sprouted, adding greatly to their nutritional value. Nuts and seeds are an excellent source of some of our most important mineral, protein and EFA [Essential Fatty Acids] requirements, and provide easy and highly nutritious snacks. Combining and grinding pumpkin, sunflower, linseed and sesame seeds, makes a very tasty food seasoning. Almonds should always be eaten without their skins; soaking them in water overnight makes it easy to remove the skins.

Be aware of what you are putting into your body.

A lot of supermarket produce has been prematurely picked and stored for unnaturally long periods of time, devitalizing its natural goodness. As well as having been liberally sprayed with chemicals and pesticides, it is also likely to have been irradiated, a method of nuclear radiation which slows down the ripening process of the product and increases its shelf life – completely destroying the enzymes, and thus all the nutritional value, in the process. If we humans were subjected to this treatment, we would die instantly, so you can imagine what it does to the fruits and vegetables we eat! Choose your food with care.

Combining foods correctly is an important part of a healthy diet.

The way we combine foods, as well as the choice of food we make, is another important factor of a healthy diet. Fruit and vegetables, for instance, should not be eaten at the same meal as they each require a different digestive process. Different vegetables may be mixed. Fruits of the same family, such as citrus fruits, may also be eaten together. Otherwise, it is best to eat each type of fruit separately. Melon should always be eaten alone.

When eating fruit, try to avoid eating any other type of food for at least half an hour, as it takes this time for the stomach to digest fruit before it is released into the small intestines. If we eat fruit together with other food, the fruit will be held in the stomach with the other food and will begin to ferment and putrefy. By the time the food enters the small intestines, little of the nutritional benefits of the fruit remain. Ideally, after eating a carbohydrate meal such as pasta or rice, or after a protein meal, it is best to wait a couple of hours before eating fruit, giving the body time to digest these foods first.

A strict raw diet can heal disease.

Many modern diseases, such as cancer and heart failure, have been shown to be strongly linked to a stressful lifestyle and an unhealthy diet. More than this, many cancers can be healed by a strict organic semi-liquid diet: freshly juiced fruit and vegetables four or five times a day, supplemented by some raw foods and plenty of pure water, has been known to heal many people with cancer.

If you are feeling out of sorts or lethargic, if you often get headaches or colds, a switch to a juice-based raw food diet can help to get you back to vibrant health. People maintaining a raw food diet seem to get ill very rarely.

There are times, however, when recovering from illness or an operation, or in very cold weather, when eating only raw foods is not appropriate, so listen to your body and see what it needs at different times. If you feel the need for cooked foods, thick vegetable soups are nutritious and delicious.

Moving on to a raw food diet should be done gradually.

If you feel ready to embark on a raw food diet, proceed with caution as too many simultaneous toxic reactions can overwhelm the body. Very gradually remove cooked and devitalized foods from your diet and increase your intake of raw foods. If you start to get toxic reactions, such as headaches or skin eruptions, drink plenty of water and eat a little more cooked food until the body adjusts itself to the process. Then, as your body becomes acclimatized, continue to eat more raw and less cooked food.

Eating a partially cooked diet can also be a healthy option.

A totally raw diet may not be suitable for everyone. If we eat vegetarian food, cut out everything on the top two levels of the Pyramid, and eat plenty of fresh fruit and vegetables, much of it raw, a partially cooked diet is also a healthy choice.

Then it is important to eat two or three portions of whole grains each day. Recommended whole grains include brown rice, millet, quinoa, buckwheat, oats and rye, and whole grain breads. They are all highly nutritious and they release energy slowly over time, helping to maintain stable body energy levels throughout the day. They are also an excellent source of fibre, an essential ingredient of a healthy diet. Quinoa is particularly beneficial as it has a very high protein content, but it should not be eaten with other proteins.

If you decide to eat partially cooked food, a good diet should consist of raw fruit or fresh juice for breakfast, a wholegrain cereal midmorning, a raw salad for lunch, fruit or fresh juice for tea, and a lightly cooked vegetarian meal in the evening. [If you prefer, you may swap lunch and dinner.] All grains should be whole foods, which have not been altered in any way. This means that they have been neither refined, nor 'enriched'. We know that refining foods, such as white rice, bread or pasta, greatly reduces their nutrient content by removing those ingredients that provide the most nourishment. But 'enriching' food is also harmful, as the actual process of enrichment reduces its natural nutrient content.

The way in which we cook food is also important.

Some methods of cooking are much safer and less detrimental to health than others. So, if you are going to eat some cooked foods, be careful how you cook them and also which utensils you use.

In South American Shamanic communities and other native tribes, the traditional way of cooking food is in the earth. The foods are wrapped in the leaves of plants or trees, then buried in the earth above hot stones. Cooked in this way, very slowly over many hours, the food retains its nutrients and all the natural flavours of the ingredients. This method of cooking also connects the community to the four elements – fire to burn the wood and heat the stones, water from the vapour issuing from the cooking, the earth itself as oven, and air circulating inside it, rendering the preparation of food a sacred communion with nature.

Most probably you are not able to cook in this way, but a good alternative is to use unglazed clay dishes and bake the food slowly in the oven. This also retains all the goodness and flavours. Using stainless steel pots and pans, or Pyrex dishes, rather than aluminium, is also recommended.

Another healthy way to cook vegetables is to steam them lightly, so that they are still crunchy, thus minimizing the loss of vitamins, minerals and especially enzymes. Grilling or baking in the usual way also minimizes the damage sustained by the food. Boiling vegetables totally destroys their enzymes and most of their nutritional value. Frying, a menace to the liver, and roasting, should both be avoided. Oil is not recommended for cooking, but if you do use oil, use sparingly; only use virgin olive oil, cold pressed and organic, and avoid cheap vegetable oils.

Although so convenient in our modern rushed lives, microwaving food should be avoided at all costs. It distorts the molecular structure of food, particularly fish, meat, milk products, seeds, nuts and any foods with oils in them, rendering them carcinogenic and extremely harmful to the body.

If you are cooking, remember that heating food and drink to over 120 degrees, not only destroys all its enzymes, it also injures the enzymes of the stomach when you consume it.

Food serves many functions in our lives. It's often the centre of social activity, when people gather to meet, talk and have fun. Imagine weddings, birthday parties, or indeed any celebration, without food! Long business lunches and the ritual of dinner parties are an integral part of much middle class life.

Food may also be a great sensual pleasure, for which we do not need company; if we are feeling miserable or lonely, we can indulge in our favourite foods and buy illusions of happiness. And food, and indeed drink, can also be a serious comfort when unpleasant emotions that we don't want to deal with begin to surface.

We eat for all kinds of reasons: because we enjoy eating, because it is our mealtime, because we are invited to eat. Often we eat at times set by our places of work. We do not necessarily eat because we are hungry. But we do often eat because we crave certain foods; because, in fact, we are addicted.

Most people in the West have some kind of addiction to food.

When people talk of addictions, they are not usually thinking of food. As we saw in Chapter 3: Mind and Ego, there are many kinds of addictions: alcohol, tobacco, drugs, gambling, work, personal dramas, material acquisitiveness, control of others, 'victimhood', sexual promiscuity, destructive or abusive relationships, dysfunctional behaviour of all kinds.

But many of us also have addictions to food, though we may not recognize them as addictions.

The two most potently addictive substances, which are found in most of the foods we regularly consume, are sugar and salt.

Sugar is the worst offender.

When *over one third* of Americans are now categorized as clinically obese, with Europe catching up fast, and when vast numbers of others are overweight, we need to take a serious look at our consumption of sugar. Of course, all fried and other junk food are culprits too, but sugar is found in most of them as well.

We probably don't think of sugar as a drug, but it certainly is. Today the average person in the West consumes his or her own weight in sugar every year! And as our weight increases, so does our intake of sugar. The consumption of sugar depletes the benefit of the minerals and vitamins found naturally in our bodies. All forms of concentrated sugar – white and brown sugar, honey from hives where the bees are fed sugar, syrup, malt and glucose – are bad, though refined white sugar is clearly the worst of all.

Sugars are all harmful, as they are all fast-releasing, which disturbs the natural blood-sugar balance of the body, and can cause conditions such as adult-onset diabetes. If this sugar is not needed by the body, it is stored as fat. Continued ingestion of sugar can damage the pancreas's ability to produce insulin, which may create sudden changes in energy levels and increase erratic mood swings, hyperactivity and irritability. The more sugar we eat, the more the insulin levels in the body become unbalanced. This makes it difficult to maintain inner calm, meditate and do inner spiritual work. The high level of sugar in children's diets is also partly responsible for hyperactivity and out of control behaviour.

Today, sugar is found not only in sweet foods, but is also added to most processed foods, tinned products and savoury sauces. Almost everything, in fact, on the supermarket shelf that is pre-packaged will contain sugar. Even many products found in health food stores, full of healthy ingredients, also have added sugar. Those responsible know the addictive nature of sugar; their repeat sales of these products are proof! Always read the ingredients on food labels; prepared foods and sauces often contain surprising ingredients.

For an incurable sweet tooth, there are many delicious alternatives to sugar: fresh organic fruits, dried fruits such as dates, apricots [unsulphured] and raisins, unheated honey [preferably from a local supplier, and where the bees are not fed on sugar] molasses, carob and maple syrup. Vegetables such as pumpkins also have a natural sweetness, and can be made into delicious desserts. Many people who are addicted to sugar are also addicted to chocolate, which has a high sugar content. Carob is a natural and tasty substitute for chocolate.

Salt is the second offender.

Salt is not quite as bad for our health as sugar, but it runs a close second. A high salt intake is linked to high blood pressure and heart disease. If taken in its crude form, it impairs the ability of the body to utilize minerals. Salt also reduces the sensitivity of the taste buds, so that we don't really taste the food we are eating.

There are many healthy, and tasty, alternatives to the use of salt: herbs, spices, ground seeds, lemon and mustard. Salt is also naturally found in seaweeds, such as dulse and kelp, and in some vegetables. Miso and tamari, delicious substitutes for crude salt, can be used as flavourings in soups, sauces and salad dressing.

However, during sustained manual labour or strong physical workouts, or in great heat, the body does require some salt. This is best taken in its natural form or as sea salt [Celtic salt].

'Comfort food' also includes drink.

Drinks to which some of us are addicted obviously include alcohol, the most serious addiction, and the one that brings with it the most serious health risks. But there are other drink addictions. These include coffee, the worst offender after alcohol, and tea [the addiction is in the caffeine], fizzy drinks such as colas and other sugar drinks.

Though most of us recognize alcoholism as an addiction, we are generally more dismissive of our own coffee and tea drinking. There are people who drink ten cups of coffee a day to 'keep them going', but ridicule the idea that they have an addiction. We need to acknowledge that caffeine is an addiction before we can deal with it.

The 'comfort eating' of junk food is widespread.

Most of us 'comfort eat or drink' some of the time; some of us 'comfort eat or drink' most of the time. Sometimes we eat junk food because we have no time to prepare and eat healthy and nourishing fresh food. Sometimes, we 'comfort eat' to satisfy cravings, and temporarily feel good. Most often, we 'comfort eat' because we are feeling miserable or lonely; we indulge in our favourite foods, or drinks, and buy illusions of happiness. We eat and drink and delude ourselves that everything is fine.

But of course everything is not fine. And by eating junk food, we are poisoning our bodies in three ways: firstly, the junk food, with all its additives, is a source of physical toxins; secondly, by 'comfort eating' we further suppress the negative emotions that we don't want to deal with, which in turn pushes the toxins further down into the organs of the body where their toxicity flourishes; and thirdly, most comfort foods contain substances that are highly addictive, and so we keep coming back for more.

So why do we continue to poison our bodies?

Most junk food is eaten either as a quick convenience food, because we have no time or energy in our busy schedules to nurture ourselves; or it is eaten for escape and emotional comfort. While it is easy to see this with an addiction to alcohol, the stimulant of strong coffee or the tongue's craving for chocolate, cream cakes, crisps, or a jam sandwich on sliced white bread, is also imbibed for comfort. We feel down, out of sorts, sad, anxious, depressed, angry or upset, and want some form of physical indulgence. Usually, of course, we are not conscious that this is the reason; we 'just fancy' a particular snack.

Eating this junk food may well bring us temporary satisfaction, but it is also damaging to our body and prevents us from seeing what is happening inside ourselves. What it is really doing is numbing our pain so that we can more easily avoid dealing with what needs to be dealt with, the deeper issues inside that need our attention. What appears as a simple indulgence, for coffee or chocolate cake just because we 'feel like it', may become a habit, and then an addiction.

Of course, this is rarely conscious. We continue the pattern unthinkingly, poisoning our bodies with the fallout from suppressed negative emotions and toxic foods. We need to look at our food and drink addictions, acknowledge them and see what lies behind them. Then, as we bring consciousness into our lives, we will see that we have a choice: to continue as we are, poisoning our bodies and locking up our hearts, or feeding ourselves nourishing foods that bring health, energy and a zest for life to our whole being.

But while of course we need to deal with food addictions, we should be gentle and compassionate with ourselves. Don't punish yourself for an *occasional* chocolate bar or cup of coffee! As we move away from our addictions into a healthier lifestyle – spiritual and emotional as well as physical – our cravings for junk food and drink will gradually subside.

Many of us may eat a healthy diet, but may still not feel vibrantly well because we are dehydrated.

The correct consumption of the right liquid is an important part of a healthy diet.

Many of us do not consume enough healthy fluid, which leads to dehydration. We may be drinking plenty of liquids, but tea, coffee and sugar drinks actually dehydrate the body. Many illnesses, for example constipation, insomnia, bladder infections and skin diseases, are caused in part by dehydration. In order to maintain a healthy body it is essential to drink plenty of healthy fluids and eat some foods that have a high water content.

Water is the healthiest drink of all.

Our body consists of between 70% and 80% water when it is healthy, and this needs to be constantly replenished. Water should be purified [reverse osmosis or similar process] or filtered, if it is filtered in a safe way. Tap water is not recommended, as it is generally polluted with chlorine, fluoride and other poisonous chemicals and inorganic minerals. Some bottled mineral water is safe to drink but there are vast discrepancies. Spring or well water, if clean, is a fantastic source of pure water, containing natural ions and energy beneficial to the body. Whichever kind of water you choose, you should try to drink between one and two litres a day.

Freshly made fruit and vegetable juices are an indispensable part of any healthy diet.

The healthiest way to start the day is with a small glass of freshly juiced wheat grass or barley grass, which are both particularly cleansing. If these are not available, any raw green vegetable juice [cucumber, celery and broccoli are good choices] freshly made, or freshly squeezed lemon juice in a tumbler of water, are good alternatives. It is also a good idea to drink at least one other fresh juice, vegetable or fruit, each day. These juices, drunk daily, provide an excellent source of nourishment and energy to the body. They retain their nutritious value, are easy to digest so the body doesn't have to work hard, and create a feeling of lightness and general well-being.

Many drinks actually dehydrate the body.

Many of the drinks that we consume on a regular basis can actually dehydrate the body. Tea and coffee are diuretic, draining the body of fluid instead of rehydrating it. So even though they may temporarily quench your thirst, they are in fact robbing the body of essential liquids. Alcohol, and all drinks containing caffeine, are also stimulants and stress the adrenal glands, making energy levels erratic. Decaffeinated coffee, although it doesn't contain caffeine, is full of other harmful additives and should also be avoided.

Many soft drinks have a similar effect; and of course, drinks with added sugar, sweeteners or artificial additives or colourings should be avoided. Many people think that by drinking low calorie drinks and so avoiding sugar, they have chosen a healthy option; but many sweeteners are actually more harmful than sugar. Aspartame, for instance, contained in many diet drinks, and many other sugar substitutes can, if used frequently, be carcinogenic and lead to lupus syndrome and multiple sclerosis. Alcohol, as well as being hugely addictive, has a high calorie content. It is also a mild poison and over time can greatly damage the liver.

There are many delicious alternatives to these drinks, such as dandelion root coffee, barley cup, caro, fresh organic herbal teas, 'smoothies' and organic juices.

All liquids should be drunk between meals, and preferably not within half an hour before eating, and one hour after. Drinking with meals should be avoided as it dilutes the digestive juices, which means that the digestive system has to work much harder to do a less good job.

If we are used to eating an unhealthy diet and want to start eating healthy and nourishing foods, the best way to begin is by detoxifying the body; then it will be better able to absorb the nutrients that we feed it. It is also an excellent way of drawing a line under the past and marking out a new healthy beginning.

Detoxifying the body is the best way to start a healthy eating programme.

Detoxifying the body is not only a matter of eliminating accumulated toxins from an unhealthy diet and polluted air; it is also a way of releasing the toxic energy caused by the build-up over many years of suppressed negative emotion. It means bringing into our consciousness the anger, resentment, jealousy and fear that have attached themselves to the different organs of our body, dealing with them and then letting them go.

We have already talked a lot about releasing our emotional 'baggage'. We need to remember that *all* our negative emotions are held in the body, and so clearing out our body also means releasing old emotions. By bringing consciousness into our body, transformation may begin right away.

The ideal way to begin detoxifying the body is to go on a Cleansing Detoxification Retreat.

Tony runs many Cleansing Detoxification Retreats every year in many countries. At these retreats, you will drink lots of different herbal remedies that will clean out your body, ridding it not only of physical toxicity, but also of the residue of emotional baggage. You will also be nourished by delicious fruit and vegetable juices, freshly made, several times a day, and by as much purified water as you can drink, to wash away the toxins.

Tony works on the emotional and spiritual levels as well as the physical one, so emotional pain and fears are uncovered during the detox and the process of releasing them is begun. Along with physical waste matter, you begin to eliminate the negative emotions that have been held for so long in your body. Through guided meditations, visualizations and exercises, Tony guides you along your journey of letting go, on all levels, of everything that has been clogging up your system and keeping you stuck.

You can also do a Detoxification Fast at home.

If you are not able to attend a Detoxification Retreat, you can achieve good results by fasting at home. But make sure you are physically strong enough before you start to fast, and are mentally healthy. Tony actually recommends a home detox only *after* you have attended one of his cleansing detox retreats and know how your body reacts. And even then, he suggests that you proceed with extreme caution. He emphasises that any unusual symptoms be properly investigated, and if you are in any doubt the fast should immediately be suspended.

Before you begin, it's a good idea to focus on why you are doing the fast and what you would like to release. The more you bring consciousness into the process, the more effective it will be. Tony recommends that a fast undertaken at home be three days, and never more than five days, depending on your intention and your physical stamina.

On the fast, drink four large glasses of pure, freshly prepared, organic fruit or vegetable juice each day, sipped slowly; and between one and two litres of pure water. [If the juice or water is not pure, you are adding further toxins to your body.]

On the second day you might feel weak, possibly dizzy or have a bad headache, as the toxins move out of their 'home organs' and are released into the bloodstream. This is the time to stick with it! If you give up now, the toxins will simply return to their organ hosts. So, just tell yourself it's part of the process, and in another day the toxins will be eliminated from the body, and you will start to feel well, light, and probably not hungry.

Always make sure that you get plenty of rest during a fast. This is especially important on days two and three, when toxins are being dispersed.

Herbal remedies can add to the efficacy of the fast.

Taking herbal preparations during a fast can be very helpful, but make sure that they are pure and made by a reputable company.

Milk thistle is an excellent herb, able to heal hepatitis and other diseases that stem from the liver. It is important to work with the liver during a detox, because that is where we hold our anger, stress, frustration and resentment. As the liver opens up, the milk thistle moves into the liver and can help to transform the negativity that it contains.

Another great herbal detox is cayenne pepper and vinegar, taken in a little water. This is excellent for cleaning out the stomach and intestines. Although it tastes horrible, it soothes this part of the body and revitalizes the blood. The vinegar also has a strong alkaline effect on the body, which counteracts over-acidity.

Bathing is an important part of a detox fast.

A sauna or steam bath helps to eliminate many impurities through the skin. Failing this, a long soak in a hot bath at home is also beneficial. This is very relaxing and can help the process of letting go of emotional baggage, too. But be careful, you may be feeling a little weak. Always drink plenty of water while bathing, and finish with a cool shower.

Fasting is also a way of healing.

When animals are sick, they know instinctively that they need to fast; we can learn from them.

When we are sick, eating puts extra stress on the body. So if you are ill, drink plenty of freshly-made fruit and vegetable juices, and as much water as you feel you need to wash out the system. If you have a cold or the flu', herbal teas are excellent, and a little hot broth may be drunk, if it is pure. We need to give our body a rest from digesting food and let it concentrate on healing.

How we break the fast is as important as the fast itself.

It is important to break the fast very gradually, over a period of time a little longer than the duration of the fast. What follows is a guide for breaking a three-day fast. [If you fasted for four (or five) days, repeat day one (and day two) before moving on.]

Start each day with freshly made fruit or vegetable juice, a good practice to carry over into the rest of your life. And drink another glass of fresh juice later in the day.

On the first day, eat only fruit, one kind at a time, three or four times during the day. Good fruits to have are apples, watermelon, mangoes, or any juicy fruit. Oranges [too acidic] and grapes [too sugary] are not recommended. In the evening, you may eat a light miso broth cooked with one vegetable. As you begin to break the fast, eat only very small quantities to start with.

On the second day, add a little green salad for lunch, but no tomatoes or avocado, and no dressing. For dinner, again have miso broth.

On the third day, add other vegetables to the salad, and have one lightly steamed vegetable for dinner.

On the fourth day, add cereals with rice milk in the morning, but no yoghurt, a mixed salad of anything you fancy for lunch, but without dressing, and lightly steamed vegetables for dinner.

On the fifth day, you may add anything from the first, second or third levels of Tony's Pyramid of Health diet.

From the sixth day, you may eat anything. But having worked so hard to maintain your fast, it would really be a pity if you now started to eat unhealthy foods; there are so many delicious alternatives! And if you have been a meat-eater up till now, maybe this would be a good time to consider becoming a vegetarian?

Think of your fast as a marker between the life that you led before the fast and your life after it, a portal into living with increased awareness, investment in a new, healthy you.

Fasting is part of spiritual practice.

Fasting is not only a way of cleaning out the physical body and releasing negative emotions; it is also an integral part of spiritual practice. It gives us an opportunity to rest from satisfying our physical cravings for food, and also offers us an opportunity to tune into our higher selves, without the distraction of thinking about, preparing and eating food. As we release the power of our addictions to food, whatever they are, we can begin to look at, and release, other 'baggage' that dominates our lives. Fasting is a wonderful way to open ourselves up wholly to Spirit.

As well as periodic detoxes, Tony recommends fasting one day a week. This rests the body, releases negative emotions, and purifies and opens the heart. It also reminds us, on a regular basis, that we can let go of our food addictions, and therefore of any other addictions we may have.

So if you can, let fasting become a strong and regular part of your spiritual practice, a day of rest from satisfying your physical desires, a day of dedication to your spiritual journey and your connection to the Divine.

Our attitudes to food form an integral part of the way we live; they are connected to our sense of right relationship, respect for ourselves and others and the way we see the world. They represent the extent to which we perceive the sacredness and interconnectedness of all life.

The dietary choices that we make have widespread ramifications, beyond our personal physical and spiritual nourishment. They affect the ecology of the planet and influence the degree of harmony that exists among the human race, the animal kingdom and the plant world. They reflect the level of our consciousness, and are a manifestation of our relationship with nature and our understanding of the circularity and interdependence of this relationship. Without the nutrients that nature supplies, we could not survive. Our growing spiritual awareness will dictate that we give something back to the earth by taking care of it.

The foods that we choose to eat also have practical implications: for soil erosion, water supplies, air purity and the balance of nature. Individual choices add up to global influences, which affect how we take care of the planet, who has too much to eat and who has too little. The peace of the world is bound up with the issues of hunger, starvation and greed. We owe it to ourselves and the planet to make responsible choices.

Choosing to eat consciously is a recognition of this responsibility, a manifestation of our wholeness and integrity, and our profound connection to the Divine.

Chapter Nine
Freedom

"Huachuma Shamanism considers freedom as a gift of nature and the cosmos to mankind. We can fully experience freedom when we perceive life through the conscious inner Self. Real freedom is living in harmony with the natural world. True freedom comes from the inside, and does not know separation."

Tony Samara

Freedom is the ultimate goal. Freedom is the journey. All our spiritual practice has been a process of releasing the shackles of our past and moving forward into the light of true freedom, connected to our deepest selves and to the harmony of the universe.

We are born free and spiritual beings.

Freedom is the natural state in which we enter this world. It is our birthright. Our path towards freedom is our journey to regain the freedom that we have lost.

We are born of the Divine, and profoundly connected to the spirit world from which we have come. We are born, too, of our own volition: our soul has freely chosen to reincarnate at this time, in this place, to be born to these parents, to experience another lifetime on this planet in order to work through aspects of our karma, the 'unfinished business' of past lives.

The human 'I' that lives this incarnation may not know its purpose nor understand its course. But our soul, choosing always our highest good, does know and does understand. Our soul remembers its divinity, its bliss, its freedom, and brings them with us into this world when we are born.

Our soul knows that it has chosen this incarnation, yet it yearns for the infinite freedom of the non-physical world. It remembers how to fly, how to dance in the limitless expanse of the everything and the nothing simultaneously. It remembers dwelling in the unity of the eternal, the infinite, the untrammelled, and it is not at all sure that it wants to live within the confines of a human body.

Our spiritual journey in this life is our journey [back] towards freedom.

In the West we seem to have lost touch with this profound connection to the world of Spirit. The innate yearnings of our soul become buried beneath the demands of twenty-first century living.

The lives we embrace as human beings are often fraught and limited. We seem to live in one tiny corner of the realms of expanding possibility, abandoning the spiritual realm, the consciousness that informs all other levels of reality. We have lost the freedom that comes from living in our place of deepest spiritual knowing.

Our spiritual work, then, is to reclaim the infinite freedom that we have lost.

The journey of this book has been a journey towards freedom, a journey towards consciousness. Reclaiming our freedom has been the *leitmotif* running through every chapter; it underlies all our spiritual work. All Tony's work, in fact, is geared towards helping us to break free.

Freedom is the ultimate goal of our spiritual journey. It is also the way we journey. All spiritual practice, in fact, is both the journey towards the goal of Enlightenment, and the way in which we journey. The way we journey *is* the goal.

Freedom in the West has largely become abstract.

In the countries of the 'free world', we have all the great theoretical freedoms of a flourishing twenty-first century democracy. And these freedoms, hard won throughout a long history, and enshrined in law or constitution, are to be treasured. *Freedom of:* speech, assembly, worship, movement; freedom of the press, academic and artistic freedom; the freedom of democratic choice to elect our political leaders and dispose of them when they don't perform as we wish. *Freedom from*: injustice, and from discrimination of all forms: race, religion, ethnicity, gender, class, sexual orientation, age. And *freedom to*: choose if and what to study, which career to pursue, where to live, what faith, if any, to follow, whom to marry or live with, how to raise our children; freedom to conduct our personal lives as we see fit, without interference or hindrance from the State. Freedom to live the lives of our choice within the protection of the law. There are many societies, today, in the twenty-first century, purporting to be civilized, that do not honour these fundamental freedoms.

But in spite of these guaranteed freedoms, we do not live free lives. With all the modern technology at our disposal, we seem to live stressed and often difficult lives, out of touch with our true selves, with our still centre. Bogged down by the pressures of our busy and demanding lifestyle, by long days at work that often don't seem to connect to our lives, what we don't seem to have is the experience of *living* real personal freedom. The freedom to enjoy being with our children, watching the sunset, hearing a bird sing, listening to music, walking in nature; freedom to expand our creative heart, painting or dancing, planting or making music. Freedom to be the authentic person we were born to be. Freedom to follow our dreams.

What is the value of freedom if we have no time to live it?

A great example of living in freedom was Tony's first Ashram in Portugal, in a community that included Tony's two [at the time] wild and wonderful little children. The continual challenge of interacting with kids who were completely free to follow each moment wherever their heart led them, being allowed to unfold in their own unique and spontaneous and disconcertingly honest way, was an on-going challenge to all the adults. It forced everyone to look inside as 'buttons were pressed' – relentlessly, and often very painfully. But ultimately, this served as inspiring lessons for everyone, and gave the children opportunities to acquire a wealth of knowledge and real understanding as they followed their curiosity without restriction. And the children continue to grow and blossom as amazing human beings.

Freedom is not licence and Tony, though allowing his kids unlimited freedom to play and learn in their own way, would certainly not advocate licence, letting a child manipulate or exploit its parents or others, letting it harm or damage itself or anyone else. There are boundaries; freedom brings with it awesome responsibility. But a child who is allowed to grow freely in its own way, exploring where its curiosity takes it, and having the space to develop its own potential naturally and in harmony with the blessings of the universe, will learn responsibility as it grows. And surely it is preferable for a child to act out of its own sense of rightness, than out of fear of punishment or hope of reward? Or, as often happens when parents raise their children with an 'agenda' of their own, understanding the unspoken language that they need to 'buy' their parents love or approval.

We are not all so fortunate, to be raised in real freedom. For many of us, our freedom to be ourselves and follow our curiosity and spontaneity wherever they may take us, will have been seriously curtailed during our childhood.

Most parents do what they consider to be in their child's best interest. But we are all raised within the limitations that conditioned our parents, and the prevailing attitudes of our society. If our parents were not living with consciousness, if they were not coming from a place of unconditional love, if they were swayed by their own emotional needs, we will not have grown up free and autonomous, confident and happy being our own unique selves.

But as adults, we are responsible for our own lives.

As adults, we need to recognize this and take this responsibility.

Whatever 'baggage' we have from the past, whether growing up with parents who had their own 'agenda' for us, in a dysfunctional family where parental needs took precedence, or maybe even growing up with neglectful, exploitative or abusive parents – we are now adults. However much our freedom to be ourselves was curtailed, however much we were criticized or blamed or ridiculed or made to feel guilty as children, however much we may have been damaged by our parents – we are now adults. And as adults, we need to recognize the influences that shaped our childhood and understand, as far as we can, how they have led us to where we are at the moment. *And then we need to let go.*

To recognize and understand is not to approve. You should never condone behaviour that was inappropriate, selfish or cruel. But this is not about your parents. This is about you and your journey. Now. Whatever was done, is done. Now it's time to draw a line under the past. We need to stop blaming our parents, however awful our childhood might have been, and take responsibility for our own lives.

So, this is your choice: to continue blaming your parents or 'the past' for all your perceived inadequacies and failures, and then you will live your life always finding someone else to blame for everything that goes wrong; or to acknowledge that now you are an adult, and you take full responsibility for your life from now on.

Becoming mature and taking responsibility for our lives is an essential part of our spiritual work. Freeing ourselves from the past is an essential part of our journey towards freedom.

So what is real freedom? Freedom has nothing to do with externals, with the outside world, with the physical circumstances of our lives. It is our identification with the outside world, with the world created by our ego, that prevents us from living in freedom.

Being free is *living* our freedom.

Being free is having the courage to let go of the beliefs that keep us chained to self-created needs which control the unfree way in which we live.

Being free is living in the present, being in the moment, open to experiencing in our own way whatever the universe offers us, ready to receive what is already here, now, in profusion.

Being free is living from the heart, putting energy into our relationships, investing time and love in being with our children, our partners, our friends, our selves. It is tapping into the abundance and joy of what is real, without the constraints of needing to try to control or fix or change anything. Living the freedom just to be.

The joy with which we live our lives, in every moment, is the true measure of our freedom.

Real freedom is detachment.

The journey of the spiritual path is the journey through the process of detachment: detaching ourselves from everything that has kept us stuck, letting go of the mind-set that tells us that our happiness and 'salvation' are to be found in the outside world.

All the 'letting go' that we have processed up till now, leads us on to a more profound detachment: detachment from our need to control, from having an agenda, from feeling that we have to influence the outcome of anything. If we have emotion invested in a particular outcome, we are not free. This applies to everything we do.

Freedom is detachment from outcome.

If we are attached to outcome, we are not doing whatever it is for its own sake, but for the sake of a desired result. For example, if we paint a picture being attached to outcome, we will paint in a certain way so that the painting will be an expression of an idea in our mind, with the hoped-for result that the finished painting will be sold or exhibited, or at the very least admired.

If we paint without attachment to outcome, we paint from the centre of our creativity, and the painting becomes a journey of discovery, an expression of our innermost self, an exploration of the sacred. Painting without attachment to outcome liberates us from the need to attain a goal; we paint for the sake of painting. This is true freedom, and the possibilities that it contains are limitless.

And it is the same with everything we undertake. Do we study because we want to pass exams or because we enjoy learning and want to gain knowledge? Do we do our job in the best way we can because we are seeking promotion or a raise, or because we get pleasure from our job and always do our best in every undertaking? Do we help other people because we want to gain approval or popularity, or because we want to be of service?

Anything that we do that is attached to outcome is *a priori* not free.

Detachment is the realization that no one else has the power to determine your life.

When we are detached, we realize that no-one else has the power to determine the course of our life. No-one else's agenda can force us do anything, or be anything. We do not need to act out a role cast for us by others. This is real freedom. And it's awesome.

Being detached means not having any expectations of others, either practically or emotionally. And when there are no expectations, there can be no judgementalness, no blame, and no disappointment. Being detached also means that we have no expectations of ourselves, no arbitrary standard that we need to attain. So we are free to live in the moment, whatever each moment offers us, without struggling to manipulate or control in order to achieve a predetermined result.

Being detached means that we are not dependent on anyone or anything outside ourselves for our happiness. We *know* that our happiness comes from within. We are truly free to be ourselves. How amazing is that!

Detachment is being fully involved in life.

People coming to Tony's retreats often ask him why they should be detached and cut themselves off from the world. But this is to misunderstand the concept of detachment. As we have seen in Chapter 2, in letting go of emotions, detachment is not being uninvolved, distancing ourselves from life or from our feelings, or not interacting with others. On the contrary, it is being deeply involved with every aspect of life, open to experiencing the full potential that life offers us at every moment, but without trying to manipulate what is, without *attachment, expectation* or *need*. Only by seeing things as they really are and not 'smudging' can we be free. If we are making 'choices' in a situation where we don't see and accept things as they are, but 'colour' things the way we want them to be, we are not making free choices.

Detachment means acting not from the desire for personal gratification, but rather coming from a sense of sacred self, detached from personal want, ready to fulfil the higher purpose of our lives, the higher good of all. Detachment is living out of higher Intention, not personal Will.

Detachment is ultimately the choice to let go of the film of your life that is playing inside your head, and move to a place where you can see it as it were from above, from the vantage point of the observer; from your Higher Self. And then we are able to live truly and freely what each moment offers us.

Detachment means never making assumptions.

People are unpredictable. We should not assume that other people will behave in a certain way, or do what we would do in their situation. For instance, if someone says they love you, you might expect them to behave in the same way that you would behave when you love someone. But everyone sees the world differently and everyone behaves differently.

If people behave badly towards us, it is coming from them. It is not an excuse for us to get angry with them, nor is it an invitation to a guilt trip. We are not the cause of their behaviour; we are not to blame. We need to remind ourselves, again – and again! – *that people behave the way they do towards us because of who they are, not because of who we are.* At the same time, if we feel angry, we should see this as an opportunity to question and learn, to see what buttons they are pressing, what unfinished emotional business of ours they are tapping into.

And of course, we also need to ask ourselves what the people in our lives mirror for us, and why we have invited this into our life. Another paradox, perhaps: that the way others behave towards us is not personal, and at the same time we should question the mirror.

Our spirituality is shaped by the paradoxes we experience and are able to hold in our hearts. Both parts of a spiritual paradox are always true. They may be beyond our mental understanding, but they greatly enrich our wisdom.

Detachment means never taking anything personally.

Taking things personally is allowing yourself to live on someone else's agenda, and is the cause of a formidable loss of personal power, as well as a great deal of suffering. It is reacting instead of acting.

Taking things personally is one of the major causes of a sense of victimhood, the cast that imprisons our suffering. ["Why is he/she treating me like this? Why is life so cruel to me? Why am I the only one with no money to do the things I want to do? Why is it always me that is sick, sacked, dumped, cheated? Why doesn't anybody love me? Poor me!"]

Freedom is being detached so that you see the bigger picture; you do not *react* from inside your ego mind, but rather *act* from a perspective of the higher good, for you and for others.

At one of Tony's retreats, a woman told an incident that had deeply hurt her: one of her closest friends hadn't come to her fortieth birthday party. This was a big occasion for her, and she had felt snubbed and rejected. In fact she was so upset that she didn't enjoy the party at all, although she'd worked hard for weeks to prepare it. She also spent the next day churning over and over in her mind what she could possibly have done to offend her friend. But it transpired that her friend had been involved in a road accident the morning of the party and had been taken to hospital with concussion. Don't take things personally!

Freedom is being able to detach yourself from other people's opinions and agendas. To stay centred and act out of your own integrity, no matter what anyone else thinks of you. To be equally unmoved by criticism or approval. To reach this point is truly to inhabit your freedom.

Freedom means accepting the perfection of Creation as it is. Not trying to control anything. Not trying to change anything. And not trying to hold onto anything.

Freedom means relinquishing our belief in permanence.

The idea of permanence holds a great deal of power over all of us. It gives us our sense of security; it is familiar and comforting and it creates stability in our life. We know where we are. We want to hang onto it at all costs.

But nothing is permanent, certainly not in the physical world; nor, perhaps, in the world beyond the physical, where things are also impermanent, although they are eternal.

Spirituality has no 'rules', because rules limit us in permanence. But nothing in Creation is fixed, nothing is permanent, though it is limitless. As the world turns, plants and animals and people die and new life is born. Each dawn brings us a whole new world to inhabit.

Nothing in life is permanent. When we are able to let go of our worldview that clings to permanence and move more deeply into our own spiritual centre, we discover that our world expands. As we uncover and let go of more layers of resistance – perhaps now we are reaching our last vestiges of resistance – we see that the world unfolds in an infinite blaze of glory, taking us into ever expanding realms of choice, unfettered, unbounded, unlimited.

Nothing is permanent. Everything changes, all the time. No-one will be quite the same tomorrow as they are today. No situation will continue to be exactly as it is now. No love will remain the way it is, for love is continual movement; a direction, not a possession. Trying to keep things as they are, is not only impossible but also a useless waste of energy.

The only constant in this life is constant change. When we realize this and are able to make this leap of faith, when we can welcome change and the unknown without fear, the most profound transformation occurs. We find that we are living in total freedom.

To be free is to hang on to nothing and be open to change at every moment. It is good to remind ourselves that we do not see the whole picture, the higher purpose. But all change is part of the greater purpose of life. When we flow with it as it unfolds and changes, our whole universe expands and we are open to receive and embrace the gifts and blessings of each moment. Reminding ourselves that allowing ourselves to receive is also a blessing.

To be free is to acknowledge that life unfolds in its own perfect way, that everything begins and everything ends at the appropriate time. Although beginnings and endings belong to world-created time. When we move more deeply into our spirituality, we realize that actually there are no beginnings and no ends. Everything just is.

Freedom is an attitude to life, an awakening of consciousness, that comes from within. It is a deep knowing that nothing and no-one owns us, or binds us, or limits us.

Freedom is both the goal and the way.

Freedom is both the goal and the way. The path *towards* freedom is also the path *of* freedom.

The goal *is* the way. This brings another layer to our experience of life that informs all the others. This is simply freedom; neither freedom *from*, the constraints of the external world; nor freedom *to,* live the way we choose to live. Just freedom, with no qualifications.

This is freedom with a cosmic smile, a conscious expression of our connection to the Divine.

Freedom is a state of being.

Being free is an inner state of being, manifest at all times, not dependent on our physical circumstances or the 'reality' around us. A pauper may be freer than a king. A traveller, with everything s/he owns in one small rucksack, may be freer than a millionaire tied to the demands of his wealth. Nelson Mandela, incarcerated on Robin Island for more than a quarter of a century by the South African apartheid government, was certainly free in a way that his prison guards were not.

Freedom is the choice to live in wholeness, in consciousness, connected to the sacred and to all of life, no matter what are our physical circumstances.

Freedom is the road we walk, in trust, from the bondage of attachment to the unfolding of our limitless potential. Freedom is freedom to choose – whom or what we serve, our own path in life.

But the ultimate choice is to let our life unfold in its own way, in all its mystery, in all its perfection. To surrender to the divine intention of our life, and allow it to fulfil its own purpose for us without needing to control it.

Surrendering to the Divine is not passive, 'waiting' for our life to happen to us. Rather it is our conscious choice, and in choosing consciously, we are acting, not reacting.

One of the great spiritual paradoxes is that freedom is both a surrendering of ego will to the higher good, and also the ability to choose in every moment. It is the simultaneity of having free will, and knowing that everything will unfold from the Source in its own perfect way.

But perhaps it isn't a paradox. For only by surrendering to life, to the Sacred, does free choice become real, and so meaningful. Only by recognizing the perfection of the All That Is can we freely recreate it in our own lives. Freedom is both process and result; the journey and the goal.

Freedom is conscious evolution.

As we begin to live in real freedom, we realize that our journey towards freedom is actually our journey towards Enlightenment. And, in fact, ultimate freedom is Enlightenment.

Freedom to choose in every moment is consciousness in action, the power of presence made manifest.

Freedom is not so much 'free choice' in any given circumstance, as 'liberated life'.

Your choice…

Chapter Ten
Exercising: Physical and Spiritual

"When a baby takes its first breath, Spirit enters its physical body. In that split second between the in-breath and the out-breath, the baby says 'yes' or 'no' to life. And whatever choice he makes, it is reinforced throughout his life by the way he breathes. Are we saying 'yes' to life by breathing deeply, consciously? All spiritual practice starts with the breath."

Tony Samara

Spirituality is wholeness, the integration of mind, body, heart and soul. Exercise is one of the best ways that we can both access and practise our spirituality. Committing ourselves to walk the spiritual path means establishing a habit of regular exercise, both physical and spiritual.

This will include conscious breathing, meditation and visualization, focusing on releasing the games of the ego mind – one of the greatest causes of stress and tension in the Western world, which affects our bodies as well as our minds – and a regimen of daily physical exercises. Together, this can bring vibrant health to our bodies, open our hearts and help us to connect to the Sacred.

Physical and spiritual exercises are not separate practices.

Physical and spiritual exercises are not two sets of separate exercises. Each is a tool that includes the practice of the other. Like everything else they are interconnected, each contributing to a holistic whole.

When we exercise the body, we bring our total awareness into the body, into the moment, inhabiting it fully; this is spiritual. Think of running a marathon, an enduring physical task. But you cannot do this unless you are fully in the moment, and this often brings with it a kind of spiritual ecstasy – as well as sore feet!

When we sit and meditate, a 'spiritual' exercise, we infuse our body with healing light and energy – physical enhancement. Again, chanting sacred sounds, a profound spiritual practice, opens the lungs and oxygenates the entire blood system.

So, where does physical exercise end and spiritual practice begin? Or *vice versa*?

As you read the exercises, you will see how difficult it is to categorize them. Is a physically dynamic shaking exercise to let go of the ego mind and become fully present in the moment, physical or spiritual? Is the seed/sapling/tree visualization that connects to all parts of our body, in which we grow physically and also connect to the Cosmic Tree of Life, spiritual or physical? Are the gland exercises, in which we cleanse the pineal and pituitary glands, and also open the crown chakra to spiritual receptivity, physical or spiritual? Is the breathing exercise that opens the airwaves and oxygenates the blood, but also invites the sacred energy of *Hu,* into our hearts, spiritual or physical?

In our exercises, we tap into the circularity and inclusivity of the All That Is. This is much more profound than a mere 'overlapping' of borders. It is tuning in to the essence of creation, where each part is not only connected to each other part; it also includes within it the whole. So, too, our exercises become a manifestation of this perfection. Everything is complete within itself.

But for easier accessibility, these practices are divided into six groups:
1. 'Ordinary' physical exercises
2. Breathing exercises
3. Meditation
4. Visualization
5. Gland and internal organ exercises
6. Shamanic energy exercises and animal postures.

Physical Exercises

Regular physical exercise is essential for maintaining optimum health, and is also an important component of spiritual practice.

The best physical exercise is also the simplest, and the cheapest: brisk walking. Its benefits cannot be overstated; walking helps to achieve and maintain good health and prolong life. You should walk at a brisk pace, breathing deeply with total awareness. Synchronize your breathing with the pace and rhythm of your movements. To obtain the maximum benefit, walk in nature, where the fresh air and the blessings of the natural world are most advantageous. Be aware of all the sights and sounds around you. Leave your mind behind and immerse yourself in the elements of nature and the sheer joy of being alive. Try to do this for at least twenty minutes each day.

Any kind of aerobic exercise is in fact excellent. This includes jogging, and any kind of sport that involves running [football, cricket, tennis, etc.]. All aerobic exercises revitalize the body. They will get your cardiovascular system going, increase the general physical fitness of your body and help you to breathe more deeply, which oxygenates the whole system. They should also bring you enjoyment and a general feeling of well-being.

You can add to this list washing the floor, vacuuming the carpet, digging, gardening and any kind of manual labour. Also, going to the gym and working out, and working with weights. Any aerobic exercise that gets the heart moving and stretches the muscles and joints is fine. All exercise, if you are really focused, is a way of stilling the mind and bringing you into the moment as you tone, rejuvenate and revitalize your body.

All exercise should be done on a regular basis to reap the greatest rewards. Fifteen minutes every day is far more beneficial than two hours once a week. Half an hour every day is better!

While all physical exercise has a spiritual connection, some exercises are more associated with spirituality than others. These are exercises that help to release blocked energy stored in the body, and return us to a state of physical and spiritual balance, in harmony with ourselves and the universe.

By far the best system, and also the oldest, is yoga, which combines physical exercise with deep breathing and spiritual practice. The practice of yoga has many advantages: it can help to relieve stress and tension, alleviate pain in the muscles, keep the joints loose and supple, release blockages that have built up over time and keep the spine flexible, all of which maintain a healthy flow of energy in the body. The regular practice of yoga postures also helps us to let go of the constant buzz of our minds and move into a place of quiet stillness, at peace with ourselves and the world. It can connect us to our spiritual centre, and align us with the wholeness and harmony of the All That Is. Yoga is highly recommended as a portal into spirituality.

Tai Chi is also a form of physical exercise that brings with it profound spiritual benefit. Believed to have been started by a Taoist priest during the Sung dynasty, it consists of a sequence of very specific movements, which have deep symbolic meaning. Although it is a form of martial art, it is non-combative and performed by each person individually; it is slow, measured and gentle. There are two main sequences of Tai Chi: the full sequence, taking about forty-five minutes, and the short one, which lasts twenty minutes. Performing Tai Chi on a regular basis helps to maintain a healthy body, a quiet mind and spiritual well-being. Chi Gong has similar benefits to Tai Chi.

Physical exercise is an important ingredient of the spiritual life. When we exercise the body, we bring our total awareness into the body, into the moment, inhabiting it fully. It is not possible to be really involved in physical exercise and not be in the moment. And being in the moment is, as we know, the place where spirituality lives.

Breathing

Breathing is the most natural thing in the world. Every living creature breathes. If we stop breathing, we die. We breathe automatically; even if we are living on 'automatic pilot', we are still breathing.

But many of us grow up breathing in a shallow and superficial way that nourishes neither our body nor our soul; they wither with each shallow and unconscious breath we take. This form of shallow breathing into the chest, clavicular breathing, creates a separation from life, from fully embracing everything around us.

Breathing unconsciously also causes stress to the lungs as they are not receiving sufficient oxygen, and this leads to feelings of lethargy and fatigue. It is also the first cause of many ailments that then may turn into more serious illnesses.

Breathing consciously is an act of loving and nurturing ourselves.

Breathing consciously is an investment in our health – physical, emotional and spiritual. It is a commitment to nurture and love and cherish ourselves.

Physically, correct breathing nourishes and revitalizes our body, bringing vital oxygen to every cell, organ, muscle and tissue. It purifies the blood, cleanses the lungs and helps to eliminate toxins. Deep breathing can help us to let go of stress, tension and anxiety, all of which are held in the body. Resentment and anger can be dissolved through the breath; you cannot scream or have a temper tantrum while you are focused on deep breathing!

Correct breathing not only enhances our physical health and rejuvenates our body, it is also the best tool we have for letting go of the constant buzz of our mind, and focusing our awareness in the present moment. Through conscious breathing we can control the flow of energy into and out of our bodies. By mastering our breath, we can also master our minds and our emotions, instead of letting them master us. The mind is limited, and it is difficult to extricate ourselves through the mind from situations created *by* the mind. We have to go beyond the mind, and a very good way to go beyond it is to free our breath. Liberating the breath takes us beyond the limitations of the mind.

Correct breathing is the basic tool for creating balance and harmony in our lives.

Huachuma Shamanism sees correct breathing as a direct way of creating balance and harmony in our lives. To become harmonious with the breath of *Pachamama* takes time and practice. By beginning to understand our breath, we are able to understand that transformation has its foundation in the body and that deep breathing is the bridge to those parts of ourselves that are not fully embracing life and need to be brought back into harmony with the power of *Pachamama.* Shamans say that correct breathing is as important as food.

Shamans can know who we are just by watching the way we breathe.

Shamans will tell you that they can know everything about you just by watching the way you breathe. They believe that the way we breathe expresses the whole of our being, our attitudes to life and to ourselves, going back to the moment of our birth. Our whole history is encapsulated in every breath we take. And repeated in every breath.

So if we are breathing in an automatic and shallow way, we can break the pattern by bringing consciousness into our breathing, and by breathing deeply transform it into a life-affirming process. This will begin to have repercussions in every area of our lives. And of course, our state of health is expressed in the way we breathe: is it open, expansive, life-affirming, or shallow, constricted and afraid? The way we breathe is the first thing a Shaman will look at to diagnose illness. Changing our breathing can also be the first tool of healing.

When Tony begins to work with breath at his retreats, participants are usually very enthusiastic, eager to learn any techniques that can help them.

In the first flush of excitement, everyone promises to practise regularly every morning, hoping that this will give them a complete understanding of breath and breathing, and so miraculously transform their lives. Tony just smiles gently. He knows that conscious breathing is taking the lid off Pandora's box.

Conscious breathing opens us up to all of ourselves.

Conscious breathing is an affirmation of life – all of life. By affirming life, by opening ourselves up to everything that life has to offer us, we are also opening ourselves up to every aspect of ourselves – including those parts that we may not like, those parts that we may have suppressed for years; our shadow selves, the dark side that we have been afraid to expose to the light.

Breathing consciously means finding the courage to experience all parts of ourselves, to look deeply within and face the shadows that so far we have been afraid to look at. It means being with ourselves in stillness, in silence, being fully in the moment, with no outside distractions, totally inhabiting our bodies. It means doing nothing, in fact, but concentrating on our breathing. Breathing in and breathing out. Breathing into the deepest part of ourselves, bringing the breath of life, into our bodies and into our hearts. Staying in this place of stillness, allowing ourselves to be with the hurt and the pain, not trying to run away from it, suppress it, or numb it. And as we stay with the breath, with the emotion, allowing ourselves truly to inhabit it, it gradually becomes transformed.

As we begin to breathe more deeply, it is quite amazing to see how dramatically our health improves, how our energy and vitality increase, how vibrant and light our bodies begin to feel. And so we create a virtuous circle. As we focus on our breathing, in the moment, we let go of the noise and distraction of our minds, and connect more deeply with our intuition, our imagination, our spontaneity. Breathing deeply enhances our consciousness; consciousness feeds our breathing.

Spirituality starts with the breath.

The process of opening up to our spirituality begins with the breath. If we are feeling angry, resentful or depressed, our breathing will reflect this and be rapid and shallow. Conversely, you cannot continue to manifest negative emotions if you are breathing deeply, with awareness. So, if you feel fear or anger or negativity, bring your awareness into your breath, breathe deeply, focus on your breath and let go of the emotion. Changing the way we breathe is actually changing the way we interact with life.

People attending their first retreats with Tony often become wildly enthusiastic and go back home resolved to do breathing exercises for an hour twice a day. After two days, when they realize how difficult this is in their current life-style, they become disillusioned and give up altogether. So be realistic; start with ten minutes, or even five minutes, and do it regularly. Work towards increasing the time later. Do one exercise twice each day, then change, so that in time you move through all the exercises.

As well as doing your regular breathing exercises, it's beneficial to practise conscious breathing as an on-going activity, whenever you think of it, and particularly if you are feeling tense or stressed. Notice your breath, bring yourself into the moment, relax your body, and fill your lungs with deep breaths, then really let go of everything you're holding on to: thoughts, emotions, worries, everything.

As you breathe, visualize inhaling peace and love into your whole body and exhaling all your stress and tension. Be right here, focused, in the moment. Breathe deeply, in and out. Breathe. You can do this wherever you are: at work, in the supermarket, stuck in a traffic jam. It is amazing how, simply by using conscious breathing, you can transform a stressful tube journey or shopping trip into an oasis of peace, an affirmation of life. Breathing deeply, with affirmation, is an exercise in consciousness and it influences everything we do.

Deep breathing is a portal into consciousness and spiritual growth.

As well as helping to keep the body healthy, vibrant and strong, the practice of conscious breathing is also essential in opening ourselves up to the path of spiritual Enlightenment. If we are breathing deeply, we are breathing in the energy of *prana,* the universal life force, the sacred breath of the All That Is. So, if we are feeling fragmented, not centred or grounded, we should focus on our breath and begin to breathe deeply. As we do this, we centre ourselves in the moment, confusion disperses, and we begin to move towards spiritual awakening.

Breathing Exercises

The following breathing exercises are aimed at helping you to connect to *prana,* the vital energy of the universe, revitalizing your body and helping to open up your consciousness. Practising them for ten minutes morning and evening is a good start, and something that is easy to keep to.

Choose a quiet place where you won't be disturbed. Unless otherwise stated, sit comfortably in an upright position with a straight spine. The ideal position is sitting cross-legged on a cushion, aligning the head, neck and spine, and keeping the shoulders straight but relaxed. This keeps the energy channels open and helps the smooth flow of *prana.* Always breathe through your nose [unless otherwise stated]. The hairs in our nostrils filter out impurities, pollution, dust and germs.

Close your eyes and focus with full awareness on your breathing. If any thoughts come into your mind, just observe them and then let them go. Focus on your breathing, which should be rhythmic, slow and smooth, gently breathing in and breathing out. Nothing should be forced; just be aware of your breathing and observe it. If your mind wanders at any time, bring your focus back to your breath. Again. And again.

Try to practise the exercises twice a day, morning and evening. Ideally, you should start by doing each exercise for ten minutes and then gradually increase the time to half an hour. If you feel tired while doing any of the exercises, stop and rest and continue at another time.

1. Mirror Exercise [this should be done standing up]:

The power of breath comes from within ourselves. This exercise shows you how you are breathing and what you may need to do to improve. Start by looking at yourself in a full-length mirror. Observe your posture, your abdomen, your shoulders, how your feet are placed. Are you standing upright or slouching? Are you fully inhabiting your body? Is the expression on your face tense, angry, happy, sad? Watch the way you are breathing.

Now hunch your shoulders as hard as you can, and try to breathe. Notice how the breath is constricted. Now relax your shoulders, let go completely, and breathe. Notice the difference. The way your breath is constricted when your shoulders are hunched, is exactly the way that most of us breathe all the time. Practise this exercise in front of the mirror, hunching your shoulders, then releasing. As you breathe out, letting go completely of all tension, all stress, all anxiety, you create a body memory; this is the correct way to breathe. As you practise, your body begins to remember.

2. Conscious Breathing – one:

This exercise is to get you used to breathing consciously. Then, of course, consciousness needs to be applied to every exercise. Sit comfortably and watch your breath. Take a deep breath in, and be aware that you are inhaling deeply. Now breathe out all the air you have inhaled, and be aware that you are exhaling deeply. As you breathe in as deeply as you can, be aware that you are breathing in as deeply as you can. As you breathe out, expressing all the air you have inhaled, be aware that you are breathing out all the air you have inhaled.

3. Conscious Breathing – two:

Do the exercise as above, but to help you stay focused count your breaths. Inhale and exhale once, and count one. Inhale and exhale again and count two, then three, four and so on, up till ten. Then start counting again from one. Counting like this brings your consciousness into your breath.

If you lose count, start again from one. Be aware of how many times you lose count in a ten-minute session. When you are fully conscious, you will not lose count. Then you may abandon the counting and do the exercise as above, focusing solely on the breath.

4. Energy Circuit Breathing:

Close your eyes and become aware of your body. Tense up and then relax each part of your body in turn, letting go of any stress or tension your body is holding. Bring your attention to your breath, and watch your abdomen gently rising and falling as you inhale and exhale. Now bring your thumb and index finger together on each hand. Then on each in-breath, inhaling deeply, move your thumb to the next finger. Keep this going from one finger to the next with each in-breath. This exercise helps to energize the whole system.

5. Extension Breathing:

Breathe naturally in your own rhythm and watch your breath. Count the length of the exhalation. On the next out-breath increase the count by one, then by two, then by three. Exhaling for longer than we inhale ensures that all the stale air is removed from our lungs and we have space to inhale clean, pure air. You can vary the count as long as the out-breath is three counts longer than the in-breath.

6. Healing Breathing:

Inhale deeply, breathing into the stomach, then bring the breath up into the ribcage, then up into the chest. Hold for a count of three, then exhale in reverse order. Breathe in as deeply as you can, and make sure you express all the breath on the exhalation. As you inhale, visualize breathing white healing light into your body; as you exhale imagine that you are breathing out all the stress, tension and negative emotions held in the body. You can also put your hands on your stomach and move them up to your ribcage and chest as you breathe, feeling how each part expands as you inhale and contracts as you exhale.

7. Slow Heartbeat Exercise:

After focusing on your breath for a couple of minutes, inhale deeply, hold the breath for a count of five, then exhale deeply, pushing out all the breath you have inhaled and hold for a count of five. This will begin to slow your heartbeat. Consciously slowing the heartbeat through deep breathing helps to oxygenate the blood and relax all the muscles and organs of the body. It also brings a great feeling of peace and well-being. And as we become more relaxed, we allow ourselves to move more fully into consciousness and gradually open up to change.

8. Mother Earth Breathing:

This exercise brings us into harmony with the rhythms of Mother Earth. Breathe in for a count of seven, hold the breath for a count of two, breathe out for a count of seven and hold for two. This is an excellent exercise to do if you are feeling out of balance with yourself, fragmented or not centred. It will bring you back into harmony with the rhythm of the earth. Remember, the earth is alive and breathes in harmony with everything in nature. As you breathe in this universal rhythm, you will tune into the great life force, and become energized and empowered.

9. Single Nostril Breathing:

Cover your left nostril with the middle finger of your right hand, breathe in deeply through your right nostril to a count of four, then exhale to a count of eight. Repeat ten times. Then cover your right nostril with the middle finger of your left hand, breathe in deeply through your left nostril to a count of four, then exhale to a count of eight. Repeat ten times. This exercise clears the sinuses and the head, and increases mental alertness.

10. Alternate Nostril Breathing:

Cover your left nostril with the middle finger of your right hand, breathe in deeply through your right nostril for a count of four, hold the breath for a count of eight, then place you right thumb over your right nostril, release your middle finger, and breathe out through your left nostril for a count of eight. Now breathe in through your left nostril for a count of four, hold the breath for a count of eight, place your middle finger over your left nostril, release your thumb and breathe out through your right nostril for a count of eight. Continue breathing in and out through alternate nostrils, and holding the breath. Notice if one nostril feels more blocked than the other. Blockages in our nostrils signify blocks on that side of the brain. Right brain is associated with intuition, creativity, spontaneity and femininity; left brain with logic, planning, mental focus and masculinity. So blockages in our nostrils can draw our attention to where we need to focus healing energy. This breathing exercise also works with subtle masculine and feminine energies to harmonize these aspects of ourselves.

Meditation

The practice of meditation is found in some form in most ancient religions, and is seen as one of the greatest tools for connecting to the spiritual. It is most closely associated with Hinduism and Buddhism. In Hinduism it became part of the tradition of yoga, *dhyana.* [Sanskrit for "deep concentration".]

Meditation is a process of integration, of letting go of our feelings of separateness, of balancing the disparate parts of ourselves, and reaching a state of harmony with the All That Is. It offers us a quiet space in which we may strip off the masks of our ego mind and return to a state of innocence. It can expand our consciousness, helping us to tune in to our higher selves and our own deepest wisdom and bring great inner peace.

Meditation offers the best way of connecting deeply to our heart and soul.

Zen Buddhism, which is the tradition of the monastery in which Tony lived in Los Angeles, advocates *zazen,* a sitting meditation in which one enters a profoundly meditative state, emptying oneself of every worldly connection in order to reach Enlightenment. The logical mind is suspended, as are all desires and judgements. *Zazen* focuses on letting go of all attachment, belief and thought, entering an ego-less state of here/now nothingness. This practice was brought to prominence by Dogen, who considered it not only to be a method of moving towards Enlightenment but also, if properly experienced, to constitute Enlightenment itself.

The purpose of meditation is to release the power that the mind has over us. It is not about acquiring knowledge; rather it is about emptying our minds of all its thoughts, certainties and beliefs, plans and 'agendas', and reaching that still place, beyond the mind, of 'inner knowing'. Meditation can bring us to a state of no-mind, what Buddhists call *mushin*. In this state, we see things as they truly are; we become an empty vessel with no attachments of any kind.

Meditation offers us a way of transcending the limitations of our everyday lives and moving beyond into the unknown. It is a communion beyond words, allowing ourselves to connect to the deepest truth within us, and to the sacred Source.

Meditation is an art.

Meditation should be approached with humility, without preconceptions of how it should be or expectation of anything particular happening. If we 'try' to meditate, we generally go round in circles, as a battle ensues between the busyness of our 'monkey mind' and our attempts to overcome it. In fact, the more you try to overcome the 'monkey mind', the more games it will play to keep you stuck. Remember, the 'monkey' is very clever; 'we' need to be wise. So don't fight it, just observe it, then let it go and refocus on your breath.

To reap the most benefit from meditation, it should become a regular practice. Twice a day is recommended. The best times are dawn and dusk, times when the world is in transition, the light is changing and the energies are most fluid. An hour each time is recommended; if this seems beyond you at the moment, start with fifteen minutes and gradually increase when you are ready.

Choose a quiet place in which to meditate, where you will not be disturbed. If you can, meditate in the same place each day. This creates a sacred 'meditation space', and builds up positive relaxing energies that benefit the process. Generally it is not a good idea to lie down to meditate, as there is a danger of falling asleep; as a regular practice it is better to sit.

The ideal position to sit in, if you can manage it, is the lotus position [sitting cross-legged with each foot resting on the opposite thigh], the half lotus [one foot resting on the opposite thigh] or simply cross-legged on the floor. If this is not comfortable, sit on a chair with your legs uncrossed and your feet placed firmly on the ground. Most of us, unless we have been practising yoga or gymnastics for many years, will not be flexible enough to manage the lotus or half-lotus position. Even sitting cross-legged on the floor may prove difficult at first. It's most important to be comfortable when you meditate so that you are not distracted by the way you are sitting. So sit in whichever way you feel most comfortable and relaxed.

Whichever position you choose, sit with your back erect with the crown of your head reaching up to the ceiling, and your shoulders relaxed; your hands should rest lightly on your knees, palms facing up. Now go through each part of your body, tensing and relaxing, until your whole body is relaxed and peaceful. It's a good idea to name each part of your body as you do this: I am tensing my feet, now I am relaxing my feet; I am tensing my ankles, now I am relaxing my ankles, etc. Remember also to relax your face and jaw, and let your jaw hang slightly open. [The jaw often holds a great deal of tension.]

Close your eyes and watch your breathing. Then begin to slow your breath, and breathe more deeply, slowly breathing in and breathing out. If any thoughts come into your mind, just watch them and then let them go. Don't chase them away – this leads to a battle with your mind. Just allow them to float away and bring your focus back to your breath.

Tony's 'basic meditation'.

If you have not meditated before, or if you would like more guidance, Tony offers a very simple meditation, a way of getting out of your mind and connecting to your heart.

Close your eyes and focus on your breath. Let go of any thoughts, emotions, worries, any plans, work problems, schedules, ideas. Let go of every attachment and focus on your breathing. Come to a still place inside yourself. Slowly, breathe in and breathe out. As you breathe in, be aware that you are breathing in the life force, energizing the whole of your being. As you slow your breath, the mind stills, and you breathe into your heart.

Now start to focus on your spiritual centre, letting go of everything else, just being aware of this place of stillness within. As you open up to your spiritual self, you feel yourself expanding, moving beyond your physical self, beyond the individual you, merging with everything and everyone around you, merging with love. With each breath you take, you merge more profoundly with this love, with the All That Is. Stay in this place of perfect stillness, perfect love. [You can stay as long as you like, but at least fifteen minutes is recommended.] When you are ready, open your eyes and come back to the room.

There are many different forms of meditation.

Meditation can take many forms, so you should find one that suits you. The most common is the silent meditation, in which you sit in total silence and concentrate on 'emptying out' and letting go. If your mind wanders, bring your focus back again, and again, to your breath. Gradually you will reach a place of stillness.

Some people find silent meditation difficult as their mind refuses to be silenced. An excellent alternative is to use a mantra, the repetition of a single syllable, word, or text, which can be repeated over and over silently in your head, or chanted. A mantra may be any word or phrase that is meaningful to you, or one given to you by a spiritual teacher. Many New Age traditions advocate a personal mantra for each individual, but this has been open to abuse as some gurus sell mantras for large amounts of money.

Chanting meditation can be very powerful.

Chanting meditation can be very powerful and is most popular in groups. According to Shamanic tradition, sound was the first thing to be created, and the whole history of the cosmos is imprinted in sound. The universe is full of sounds, not only the cries of animals or birds, but also the sounds of plants, trees, rocks, the sky, the earth. These sounds are beyond our everyday hearing; we need to be spiritually attuned to the silence of the universe, which is imbued with the essence of these sounds, in order to be able to hear them. Each human soul also has its own unique sound, audible only to the spiritual traveller.

Chanting meditation can connect us to universal spirit through tapping into universal sound. There is a vast number of sounds and chants, but Tony follows the tradition based in India and chants the sound of Omm. Omm [or Aumm] is believed to be the original sound of the universe, a sacred sound. So when you chant Omm, you are inviting the primary agent of creation into your life. In the chant of Omm lies the power to create new beginnings…

In every meditation, the breath plays a central role. In chanting meditation, it is even more important, as the chant and the breath need to fuse, to become one. The breath carries the sound, the sound flows from the breath. Relax your body completely and breathe in deeply, filling your whole body with the breath. Then on the out-breath, chant Omm, sending the sound out into the universe, into infinity. Hold the breath and the chant as long as possible, then take in another deep breath and start again. The breath and the sound of Omm become fused, a circular dance, reaching from the deepest part of you out into the universe. Omm…

Drumming can also be a powerful way of meditating and a profound portal into reaching a deeper consciousness. This is best done in a group.

Moving meditation.

If you find sitting meditation difficult, there are other ways to meditate. A walk in nature, if you bring to it consciousness and Intention, can be a profound spiritual experience. Walking through fields or in a forest on a warm spring day; looking at the beauty of nature blossoming on the hillside; a walk by the sea, breathing in the fresh sea air and feeling connected to the power of the waves; walking beneath a star-filled sky on a clear summer night; walking in the rain and feeling the power of the elements. All these offer us opportunities to let go of the control of our minds and connect to the one-ness of all creation. They are all ways of meditating, ways of touching the core of our own spiritual being and reaching the stillness within.

Some people find meditating through movement very powerful. Gentle music can act as a gateway to meditation, and working in a group can raise the energy and help us to connect more deeply. Sacred circle dance and trance dance can both be powerful; but it doesn't matter what kind of dance or movement we do, as long as we do it with Intention to reach a deeper consciousness. You can do it alone or in a group, although trance dance particularly is more powerful in a group. The best way is to close your eyes and let the music transport you to other realms.

Tony's 'Dynamic Meditation'.

If you who would like a really active meditation, try this. It may not be everyone's idea of meditation, but it illustrates how we shouldn't make assumptions about anything! The purpose of this meditation is to shake free dormant energies and awaken the vibrant energy in the centre of the body. In this meditation, we can reach through the body that place of perfect stillness within where we completely let go of the mind. This meditation is best done early in the morning. It is in three parts:

Part 1: Stand up and let your whole body shake, every part of you, not just your arms – your head, your face, your upper body, your torso, your legs, your feet. Be loose and really let yourself go, shaking every part of your body with full energy. Feel the energies moving through your whole body. Let go everywhere. Become the shaking. Continue for fifteen minutes.

Part 2: Sit down with your eyes closed. Open your mouth and let your jaw drop loosely. Gently rotate your body from the waist, like a reed blowing in the wind. Feel the wind blowing you, and allow your body to go with it. Don't force anything. Continue for fifteen minutes.

Part 3: Lie down and close your eyes. Focus on breathing deeply and slowly. Feel the stillness. Continue for fifteen minutes. As you finish, focus on bringing this stillness back with you into the rest of your day.

Visualization

Visualization is actually another kind of meditation. But many people find visualization easier, as it gives us something positive to focus on, rather than trying to 'empty out' and reach a state of 'no-mind' nothingness. Generally, it is good to do visualizations lying down.

Tony does many visualizations at his retreats. The purpose of all of them is to help us to let go of the limitations of the reality that we have created, to leave behind our busy controlling minds and come into a place of stillness, where we may expand our hearts and move more deeply into our spirituality.

Space allows for just a few examples, but they will give a taste of what this work involves. Once you feel comfortable doing visualizations, you can also create your own. You can stay as long as you like in each of the visualizations, but at least fifteen minutes is recommended.

Beyond the Clouds Visualization:

Close your eyes and focus on your breath. Let go of any thoughts, emotions or worries, and focus on your breathing. Come to a still place inside yourself. Begin to slow your breath, and as you do you connect to the wonderful energy of the earth. Now see yourself drifting to a beautiful place in nature. Flowers abound, birds are cooing, a gentle breeze is blowing through the leaves; the sun is shining and the air is warm. You hear the gentle rushing of a stream nearby, and watch the clouds slowly drifting by. Your body is deeply relaxed.

As you breathe in, you let go: of your mind, your thoughts, of everything; you feel profoundly relaxed and peaceful. Then in the distance you see an eagle soaring upwards, higher and higher into the clouds, a beautiful majestic bird, its wings spread open. And your soul flies up to this eagle, and together you soar. As you look down, the trees become smaller and smaller. You soar higher and higher with the eagle, into the clouds, beyond the clouds. The earth becomes a tiny distant object.

You soar higher, above the clouds, and look down on the clouds beneath you. You fly higher still, moving into the light beyond the clouds. You breathe in deeply, deeply, breathing in the light. And then you dissolve into the light, you become one with the light. Now you can travel anywhere, you are not limited by gravity, by your physical body. And you float away with the light, at one with all of creation. Stay in this place of perfect stillness, perfect light, perfect love.

When you are ready, gently begin to come down. As you descend, be aware that your body retains the light; it is open to all the subtle energies of the universe. As you focus on your breathing, bring this light back with you into your everyday life. Then gently open your eyes and come back to the room.

Aura Cleansing Visualization:

This gentle visualization is one of Tony's favourites. It is a very effective way to balance yourself and bring you into harmony with the natural world. Close your eyes and watch your breath as you gently breathe in and out. Begin to breathe more slowly and deeply. Then with every out-breath, feel your body sinking into the ground, every part of your body sinking more and more deeply into the earth, feeling the warmth of Mother Earth embracing your whole being, flooding all the cells of your body with love.

Now you find yourself in a beautiful cave, with a crystal clear stream flowing through it. You listen to the gentle sounds of the stream, which carry you deeper and deeper into the earth, into the cave, into yourself. Every in-breath takes you more deeply into yourself; with every out-breath, you let go of the outside world, allowing the energy of Mother Earth to cleanse every part of your body, renewing your body with energy, vitality and strength.

As you lay there, surrounded by light, you begin to sense that there are other people in the cave with you. They are wise ancient people and they have come to help you. They start to blow smoke on every part of your body, clearing the energy, cleansing your aura, blowing away all the impurities, the stagnant energy and emotions that are stuck in your body, the pain that is held in every cell of your body. They continue to blow smoke over you until your aura is cleansed and free and shining with light.

Now you notice that your right hand is holding a beautiful object, a gem, a jewel that is sparkling, full of pure energy, radiating with a wondrous coloured light. This light surrounds and also enters your body, so that your whole body shines as brightly as this gem. This is a gift from the wise people who have come to you. Gently you place this gem next to your heart and it fuses with your heart, and your heart begins to open and shine with sparkling energy, shining for everyone to see. And you know that this gift is yours forever. You stay for a while in the cave, holding this precious gift.

When you are ready, holding the gift in your heart, you bring it back with you into this world. Then slowly open your eyes and come back to the room.

Tibetan Bowl Visualization:

Close your eyes and watch your breath, gently breathing in and out. Begin to breathe more slowly and deeply, letting go of any tension in your body. As you sink deeply into the ground, you find yourself lying on soft grass, resting beside a beautiful tree. You are totally relaxed, enjoying the cooing of birds, the sounds of insects, the rustle of the breeze in the trees. You feel the earth beneath you supporting you, the tree shading and protecting you. As you sink deeply into the earth, you find yourself moving down into the roots of the tree. You go down, further and further, deep into the earth, and you find yourself entering a large cave, full of light.

A deep stillness and peacefulness pervades the cave. You realize that you are not alone. Standing in front of you, you see a wise old person. This is your guide. He/she looks at you full of love, then stretches out her/his hands and offers you a golden bowl. You take the bowl, and as you touch it you sense immense power coursing through your body. Then you place in the bowl everything that is holding you back in your life – your beliefs, your emotions, your fears, your anger, your judgementalness, all your shadows – everything that you want to let go of, you put into the bowl. Then the light swirls around in the bowl and swallows them up. And the bowl is transformed into light.

You sink deeply into the light, and the deeper you go, the more you feel the light expanding, expanding beyond your body, reaching out into everything around you. And the light shines in you and through you and opens your heart, and gives you power, strength and courage to move forward. Nothing can stop this light; it is burning as brightly as the sun, pouring into the deepest parts of you, flooding your heart with light as it expands outwards. You feel great joy and peace. And you stay bathed in this light.

When you are ready, bring the light back into your body, bring your body back into the cave and thank your guide. You know that you can return to the cave at any time, and your guide will always be there, waiting for you. Then you climb back up the tree trunk, and find yourself lying on the grass by the tree. Gently come back into your body, open your eyes and come back into the room.

Gland and Internal Organ Exercises

These glandular exercises are very important, not only for physical health, but also for toning and protecting the emotional and energetic body from the bombardment of daily stresses, and bringing calm and peace to the spirit.

These exercises invigorate the glands of the body, help you to feel and stay youthful, and can balance your weight. If you are overweight, you will lose weight, if you are underweight, you will gain. Unlike with fad diets, you will reach and retain your optimum weight, as the glands bring balance to your body.

Find a comfortable sitting position, preferably cross-legged on the floor. Keep the spine straight and relaxed and your head upright. Make sure that your shoulders are relaxed and that you let go of any tension in the face. Relax your jaw and let it drop open slightly. Breathe deeply and become aware of your environment, the sounds and smells around you. Tune into your body and focus on your breath at the start of each exercise.

These exercises are best done between 5 and 7 p.m. and for optimum results should be done sequentially.

1. Balancing the breath:
Breathe in through the nose for a count of seven and hold for a count of two; breathe out for a count of seven and hold for a count of two. Continue for five to ten minutes.

2. Pineal and pituitary exercise:
The pineal gland, situated behind the third ventricle of the brain, and the pituitary gland at the base of the brain, not only control many physical aspects of the body, including growth; they are also believed to be essential for spiritual development, as they help to open the crown chakra and the third eye by secreting a special fluid deep in the brain [known to Hindus as *Amrit*]. This fluid helps to align the cells of the body as you begin to undergo spiritual transformation.

Place the tongue on the roof of the mouth. Rotate the body slowly from the hips up in a circular, clockwise direction. After a couple of minutes, start to hum gently. These movements activate the pituitary and pineal glands, releasing the *Amrit* fluid, which then flows to the throat and nourishes the thyroid gland. After a while, you will begin to sense the liquid moving down from the pituitary gland onto the tip of your tongue and into the thyroid. Continue rotating with awareness for about ten minutes to help the fluid move through your body and then gently bring your body to a standstill. Sit quietly for a few minutes before getting up.

3. Thyroid exercise:

This exercise works on opening the thyroid gland. The thyroid is important for balancing the emotions and helping to prevent severe mood swings. It is also responsible for controlling weight, and the aging process.

Keeping your body relaxed, focus on your breathing, and do all the movements very slowly. Gently bring your head down so that your chin rests on your chest and you feel a strong stretch in the back of your neck. Breathe in deeply, hold for a few seconds, then exhale, in each position. Bring your head back to the up-right position, then gently let it fall backwards and again hold for a few seconds. Bring your head back to the upright position, and breathe. Now bring your head over to rest on the right shoulder, hold for a few seconds. Bring your head back to the upright position, then over to the left shoulder and hold for a few seconds. Repeat the whole sequence ten times.

4. Thymus exercise:

The thymus is located in the neck, where it produces T-lymphocytes to stimulate the immune system. As well as its importance for boosting the immune system, this exercise also has a strong influence on our emotions and can protect us from outside emotional stress.

Breathing rhythmically, bring your awareness into your thymus. Breathe in, and on the out-breath massage down the outer sides of your neck with your fingertips from the ears to the shoulders. Alternatively, tap gently and rapidly around the thymus. Both actions will stimulate the thymus, and send it messages to begin to transform any sadness into joy.

5. Draining the lymph fluid:

Breathe deeply and slowly for a few moments. Then breathe in and cross your arms across your chest. On the out-breath press in and down a couple of inches under the armpits. This helps to drain the lymph fluid. Continue for five minutes.

6. Kidney exercise:

This exercise helps to drain impurities and toxic waste from the kidneys and keep them running smoothly [forgive pun]. Make fists with both hands and bring them to the top of the kidneys. Breathe deeply. On the out-breath, massage downwards strongly. Repeat a few times. Then rub your hands together rapidly, place them on your kidneys, and feel the warmth penetrating this area. Repeat the whole sequence ten times.

7. Bladder and lower back exercise:

Breathe normally and watch your breath. On the out-breath, find the mid point on the backs of your knees and press in firmly. Repeat twenty times. This helps to keep the bladder and kidneys flowing, and relieves pressure on the lower back.

8. Spinal tap:

All parts of the body have nerve endings in the feet, so pressing on different parts of the feet works to alleviate pain or symptoms of ill health in the corresponding parts of the body. [This is the principle of reflexology.] This exercise works on the whole of the spine. Focus on your breath. Breathe in and on the out-breath massage firmly down the inner sides of the feet, working from the heal to the toes. Continue for ten minutes.

9. Freeing the solar plexus:

Focus on your breath. Breathe in and on the out-breath find the point half way down in the middle of the foot and press firmly inwards. Repeat twenty times. This pressure works on freeing the solar plexus area.

10. Opening the heart:

Focus on slowing your breath. Place your hands, palms up, on your knees and start to bring your attention to the area of your heart. On the in-breath, bring the thumb and middle finger of each hand together to form a circle. On the out-breath, squeeze gently and open your hands; at the same time, make the sound 'Aaaahhh' and feel it resonate around your heart. Continue for five minutes. Finish with several minutes' silence, keeping your awareness in the heart area. Bring this peace and stillness back with you into your daily life.

In Conclusion:

When you have finished the exercises, close your eyes and focus on your breath. Spend ten minutes in silent meditation, bringing your awareness into your breath, breathing in and breathing out slowly and deeply.

Shamanic Energy Exercises

Huachuma Shamanism, the 'branch' of Shamanism with which Tony was most closely connected, has an ancient tradition of Energy Postures that help us to align physically, emotionally and spiritually with the cycles of nature and the harmony of the natural world. These Energy Postures have been practised by Shamans and other ancient peoples for thousands of years.

These postures are similar to exercises found in Tai Chi and Yoga, and are considered by many to be the origins of these disciplines. Gradually, if we practise these postures diligently, we begin to understand their meaning and the profound wisdom that they carry. For not only can they help our body physically to become fitter and stronger, they can also help us emotionally and spiritually to align to our deepest self, our inner power, and the power of nature.

These exercises help to ground us and are a perfect portal into spiritual practice. Grounding essentially means being completely in your body, aware of your surroundings and fully present to whatever is happening in the moment. The goal of spiritual practice is not to transcend the physical, but rather to be fully consciously in the body, and so transcend the limitations of our minds and the physical plane. Some of these exercises are best practised at certain times of the day [where stated] so we may best tune in to universal energy, which is different in the morning, at noon and at night. All exercises should be done in a quiet place where you won't be disturbed.

1. Clearing Energy:

This is a simple exercise and a very good one to shake us out of 'stuckness'. It is also good to do at the start of an exercise regime as it loosens up the whole body. You can also do it at any time if you are feeling overwhelmed or stressed, as it helps the body to release stagnant energy and really helps us to let go of the masks that we all hide behind.

Stand up, place your feet firmly on the ground and close your eyes. Connect your feet to the earth and feel the earth's energy rising through your body. Take a few deep breaths, then start to shake your whole body, really shaking every part of your body, as vigorously as you can – and then more! Every part – hands, arms, feet, legs, hips, trunk, head, face, jaw; the parts you are used to moving, and those you may have forgotten you have! On each out-breath sigh and vocalize, as you let go of all the tension in your body, everything your body is holding on to. Concentrate on releasing tension as you shake, especially around the face and jaw, which often get neglected. Try to keep going for twenty minutes. If you can't manage this, start with five minutes and gradually increase the time. [Not recommended if you have heart or spinal problems, or if you are pregnant.]

2. Basic Grounding Exercise:

This is an excellent exercise for grounding yourself if you are feeling disconnected or out of balance. Stand in a relaxed position and gently raise your body up from the ground onto the balls of your feet. Come back down hitting the ground with your heels quite firmly, and then let your whole body flop completely. As you do this, make the sound 'hu'. Repeat this half a dozen times. This exercise helps to ground the energy to the base chakra, bringing the energy out of the head and back into the body. [Not recommended if you suffer from spine or neck problems.]

3. Grounding Cord Exercise:

Another excellent exercise for grounding yourself, this is recommended as a regular part of your spiritual practice. Sit in a chair, spine straight but relaxed, both feet firmly on the floor, hands resting on your lap. Close your eyes and bring your attention to the centre of the head. Become aware of your breathing, allowing your body to expand with each in-breath. Now bring your awareness into the first chakra and visualize a cord of light about 4–6 inches in diameter attaching itself to the base of your spine. Follow this grounding cord visually and see it extend into the earth, moving through the layers of the earth until it reaches the centre of the planet where the magnetic core is located. See or feel the grounding cord anchoring. Breathe in deeply, bringing the energy of the earth up through the cord into your body and feel it energize your whole body. As you exhale release any stress or tension or stagnant energy back down the cord into the earth, where it can be transformed.

Begin to visualize the grounding cord changing colour. Experiment with each colour of the rainbow, and notice how you feel with each one. See which colour induces calm, confidence, strength, joy. When you are ready, detach the grounding cord from your spine by pulling it down and releasing it back into the earth. Open your eyes and come back into the room.

Once you know which colours induce which feelings, you can repeat this exercise with a particular colour cord that fits a particular need.

4. Strengthening the Heart – the ideal time to do this exercise is between 4 and 5 am:

Sit comfortably cross-legged on a cushion with your back straight. Relax your shoulders and release any tension you are holding in your body. Close your eyes and just watch your breath. Then start to breathe slowly and deeply. Place your hands in a relaxed fashion on your knees, palms upwards. When you feel centred, bring your awareness to your heart area. Then, taking a deep breath into the abdomen, bring your thumb and middle fingertips together on both hands and squeeze gently, holding the breath. As you exhale, relax the whole body and utter the sound 'hum'. Repeat this exercise 15–20 times using deep in-breaths and relaxed out-breaths.

5. Uniting Heaven and Earth – the ideal time for this exercise is dawn, and outside is best:

Stand with your feet shoulder-width apart, knees slightly bent, pelvis and chin tucked in. Feel your feet rooted to the ground connecting with the earth. Bring your hands together pointing downwards, welcoming the energy of Mother Earth. Bring this energy with you as you bring your hands up to your naval, then turn them upwards and stretch up as high as you can, reaching up towards heaven. Open your hands, palms up to the sky, collecting energy from the sun.

Then slowly bring your hands down to the earth. Repeat half a dozen times. This exercise helps to clear the chakras. At the end, lie down for ten minutes in silence, breathing deeply and feeling the energy circulating through your body.

6. Third Eye Exercise – the ideal time for this exercise is between 1 and 2 pm:
This exercise is good for bringing energy up through the spine and opening the third eye. Sit comfortably cross-legged on the floor and straighten your back, pushing your chest out and keeping your head perfectly aligned with your spine. Interlock your fingers and place your hands on the back of your neck. Take a deep in-breath, then exhale slowly, bringing your forehead down to touch the floor if possible, or as near as you can get. Hold the out-breath for as long as you can. When you need to breathe, gently bring yourself back to an upright position, slowly breathing in and visualizing the third eye opening. Feel the energy move through your body. Repeat this exercise 5–10 times. [Not recommended if you suffer from lower back problems.]

7. Liver Exercise – the ideal time for this exercise is sunrise or sunset and should be done outside:
This is a very powerful detox exercise and is especially good to do during a fast. Stand facing the sun and relax your body. Bend your knees slightly with your feet shoulder width apart, and your eyes looking comfortably towards the sky. As you breathe deeply, visualize the energy of the sun pouring into your body through the solar plexus area [just above your navel]. Bring your hands together and place them on your solar plexus with your middle fingers touching. As you exhale, make the sound, 'aaahh', and feel your liver open up to release its toxins. As you release the toxins on the out-breath, feel the energy of the sun, feel your liver bathed in its heat, warmth and light. Continue for ten minutes.

8. Fire Ball Exercise:
Standing up with your feet rooted to the ground, bend your knees slightly and stretch your arms outwards in front of you, palms down. Visualize a large ball of fire coming up from the ground into your hands. This ball contains powerful energy rising up from the depths of the earth into your hands. Breathe in deeply and move this energizing power around your whole body.

9. Tree Exercise:
This exercise is especially good for counteracting negativity, your own, other people's, or that of the world around you. You can do this exercise with a real tree, or you can visualize one. Squat in front of a beautiful tree. With both hands, hold onto the trunk of the tree and balance your body. If you find it difficult to squat, you can do this exercise standing up. Visualize the strength of the tree supporting you as you let go of everything that is overwhelming you in your life.

Feel your body release all its negativity, through your hands, into the trunk of the tree. Watch as the energy sinks down into the roots of the tree and down into the earth where it is transformed into balanced energy.

Begin to breathe deeply; with each in-breath, feel the life force of the tree strengthen and support your whole body, particularly your spine. You may begin to feel a tingling sensation move through your body. Focus on being at one with the life force and spirit of the tree. When you feel complete, thank the tree for the healing it has just given you. You might like to follow Shamanic custom and leave a simple gift, such as ground corn, sage or any herb, in appreciation to the tree.

10. Seed/Sapling/Tree Exercise:

Curl up into a ball in the foetal position, as small and tight as you can. You are a seed, lying dormant in the winter earth. Connect to being a seed, buried deeply in the ground; how does it feel?

As spring approaches, you start to wake. Very slowly you begin to come to life, uncurling your body, a little bit at a time, as your tiny seed begins to grow into a sapling. You uncurl more, as your sapling begins to grow into a tree. You stretch out your arms, your branches, reaching upwards, further towards the heavens, your feet, your roots, still firmly planted in the earth. Now stretch up as high as you can. Feel your rootedness, and your power to expand as you stretch upwards. As well as stretching every muscle in your body, this is an excellent exercise to do to overcome limitations and grow to your full potential. Done regularly, it can be transformative.

Shamanic Animal Postures

Tony first became interested in these Shamanic Animal Postures while he was living in South America and exploring the ancient temple sites and ruins. Studying some of the symbols on these temples walls, he found animal carvings and drawings depicting unusual postures. He spent many hours in the temples, copying these postures, standing by the original carvings and holding the pose for several hours at a time. Gradually, he realized that they were Animal Healing Postures, holding within them ancient wisdom and profound spiritual knowledge.

Every animal possesses a spirit that can teach us how to achieve balance. The teaching that comes from each animal species is unique. We can call on the spirit of different animals to guide us and transform difficult situations. We can ask animals to become our totems and help us in an ongoing way in our lives. We can invoke the spirit of different animals and their power by copying the Shamanic Animal Postures. If we can't actually go to see these animals in the wild, we can watch films or videos or see photographs, study the way they move and the way they stand, and then take on the posture that most connects us to their physical essence and their spirit.

Here are examples of the qualities of just three animals, and the ways that connecting to them can help us. [The scope of this book doesn't allow more detail, but there are many books on Shamanism that give a comprehensive list.]

The Cougar, also known as the Puma, is the big cat of the mountains, and has great affinity with the wildness of a mountain landscape. It represents strength, determination, great courage, and can teach us to take responsibility for ourselves and our actions, encourage us to overcome difficult situations and develop our qualities of leadership.

The Wolf is *the* animal symbol of Shamanism in North America. A legendary hunter and path-finder, always returning to the pack to share and teach its medicine, it can show us how to find our right path through life. Wolf is connected to moon energy, the unconscious that holds secrets of wisdom and new knowledge. It symbolizes fierce intelligence, emotional sensitivity, strong vision and communication. Wolf can teach us about being a faithful friend, and being true to ourselves.

The Hawk awakens buried memories and teaches us new ways of seeing, paying attention to detail while seeing the broader vision. It is the messenger of the sun, bringing divinity to earth and enlarging our spiritual horizons. It encourages us to examine our everyday lives, to observe with awareness everything we do, to see the signals that life is sending us, to be alert to possible dangers or obstacles. Hawk offers us the qualities of protectiveness, independence, intrepidness and decisiveness, and may help us towards material prosperity.

There are hundreds of species of animals that can teach us and bring us wisdom. By taking on the posture of an animal whose spirit resonates with us, we bring its energy into our physical body and can also learn a lot about opening up to our spirituality.

A couple of examples of how to approach the postures follow; the same technique can be used with any animal. Start by focusing on your breath, quietening your mind and coming to a still place within. Enter into the posture of your chosen animal and breathe deeply. You don't have to hold the postures for hours at a time; start with five minutes, and gradually increase if you can.

The Bear Posture – this is best done between 8 and 9 in the morning:
This posture can help to strengthen the abdomen and the intestines, and is especially good for people with constipation or weak stomachs. It is also good for strengthening the ankles and increasing muscle tone to the rest of the body.

Squat on a flat surface with the weight of your body close to the ground, your back straight, and your head looking straight ahead. For women who want to help strengthen and loosen the pelvic muscles for giving birth, move the feet slightly further apart. Breathe naturally, making sure that your face and shoulders are completely relaxed.

Moving from the simple squat, lift yourself up onto the balls of your feet, balancing on your toes. Your body should be completely relaxed and the only tension should be around your ankles. Breathe deeply, feeling your lower body connected to the heels of your feet. Then move your hands upwards towards your shoulders, leaning your elbows gently on your calves and making sure your face is still looking straight ahead. Hold this posture for three minutes to start with, gradually increasing to fifteen if you can.

The Eagle Posture – this is best done between 8 and 10 in the evening:

This posture was often used in South America during initiations when Shamans were tested to find hidden objects. Its purpose for us is to locate something we've lost, not usually physical, or forgotten memories.

Stand with your hands relaxed by the sides of your body, and your head facing forward. Relax your shoulders. Close your eyes and feel your body from the inside. Now visualize an image of an eagle and bring it into your body. Feel your body begin to change and become one with the eagle. As you inhale, bring your arms out from your sides up towards your shoulders, with your fingers pointing towards the ground. On your next in-breath begin to sway gently. As you sway, move your arms up and down in a flying motion and imagine you are beginning to fly. Keeping your eyes closed, observe everything that is around you.

Continue to sway gently and bring your focus to your third eye. Just be present to yourself, feeling the swaying of your body taking you more and more deeply into yourself, being present to something that you need to find. It may happen that what you think you need is completely different from where the eagle takes you. Just be present to the process and allow the information to come through to you without trying to make sense of it logically.

Eagle can bring us a different perspective on our lives. As it flies, it can move beyond human limitation and bring us new vision and greater clarity. Hold this posture for five minutes to start with, gradually increasing to fifteen if you can.

Imitating these Shamanic animal postures on a regular basis can help to revitalize our health, strengthen our body, and bring new vision and perspective to our lives.

All these exercises and practices, if undertaken regularly, help to bring our mind, body and heart into balance, help us to live more, and more joyfully, in the moment, increase our awareness and consciousness, and connect us more deeply to our spirituality.

Chapter Eleven
The Path of the Heart
Healing Ourselves, Healing the Planet

"Spiritual action for me is Karma Yoga, selfless service. By observing and respecting the purpose of all that lives on this planet, we tune in more and more to the vibration of Life and Love that permeates us and the planet. As we become more in tune with Life, we feel Life's desire: the desire to love, nurture, provide and care for all that lives."

Tony Samara

Tony calls the journey that he takes us on "The Path of the Heart": letting go of our ego attachments and awakening to consciousness; opening our hearts and allowing ourselves to live in that deep and magical place of love.

Every life is unique and meaningful and serves a divine purpose, though we may not know what this is. Our journey through life is a journey of discovery, discovering who we really are and what our life's purpose may be. Before we are born, our soul chooses the tasks it will perform in this lifetime, in order for us to learn the lessons that we need to learn and bring more light to the world. If we do not fulfil our soul's mission in this lifetime, it will not be fulfilled; not for us and not for the world. So how important is each individual life! How important is your life. The spiritual imperative of life is to know yourself. And then to be yourself; the most yourself that you are able to be.

One of the greatest gifts that spirituality bestows upon us is that of being able to accept that our life unfolds according to its divine purpose. Our task is not to try to control its purpose, nor even understand it, but to allow it to unfold in its own way. And to accept that we do not need to know what it is; we just need to allow ourselves to experience it. 'Needing to know' brings with it assumptions and judgementalness, expectations and blame. Preconceived perceptions of how things ought to be limit our openness to what is.

Tony often tells stories in his retreats, allegories that illustrate profound spiritual truths. A farmer had a horse, his prize possession. One day, the horse ran away. When his neighbour heard about this, he ran over to the farmer and commiserated with him. "That's terrible," he said. And the wise farmer said, "You never know." A few days later, the horse returned, but it was not alone; it was leading two wild horses. When the neighbour heard about this, he ran over to the farmer joyfully. "That's wonderful," he said. And the wise farmer said, "You never know." A few days after this, the farmer's son was training one of the wild horses, when he fell off and broke his leg. When his neighbour heard this, he ran over to the farmer and commiserated with him. "That's terrible," he said. And the wise farmer said, "You never know." The following week, the Cossack army came riding through the countryside, recruiting every able-bodied young man for the army. But they didn't take the farmer's son because of his broken leg. When the neighbour heard this, he ran over to the farmer joyfully. "That's wonderful," he said. And the wise farmer said, "You never know… "

We never know what divine purpose has in store for us just round the corner; something that appears quite negative may turn out to be in our best interests after all. Our task is simply to allow ourselves to be open to receive whatever the universe offers us, to trust the journey into the unknown and welcome it without fear. By overcoming the fear of what lies ahead, by celebrating the risks that we take on our adventure through life, we awaken to the splendour of our hearts.

The Path of the Heart is the unity of love. And this path is paved with many bricks: harmlessness, gratitude, humility.

The practice of harmlessness is an essential part of our spiritual journey. You may think that practising harmlessness is not a very lofty aspiration. But if everyone did no more than practise harmlessness, there would be no evil in the world. Just think: *no evil.*

But harmlessness is not just a matter of passively not causing harm; though even to do this demands that we be ever vigilant and alert to the life around us. Harmlessness is a conscious act of engaging with everything and everyone in our environment and acting for the higher good of all. If we are living with Intention, we are practising harmlessness. We recognize that every life serves a divine purpose, and no life is more or less important than any other; ours included.

Harmlessness is not to be underestimated.

As we awaken to an ever-deepening consciousness, we realize that gratitude is an essential part of spirituality. Showing gratitude is a way of acknowledging that our blessings are bestowed upon us by grace; they are not ours by right, and we do not own them. Showing gratitude is a way of thanking the universe for the manifold gifts showered upon us each day; it reminds us of our relationship with Great Spirit. Miracles are strewn across our path and our unseen guides are with us at all times.

The more we show gratitude, the more we open ourselves up to experiencing our blessings, and the more we realize how blessed we are. When we express gratitude, it is impossible to feel alone, isolated or disharmonious. When we express gratitude, we connect to the sacred within us and within the All That Is, and so enrich our life.

Another essential expression of our spirituality is humility. Humility is a deep feeling, a state of being; it has nothing to do with humbleness, which is a false emotion. Humility is not a matter of putting ourselves down; far from it. It is knowing our true worth, and so not needing to trumpet it. Humility is the opposite of arrogance. Humility is contained within unconditional love. Another spiritual paradox perhaps, but we cannot feel unconditional love for ourselves without also feeling humility. For unconditional love connects us to the sacred; humility is our acknowledgement that this is the source of all our blessings.

When Tony was living in the Amazon Rain Forest, he was told this traditional Shamanic folktale. In ancient times, ants were believed to be very wise people. They lived and worked within the laws of nature, understanding the energies of the cosmos to such a degree that they were able to build large cities, more powerful than any others and marvellous to behold. But gradually, caught up in their hectic lives of building and running yet more fantastic cities, glorifying in their own power and success, they forgot the teachings of Great Spirit. They forgot gratitude and humility. Great Spirit became angry, and punished them by turning them into ants.

Acting with humility is acknowledging who we truly are, and the true measure of all our relationships. It is recognizing that we come from the Divine and that we are worthy of unconditional love. It is being mindful of the immutable laws of the natural world and knowing our own place within the cosmos.

Consciousness is the marriage of humility, gratitude and unconditional love.

The language that we use is also a reflection of our spirituality. Language has a power of its own. So it behoves us always to try to be impeccable in our word; to use words that come from our wholeness, that communicate something real from our heart to the heart of our listener; to speak what is true and what adds to the harmony of the universe. And if we are ever tempted to say something that does not come from our highest integrity, then it is better to remain silent. And of course speaking behind someone's back, or speaking or listening to gossip, is out of the question.

Words have power, just as thoughts have power, to create the reality that we inhabit. If we say something negative about someone, we are sending out a sound of disharmony, which reverberates out into the universe, to infinity, and also creates a strong negative reality for ourselves. We should always ask ourselves if the words we speak add to the good in the world, or not; if they are compatible with living in our sacred centre.

Words have power. When we express ourselves directly and honestly from the heart, language too serves to raise consciousness to a higher level; language, too, becomes a tool of divine work.

The Path of the Heart is the path of healing. Healing comes about through unconditional love. And it starts by giving *ourselves* unconditional love.

This love comes through consciousness. It asks nothing in return, not even love. It simply is. It expresses itself in the way you live your life and is not dependent on any 'love object'. You live this love deeply, manifesting it through the way you relate to everyone and to the universe. We all have this love inside us; it is an expression of our divinity.

Love is our connection to the sacred within us, and the manifestation of consciousness of the sacred in every aspect of our lives. It is knowing God within, not as a separate being outside ourselves, but as our deepest essence; not as a Patriarch, that demands obedience and self-sacrifice, but as Spirit, that loves us unconditionally.

As we connect to God's unconditional love within us, how can we *not* also love ourselves unconditionally? And this means accepting ourselves as we are. It doesn't mean that we don't make mistakes. Indeed, making mistakes is part of what it is to be human; it is how we learn. The appropriate response is to acknowledge our mistakes, accept responsibility for them without emotional attachment, learn from them and then move on. We do not need to be judgemental or self-critical, to apportion blame or indulge in guilt. *And we do not stop loving ourselves unconditionally.*

Unconditional love is the greatest medicine. It can heal all wounds. And it heals, not by sticking plaster on wounds, but by healing them from the inside; not by alleviating symptoms, but by healing the causes. Loving ourselves brings about the most profound healing: healing our bodies, healing our hearts, healing our souls.

And healing the planet. For loving ourselves unconditionally embraces loving the perfection of the universe and everything within it. And so taking care of it. This is our sacred duty.

For a long time Western civilization has been suffering from a deep sickness of the soul. Of course 'Western civilization' is not a unified entity; it is made up of diverse and often discordant elements. But our disaffection with spiritual values seems to be shared among us all. The loss of our connection to our roots; our negligence towards nature and our systematic destruction of the environment; our greed, selfishness, violence, prejudice, racism and disrespect for other cultures; our limited world view and our abandonment of the sacred – all these factors have been hurtling the human race towards its own self-destruction. And the scientific solutions to all these problems have simply reinforced this material reality. The hard face of science became the god of the twentieth century.

The world as we know it in our everyday lives is careering out of control towards insanity. The destruction of the rain forests, global warming, oppression and wars, are the manifestation of a deep sickness within us. Trying to control our environment, we live out of tune with the earth and with our true selves. Humans are the only species bent on the destruction of everything in the natural world that supports us. We need to understand that if we are bent on destroying the planet, it will destroy us first.

So how can we change this? One way would be to embrace the Shamanic worldview that sees the human race as custodians and protectors of the planet.

Just as Mother Earth sustains and nourishes us, so it is our job to care for her in return. It would help us if we were to welcome the gifts of our Shamanic roots, the lost heritage of our ancestors who walked the earth in balance and harmony. Perhaps we will be able to discard our arrogance and live as a harmonious part of the cosmos, interconnected with "all our relations". Perhaps we can return to a sacred relationship with Mother Earth, serving her with love and compassion, that will be of mutual benefit to us all. Perhaps we can again embrace the mystery and magic and magnificence of the All That Is.

As we evolve spiritually, we realize that our journey through this life is not only about ourselves. It is also about serving others. This is the practice of Karma Yoga, selfless service.

This has nothing to do with a moral concept of 'duty', that may have been instilled into us as children, and which we may have continued to follow. Duty is often motivated by fear of punishment if we don't 'do our duty'; or hope of reward if we do. Duty ultimately serves no-one. It disempowers the receiver and may bring a sense of self-righteousness or even smugness to the giver.

Service, on the other hand, comes from a place of love and is given for its own sake; it is a transaction between equals, joined by love. It is a manifestation of the concept: "I am not free as long as you are in chains". Real service comes from accepting that all people are our relations, and that giving from a place of love is blessed.

Spiritual practice incorporates serving others through love and compassion, a commitment to giving time and energy and resources to others. And it includes the giving of material goods and money. It seems extraordinary that so many people seem to find money the hardest thing of all to give. Even people who are generous with their time, their energy, their friendships, their compassion – all the important things – often find it extremely difficult to part with money.

When Tony first started conducting retreats in Europe he made no charge, but instead he asked participants to make a donation to the Samara Foundation, a non-profit organization he had established with Sylvia to spread his teachings. People would come up to him at the end of the retreat, thank him profusely for his help, often telling him that he had transformed their lives and they were now consciously walking their spiritual path. And then they would walk away without making even a small donation.

What is our obsession with money? Are we still buying into the prevalent culture of the West, which sees money as a symbol of status, control, ownership, success, authority, power? If we find it difficult to part with money, we need to look at what it symbolizes for us. For *these* are the things we are finding it so hard to part with. These are our attachments. If we are not able to let go of money and material possessions, how can we truly let go of those things that are more deeply entrenched, such as our beliefs, our fears, our judgementalness, our ego, our illusions, our doubts?

In the Bible, we are enjoined to give "tithes", that is, a tenth of everything we own and everything we gain. In Biblical times, farmers would leave part of their grain round the edges of their fields at harvest time, so that poor people could come and glean. We need to follow this example and give away at least ten percent of all that we have and all that we earn. This can be to any charity, good cause or people in need.

This selfless giving not only serves the people to whom we give, it also helps us to let go of our attachment to money and possessions. Giving to charity is a fundamental part of spiritual practice.

As we become more conscious, more awake, we may feel that we are opening up to our spiritual journey, that we are progressing, moving along our path in the right way.

But actually, to describe our spiritual journey as 'moving on', or 'progressing', is not really accurate. We use these terms to help make the spiritual path more accessible when we start our journey. They are concepts that may help us at the beginning of our way, a measure by which we can mark our spiritual development. These words give us a vocabulary with which to communicate about our spirituality, a language to articulate it for ourselves. But all these words – progress, movement, even the concept of a journey – are ultimately meaningless.

Spirituality is not 'moving forward', and there is no 'journey', for we are already 'there'. *Here* is *there.* Wherever we are is where we need to be. We are born fully conscious, spiritual beings. Our task in this life is simply to remove the blinkers that keep us from recognizing our spiritual centre, our one-ness with all of Creation; to recover what we knew in the moment of our birth, the perfection of our soul.

The only journey that we have to make is perhaps the longest journey of all: the journey from our head to our heart.

The purpose that our soul has chosen for us for this life is the creation of those situations that will best teach us the lessons we need to learn in this life: to know ourselves, to open our hearts and to love better.

The universe is the manifestation of the perfection and oneness of everything in Creation. It is only when we separate ourselves from this oneness that we suffer. And we really suffer, because we suffer alone. Our greatest source of misery, in fact, is our separation from our divinity, from our true selves. And then we also feel that we are separate from everyone else.

Each soul has an inborn longing for connectedness, a profound yearning to merge with the whole, for its uniqueness to be harnessed to the perfection of the universe. As we have separated ourselves from this oneness, our soul's 'journey' is to be rejoined with the spirit of life that is within all Creation, with the unity of divinity that is waiting to embrace us, calling us back to our essence.

The ultimate intention of spiritual practice is the merging of our selves with the infinite, the individual with the All That Is, the human with the Divine. But as we feel that we are moving towards this union, the mind gets scared: it does not want to 'merge' with anything, for then it would lose its individual identity, its control. And so its tricks become ever more sophisticated. It knows that we are now 'spiritual', and so it uses the language of spirituality to trap us. We need to be ever alert to the games of our ego mind and the 'spiritual perceptions' that it creates. The more spiritually conscious we become, the more subtle and ingenious the tricks of our ego mind will be. Be aware and beware!

There is a danger too that as we feel ourselves becoming more spiritual, we may start to feel 'virtuous', and so 'better than' others, who are less spiritual. A slight feeling of superiority or smugness may creep in, uninvited – the mind keeping us from reaching Enlightenment. We need to be ever vigilant and make sure that we are not 'spiritualizing the ego', but rather transforming the heart.

Nothing in life is random, and everyone who comes into our lives may teach us something, if we are ready to learn.

As we evolve spiritually, we become more open to receive the lessons that strew our path, from whatever source. We may learn from a partner or others close to us, from our dreams, from a totem animal, from trees or anything within the natural world. We may learn from people and situations that we perceive as negative or difficult, and who often have the most to teach us.

But at different times in our lives, we also need spiritual teachers who are masters. As the saying goes, "When the student is ready, the teacher appears.". We may be greatly helped by reading spiritual books and attending spiritual workshops. But the depth of our experience will depend upon our own readiness to receive such knowledge and experience.

As Tony works with each person's Higher Self, he can teach us many things. He can show us who we really are, and help us to open our heart and experience a spiritual way of life. He can help us to let go of everything that is keeping us stuck, fearful, blinkered, and lead us to a place of harmony and love. If we are open to receive, we may find his teachings inspirational and life transforming.

Nothing in life is random. As this book of Tony's teachings has come into your life at this time, the chances are that you are ready to receive its wisdom. The job of a spiritual teacher is to light your flickering log so that it may burn ever more brightly, helping you to relinquish the domination of your ego mind and emotions and connect more deeply to your highest self. He can help you to reflect upon the invisible world beyond the borders of your rational mind, beyond the role you see yourself as playing, beyond your perceived need for material acquisitions or worldly achievements.

Sometimes, as our mind finds it difficult to understand what is beyond itself, the guidance of a spiritual teacher may seem incomprehensible. And so we need to find our place of trust. For ultimately, through trusting him and trusting your own Higher Self, you may come to inhabit a world without borders, a world of infinite possibilities, and an experience of life that is filled each moment with joy, love and profound peace.

And so we move towards Enlightenment. And what actually is Enlightenment?

When Zen Buddhist Masters were asked this question, they are quoted as saying, "Before Enlightenment: chop wood, draw water. After Enlightenment: chop wood, draw water." As though to tell us that nothing in the outside world has changed – but everything has changed within us. Enlightenment changes the way we see the world, the way we are in the world; the way we live.

It spreads light where before there was darkness.

Enlightenment is beyond words. It is a profound mystery, a world of infinite dimensions inconceivable to the limitations of our mind and emotions.

Enlightenment is consciousness; and consciousness is love.

The Path of the Heart opens us up to this profound knowing: consciousness is love, love is consciousness. Unconditional love informs everything, but is attached to nothing. When we have let go of all our attachments, what is left is pure love.

When you are living in a state of consciousness, you *are* love. *You are love.* Unconditional love is the essence of who you are. It is the doorway to Enlightenment. And, in fact, unconditional love *is* Enlightenment.

So, what remains for us to do? Nothing. Just let go; let go of everything. Let go – and be.

For Enlightenment cannot be attained. It may come upon us unexpectedly. But we do not 'reach' Enlightenment. Rather, it may reach us. All we can do is open our hearts and be ready – to allow, to receive, to welcome with a smile. And then wait patiently, for grace.

Epilogue

When I'd finished the final draft of the final chapter – The Path of the Heart – something felt not quite right. Everything that needed to be in the book was there. Everything seemed to be in the right place. But something troubled me. It was as though the book were still somehow incomplete; it had not come to rest.

I waited for a couple of days to see what would happen. This feeling that somehow I had not completed the book, that the last note was missing, didn't leave me. But I couldn't see what was needed.

I woke early the next morning and decided to go on a Vision Quest. The sun was up and beckoning, although the day was still cold. I walked across the wilder parts of Hampstead Heath, off the beaten track, where the density of trees and undergrowth form a kind of forest, and where there were no people to disturb my peace. I could feel the earth beneath my feet; I was intensely aware of the different sounds of birdsong and the crackling of twigs underfoot. I walked without expectation, with my mind turned off and my heart open to whatever would be...

A perfect round black stone caught my eye. The stones all around it seemed to be embedded in the earth, but this one was loose, as though it didn't belong to that spot, as though it were waiting... I picked it up and held it; then I decided to take it home, to join others that I'd found at different places during the last few years, that had special meaning for me.

I continued walking, feeling intensely alive and aware and embraced by nature. Then in the distance, I saw a tree that seemed to be calling to me. Its trunk was divided into two; it immediately came to me that this represented the head and the heart. As I drew nearer, I saw that out of the two trunks, a little higher up, a third trunk was growing, reaching up higher than the other two – the soul, of course. I sat on the ground with my back leaning against the tree, and asked for guidance.

I sat for a long while, feeling deeply at peace, with myself, with the world.

And then it came to me, the guidance that I'd asked for, in all its profound simplicity; the summation of everything that I'd learnt through Tony: Walk your path, for love greets your every step.

This is the Path of the Heart. We need no more words.

I wanted to leave something for the tree, in gratitude. All I had was the black stone I'd picked up earlier. I left the stone on the tree, where the three trunks joined...

Afterword
Tony's Work Today

"The more highly evolved one is, the more one needs silence. Silence is not emptiness. Silence is impregnated with fullness, producing a state of harmony, poetry and inspiration. Silence is the birth of the profound meaning contained in life."

Tony Samara

The Samara Foundation, created by Tony and Sylvia Samara, was set up to help realize the evolution of human consciousness, using the guidelines of Tony's spiritual teachings. It is a non-profit organisation established to spread Tony's teachings throughout the world.

The Foundation does this in many ways: through workshops and retreats, by producing teaching and inspirational materials such as videos, CD's, tapes and booklets, through educational workshops on spirituality for children, by creating bursaries to help people in real economic hardship to attend retreats, by establishing places where people who are dedicated to their spiritual path may come and practise this living form of spirituality, and by creating various healing projects.

The Samara Foundation embraces the goal of working towards self-realization and personal liberation. As we move beyond the simple gratification of individual needs and connect more deeply with our higher self, we take responsibility for our own processes, raise our consciousness and find the love and the light in each situation, creating a reality of harmony with our spiritual aspirations.

Tony's work takes him all over the world. He holds retreats and workshops in many countries, including Eastern and Western Europe, South America, and Australia and New Zealand. He also gives introductory talks in many places, and one day 'experiential days'.

All Tony's retreats – no matter what their title, or what 'subject' participants may expect – are actually guided journeys into our selves. The emphasis may be different, but they are all journeys that help us to move more deeply into ourselves, showing us how we can take off our masks and become the beautiful person we are born to be. Through exercises, visualizations and many different kinds of meditation, Tony's gentle voice guides us through his teachings, bringing us back to our true selves.

In these retreats, we explore our connection with the power and wisdom of nature, we look at our dreams, our relationships, we confront our resistance to letting go of our ego mind and its games, and the false reality and 'needs' that it creates for us. The retreats open us up to our spirituality and take us on a journey towards deeper consciousness, freedom and unconditional love. Unless it's a cleansing detoxification retreat, delicious vegetarian food is served.

Tony's retreats are based on ancient *Huachuma* Shamanic practices, integrated with his own teachings, which have grown and developed through his many years of spiritual questing. They lead us towards self-healing and personal growth, creating an amazing journey of self-discovery and reclamation of spirit. Tony works on the energetic level and the physical level at the same time, which may account for the seeming random and chaotic nature of his work. He says that he works in the moment, with each person present, simultaneously tuning in to where each individual is stuck, and giving each one what he/she needs at that moment to move on.

Tony is often asked by people seeking his help, "Isn't there an easier way? Isn't there a quick solution?" He tells them that this is like asking for a McDonalds in a gourmet restaurant. There are no quick fixes, no express trains to Enlightenment. Tony's retreats offer us a cosmic nudge on our journey. If we bring to them an open heart and a willingness to learn, to receive, without judgement, they can be life transforming.

As Tony says: "Our essence can be celebrated, our dreams can be realized, our feelings can be fulfilled, and in this limitless celebration we can discover who we really are."

Listed below are the main events of Tony's year. Remember, though, that all the retreats are actually a journey into the wholeness of spirituality, but with slightly different emphases.

The Cleansing Detoxification Retreat:

Our physical body is a temple, and this temple should be glowing with light. However, we often forget about our body and take it for granted – until we get sick. So, cleansing retreats form an intrinsic part of this spiritual path.

These are fasting retreats, offering a very powerful cleansing and detoxification programme, lasting over a number of days. They offer a combination of freshly made organic fruit and vegetable juices, liquid super-foods, and as much purified water as you can drink [between one and two litres a day is recommended]. They also include special cleansing herbs and herbal detox preparations, and Theriaca, Tony's specially created healing elixir.

These cleansing retreats offer morning and afternoon talks and satsangs [see below] interspersed with energy exercises, dream work, gentle exercises such as journeys to the heart and journeys to the essence, visualizations and meditations that harmonize mind and body and mind and emotions, strong meditation practices such as the whirling meditation, breathing exercises, and group exercises drawn from Tony's wealth of experience with ancient Shamanic, oriental and Zen Buddhist traditions. Participants are also able to pamper themselves with a massage, available at a small extra cost. And there is some free time for walks in nature, for writing in journals and for integrating the wisdoms of the various satsang sessions.

The purpose of these retreats is to help us to clean out and detoxify the body, but also to enable us to let go of emotional and spiritual 'baggage'. Along with the physical toxins that we eliminate, we also let go of an amazing amount of emotional 'rubbish'. By the end of the retreat, we usually feel 'purged', light, not hungry, energetic, shining with vitality and good health, more self-aware, more loving, more spiritual, and often transformed.

Tony sees these retreats as a journey though the complexity of what it means to be a human being in a multi-faceted world. This journey offers us an opportunity to increase our physical health and vitality and strengthen our resistance to illness. At the same time, it helps us to nourish our body, heart and soul, enabling us to engage more fully and deeply in all aspects of life. As we cleanse and rejuvenate our body, we also nourish the spiritual roots of our health and well being, connect more profoundly with our life force and root ourselves more deeply in spiritual blessing.

Come and reclaim your connection to the wisdom within.

The Satsangs:

A Satsang is something between a meeting and a talk, but is more than both. The word 'Satsang' comes from the Sanskrit word used in India, and doesn't have an exact equivalent in English. The nearest explanation would be a meeting of people who come together in order to hear words of wisdom from an enlightened person. But it is more than a talk, as something more than words are exchanged.

At a Satsang, Tony guides us along a path of discovery of profound transformation, evolution of consciousness and inner peace. This path is open to all people from all walks of life, who seek health, happiness and inner wisdom. The Satsang programmes offer an opportunity to be present to your Higher Self and let your wisdom lead you to a space of inner peace.

Each individual has to experience this inner peace and truth in his/her own heart. But at a Satsang, Tony empowers us to have the courage to move more deeply into our own experience, and to open up to receive the wisdom and spiritual consciousness that he offers.

The Relationship Retreat:

The way we relate to others is at the heart of spirituality. Bringing consciousness into all our relationships – partner, parents, children, friends, strangers – is a basic part of spiritual practice. At these retreats, Tony takes us on a journey through this process.

But he starts the retreat by examining our relationship with our own inner self. We look at the masculine and feminine energies that are part of each of us [they are also present in the DNA structure of our cells] and see how we do, and don't, harmonize these aspects of ourselves. When they are balanced, we can connect more deeply to the divinity that is our centre, helping us to overcome feelings of separateness, loneliness and alienation.

Right relationship with ourselves, balancing our masculine and feminine energies, and living from our highest integrity, form the basis of all our relationships, with ourselves and with others. Tony takes this process further by working with the natural life force, the kundalini. Through powerful exercises, he helps us to connect more deeply to the divine energies of our masculine and feminine qualities. As the kundalini rises, we find that we have more strength and courage to dissolve old limitations, unwanted ancestral patterns, guilt and fears – all the 'baggage' that we have so far been unable to release.

On these retreats, Tony works with energy exercises, strong meditation practices, dream work, visualizations and group exercises. Although his work is energetic rather than verbal, he also talks, and allows plenty of time for questions.

The Silent Retreat:

The more highly evolved we are, the more we need silence in our lives. So often, the miracle of life is forgotten because of the thoughts and emotions that well up and colour the simplicity of each moment and its unique gifts. Often we get lost in this world, feeling empty and sad because we have paid attention to everything except what is really important. Often, we focus on the 'reality' outside and do not see what is real.

Let us stop for a moment and be silent. In silence, we may experience a magical connection to our own hearts. When we are silent, we can connect more profoundly to Mother Earth and tune in to the Universal Breath of Life. In this silent stillness, we can connect more strongly to our essence and experience the joy of just being, in the moment. Intensely. Profoundly. Continuously.

It is in this stillness and silence that Tony can work more profoundly with us. In his Silent Retreat, he can boost our experiential awareness and deepen our spiritual practice. The more highly evolved we become, the more we understand the blessings of silence, and the more we realize that we need to spend time living and being in silence. For in silence we may find an ever-deepening consciousness, profound inspiration, harmony and peace. It is in this stillness that we can simply be, that we can look in the mirror and see a most wonderful being, and start loving ourselves, as we are, unconditionally. And so we may become a being of light and love, expanding into the miracle of the universe.

The Forty Day Retreat:

This is definitely not for the faint-hearted! This retreat is always held in a powerful place in nature, either by the sea, near mountains, or in glorious countryside, and usually in an exotic setting. Recent Forty Day retreats have been held in the Sinai Desert and Costa Rica.

The Forty Day Retreat is a fasting programme, and you need to check beforehand that you are physically strong enough to do it. Over the course of forty days, Tony slowly moves each person's physical body away from eating solid foods, and introduces juice fasting. This includes delicious and nourishing fruit and vegetable juices and 'smoothies', special detoxing herbal drinks and plenty of pure water. For a period in the middle of the forty days, many people fast only on water, deciding for themselves the length of this water fasting period. [Tony will say if he feels that this is not appropriate for you.] Towards the end of the forty days, Tony will gradually reintroduce more solid foods again, preparing the body for re-entry into the 'real' world again.

This retreat includes meditation, visualizations, gentle exercises, karma yoga and chanting. Most of the retreat is held in silence. Although participants journey together, each one also walks his/her own unique path alone, moving more deeply into their own 'beingness'. Fasting for this length of time can bring about a profound spiritual experience. In the silence and stillness of nature, a deep mystical and alchemical process may occur, invaluable to the evolution of human consciousness.

No-one who does this retreat is ever quite the same again!

Ceremony:

Ceremony is the profound experience of working with Tony, with the sacred drink that he discovered when working with the Shamans in Peru, and moving along the wondrous spiritual journey that this awakens. Tony always holds Ceremony at night, as he feels that the energies of the moon and the night are gentler and more providential than those of the day.

This sacred drink, made of specially grown plants and herbs, is a strong, vile-tasting, slimy green concoction. On the physical level, it purifies the blood, cleans out the bowels and eliminates toxins from every cell of the body. But it does much more than this. It also opens up a space inside that is normally hidden. When taken in Ceremony, and guided by an initiated Shaman, it can help us to let go of the limitations of the material world and transcend the limits of our ego minds. It has a gentle, feminine energy, and works with the individual, with what each person needs to work with in the moment. There may be fifty people in the room all doing Ceremony, but each will experience an individual and unique journey.

This wondrous drink mirrors the reality in which you are at the moment: if you are deeply into spiritual consciousness, then this is the level on which it will work for you. If you are not, it will start its work with you wherever you are on your journey at the moment. As Tony says, he likes to move people along gently, not jolt them out of their senses. But the greatest power of this drink is manifest only when we are in true harmony with ourselves, with nature, and with all the dynamics around us, truly conscious of our place within the cosmic scheme of things. Then it can take us to amazing and extraordinary places.

Working with Tony in Ceremony is a magical, mystical experience that awakens us to our deepest selves and opens portals to infinite worlds beyond.

And this is where we came in. My first experience of working with Tony was in the valley at Monte Mariposa, in Ceremony. We have come full circle...

For more information about Tony Samara and the work of the Samara Foundation, please visit the website: www.tonysamara.org

INDEX:

Note 1: For more information about Tony's Theriaca Tea, please visit **www. theriaca.org**

Note 2: For Tony's newsletter about the light in various foods, please visit **www. tonysamara.org**

Note 3: A Vision Quest is a journey through nature, into ourselves; a powerful opportunity for us to reclaim our connection to the wisdom of Mother Earth and open us up to the mystery of the natural world and its transformative power.

Contributions from people
who have worked with Tony

Over the years, Tony has worked with many thousands of people. What follows are the experiences of a tiny sample of people who have ech worked closely with Tony over several years. They have written in their own words, in their own distinctive style, in English, which is not the first language of any of them. Apart from correcting an occasional grammatical error, I have not changed or edited their texts in any way. They speak in their own voices.

The contributions appear in the order in which I received them. After each person's name, is their country of origin or background or where they live, to give a flavour of the diversity of people who work with Tony.

"For me it has been a greater joy than imaginable to meet and 'rise' in Love with this amazing mystery referred to as Tony Samara. It is not possible to put into the very limited medium of words, the Ecstasy of being enraptured by the Love flowing through this being. It has been a feeling of melting. Merging. A feeling of coming back home. It seams unbelievable that such an ordinary looking guy is blessing us with such a limitless, ever-present, inexhaustible Love.

"Since I met Tony it feels like most of the time I don't have a clue what is going on in the bigger picture of this Life. But instead Life has become a joyous learning opportunity, where everyday is filled with wonder at the mystery of being Alive, and Loved through every moment. The gratitude I feel is inexpressible, therefore it is a joy to know that he knows without words. It is the most intimate relationship imaginable. It is such an intimate feeling that I once said it almost feels silly to see him in the physical reality, comparing with unlimited wonder I have experienced through him. So simple. Yet so… inexpressible. Thank you…"

Satprem [Sweden]

"No words nor all the words of the world could ever describe who Tony is, nor what exactly he does. He must be experienced and yet, the only one I got to know better during my time with him, is me.

"Tony has been a guide to me, besides being a clever trickster and a loving friend. He showed me places I never knew existed and other places I never wanted to know existed. Guiding me patiently… very patiently along my path like a beacon of light. Lighting up the way, allowing me to stop and look at the sticks and stones and the nitty-gritty. Always there as a loving presence, whether I experienced ecstatic moments of joy or destructive moments of doubt and frustration. For that same reason, I have loved and hated him, for the sheer fact of loving me for who I am at any given time in life. Giving me the space to remember. In such moments of clarity, deep trust arises and I see his devotion and unconditional love… and that is when I recognise and thank him for being who he is and helping me to be who I am."

Nura [Germany/Thailand]

"I met Tony in 2001 just when my spiritual awakening started happening. That was when I asked him to start to work with me. It was one of the most important things that happened in my life, if not the most significant.

"But at that time nothing could foretell the great, enthusiastic, and perfect, wonderful path, full of light, towards the discovery of the inner self, step by step into the moment. A voyage into myself started and still goes on, through ups and downs, through dreams that came true and others that were dropped, meeting all sorts of people, simply having the deepest experience of my life. My inner wisdom tells me now that this is possible when the true trust in one's heart to the work of the Master exists. The Master, the Friend, the Love Affair that every day and every moment unveils the true work that lies behind the mundane, the material, the mind and the body.

"My experience is unique to me and each one has a different one. But when Love becomes the centre of the path we all share the wisdom of Tony's teachings, the Path of Love. My invitation and dream is that you also have the freedom to jump as high as you can into Tony's work, thus into your deepest self. In my opinion this is not an easy path nor does it make you always happy and fulfilled and glowing with light; instead it enables us to drop the masks and layers upon layers that hide the Truth of our hearts.

"I'm sure that Tony's teachings will be experienced by everyone that truly seeks that something that cannot be told by words or concepts. I believe that in silence and stillness every door of our true nature opens to our experience of the moment, to the unity and one-ness where we all came from. I trust that in that moment real freedom becomes the experience of selfless and effortless work, joy and happiness. This and more were the things that I learned from being with Tony Samara. Thank you Tony for being."

Wahido [Portugal/Germany]

"The first time I met Tony was in Mafra, Portugal in the beginning of the 2002 Autumn. I had just begun looking for a sense of spirituality in my life six months before, which coincided with the beginning of my first truly deep relationship with a woman. All three events were and still are deeply intertwined in a web of actions and consequences that ripple into life through an understanding that extends beyond the mental grasp.

"The week before my meeting with Tony, I had the strangest dreams I'd had up till then, such as dying and being resuscitated by a snake springing out of its sleeping coil and meeting my totem animal laughing at me as he flew over me while I danced in an ancient stone circle around the fire. At the time these made absolutely no sense to me because I could not relate to the importance of dreams and their messages even though on some level there was a curiosity that pulled me to go beyond the idea that these were 'just dreams'. Later I understood the messages and the reason of the timing of these manifestations of the formative world into this plane.

"In Mafra a weekend workshop was taking place. At first I was totally unimpressed by Tony, in fact, I didn't make much of him and my first incredulous thoughts were 'This guy is a Shaman???' My ideas and expectations had not been fulfilled in any way; the person who appeared in front of me was a man with a silly haircut, a strange posture and a T-shirt tucked into his trousers, seemingly very shy and non-sociable. It is only when the workshop began that I started to feel something inside me speak louder than my mind and that the meditations and other exercises began their transformative process. In two days my whole world had been shaken.

"Before meeting Tony I had gone through a deep depression that lasted for some years and within it had abused various kinds of drugs, varying between the soft and hard ones and had absolutely no sense of what being healthy meant. I could not find anything in the world that deserved any kind of investment; the modern world offered no challenge to me, consumer society seemed like a pointless and doomed venture and so I was at loss, not knowing where to direct my energy.

"My first wake-up call to the possibility of the existence of other unseen dimensions in life was in the stone circle that I mentioned in the dream above. Our encounter was a bit like when one goes for a treasure hunt; after six months I had finally found the person who could guide me clearly to what I had been searching for. Within three months of meeting Tony, I had stopped drinking alcohol, stopped smoking tobacco and started a dietary change towards vegetarianism by stopping meat consumption completely. I could not explain the reason behind these very quick changes. I could only feel that this was something that I needed to do because I had found something to do in life now. I knew that I wanted to be free, that I was meant to dedicate myself to becoming one with Nature and that this was possible because I had met a living example of this.

"Four years later, after having cleaned many compost toilets, been sent to the other side of the ocean with a hundred dollars in my pocket, been thrown off a ten-metre waterfall, taking part in many very scary Ceremonies, confronting big old demons and obsolete magic amongst a string of other strange events and happenings, I can truly say that I am blessed with the guidance of an enlightened Guru in the literal sense of the Sanskrit definition.

"In today's work, we are forming a community of people dedicated to the evolution of consciousness through Tony's guidance and I am very happy to be part of this creation. Together we work through the mirrors of each other's presence, and with Karma Yoga. In the simplest things, Tony is there, manifested as an aspect of everything; within All he becomes more than just a physical being and he turns into the consciousness that is ever present."

Sud Ram [England/Belgium/India]

"Tony taught me how to look beyond and stay centred. In the beginning – I tried – and even when I didn't see, I believed. The truth in him is the truth in me. In all."

Soraya [Portugal]

"I first worked with Tony when I went on a Vision Quest [for more information on Vision Quests, see Index, note 3]. It was an extraordinary experience for me: magical and transformative. The retreat was held in a beautiful place by a river, and was conducted in silence; each person journeyed alone.

"When we arrived, I did as Tony told us and walked around on my own until I found a place I felt strongly connected to, and pitched my tent there. Then I sat in the stillness, rolled a cigarette and smoked it, feeling very peaceful. Then we all gathered by the river.

"As I approached the river, I saw Tony looking at me. He waved me over and asked me if I had just smoked a cigarette. I said 'Yes'. But he could not possibly have seen me smoking; how did he know? Then he told me that cigarettes, alcohol and drugs of any kind were not allowed on the retreat. He asked me if I would like to give him my tobacco, and said that if I felt I really needed to smoke, I should do so in his presence. I had been a serious smoker for twenty-five years, and had been trying to stop for the previous five years, but couldn't. I gave my tobacco to Tony, and wondered how I would manage.

"It didn't take long before I felt the urge to smoke, and I got up to go to Tony. But when I was within twenty yards or so of him, I felt that I didn't need the cigarette. This happened many times during the Vision Quest. At the end of the retreat, Tony asked me if I wanted my tobacco back. I just said, 'Well, I think it's better if it stays with you.'.

"On my way home I passed a shop selling cigarettes, and asked myself if I should get some. But I felt I could pass this shop by easily without going in. And with each shop I came to, I was able to say, 'This one I can pass by, too.'. This continued all the way home; each shop I came to I was able to pass by and not go in. Then I went into the supermarket, and my brand of cigarettes was right there in front of me; and what amazed me was that I didn't feel any connection with them. It was interesting; I felt neither attracted nor disgusted by the cigarettes, just totally indifferent. I have never smoked since."

Sabrina [Germany]

"In the 1990s, a woman called Marion treated a wound in my head in my tenth body, something that had been planted there in a previous life in ancient Egypt, so she said.

"When I started to work with Tony [or he with me – until today I'm not sure who works with whom] I was hoping to get more background information on the Egyptian story, but Tony simply asked, "Why do you want to know *that?*" and suggested that I carry on with the healing job, preferably at a *Huachuma* Ceremony. Marion used to put me in a Tachyon field; Tony had me put the high vibration energy into myself. I came to Ceremony – and stepped into a new life.

"The Ceremonies were extraordinary experiences. Finding it hard anyway to stop my mind, I need to underline that I could at all times use my 'daytime' awareness, if I wished to do so. At least, that's what I imagine. The sacred drink made me feel soooo sick. But I didn't go as far as vomiting. I hated it and at the same time every cell of my being knew that I wanted to go on with that cleansing. For a long while, I kept seeing films that would have been classified as psychedelic in the Sixties.

"I never had a 'horror-trip'. It took me years to understand that those patterns I saw were my very personal patterns, the patterns of the logical mind. Later on, earthquakes came to shake the patterns.

"If I hadn't been on the verge of vomiting most of the time I might have enjoyed those nights at the movies without any restrictions. So I just paddled through the night observing, trying to take mental photos and to understand; wondering, knowing that at the delicious fresh fruit breakfast at sunrise, I would feel like being reborn.

"Afterwards Tony would help me, and all the others, to decipher the messages that came through from some higher wisdom. This included practical things like a plant that would help me with a specific physical condition, or the name of a person that had something to do with me, etc.

"Then there came a time when I actually learned to vomit. And the world didn't stop turning. And then there was a time where I didn't feel nauseous any longer. And the last time I participated in Ceremony I could actually see people, the human family! What else is there to come yet? And I'm still healing. Isn't that wonderful?"

Jutta [Germany/Portugal]

"I am afraid that in the same way Tony repeats himself over the years, at least to those who have been with him for long enough, although his simple message is as rich and magical as his repetitions, in the same way to expand on the impressions of working with him, have no other outcome than a merry-go-round of words utterly nonsensical for the outside reader... Or, it may sound like brain-washing, or fanaticism... Simply because words can definitely not convey profound love, profound respect and reverence, total trust or all of the other feelings that link me to Tony Samara... But I will try, for the sake of all of us who might profit even a drop by my 'insane trial' of trying to expand on Tony's work.

"Tony can be speaking about my wounded toenail, and I can hear his love flowing towards so many wounds in me that are crying silently for healing while I give such attention to the little whitish skin around my toenail... In his practical advice that sometimes sounds like the simplest of chats, he pours love, simplicity, clarity and so much more to whoever cares to listen carefully.

"After many years around him, I delight at any opportunity to have him addressing any matter, from the silliest to the deepest, as in any interaction with him his words are, for the experienced listener, of profound meaning, although his choice of words, his tone, delude the listener who does not make some space inside himself while listening... What a sweet trick that leaves many wondering what is that tingle in their hearts even though the mind has not grasped a single meaning in the words that were just spoken to him/her, what is that sensation of wanting to cry or laugh, all that emotion that surfaces if one let's even a tiny window of availability be present when talking to him...

"Of course, I have seen many go away untouched also. Everything is possible, but for me every single one of the thousands of interactions with him have brought light and clarity to the incredible confusion that I create and recreate as fruition of my hyperactive mind and emotional heart.

"For me meeting Tony has utterly, totally and so beautifully changed my present life. It has made it far richer, far more understandable [as much as raising new doubts in understanding]; it has brought and keeps on bringing so much wisdom on all topics that are 'passed' through him, from health to happiness, from relationship issues to practical decisions, every inch of my life is full of him.

"I like so much to watch the corner of people's mouths twitch when I openly say that Tony Samara is for me a true master, an infinitely compassionate and truthful being, that I have no doubts about his total honesty, commitment to his work of liberating his fellow human beings, that I am at peace with all of these beliefs I have in him, and that believing him totally has been and is maybe the greatest trick that has helped me to evolve more quickly, to utilize time in a more intelligent way by not wasting it in doubts [I am not saying that doubts cannot be and are important in some matters] and to practise trust/devotion/surrender [often described as 'the eastern way of master/disciple'] while living a totally western-style life.

"The decision to trust one human being totally has brought me indescribable gifts and I am presently a much more balanced being than I was before I met Tony, in every single sense. I might look madder also, and probably am, as so many new questions have arisen in my being, but I can deal with my greater madness in a more cool way. And, as I recently heard a scientist say in a movie: 'If you are a scientist and if you have studied science deeply and you have not become madder, then you have not understood science at all.'!!!

"Tony has my total trust, my total love [as total as I have ever experienced], my devotion and my support. His work has revealed so many positive changes in people around him that I can only feel very honoured to live and grow close to him."

Kaya [Brazil/Portugal]